Active Learn

Microeconomics
Principles and Applications
THIRD EDITION

Robert E. Hall
Stanford University

Marc Lieberman
New York University

Prepared by

Geoffrey A. Jehle
Vassar College

THOMSON
SOUTH-WESTERN

Australia · Canada · Mexico · Singapore · Spain · United Kingdom · United States

THOMSON
SOUTH-WESTERN

Active Learning Guide to accompany
Microeconomics: Principles and Applications, 3e

Robert E. Hall and Marc Lieberman
Prepared by Geoffrey Jehle

Vice President / Editorial Director:
Jack W. Calhoun

Vice President / Editor-in-Chief:
Michael P. Roche

Publisher of Economics:
Michael B. Mercier

Acquisitions Editor:
Michael W. Worls

Sr. Developmental Editor:
Susanna C. Smart

Executive Marketing Manager:
Janet Hennies

Sr. Marketing Coordinator:
Jenny Fruechtenicht

Production Editor:
Daniel C. Plofchan

Manufacturing Coordinators:
Sandee Milewski, Rhonda Utley

Media Technology Manager:
Vicky True

Technology Project Editor:
Peggy Buskey

Media Editor:
Pam Wallace

Compositor:
OffCenter Concepts House
Soldotna, AK

Sr. Design Project Manager:
Michelle Kunkler

Cover and Internal Designer:
Ramsdell Design, Cincinnati

Cover Image:
© Getty Images, Inc. and Masaaki Toyoura/Photonica

Printer:
VonHoffman Graphics
Frederick, MD

COPYRIGHT © 2005
by South-Western, a division of Thomson Learning. Thomson Learning™ is a trademark used herein under license.

Printed in the United States of America
1 2 3 4 5 07 06 05 04

For more information
contact South-Western,
5191 Natorp Boulevard,
Mason, Ohio 45040.
Or you can visit our Internet site at:
hyyp://www.swlearning.com

ALL RIGHTS RESERVED.
No part of this work covered by the copyright hereon may be reproduced or used in any form or by any means–graphic, electronic, or mechanical, including photocopying, recording, taping, Web distribution or information storage and retrieval systems–without the written permission of the publisher.

Book ISBN: 0-324-26045-8

For permission to use material from this text or product, submit a request online at http://www.thomsonrights.com.

Any additional questions about permissions can be submitted by email to thomsonrights@thomson.com.

Contents

Preface   v

Chapter 1   What is Economics?   1

Chapter 2   Scarcity, Choice, and Economic Systems   11

Chapter 3   Supply and Demand   21

Chapter 4   Working with Supply and Demand   39

Chapter 5   Consumer Choice   53

Chapter 6   Production and Cost   75

Chapter 7   How Firms Make Decisions: Profit Maximization   93

Chapter 8   Perfect Competition   107

Chapter 9   Monopoly   121

Chapter 10   Monopolistic Competition and Oligopoly   135

Chapter 11   The Labor Market   149

Chapter 12   Income Inequality   165

Chapter 13   Capital and Financial Markets   177

Chapter 14   Economic Efficiency and the Role of Government   191

Chapter 15   Comparative Advantage and the Gains from International Trade   209

Final Exam in Microeconomics   221

Answer Key   237

Economics: Principles and Applications, 3e	Microeconomics: Principles and Applications, 3e	Macroeconomics: Principles and Applications, 3e
PART I: PRELIMINARIES		
1. What is Economics?		
2. Scarcity, Choice, and Economic Systems		
3. Supply and Demand		
4. Working with Supply and Demand		
PART II: MICROECONOMIC DECISION MAKERS		
5. Consumer Choice		
6. Production and Cost		
7. How Firms Make Decisions: Profit Maximization		
PART III: PRODUCT MARKETS		
8. Perfect Competition		
9. Monopoly		
10. Monopolistic Competition and Oligopoly		
PART IV: LABOR, CAPITAL, AND FINANCIAL MARKETS		
11. The Labor Market		
12. Income Inequality		
13. Capital and Financial Markets		
PART V: EFFICIENCY, GOVERNMENT, AND THE GLOBAL ECONOMY		
14. Economic Efficiency and the Role of Government		
15. Comparative Advantage and the Gains from International Trade		17. Comparative Advantage and the Gains from International Trade

Economics: Principles and Applications, 3e	Macroeconomics: Principles and Applications, 3e
PART VI: MACROECONOMICS: BASIC CONCEPTS	PART II: MACROECONOMICS: BASIC CONCEPTS
16. What Macroeconomics Tries to Explain	4. What Macroeconomics Tries to Explain
17. Production, Income, and Employment	5. Production, Income, and Employment
18. The Monetary System, Prices, and Inflation	6. The Monetary System, Prices, and Inflation
PART VII: LONG-RUN MACROECONOMICS	PART III: LONG-RUN MACROECONOMICS
19. The Classical Long-Run Model	7. The Classical Long-Run Model
20. Economic Growth and Rising Living Standards	8. Economic Growth and Rising Living Standards
PART VIII: SHORT-RUN MACROECONOMICS	PART IV: SHORT-RUN MACROECONOMICS
21. Economic Fluctuations	9. Economic Fluctuations
22. The Short-Run Macro Model	10. The Short-Run Macro Model
PART IX: MONEY, PRICES, AND THE MACROECONOMY	PART V: MONEY, PRICES, AND THE MACROECONOMY
23. The Banking System and the Money Supply	11. The Banking System and the Money Supply
24. The Money Market and the Interest Rate	12. The Money Market and the Interest Rate
25. Aggregate Demand and Aggregate Supply	13. Aggregate Demand and Aggregate Supply
PART X: MACROECONOMIC POLICY	PART VI: MACROECONOMIC POLICY
26. Inflation and Monetary Policy	14. Inflation and Monetary Policy
27. Fiscal Policy: Taxes, Spending, and the Federal Budget	15. Fiscal Policy: Taxes, Spending, and the Federal Budget
28. Exchange Rates and Macroeconomic Policy	16. Exchange Rates and Macroeconomic Policy

PREFACE TO THE THIRD EDITION

TO THE STUDENT

There's a secret to learning economics. Those who discover it learn economics more quickly, understand it more deeply, and do better on exams than those who don't. The secret is this: Economics must be learned actively, not passively.

Passive learning relies on "taking things in." Merely listening to your professor, reading the book, flipping through your notes, and feeling like you "get it" because it all makes sense when someone else says it—these are the hallmarks of passive learning. While passive learning can work in some subjects, generations of students have discovered it does not work very well in economics.

Active learning, by contrast, works very well in economics. Active learning means periodically closing your book, closing your notes, and reproducing the material on your own. It means knowing how to *use* the vocabulary of economics—not just recognizing terms when you hear them. It means drawing graphs on your own, explaining what happens as we move along a curve, and what makes a curve shift—not just making sense of a graph when someone else draws it for you. It means solving problems from the ground up—not just following along as someone else solves them for you.

This Active Learning Guide will help you to study economics actively. Other than this preface, you will find nothing here for you to just read, review, or merely "take in." As soon as you turn the page, you will be asked to *do* things—again and again and again.

Each chapter of this study guide corresponds to the same numbered chapter in Hall and Lieberman's *Microeconomics: Principles and Applications, 3rd edition*. In every chapter, you will be asked to:

- *Summarize the Chapter* by identifying missing parts of important conclusions from the text;

- *Learn the Lingo* by filling in key vocabulary terms when you are given their definitions;

- *Build Your Skills* by solving quantitative problems and using graphs—plotting them, interpreting them, and drawing conclusions from them;

- *Test Yourself* by answering multiple choice, true/false and short-answer questions to help you decide when you've mastered a chapter of the text, and what you need to go back and review.

To help gauge your mastery of *all* the material, not just that of any single chapter, you may challenge yourself more comprehensively by completing the included:

- *Sample Final Exams in Microeconomics* offering multiple choice exams, carefully coordinated with the text, along with answers and full explanations.

TO THE INSTRUCTOR

Nothing is more frustrating than inconsistency between a textbook and its associated study guide. I know this firsthand. Over the years, I've suffered—as have my students—with study guides and texts that seem to come from different planets.

In writing this updated Active Learning Guide, I've worked closely with the textbook's authors, Bob Hall and Marc Lieberman, to ensure complete consistency in approach, language, and content. Indeed, the authors themselves contributed many of the questions and problems in this guide. From the beginning our goal has been to make the transition from text to study guide—and back again—as seamless as possible. If, despite our efforts, you discover errors or omissions in this guide, I would be very happy to hear from you at the e-mail address, below.

ACKNOWLEDGEMENTS

Bob Hall and Marc Lieberman have written a gem of a text, and it was a pleasure to prepare this Active Learning Guide with them. Their devotion to their subject, and to their reader, is inspiring. I would also like to offer special thanks to my assistant, Erick Sager, whose keen eye, careful attention to detail and hard work have contributed greatly to this guide.

Geoffrey A. Jehle
Vassar College
jehle@vassar.edu

CHAPTER 1
WHAT IS ECONOMICS?

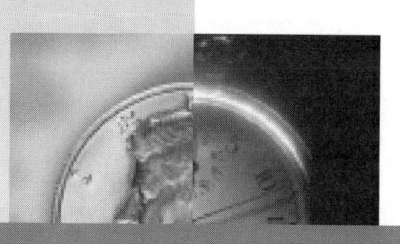

SUMMARIZE THE CHAPTER

Construct your own chapter summary by filling in the blanks. If you have difficulty, review the highlighted points in the chapter, then try again.

- Economics is the study of choice under conditions of _____ .

- As individuals, we face a scarcity of _____ and spending power. Given more of either, we could each have more of the goods and services that we desire.

- As a society, our resources—land and natural resources, labor, _____ and entrepreneurship—are insufficient to produce all the goods and services we might desire. In other words, society faces a scarcity of resources.

- A _____ is an abstract representation of reality, and should be as simple as possible to accomplish its purpose.

- Economic models contain two types of assumptions: simplifying assumptions and _____ assumptions.

- Mathematical Appendix:

- A graph between two variables X and Y is only a picture of their relationship when all other variables affecting Y are _____ .

- Suppose Y is the dependent variable, which is measured on one of the axes in a graph. If the independent variable measured on the other axis changes, we _____ the line. But if *any other* independent variable changes, the _____.

- To solve for X in any equation, rearrange the equation, following the rules of algebra, so that X appears on one side of the _____ and everything else in the equation appears on the other side.

LEARN THE LINGO

Fill in each blank with the appropriate word or phrase from the list provided in the word bank. (For a challenge, fill in as many blanks as you can *without* using the word bank.)

_____ 1. The study of choice under conditions of scarcity.

_____ 2. A situation in which the amount of something available is insufficient to satisfy the desire for it.

_____ 3. The labor, capital, land and natural resources, and entrepreneurship that are used to produce goods and services.

_____ 4. The time human beings spend producing goods and services

_____ 5. Something produced that is long-lasting and used to produce other goods.

_____ 6. The part of the capital stock consisting of physical goods, such as machinery, equipment, and factories.

_____ 7. The skills and training of the labor force.

_____ 8. The total amount of capital in a nation that is productively useful at a particular point in time.

_____ 9. Land as well as the naturally occurring materials that come with it.

_____ 10. The ability and willingness to combine the *other* resources—labor, capital, and natural resources—into a productive enterprise.

_____ 11. Anything (including a resource) used to produce a good or service.

_____ 12. The study of the behavior of individual households, firms, and governments, the choices they make, and their interaction in specific markets.

_____ 13. The study of the behavior of the overall economy.

_____ 14. The study of how the economy *works*.

_____ 15. The study of what *should be*; it is used to make value judgments, identify problems, and prescribe solutions.

_____ 16. An abstract representation of reality.

Chapter 1 What Is Economics?

_____ 17. Any assumption that makes a model simpler without affecting any of its important conclusions.

_____ 18. Any assumption that affects the conclusions of a model in an important way.

Word Bank

capital	microeconomics
capital stock	model
critical assumption	natural resources
economics	normative economics
entrepreneurship	positive economics
human capital	physical capital
input	resources
labor	scarcity
macroeconomics	simplifying assumption

BUILD YOUR SKILLS

Note to the Student: Some of the basic principles of graphs and graphing are reviewed in the Appendix to Chapter 1 in your text. If it has been a while since you used graphs you might want to take a look at that section of the text before you do these exercises. Those already comfortable with graphs can proceed with the exercises.

For each of the following items, write the correct answer in the blank or circle the correct answer.

1. This table reports estimates of the United States' population (in millions) each year during the 1980s. The data are population in millions by year.

Year	US Population
1980	228
1981	230
1982	233
1983	235
1984	237
1985	239
1986	242
1987	244
1988	246
1989	248

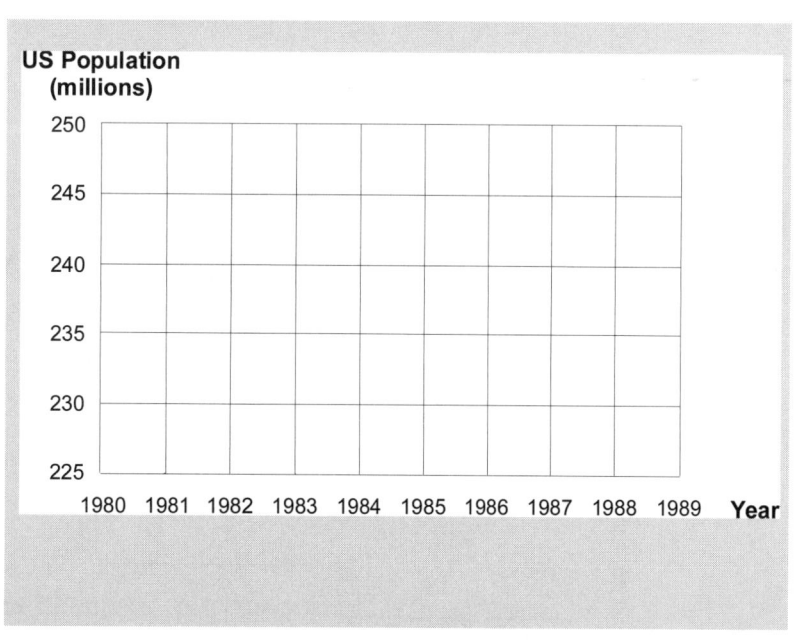

a. On the axes provided, carefully plot the data from the table.

b. Looking at your graph in (1), which of the following best describes how population changed in the 1980s? _____
   i. Population generally decreased over the decade.
   ii. Population stayed roughly constant over the decade.
   iii. Population increased and decreased erratically over the decade.
   iv. Population increased at a roughly constant rate over the decade.

c. On your graph for (1) use a ruler and draw in a single straight line which seems to best fit the data you plotted.

d. Slope measures the rate of change in the y-axis variable for a one unit change in the x-axis variable. Bearing this in mind, what is the rate at which population changed over the decade of the 1980s? _____

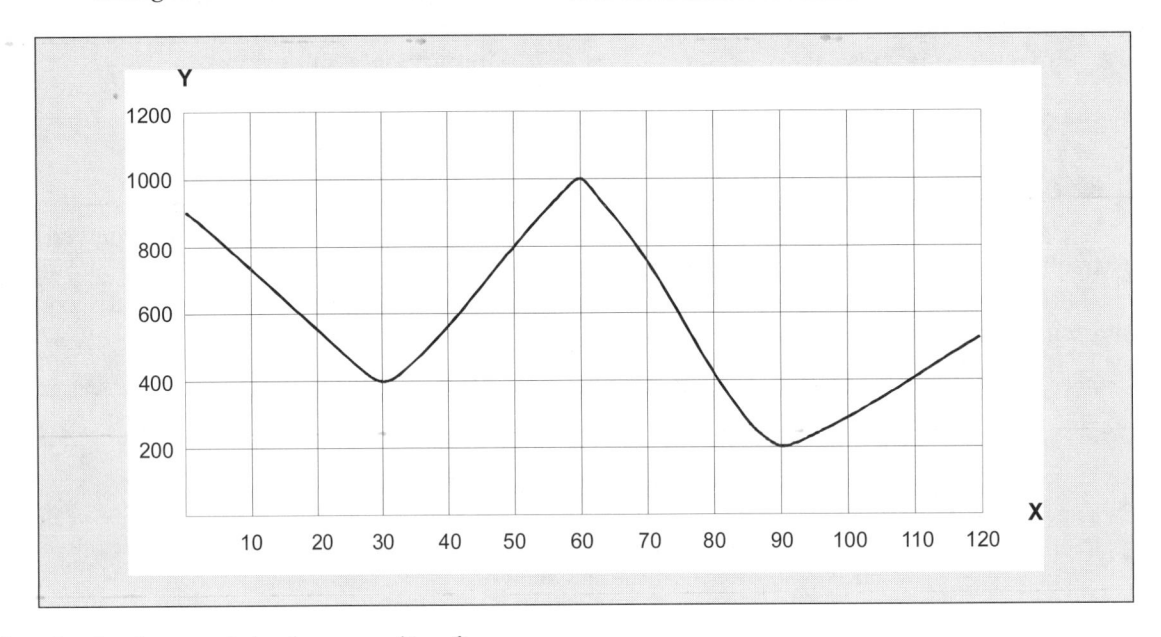

2. Study the graph in the preceding figure.

   a. In the figure, Y increases when X increases from _____ to _____, and then again when X increases from _____ to _____. In these two regions, the slope of the relationship between X and Y is (positive/negative/zero).

   b. In the same figure, Y decreases when X increases from _____ to _____, and then again when X increases from _____ to _____. In these two regions, the slope of the relationship between X and Y is (positive/negative/zero).

   c. Y reaches its maximum value of _____ when X has the value _____. Y reaches its minimum value of _____ when X has the value _____.

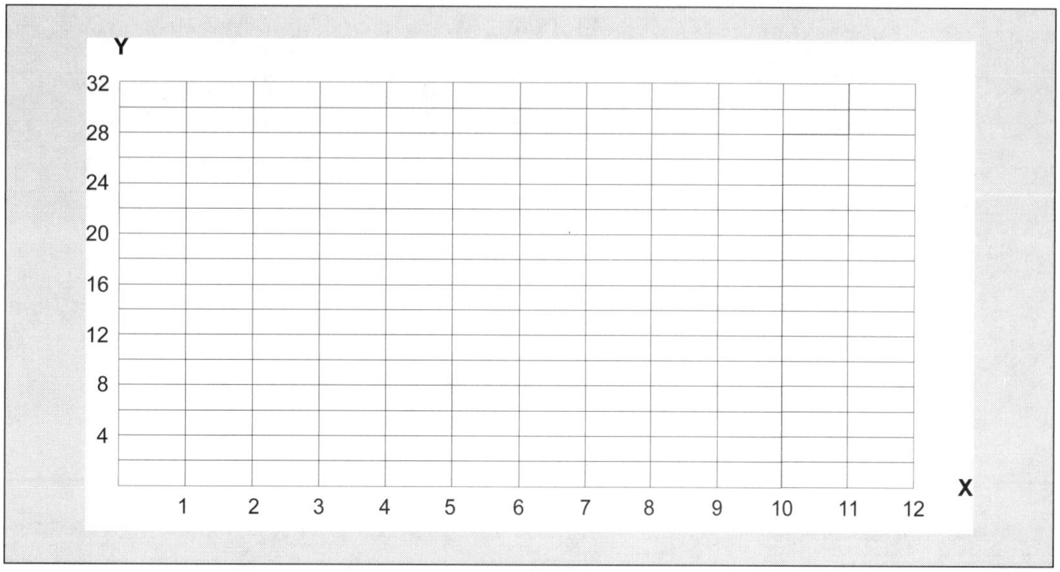

3. Graph each of the following equations on the grid provided. Then describe your graph by filling in the blanks.

   a. Y = 2X + 10
   This graph has a vertical intercept of ____________________ and a constant slope of ____________________. As X increases, Y always (increases/decreases) at a (constant/changing) rate.

   b. Y = 2X + 5
   This graph has a vertical intercept of ____________________ and a constant slope of ____________________. As X increases, Y always (increases/decreases) at a (constant/changing) rate.

   c. Y = X + 10
   This graph has a vertical intercept of ____________________ and a constant slope of ____________________. As X increases, Y always (increases/decreases) at a (constant/changing) rate.

   d. Y = 30 – 5X
   This graph has a vertical intercept of ____________________ and a constant slope of ____________________. As X increases, Y always (increases/decreases) at a (constant/changing) rate.

   e. Y = 30 – 3X
   This graph has a vertical intercept of ____________________ and a constant slope of ____________________. As X increases, Y always (increases/decreases) at a (constant/changing) rate.

4. Your text describes a method you can use to calculate the slope of a curved line at a specific point along it by drawing a tangent line to the curve.

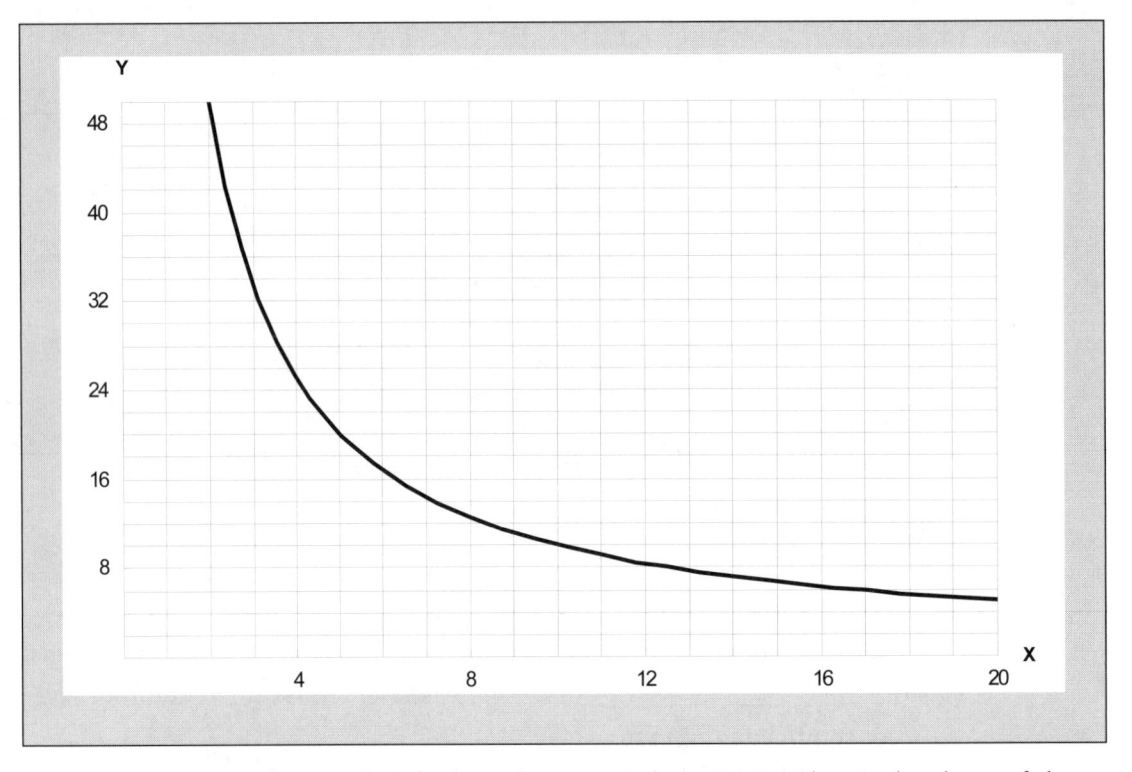

a. Draw a tangent line to the point on the curve where X=5. What is the slope of the curve at that point? _____

b. Draw a tangent line to the point on the curve where X=10. What is the slope of the curve at that point? _____

5. Remember Len and Harry, the Texas ice cream makers? Seems they've solved their advertising problems and turned their full attention to that other problem facing their business: the weather. Len and Harry know that both rainfall *and* temperature affect ice cream sales, but they do so differently. Other things equal, the greater the average daily amount of rainfall, the lower monthly ice cream sales; while the greater the average daily temperature, the higher ice cream sales.

a. If we think of monthly ice cream sales (S) as the dependent variable, we would say that average daily rainfall (R) and average daily temperature (T) are two (dependent/independent) _____ variables affecting S. Moreover, from what we know, S and R have a (positive/negative) _____ relationship, while S and T have a (positive/negative) _____ relationship.

In the lefthand panel below, the relationship between S and R has been graphed for three different values of the (ungraphed) variable T. In the righthand panel, the

Chapter 1 What Is Economics?   7

relationship between S and T has been graphed for three different values of the (ungraphed) variable R. Let's get some practice using the technique described in the text for determining whether movements along a curve, or shifts in the curve, occur.

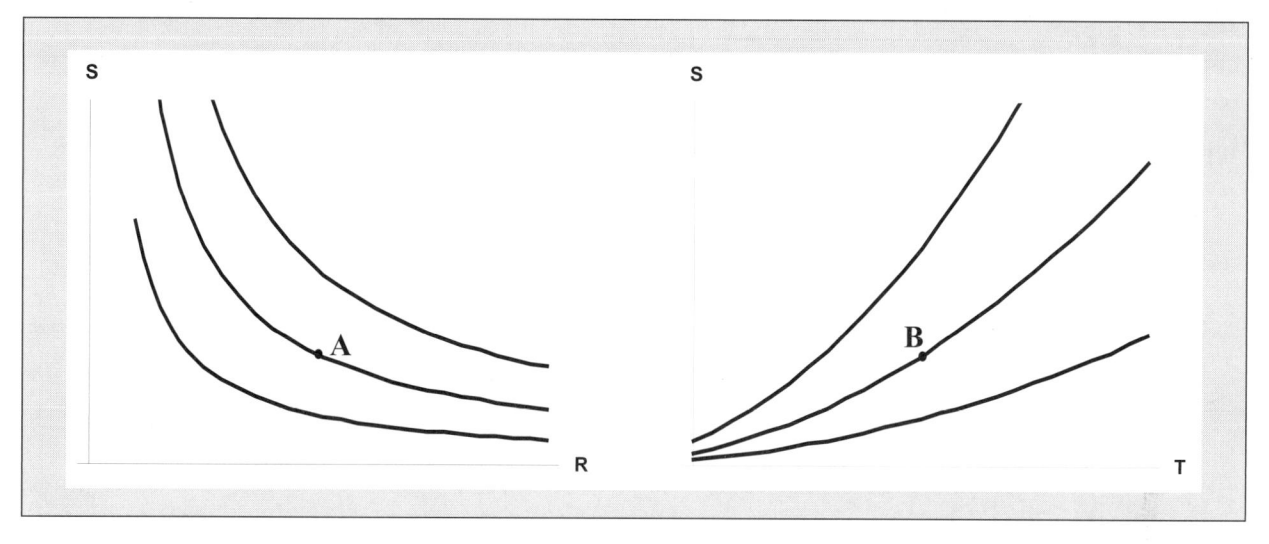

Place a pencil on the point A in the lefthand panel, and answer the following questions.

b. From what we know about the relationship between S, R and T, other things equal, a decrease in rainfall from that associated with point A would lead to (a leftward movement along the curve through A / a rightward movement along the curve through A / an upward shift in the curve through A / a downward shift in the curve through A.) _____. By contrast, an increase in temperature would lead to (a leftward movement along the curve through A / a rightward movement along the curve through A / an upward shift in the curve through A / a downward shift in the curve through A.) _____, while a decrease in temperature would lead to (a leftward movement along the curve through A / a rightward movement along the curve through A / an upward shift in the curve through A / a downward shift in the curve through A) _____.

Now place your pencil on the point B in the righthand panel, and let's answer those same questions, but from this new perspective of the graph between S and T.

c. From what we know about the relationship between S, R and T, other things equal, a decrease in rainfall from that associated with point B would lead to (a leftward movement along the curve through B / a rightward movement along the curve through B / an upward shift in the curve through B / a downward shift in the curve through B.) _____. By contrast, an increase in temperature would lead to (a leftward movement along the curve through B / a rightward movement along the curve through B / an upward shift in the curve through B / a downward shift in the curve through B.) _____ , while a decrease in temperature would lead to (a leftward movement along the curve through B / a rightward movement along the curve through B / an upward shift in the curve through B / a downward shift in the curve through B) _____ .

TEST YOURSELF

To see what you *really* know and remember, take the test at least a day *after* you've read the chapter in the text and completed the exercises in this study guide.

Multiple Choice: Circle the letter in front of the single best answer.

1. Economics can be defined as the study of
   a. business firms and how they can increase their profit.
   b. financial markets, like the stock market and the bond market.
   c. choice under conditions of scarcity.
   d. how households allocate their income to different uses.
   e. how businesses and government agencies allocate their revenue to different uses.

2. *Micro*economics studies the economic behavior of
   a. very small nations.
   b. very small people.
   c. individual businesses only.
   d. individual households only.
   e. individual decision-makers, including households and businesses.

3. Which of the following is a *resource*, from society's point of view?
   a. Meat
   b. Clothing
   c. The income tax
   d. An office building
   e. Electricity

4. Regardless of its truth or falsehood, the statement "A tax cut will cause faster growth in total output than an increase in government spending" is an example of
   a. positive microeconomics.
   b. positive macroeconomics.
   c. normative microeconomics.
   d. normative macroeconomics.
   e. none of the above.

5. Which of the following is the best example of a *model*?
   a. A dollar bill
   b. A coffee cup
   c. A drawing of a house
   d. A stop sign
   e. A laptop computer

6. The best way to study economics is
   a. *passively*, reading the book over and over again until you can follow the logical flow.
   b. *actively*, making sure you can reproduce the material on your own.
   c. with a phone in one hand and a remote control in the other.
   d. bent at the waist, making a 90-degree angle with your upper torso.
   e. with Country-and-Western music in the background.

True/False: For each of the following statements, circle T if the statement is true or F if the statement is false.

T F 1. All assumptions in an economic model are *simplifying* assumptions.

T F 2. Economists classify resources into three categories: labor, physical capital and human capital.

T F 3. Normative economics deals with how the economy normally functions in ordinary times.

T F 4. In economics, we assume that individuals face scarcities of time and spending power.

T F 5. *Macro*economics studies large global markets, such as the market for oil.

Short Answer: Fill in the blanks with brief answers.

1. State whether each of the following questions is primarily *microeconomic* or *macroeconomic*, and whether it is primarily *positive* or *normative*. Don't worry about the actual answers to the questions themselves—just classify them. (For example, the first question is a microeconomic, positive question.)
   a. If the price of compact discs rises, what will happen to the equilibrium price of cassette tapes?

   _____   _____

   b. If we raise the social security tax on wages and salaries, what will happen to total employment in the United States?

   _____   _____

   c. How much have pollution-control devices raised the price of automobiles?

   _____   _____

   d. Should the federal government use our tax dollars to support the arts?

   _____   _____

   e. What policies would help improve the average standard of living in less-developed countries?

   _____   _____

f. Should less-developed countries like Ethiopia or Ghana use government funds to subsidize basic necessities like bread or milk?
_____   _____

g. Which is worse for society: a one percentage-point rise in the unemployment rate, or a one percentage-point rise in the inflation rate?
_____   _____

2. Each of the following is an example of one of the four categories of resources. In the blanks, identify the categories.
   a. A surgeon's time in performing an operation _____
   b. The surgeon's scalpel _____
   c. The surgeon's skills and training _____
   d. The iron ore used to make steel _____
   e. The workers who make steel out of iron ore _____
   f. The factory in which iron ore is made into steel _____
   g. The services performed by a waiter at a restaurant _____
   h. A restaurant's pots, pans and dishes _____
   i. The individual who spots a neighborhood that doesn't have a restaurant, borrows money, and opens one up. _____s

CHAPTER 2

SCARCITY, CHOICE, AND ECONOMIC SYSTEMS

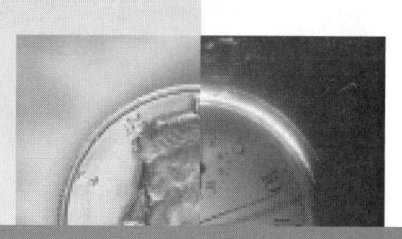

SUMMARIZE THE CHAPTER

Construct your own chapter summary by filling in the blanks. If you have difficulty, review the highlighted points in the chapter, then try again.

- The opportunity cost of any choice is what we must forego when we make that choice. It is the best among the available _____ to that choice.

- The opportunity cost of a choice includes both explicit costs and _____ costs.

- The _____ (or direct money) cost of a choice may only be a part—and sometimes a small part—of the opportunity cost of a choice.

- Virtually all production carries an opportunity cost: To produce more of one thing, society must shift _____ away from producing something else.

- According to the law of _____ , the more of something we produce, the greater the opportunity cost of producing even more of it.

- A firm, an industry, or an entire economy is productively _____ if it could produce more of at least one good without pulling resources from the production of any other good.

- A technological change or an increase in the _____ stock, even when the direct impact is to increase production of just one type of good, allows us to choose greater production of all types of goods.

- In order to produce more goods and services in the future, we must shift _____ toward R&D and capital production, and away from the production of things we'd enjoy right now.

- _____ and exchange enable us to enjoy greater production, and higher living standards, than would otherwise be possible. As a result, all economies exhibit high degrees of _____ and exchange.

- A person has a _____ in producing some good if he or she can produce it with a smaller opportunity cost than some other person can.

- Total production of every good or service will be greatest when individuals specialize according to their _____. This is another reason why specialization and exchange lead to higher living standards than does self-sufficiency.

- When resources are allocated by the _____, and people must pay for their purchases, they are forced to consider the _____ to society of their individual actions. In this way, markets are able to create a sensible allocation of resources.

- An _____ is composed of two features: a mechanism for allocating resources and a mode of resource ownership.

LEARN THE LINGO

Fill in each blank with the appropriate word or phrase from the list provided in the word bank. (For a challenge, fill in as many blanks as you can *without* using the word bank.)

_____ 1. What is given up when making a choice or taking an action.

_____ 2. The dollars sacrificed—and actually paid out—for a choice.

_____ 3. The value of something sacrificed when no direct payment is made.

_____ 4. A curve showing all combinations of two goods that can be produced with the resources and technology currently available.

_____ 5. The more of something we produce, the greater the opportunity cost of producing one more unit.

_____ 6. A situation in which we could produce more of one good without sacrificing production of any other good.

_____ 7. A method of production in which each person concentrates on a limited number of activities.

_____ 8. The act of trading with others to obtain what we desire.

Chapter 2 Scarcity, Choice and Economic Systems   13

_____ 9. The ability to produce a good or service using *fewer resources* than other producers use.

_____ 10. The ability to produce a good or service at a *lower opportunity cost* than other producers.

_____ 11. A method of determining which goods and services will be produced, how they will be produced, and who will get them.

_____ 12. An economy in which resources are allocated according to long-lived practices from the past.

_____ 13. Two names for an economic system in which resources are allocated according to explicit instructions from a central authority. (Two terms here)

_____ 14. An economic system in which resources are allocated through individual decision making.

_____ 15. A group of buyers and sellers with the potential to trade with one another.

_____ 16. The amount of money that must be paid to a seller to obtain a good or service.

_____ 17. A type of economic system in which most resources are owned in common.

_____ 18. A type of economic system in which most resources are owned by the state.

_____ 19. A type of economic system in which most resources are owned privately.

_____ 20. General term for a system of resource allocation and resource ownership.

Word Bank

absolute advantage
capitalism
centrally planned economy
command economy
communism
comparative advantage
economic system
exchange
explicit cost
implicit cost
law of increasing opportunity cost

market
market economy
opportunity cost
price
production possibilities frontier (PPF)
productive inefficiency
resource allocation
socialism
specialization
traditional economy

BUILD YOUR SKILLS

For each of the following items, write the correct answer in the blank or circle the correct answer.

1. By using its existing resources efficiently, an island society can produce the following alternative combinations of mangoes and oranges each day.

Daily Production of:	
Mangoes	Oranges
A 0	50
B 5	49
C 10	46
D 15	40
E 20	30
F 25	0

a. Plot this society's production possibility frontier (PPF) on the axes provided. Label the points A–F on your graph.

b. Assume the islanders are currently producing at point A, devoting all their resources to orange production. In moving to point B, this society gives up _____ orange(s). The resources released from producing oranges are then able to produce _____ mangoes. The opportunity cost to society of these first _____ mangoes is _____ orange(s).

Starting at point B, this society can move to point C and produce an additional _____ mangoes only if it foregoes an additional _____ oranges. The opportunity cost of the additional mangoes obtained in moving from B to C is an additional _____ oranges foregone.

In moving from C to D, the opportunity cost of _____ additional mangoes is _____ more oranges. In moving from D to E, the opportunity cost of _____ more mangoes is _____ more oranges. In moving from E to F, the opportunity cost of _____ more mangoes is _____ more oranges.

Moving along the PPF from A to F, the opportunity cost of mangoes is (increasing/decreasing/constant) as more and more mangoes are produced.

c. Now assume the islanders are currently producing at point F, devoting all their resources to mango production. In moving to point E, this society gives up _____ mangoes. The resources released from producing these mangoes are then able to produce _____ oranges. The opportunity cost to society of these first _____ oranges is _____ mangoes.

Starting at point E, this society can move to point D and produce an additional _____ oranges only if it foregoes an additional _____ mangoes. The opportunity cost of the additional oranges obtained in moving from E to D is an additional _____ mangoes foregone.

In moving from D to C, the opportunity cost of _____ additional oranges is _____ more mangoes. In moving from C to B, the opportunity cost of _____ more oranges is _____ more mangoes.

Moving along the PPF from F to A, the opportunity cost of oranges is (increasing/decreasing/constant) as more and more oranges are produced.

2. On the graph above, plot the point representing total production of 10 mangoes and 30 oranges. Label this point G. Plot the point representing production of 15 mangoes and 50 oranges. Label this point H.

   a. At point G, the islanders (are not/are) wasting resources. Starting from point G, the opportunity cost of an additional 5 mangoes would be _____ oranges. The opportunity cost of an additional 5 oranges would be _____ mangoes. At point G, does this society achieve productive efficiency (yes/no)?

   b. The point H represents a combination of mango and orange production that this society (can/cannot) achieve with existing resources and technology. To achieve point H, the economy would have to experience technological change, or it would have to (acquire more/use fewer of its) resources.

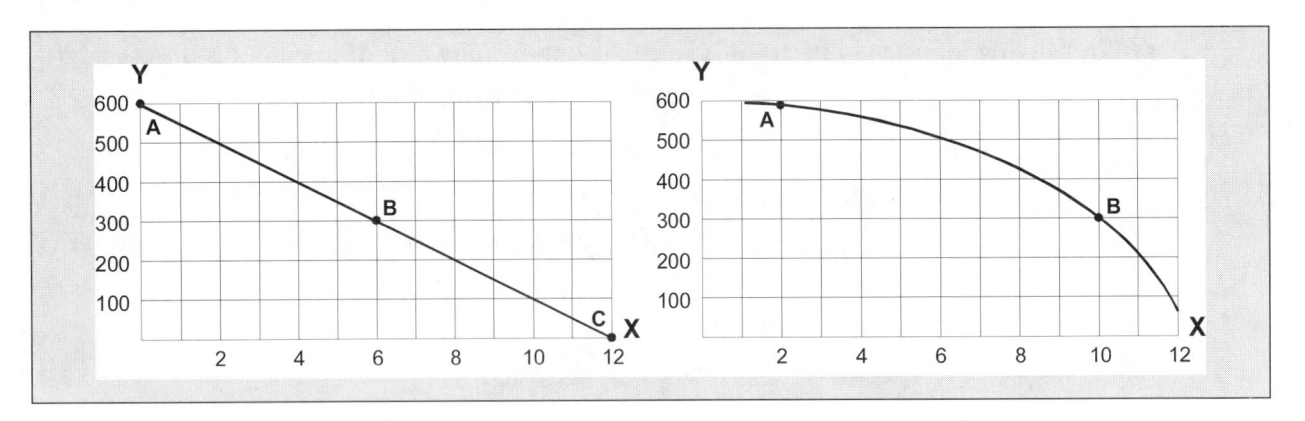

3. In the panel on the left above, the absolute value of the PPF's slope is (constant/increasing/decreasing) as we move from A to B. Starting at A, the opportunity cost of the first unit of good X will be _____ units of (X/Y). Starting at B, the opportunity cost of one more unit of X will be _____ units of (X/Y). If we begin at point C, the opportunity cost of one more unit of X will be _____ units of (X/Y). With this PPF, as we move from A to B to C, the opportunity cost of additional units of X is (constant/increasing/decreasing).

4. In the panel on the right above, as we move from point A to point B, the absolute value of the PPF's slope (remains constant/increases/decreases). At point A, the opportunity cost of an additional unit of X is (the same as/greater than/less than) the opportunity cost of an additional unit of X at point B. At the same time, at point A the opportunity cost of an additional unit of Y is (the same as/greater than/less than) the opportunity cost of an additional unit of Y at point B.

5. Each entry in the following table gives the number of hours it takes a typical worker in the given country to produce one unit of the indicated good. Thus, it takes a worker in Norway two hours to produce one sweater, and four hours to catch a fish, and so forth.

	1 Sweater	1 Fish
Norway	2 hours	4 hours
Sweden	6 hours	2 hours

a. From these data, we can see that Norway has an absolute advantage in producing (sweaters/fish/both goods/neither good). At the same time, Sweden has an absolute advantage in producing (sweaters/fish/both goods/neither good).

b. From these same data, we can see that the opportunity cost of producing a fish in Norway is _____ sweater(s). The opportunity cost of producing a fish in Sweden is _____ sweater(s). From this we can conclude that Sweden has a comparative advantage in producing (sweaters/fish/both goods/neither good), while Norway has a comparative advantage in producing (sweaters/fish/both goods/neither good).

TEST YOURSELF

To see what you *really* know and remember, take the test at least a day *after* you've read the chapter in the text and completed the exercises in this study guide.

Multiple Choice: Circle the letter in front of the single best answer.

1. The opportunity cost of any choice is
   a. the money given up for that choice.
   b. the time given up for that choice.
   c. what is actually sacrificed to make that choice.
   d. the sum of the values of every alternative to that choice.
   e. how much you would pay to avoid that choice.

2. For society, opportunity cost arises because of a scarcity of
   a. technology.
   b. land.
   c. money.
   d. resources.
   e. markets.

3. As we move rightward along a production possibilities frontier, we also move
   a. downward, and the frontier becomes steeper.
   b. downward, and the frontier becomes flatter.
   c. upward, and the frontier becomes steeper.
   d. upward, and the frontier becomes flatter.
   e. neither upward nor downward, and the slope of the frontier remains unchanged.

4. A point inside a production possibilities frontier might represent
   a. productive efficiency.
   b. a recession.
   c. a situation of very high opportunity cost.
   d. full employment of resources.
   none of the above.

5. The production possibilities frontier is concave shaped (like an upside-down bowl) because of
   a. the scarcity of resources.
   b. the law of increasing opportunity cost.
   c. productive inefficiency.
   d. absolute advantage.
   e. none of the above.

6. Which of the following is consistent with specialization according to comparative advantage?
   a. Famous attorney Alan Dershowitz prepares and addresses his own bills and takes them to the post office each day.
   b. John Travolta walks his own dog.
   c. The President of the United States drafts his own speeches.
   d. All of the above.
   e. None of the above.

7. Which of the following is a reason that specialization and exchange lead to greater production?
   a. comparative advantage.
   b. the development of expertise.
   c. the time saving from not having to switch tasks.
   d. all of the above.
   e. none of the above.

8. Which of the following is a method of resource allocation?
   a. Capitalism
   b. Socialism
   c. Command
   d. All of the above
   e. None of the above

9. Which of the following questions is answered by the economy's method of resource allocation?
   a. How are the economy's goods and services produced?
   b. What determines the rate of unemployment?
   c. How can business firms increase their profit?
   d. How can an economy avoid a recession?
   e. All of the above.

10. Under *market capitalism*, resources are
    a. owned by society as a whole.
    b. owned by the market itself.
    c. owned by no one.
    d. allocated in an entirely random way.
    e. none of the above.

True/False: For each of the following statements, circle T if the statement is true or F if the statement is false.

T F 1. The correct measure of the cost of a choice is the time used up by that choice.

Chapter 2   Scarcity, Choice and Economic Systems

T   F   2. The law of increasing opportunity cost tells us that the opportunity costs of our choices tend to rise over time.

T   F   3. If we can produce more of one good without producing less of any other goods, the economy is productively inefficient.

T   F   4. An individual has a comparative advantage in producing a good if he or she can produce it at a lower opportunity cost than some other individual.

T   F   5. The United States is an example of a pure market economy, in which all resource allocation is accomplished through the market.

T   F   6. An economic system is comprised of two components: a method of resource allocation and a mode of resource ownership.

T   F   7. A recession can be illustrated by a movement downward and rightward along a country's production possibilities frontier.

T   F   8. The economic system of the former Soviet Union was market socialism.

Short Answer: Fill in the blanks with brief answers.

1. What are the three different methods of resource *allocation*?

   _____   _____   _____

2. What are the three different systems of resource *ownership*?

   _____   _____   _____

CHAPTER 3
SUPPLY AND DEMAND

SUMMARIZE THE CHAPTER

Construct your own chapter summary by filling in the blanks. If you have difficulty, review the highlighted points in the chapter, then try again.

- A market is a group of _____ and _____ with the potential to trade with each other.

- In economics, markets can be defined broadly or narrowly, depending on _____.

- For the most part, in markets for consumer goods, we'll view business firms as the only _____, and households as the only _____.

- In _____ _____ markets, individual buyers or sellers can influence the price of the product.

- In _____ _____ markets (or just _____ markets), each buyer and seller takes the market price as a given.

- The supply and demand model is designed to explain how prices are determined in _____ _____ markets.

- A household's _____ _____ of a good is the specific amount the household would choose to buy over some time period, given (1) a particular price that must be paid for the good; (2) all other _____ on the household.

- Market _____ _____ (often just _____ _____) is the specific amount of a good that all buyers in the market would choose to buy over some time period, given (1) a particular price they must pay for the good; (2) all other _____ on households.

21

- The law of demand states that when the price of a good rises and everything else remains the same, the quantity of the good demanded will _____.

- The market demand curve (or just demand curve) shows the relationship between the _____ of a good and the quantity demanded, holding constant all other variables that influence demand. Each point on the curve shows the total quantity that buyers would choose to buy at a specific _____.

- The law of demand tells us that demand curves virtually always slope _____.

- A change in the price of a good causes a _____ _____ the demand curve.

- A change in any variable that affects demand—except for the good's price— causes the demand curve to _____.

- A rise in either income or wealth will increase the demand for a (an) _____ good, and decrease the demand for a (an) _____ good.

- A rise in the price of a substitute will _____ the demand for a good, shifting the demand curve to the _____.

- A rise in the price of a complement will _____ the demand for a good, shifting the demand curve to the _____.

- In many markets, an expectation that price will _____ in the future shifts the current demand curve rightward, while an expectation that price will _____ shifts the current demand curve leftward.

- A firm's _____ _____ of a good is the specific amount its managers would choose to sell over some time period, given (1) a particular price for the good; (2) all other _____ on the firm.

- Market _____ _____ (often just _____ _____) is the specific amount of a good that all sellers in the market would choose to sell over some time period, given (1) a particular price for the good; (2) all other _____ on firms.

- The law of supply states that when the price of a good rises, and everything else remains the same, the quantity of the good supplied will _____.

Chapter 3 Supply and Demand

- The market supply curve (or just supply curve) shows the relationship between the _____ of a good and the quantity supplied, holding constant the values of all other variables that affect supply. Each point on the curve shows the quantity that sellers would choose to sell at a specific _____.

- The law of supply tells us that supply curves slope _____.

- A change in the price of a good causes a _____ _____ the supply curve.

- A change in any variable that affects supply—except for the good's price—causes the supply curve to _____.

- A fall in the price of an input causes a (an) _____ in supply, shifting the supply curve to the _____. A rise in the price of an input causes a (an) _____ in supply, shifting the supply curve to the _____.

- When the price of an alternate good _____, the supply curve for the good in question shifts leftward. When the price of an alternate _____, the supply curve for the good in question shifts rightward.

- Cost-saving technological advances _____ the supply of a good, shifting the supply curve to the _____.

- An increase in the number of sellers—with no other change—shifts the supply curve _____, while a decrease in the number of sellers shifts it _____.

- In many markets, an expectation of a future price hike shifts the current supply curve _____. Similarly, an expectation of a future price drop shifts the current supply curve _____.

- Favorable weather increases crop yields, and causes a _____ shift of the supply curve for that crop. Unfavorable weather destroys crops and shrinks yields, and shifts the supply curve _____.

- The _____ price and _____ quantity are values for price and quantity in the market that, once achieved, will remain constant—unless and until the supply curve or the demand curve _____.

- To find the _____ price and quantity in a competitive market, draw the supply and demand curves. The _____ price and _____ quantity can then be found on the vertical and horizontal axes, respectively, at the point where the supply and demand curves cross.

- A rightward shift in the _____ curve causes a rightward movement along the supply curve. Equilibrium price and equilibrium quantity both _____.

- Any change that shifts the supply curve leftward in a market will _____ the equilibrium price and _____ the equilibrium quantity in that market.

- When just one curve shifts, and we know the direction of the shift, we can determine the direction that both equilibrium price and quantity will move. When both curves shift, and we know the directions of the shifts, we can determine the direction for either _____ or _____ —but not both. The direction of the other will depend on which curve shifts by more.

The next three statements concern the three-step process that economists use again and again to answer questions about the economy.

- Step # 1 is to "_____ the Market"—to decide which market or markets best suit the problem being analyzed, and identify the decision makers (buyers and sellers) who interact there.

- Step # 2 is to "Find the _____"—to describe the conditions necessary for _____ in the market, and a method for determining that _____.

- Step # 3 is to determine "What Happens When _____ _____"— to explore how events or government policies change the market _____.

LEARN THE LINGO

Fill in each blank with the appropriate word or phrase from the list provided in the word bank. (For a challenge, fill in as many blanks as you can *without* using the word bank.)

_____ 1. The process of combining distinct things into a single whole.

_____ 2. A market in which a single buyer or seller has the power to influence the price of the product.

_____ 3. A market in which *no* buyer or seller has the power to influence the price of the product.

_____ 4. The specific amount some household would choose to buy over some time period, given (1) a particular price, (2) all other constraints on the household.

Chapter 3 Supply and Demand

_____ 5. The specific amount of a good that *all* buyers in the market would choose to buy over some time period, given (1) a particular price, (2) all other constraints they face.

_____ 6. "As the price of a good increases, the quantity demanded decreases."

_____ 7. A list showing the quantities of a good that consumers would choose to purchase at different prices, with all other variables held constant.

_____ 8. A curve showing the quantity of a good or service demanded at various prices, with all other variables held constant.

_____ 9. The amount that a person or firm earns over a particular period.

_____ 10. A good that people demand more of as their incomes rise.

_____ 11. A movement along a demand curve in response to a change in price.

_____ 12. A shift of a demand curve in response to a change in some variable other than price.

_____ 13. A good that people demand less of as their incomes rise.

_____ 14. The total value of everything a person or firm owns at a point in time, minus the total value of everything owed.

_____ 15. A good that can be used in place of some other good and that fulfills more or less the same purpose.

_____ 16. A good that is used together with some other good.

_____ 17. The specific amount a firm would choose to sell over some time period; given (1) a particular price for the good, (2) all other constraints on the firm.

_____ 18. The specific amount of a good that *all* sellers in the market would choose to sell over some time period, given (1) a particular price for the good; (2) all other constraints on the firm.

_____ 19. "As the price of a good increases, the quantity supplied increases."

_____ 20. A list showing the quantities of a good or service that firms would choose to produce and sell at different prices, with all other variables held constant.

_____ 21. A curve showing the quantity of a good or service supplied at various prices, with all other variables held constant.

_____ 22. A movement along a supply curve in response to a change in price.

_____ 23. A shift of a supply curve in response to some variable other than price.

_____ 24. Another good that a firm could produce using some of the same types of inputs as the good in question.

_____ 25. The market price that, once achieved, remains constant until either the demand curve or supply curve shifts.

_____ 26. The market quantity bought and sold per period that, once achieved, remains constant until either the demand curve or the supply curve shifts.

_____ 27. At a given price, the amount by which quantity demanded exceeds quantity supplied.

_____ 28. At a given price, the amount by which quantity supplied exceeds quantity demanded.

Word Bank

aggregation
alternate good
change in demand
change in quantity demanded
change in quantity supplied
change in supply
complement
(market) demand curve
demand schedule
equilibrium price
equilibrium quantity
excess demand
excess supply
firm's quantity supplied

household's quantity demanded
imperfectly competitive market
income
inferior good
law of demand
law of supply
normal good
perfectly competitive market
market quantity demanded
market quantity supplied
substitute
(market) supply curve
supply schedule
wealth

Chapter 3 Supply and Demand

BUILD YOUR SKILLS

For each of the following items, write the correct answer in the blank or circle the correct answer.

For each of the following items, follow the instructions, write the correct answer in the blank, or circle the correct answer.

1. In the following demand schedule, P is the market price and Q^D is the quantity of limousine rides demanded per week by buyers in Patterson, New Jersey.

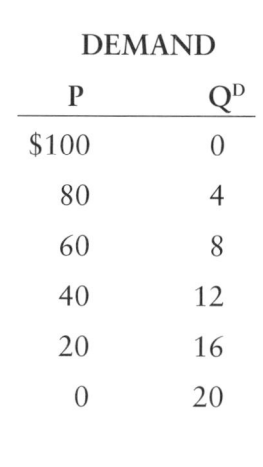

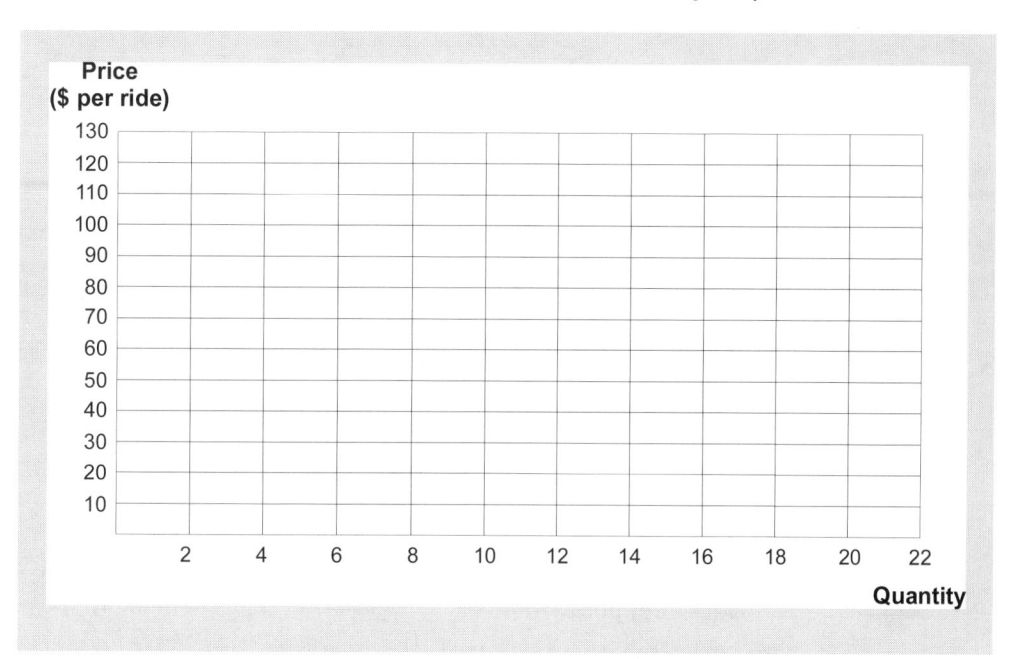

DEMAND

P	Q^D
$100	0
80	4
60	8
40	12
20	16
0	20

a. Plot the market demand curve for limousine rides. Label this curve D.

b. From this demand curve, we can see that when the market price is $50, the quantity of limousine rides demanded will be _____. If the market price rises to $90, however, the quantity demanded will (rise/fall) to _____ units per week. However, if the market price falls as low as $10, the quantity demanded will (rise/fall) to _____ units per week.

2. In the following supply schedule, P is the market price of limousine rides and Q^S is the quantity of rides supplied per week by sellers in Patterson, New Jersey.

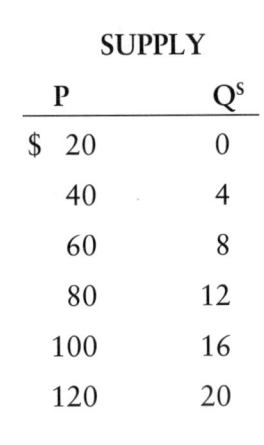

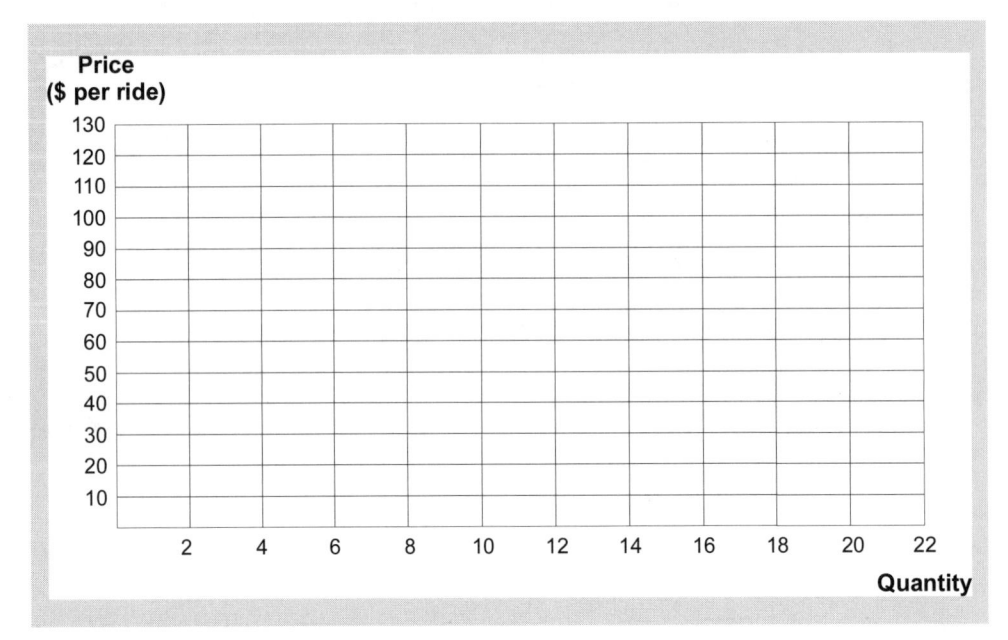

SUPPLY

P	Q^S
$ 20	0
40	4
60	8
80	12
100	16
120	20

a. Plot the market supply curve for limousine rides in the space provided. Label this curve S.

b. From this supply curve, we can see that when the market price is $50, the quantity of rides supplied will be _____. If the market price rises to $90, however, the quantity supplied will (rise/fall) to _____ units per week. However, if the market price falls as low as $30, the quantity supplied will (rise/fall) to _____ units per week.

3. In the space below, re-plot the demand curve and the supply curve for limousine rides using the data from the previous two questions.

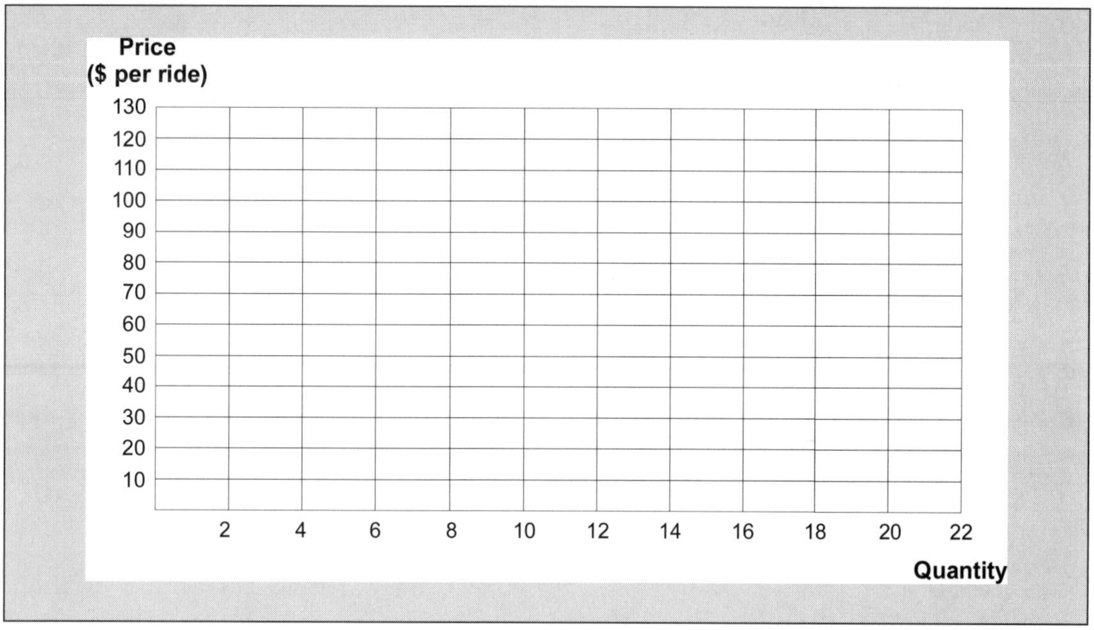

a. By examining demand and supply together, we can see that the equilibrium price in the market for limousine rides will be __________________. The number of rides bought and sold per week will be __________________.

b. At a price of $80 per week, there would be an excess (demand/supply) of __________________ units per week in this market. Market price would tend to (rise/fall) as (buyers/sellers) compete with one another to (buy/sell) more limousine rides.

c. At a price of $40 per week, there would be an excess (demand/supply) of __________________ units per week. Market price would tend to (rise/fall) as (buyers/sellers) compete with one another to (buy/sell) more limousine rides.

4. Under current conditions, the monthly demand curve and monthly supply curve for 13-inch color TVs in Golden, Colorado, are plotted below.

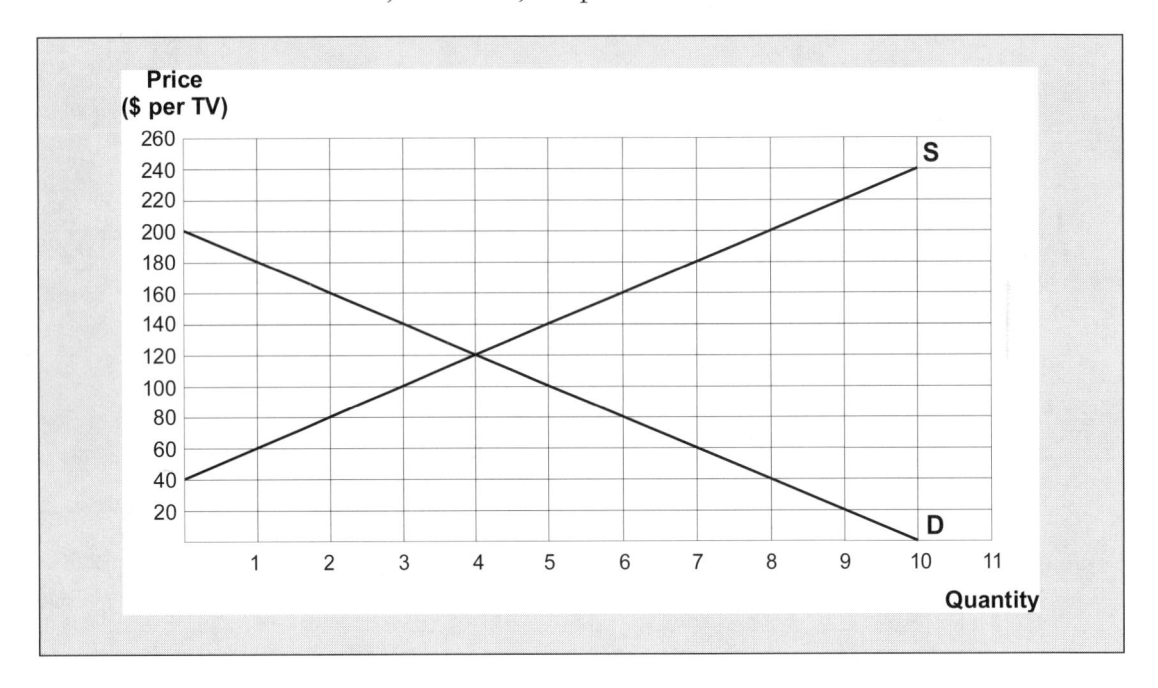

a. What is the equilibrium price of TVs? _____.

b. Suppose the price of recliner chairs, a complement to TVs, falls. This will tend to (increase/decrease) the quantity of TVs demanded every month, and so shift market demand for TVs (rightward/leftward).

The table below shows data on market demand for TVs *after* the price of recliners has fallen.

P	Q^D
$200	2
160	4
120	6
80	8
40	10

c. Plot the new demand curve for TVs on the graph above.

d. What is the new equilibrium price for TVs? _____.

e. Suppose the price of copper wire, an important component in the production of TVs, rises. This will tend to (increase/decrease) the quantity of TVs supplied every month, and so shift market supply of TVs (leftward/rightward).

Data on market supply of TVs after the price of copper wire has fallen are recorded in the table below.

P	Q^S
$120	2
160	4
200	6
240	8
280	10

f. Plot the new supply curve for TVs on the graph on the previous page.

g. What is the new equilibrium price for TVs after this latest change?
_____.

5. Monthly data from Tuscaloosa on market demand and market supply of leather handbags have been graphed below.

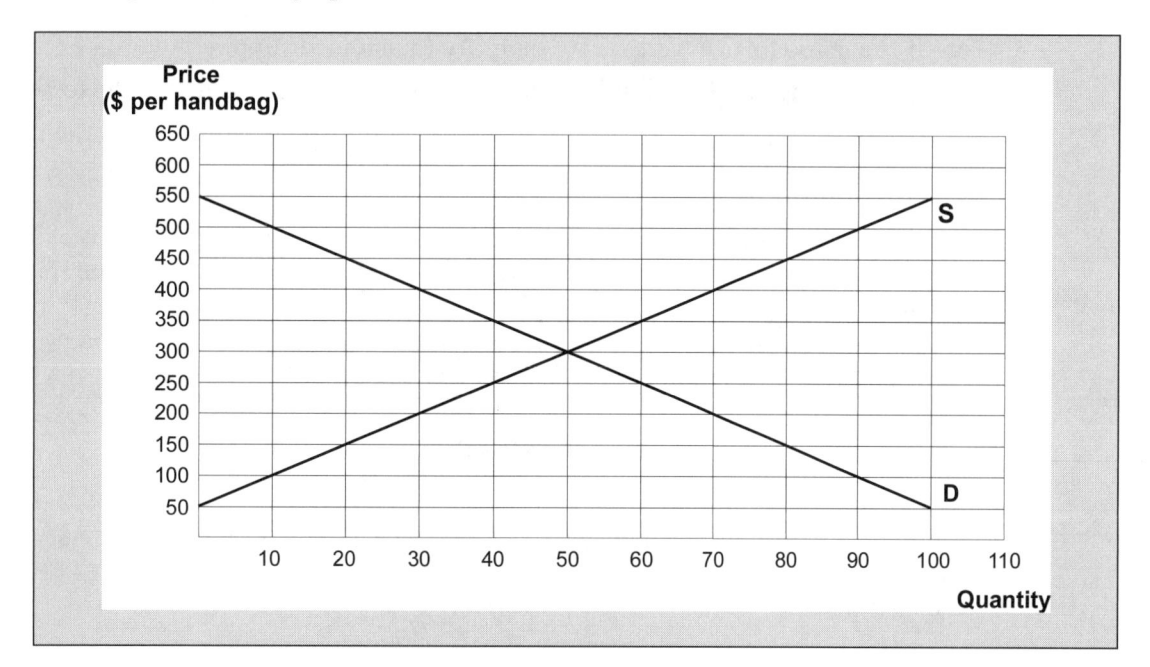

a. Complete the combined demand and supply schedules for leather handbags.

P	Q^D	Q^S
$450	____	____
400	____	____
350	____	____
300	____	____
250	____	____
200	____	____
150	____	____

b. If the market price were $400, quantity (demanded/supplied) would exceed quantity (demanded/supplied) and there would be an (excess demand/excess supply) equal to _____ units per period. This would cause the market price to (rise/fall) toward its equilibrium level of _____.

c. If the market price were $150, quantity (demanded/supplied) would exceed quantity (demanded/supplied) and there would be (excess demand/excess supply) equal to _____ units per period. This would cause the market price to (rise/fall) toward its equilibrium level of _____.

6. So far, we have studied market demand and market supply either as tables or as graphs. Sometimes, however, it is more convenient to express those same relationships in the form of equations. For example, suppose we know that, every week, the quantity of deep sea fishing trips buyers will demand (Q^D) is related to market price according to the equation

$$Q^D = 20 - P/15,$$

while the quantity of fishing trips supplied (Q^S) is related to market price according to the equation

$$Q^S = P/12 - 2.5.$$

Using these equations, complete the combined demand and supply schedules below. (To fill out the table, just plug market price into the demand or supply equation given above and solve for the corresponding quantity demanded or supplied.)

P	Q^D	Q^S
270	___	___
210	___	___
90	___	___
30	___	___

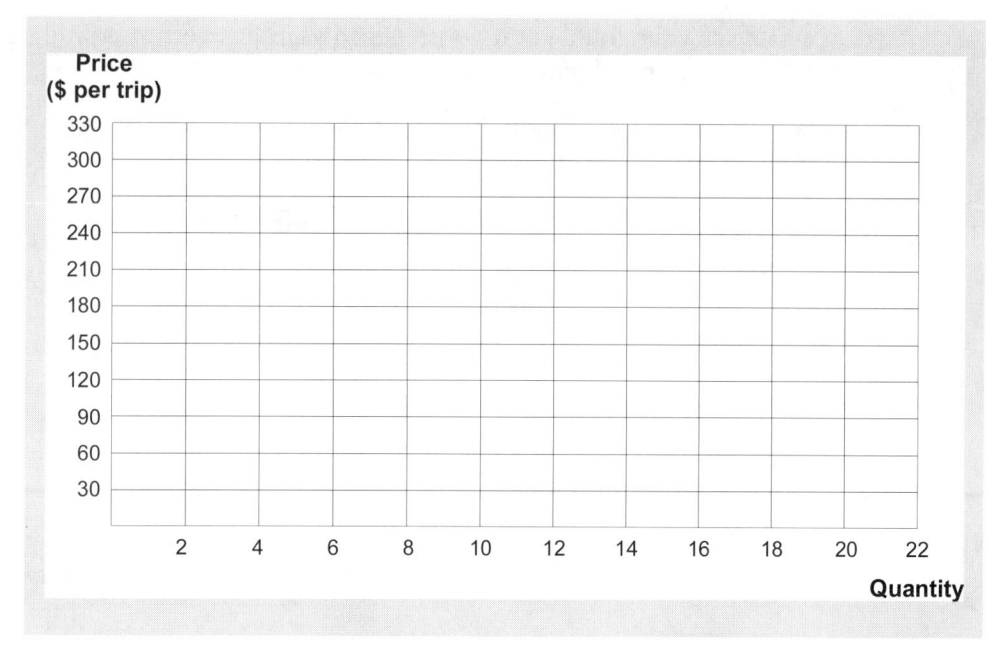

Price ($ per trip) vs **Quantity** (grid from 0 to 330 on price axis, 0 to 22 on quantity axis)

Now look at the table you just completed. Notice that at very low market prices, quantity demanded exceeds quantity supplied, while at higher prices quantity supplied exceeds quantity demanded. Just by looking at the data in these demand and supply schedules, we are therefore unable to determine the equilibrium price in this market.

But we *can* find the equilibrium with our equations. Suppose we let P_e stand for the unknown value of the equilibrium price in this market. While we do not know P_e, we know it is special: it is the only price at which quantity demanded will equal quantity supplied. To find P_e, we therefore simply set the equation for quantity demanded equal to the equation for quantity supplied. Setting $Q^D = Q^S$ in this way, we obtain

$$20 - P_e/15 = P_e/12 - 2.5.$$

To solve for P_e, we add 2.5 to each side, then add $P_e/15$ to each side, and get

$$22.5 = P_e/12 + P_e/15.$$

Next, putting the two terms on the righthand side over the common denominator $12 \times 15 = 180$, we obtain

$$22.5 = 27P_e/180.$$

Finally, by multiplying both sides by 180 and dividing by 27, we get the final answer

$$P_e = (22.5)(180)/27 = 150.$$

7. Using the data you generated in the preceding exercise, plot the market demand and supply curves in the space provided there. Once you've completed your graphs, locate the equilibrium market price. What is that price according to your graphs? _____ Is it the same price you obtained by solving the demand and supply equations? _____ It should be, so if it is not, go back and see what you did wrong.) What is the equilibrium quantity? _____ Is it

the same as you would get if you plugged your answer for equilibrium price into the market demand and market supply curves? _____ (It should be.)

8. Annual market demand and market supply for tons of California cumquats are given, respectively, by the following equations

$$Q^D = 500 - P/8$$
$$Q^S = P/2 - 500.$$

Without plotting graphs for demand or supply, answer the following questions.

a. In equilibrium, the price of California cumquats will be $_____. The quantity of cumquats bought and sold will be _____ tons.

b. If market price were $1,200, quantity demanded would be _____ tons and quantity supplied would be _____ tons. There would be (excess demand/excess supply) equal to _____ tons of cumquats per year.

c. If market price were $2,000, quantity demanded would be _____ tons and quantity supplied would be _____ tons. There would be (excess demand/excess supply) equal to _____ tons of cumquats per year.

TEST YOURSELF

To see what you *really* know and remember, take this test at least a day *after* you've read the chapter in the text and completed the exercises in this study guide.

Multiple Choice: Circle the letter in front of the single best answer.

1. In economics, a "market" is
   a. a geographic location where buyers and sellers trade with each other.
   b. virtually always defined locally, rather than nationally or internationally.
   c. virtually always defined nationally, rather than locally or internationally.
   d. defined only *after* an exchange actually takes place.
   e. a group of buyers and sellers with the potential to trade.

2. A perfectly competitive market is one in which
   a. buyers and sellers never actually meet each other.
   b. no buyer or seller can influence the price of the product being traded.
   c. a few very large firms directly compete with each other for customers.
   d. there are no limits to the tricks sellers can play to drive their rivals out of business.
   e. all of the above.

3. Which of the following would cause a rightward shift of the demand curve in the market for fresh eggs in St. Louis?
   a. A technological advance in the egg-producing industry
   b. An increase in the number of firms in the egg-producing industry
   c. An increase in the price of chicken feed
   d. An increase in the price of powdered eggs, a substitute for fresh eggs
   e. None of the above

4. If used books are an inferior good, then a decrease in income will cause a
   a. rightward shift of the demand curve for used books.
   b. leftward shift of the demand curve for used books.
   c. rightward shift of the supply curve for used books.
   d. leftward shift of the demand curve for used books.
   e. shift in both the demand and the supply curves for used books.

5. If the price of oranges is expected to rise, then
   a. the demand curve for oranges will shift rightward.
   b. the demand curve for oranges will shift leftward.
   c. the supply curve for oranges will shift leftward.
   d. both *a* and *c*.
   e. both *b* and *c*.

6. Which of the following would shift the supply curve for a good leftward?
   a. A rise in the price of a complement
   b. A rise in the price of an input used in producing the good
   c. A cost-saving technological advance in producing the good
   d. All of the above
   e. None of the above

7. If there is an excess supply of a good, we can generally expect
   a. the price of the good to rise.
   b. the price of the good to fall.
   c. the demand curve to shift rightward.
   d. the supply curve to shift leftward.
   e. both *c* and *d*.

8. A rise in the price of a substitute for a good will cause
   a. the equilibrium price of the good to increase and the equilibrium quantity to decrease.
   b. the equilibrium price of the good to decrease and the equilibrium quantity to increase.
   c. both the equilibrium price and the equilibrium quantity of the good to increase.
   d. both the equilibrium price and the equilibrium quantity of the good to decrease.
   e. no change in either the equilibrium price or equilibrium quantity of the good.

9. Which of the following is one of the three steps in the three-step process that economists use to solve problems?
   a. Graph the Equations.
   b. Find the Equilibrium.
   c. Solve for the numbers.
   d. Find the Calculator.
   e. Drink the coffee.

10. In the market for potatoes, a rise in the price of beef (a complement) and a rise in the wage paid to farm labor (an input) would cause
   a. both the equilibrium price and equilibrium quantity to rise.
   b. both the equilibrium price and equilibrium quantity to fall.
   c. a decrease in the equilibrium quantity, and an ambiguous effect on the equilibrium price.
   d. an increase in the equilibrium price, and an ambiguous effect on the equilibrium quantity.
   e. none of the above.

True/False: For each of the following statements, circle T if the statement is true or F if the statement is false.

T F 1. The law of demand tells us that, for most goods, a rise in income will cause an increase in quantity demanded.

T F 2. If people want to buy more of a good at any price, sellers will want to sell more of the good, so the supply curve will shift.

T F 3. A change in the expected future price of a good will generally cause both the supply curve and the demand curve for the good to shift.

T F 4. A "change in supply" refers to a movement along the supply curve.

T F 5. A rightward shift in the demand curve for cotton shirts will cause a rise in both the equilibrium price and equilibrium quantity of cotton shirts.

T F 6. A rise in the price of *rayon* shirts will cause a decrease in the equilibrium price and quantity of *cotton* shirts.

T F 7. The *first* step of the three-step process is: Find the Equilibrium.

T F 8. The *last* step of the three-step process is to ask: What Happens When Things Change?

Chapter 3   Supply and Demand

Short Answer: Fill in the blanks with brief answers.

1. List four distinct variables (and the direction of change for each) that would cause the *demand* curve for a good to *shift leftward*. (Assume that the good is *normal*.)

   _____   _____

   _____   _____

2. List four distinct variables (and the direction of change for each) that would cause the *supply* curve for a good to *shift leftward*.

   _____   _____

   _____   _____

CHAPTER 4

WORKING WITH SUPPLY AND DEMAND

SUMMARIZE THE CHAPTER

Construct your own chapter summary by filling in the blanks. If you have difficulty, review the highlighted points in the chapter, then try again.

- When quantity supplied and quantity demanded differ, the short side of the market—whichever of the two quantities is _____ —will prevail.

- A price _____ creates a shortage and increases the time and trouble required to buy the good. While the price decreases, the opportunity cost may _____.

- A price _____ creates a surplus of a good. In order to maintain the price _____, the government must prevent the surplus from driving down the market price. In practice, the government often accomplishes this goal by purchasing the surplus itself.

- The price _____ of demand (E_D) for a good is the percentage change in quantity demanded divided by the percentage change in price:

$$E_D = \frac{\%\text{ Change in Quantity Demanded}}{\%\text{ Change in Price}}$$

- A price _____ of demand tells us the percentage change in quantity demanded caused by a 1 percent rise in price as we move along a _____ curve from one point to another. When calculating elasticity, the base value for percentage changes in price or _____ is always midway between the initial value and the new value.

- Elasticity of demand varies along a straight-line demand curve. More specifically, demand becomes _____ elastic as we move upward and leftward.

- Where demand is _____, total revenue moves in the same direction as price. Where demand is _____, total revenue moves in the opposite direction from price. Finally, where demand is _____ _____, total revenue remains the same as price changes.

- At any point on a demand curve, sellers' total revenue (buyers' total expenditure) is the area of a rectangle with width equal to quantity demanded and height equal to _____.

- The more narrowly we define a good, the easier it is to find substitutes, and the _____ elastic is the demand for the good. The more broadly we define a good, the harder it is to find substitutes and the _____ elastic is the demand for the good.

- In general, the more "necessary" we regard an item, the harder it is to find substitutes, and the _____ elastic is demand for the good.

- It is usually easier to find substitutes for an item in the _____ run than in the _____ run. Therefore, demand tends to be more elastic in the _____ run than in the _____ run.

- The more of their total budgets that households spend on an item, the _____ elastic is demand for that item.

- The income elasticity of demand (E_Y) is the percentage change in _____ _____ divided by the percentage change in income, with all other influences on demand—including the price of the good—remaining constant:

$$E_Y = \frac{\% \text{ Change in Quantity Demanded}}{\% \text{ Change in Income}}$$

- A _____-_____ elasticity of demand tells us the percentage change in quantity demanded of a good for each 1-percent increase in the price of some other good, while all other influences on demand remain unchanged.

- The _____ _____ of supply (E_S) is the percentage change in the quantity of a good supplied that is caused by a 1 percent change in the price of the good, with all other influences on supply held constant:

$$E_S = \frac{\% \text{ Change in Quantity Supplied}}{\% \text{ Change in Price}}$$

Chapter 4 Working with Supply and Demand

- An _____ tax shifts the market supply curve upward by the amount of the tax. For each quantity supplied, the new, higher curve tells us firms' gross price, and the original, lower curve tells us the net price.

- For a given supply curve, the more elastic is demand, the more of an excise tax is paid by _____. The more inelastic is demand, the more of the tax is paid by _____.

- For a given demand curve, the more elastic is supply, the more of an excise tax is paid by _____. The more inelastic is supply, the more of the tax is paid by _____.

LEARN THE LINGO

Fill in each blank with the appropriate word or phrase from the list provided in the word bank. (For a challenge, fill in as many blanks as you can *without* using the word bank.)

_____ 1. A government-imposed maximum price in a market.

_____ 2. The smaller of quantity supplied and quantity demanded at a particular price.

_____ 3. An excess demand not eliminated by a rise in price, so that quantity demanded continues to exceed quantity supplied.

_____ 4. A market in which goods are sold illegally at a price above the legal ceiling.

_____ 5. Government-imposed maximum rents on apartments and homes.

_____ 6. A government-imposed minimum price in a market.

_____ 7. An excess supply not eliminated by a fall in price, so that quantity supplied continues to exceed quantity demanded.

_____ 8. The sensitivity of quantity demanded to price; the percentage change in quantity demanded caused by a 1-percent change in price.

_____ 9. A price elasticity of demand between 0 and −1.

_____ 10. A price elasticity of demand equal to 0.

_____ 11. A price elasticity of demand less than −1.

_____ 12. A price elasticity of demand approaching minus infinity.

_____ 13. A price elasticity of demand equal to –1.

_____ 14. An elasticity measured just a short time after a price change.

_____ 15. An elasticity measured a year or more after a price change.

_____ 16. The percentage change in quantity demanded caused by a 1-percent change in income.

_____ 17. A good with an income elasticity of demand between 0 and 1.

_____ 18. A good with an income elasticity of demand greater than 1.

_____ 19. The percentage change in the quantity demanded of one good caused by a 1-percent change in the price of another good.

_____ 20. The percentage change in quantity supplied of a good or service caused by a 1-percent change in its price.

_____ 21. A tax on a specific good or service.

_____ 22. The division of a tax payment between buyers and sellers, determined by comparing the new (after tax) and the old (pre-tax) market equilibriums.

_____ 23. The process by which some or all of a tax imposed on *one* side of the market ends up being paid by the *other* side of the market.

Word Bank

black market	price ceiling
cross-price elasticity of demand	price elasticity of demand
economic luxury	price elasticity of supply
economic necessity	price floor
elastic demand	rent controls
excise tax	shortage
incidence	short-run elasticity
income elasticity of demand	short side of the market
inelastic demand	surplus
long-run elasticity	tax shifting
perfectly inelastic demand	unitary elastic demand
perfectly elastic demand	

Chapter 4 Working with Supply and Demand

BUILD YOUR SKILLS

For each of the following items, write the correct answer in the blank or circle the correct answer.

1. In the space below, re-plot the demand curve and the supply curve for limousine rides using the data from questions (1) and (2) in Chapter 3, reproduced in the table below.

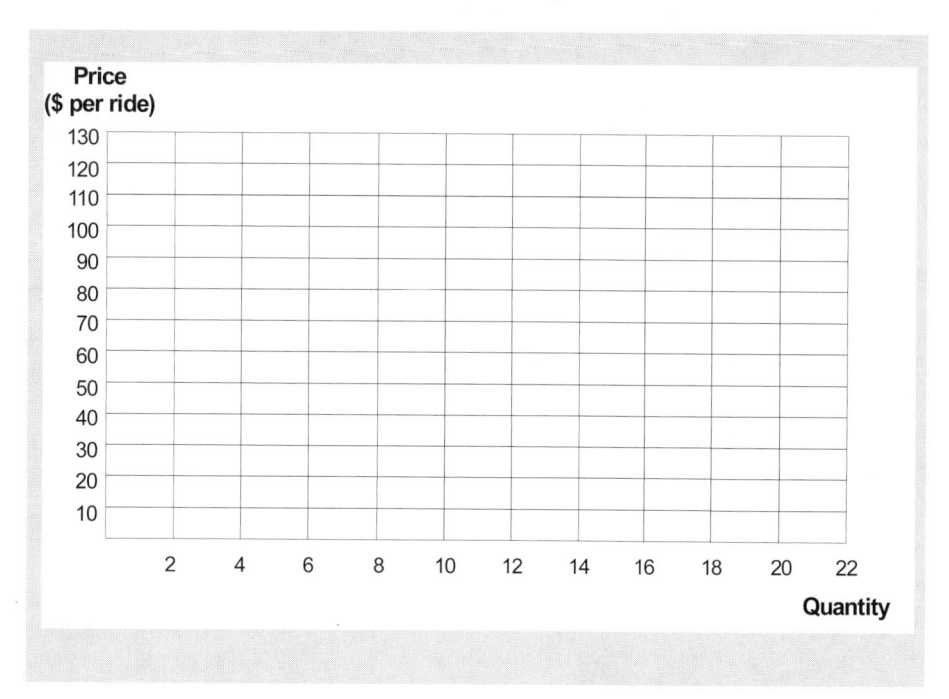

P	Q^D	Q^S
$100	0	16
80	4	12
60	8	8
40	12	4
20	16	0

a. By examining demand and supply together, we can see that the equilibrium price in the market for limousine rides will be _____. The number of rides bought and sold per week will be _____.

b. If the government were to establish and enforce a price floor of $80 per week, there would be an excess (demand/supply) of _____ units per week in this market.

c. If the government were to establish and enforce a price ceiling of $40 per week, there would be an excess (demand/supply) of _____ units per week.

d. If the government imposed a price ceiling of $40, a black market for limousine rides would likely develop. If you tried to buy rides on the black market, you could expect to pay at least _____ per unit.

For each of the following items, follow the instructions, write the correct answer in the blank, or circle the correct answer.

Reminder: **Price elasticity of demand** measures the responsiveness of quantity demanded to price, holding constant all other influences on demand. It is found by dividing the percentage change in the quantity demanded by the percentage change in the good's price, where the base value used to calculate percentage change is the *midpoint* between the initial value and the ending value.

Thus, the formula for the percentage change in quantity demanded is:

$$\%\Delta Q^D = \frac{Q_1 - Q_0}{\frac{1}{2}(Q_1 + Q_0)}.$$

The formula for the percentage change in the price is:

$$\%\Delta P = \frac{P_1 - P_0}{\frac{1}{2}(P_1 + P_0)}.$$

Elasticity is computed by taking the ratio of these:

$$E_D = \frac{\%\Delta Q^D}{\%\Delta P}.$$

2. Calculate price elasticity over the indicated range when:

   a. Price rises from $10 to $14, while quantity demanded falls from 30 units to 24 units. _____

   b. Price declines by 20%, while quantity demanded increases 15%. _____

   c. Price rises by 12%, while quantity demanded falls from 200 units to 160 units. _____

   d. Quantity demanded decreases by 2% while price rises by 4%. _____

   e. Price declines from $8 to $6, while quantity demanded rises from 100 tons to 150 tons. _____

3. Upon rearranging a bit, the formula above for price elasticity of demand can be reduced to the following "short-cut" formula:

$$E_D = \frac{Q_1 - Q_0}{Q_1 + Q_0} \times \frac{P_1 + P_0}{P_1 - P_0}$$

This formula is very useful when you are given a problem with initial and new prices and quantities. Use it to recalculate the answers to (a) and (e) in problem 2 and convince yourself the short-cut formula "works."

4. The weekly demand for new air conditioning systems in Midland, Texas, is as follows.

P	Q^D	Q^D'
1,400	0	____
1,000	12	____
600	24	____
200	36	____
0	42	____

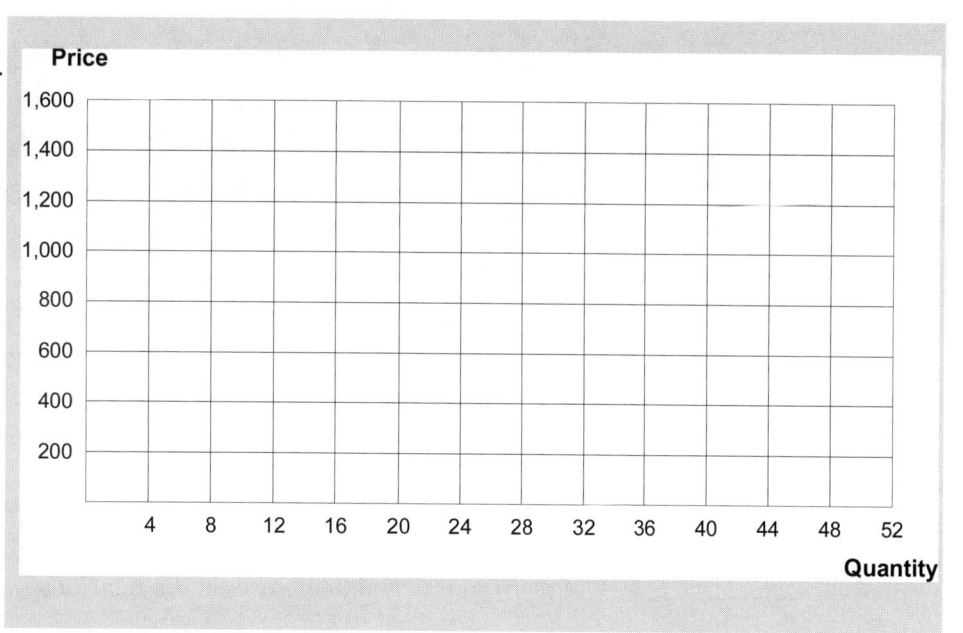

a. Plot the demand curve. (Ignore the column of blanks for now.)

b. At a price of $1400, _____ units will be purchased each week. If the price drops to $1000, _____ units will be purchased each week. Between $1400 and $1000, the elasticity of demand for air conditioning systems is $E_D=$ _____. Between these two prices, demand is (elastic/inelastic/unit elastic). From this we know that a decrease in price from $1400 to $1000 will (increase/decrease/have no effect on) the amount consumers spend on this good per week.

c. Between $1000 and $600, the elasticity of demand for air conditioning systems is $E_D=$ _____. Between these two prices, demand is (elastic/inelastic/unit elastic). From this we know that a decrease in price from $1000 to $600 will (increase/decrease/ have no effect on) the amount consumers spend on this good per week.

d. Between $600 and $200, the elasticity of demand for air conditioning systems is $E_D=$ _____. Between these two prices, demand is (elastic/inelastic/unit elastic). From this we know that a decrease in price from $600 to $200 will (increase/decrease/ have no effect on) the amount consumers spend on this good per week.

5. Now suppose that, due to a sharp rise in summer temperature, the demand for new air conditioning systems increases. In particular, at every price, consumers now demand exactly 10 more systems than they did before.

   a. Fill in the column labeled $Q^{D'}$ in the table above. Graph the new demand curve and label it D´.

b. Between $1400 and $1000, the elasticity of demand for this good is now $E_{D'}$ = _____. Elasticity between these two prices has (increased/decreased/not changed) in absolute value with the rightward shift in demand. Between $1000 and $600, the elasticity of demand for this good is now $E_{D'}$ = _____. Elasticity between these two prices has (increased/decreased/stayed unchanged) in absolute value after the rightward shift in demand. Between $600 and $200, the elasticity of demand for this product is now $E_{D'}$ = _____. Elasticity between these two prices has (increased/decreased/not changed) in absolute value after the rightward shift in demand. From the preceding, we can deduce that a rightward shift in a straight-line demand curve will always (increase/decrease/leave unchanged) the absolute value of elasticity of demand between any two prices.

6. Chapter 4 makes clear that slope and elasticity are *not* the same thing. But they *are* related. The following exercises will help you see the relationship between slope and elasticity.

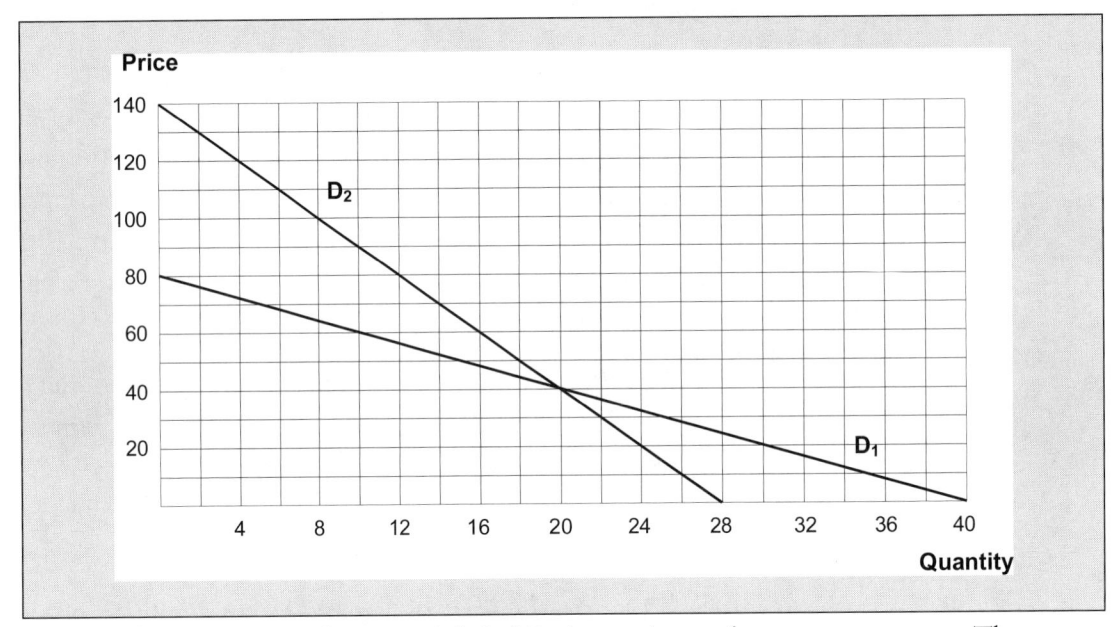

a. In the figure above, the curve labeled D_1 has a slope of _____. The curve labeled D_2 is (flatter/steeper), and it has a slope of _____. The two curves intersect where quantity demanded is _____ and price is _____ along both curves.

b. Along D_1, when price is 60, quantity demanded is _____. When price is 20, quantity demanded is _____. For a decrease in price from 60 to 20, the elasticity of demand along D_1 is E_{D1} = _____.

c. Along D_2, when price is 60, quantity demanded is _____. When price is 20, quantity demanded is _____. For a decrease in price from 60 to 20, the elasticity of demand along D_2 is E_{D2} = _____

d. Comparing answers in the previous three problems, it seems that whenever two curves share a common midpoint for the change in price and quantity demanded, the steeper curve will be more (elastic/inelastic/unit elastic) than the flatter curve over the given range.

7. **Income elasticity of demand** measures the percentage change in quantity demanded for a 1 percentage change in market income. Calculate income elasticity in (a) through (c), below, and remember to use the midpoint as your base when necessary.

   a. Income increases from 100 to 200 and quantity demanded increases from 100 to 140. _____

   b. Income decreases from 200 to 180 and quantity demanded decreases from 40 to 30. _____

   c. Income rises by 20% and quantity demanded rises by 30%. _____

8. **Cross-price elasticity of demand** gives the percentage change in quantity demanded for a 1 percent increase in the price of some other good, all other things affecting demand held constant. Calculate the cross-price elasticity of demand for rye bread in (a) and (b), below, Calculate income elasticity in (a) through (c), below, and remember to use the midpoint as your base when necessary.

   a. the price of jam rises from $1 to $1.50 and the quantity of rye bread demanded decreases by 20%. _____

   b. the price of whole wheat bread falls from $1.20 to $1.00, while the quantity of rye bread demanded declines from 140 to 120. _____

9. On the supply side of the market, we can define the **price elasticity of supply** as the responsiveness of quantity supplied to changes in price. In your text, it is computed by taking the ratio of the percentage change in quantity supplied to the percentage change in price along the supply curve:

$$E_S = \frac{\%\Delta Q^S}{\%\Delta P}.$$

Once again, percentage changes are reckoned using as a base the *midpoint* between the old and new prices and quantities. Calculate the price elasticity of supply when

   a. quantity supplied rises by 10%, while price rises by 20%. _____

   b. quantity supplied increases from 1,200 to 1,800, while price rises from $13 to $17. _____

   c. price falls from $21 to $15, while quantity supplied declines from 360 to 280. _____

   d. price falls from $150 to $120, while quantity supplied does not change at all. _____

TEST YOURSELF

To see what you *really* know and remember, take this test at least a day *after* you've read the chapter in the text and completed the exercises in this study guide.

Multiple Choice: Circle the letter in front of the single best answer.

1. Imposing a price ceiling below the equilibrium price of a good often leads to
    a. a greater supply of the good.
    b. a black market for the good.
    c. a rightward shift of the supply curve for the good.
    d. a leftward shift of the demand curve for the good.
    e. all of the above.

2. An excise tax
    a. shifts up the market supply curve.
    b. increases the price paid by buyers.
    c. decrease the (net) price received by sellers.
    d. all of the above.
    e. none of the above.

3. If the price elasticity of demand for a good is negative, we know that the good
    a. is normal.
    b. is inferior.
    c. obeys the law of demand.
    d. violates the law of demand.
    e. is inelastically demanded.

4. When the price of a good rises by 10 percent, and nothing else changes, the quantity of the good demanded falls by 5 percent. For this price change, the price elasticity of demand for this good is
    a. −5%.
    b. −5.0.
    c. −2.0.
    d. 2.0.
    e. −0.5.

5. If the (absolute value of) the price elasticity of demand for a good is greater than one, then demand for the good is
    a. inelastic.
    b. elastic.
    c. inferior.
    d. normal.
    e. paranormal.

6. As we move leftward along a straight-line demand curve, the (absolute value of the) price elasticity of demand
   a. remains constant at zero.
   b. remains constant at a value of one.
   c. remains constant and equal to the (absolute value of the) slope of the demand curve.
   d. grows smaller.
   e. grows larger.

7. If a good is normal, we know that
   a. the good's price elasticity of demand is positive.
   b. demand for the good is elastic.
   c. demand for the good is inelastic.
   d. income elasticity of demand is positive.
   e. income elasticity of demand is negative.

8. The price elasticity of demand for a good is –2.0. When the price of this good rises,
   a. quantity demanded will rise as well.
   b. the total revenue of firms selling this good will rise.
   c. the total income of those who buy the good will increase.
   d. all of the above.
   e. none of the above.

9. Which of the following would you expect to have the greatest (in absolute value) price elasticity of demand?
   a. Clothing
   b. Pants
   c. Blue jeans
   d. Levi's blue jeans
   e. All of the above would have approximately the same price elasticity of demand.

10. Among the reasons that farmers' incomes are unstable is
    a. the demand for food is elastic (with respect to the price of food).
    b. the supply curve for food can shift dramatically rightward or leftward from year to year.
    c. the income elasticity for food is very high.
    d. all of the above.
    e. none of the above.

11. Under which of the following conditions would most or all of an excise tax be paid by *buyers* of a good?
    a. the demand for the good is very price-inelastic.
    b. the supply of the good is very price-inelastic.
    c. the good is an economic luxury.
    d. the cross-price elasticity of the good and its nearest substitute is very small in absolute value.
    e. all of the above.

12. The cross-price elasticity between good X and good Y is -2. This tells us that goods X ands Y are
    a. economic luxuries.
    b. economic necessities.
    c. inferior.
    d. substitutes.
    e. complements.

True/False: For each of the following statements, circle T if the statement is true or F if the statement is false.

T F 1. If a price ceiling below the equilibrium price is imposed on a market, it will cause the quantity demanded to rise and the quantity supplied to fall.

T F 2. Rent controls are one of the few examples of a price floor in market economies.

T F 3. If the demand for mass transit in a city is inelastic, then raising fares will increase mass transit revenue.

T F 4. The cross-price elasticity of demand between Levi's blue jeans and "The Gap" blue jeans is most likely positive.

T F 5. If the demand for illegal drugs is inelastic, then government efforts to reduce the supply of illegal drugs, all else equal, are likely to cause an increase in total expenditure on them.

T F 6. Perfectly inelastic demand occurs when the demand curve is horizontal.

T F 7. All else being equal, the more important an item is in buyers' budgets, the more elastic is demand for the good.

T F 8. If the demand curve for a good is a relatively steep, straight line, then the demand for the good is inelastic at every point along that demand curve.

T F 9. If the supply curve for a good is vertical, then the price elasticity of supply for the good is very large.

Chapter 4 Working with Supply and Demand   51

    T F 10. For a given supply curve, the more elastic the demand for a good, the more of an excise tax will be paid by buyers.

Short Answer: Fill in the blanks with brief answers.

For each of the following characteristics of a good (or goods), state which type of elasticity tells us about the characteristic, and what we know about the value of that elasticity. (The first row is filled in for you.)

Characteristic	Type of Elasticity	Value
A rise in price increases total revenue of sellers of the good	Price elasticity of demand	Between 0 and -1
The good is an economic luxury		
The good is an economic necessity		
The good is a substitute for another good		
The good is normal		
The good is inferior		
The supply curve for the good is vertical		
The demand curve for the good is vertical		
The good obeys the law of demand		
Demand for the good is "elastic"		

CHAPTER 5
CONSUMER CHOICE

SUMMARIZE THE CHAPTER

Construct your own chapter summary by filling in the blanks. If you have difficulty, review the highlighted points in the chapter, then try again.

- A consumer's budget constraint identifies which combinations of goods and services the consumer can afford with a limited budget, at given _____.

- The slope of the budget line indicates the spending trade-off between one good and another—the amount of one good that must be sacrificed in order to buy more of another good. If P_y is the price of the good on the vertical axis and P_x is the price of the good on the horizontal axis, then the slope of the budget line is _____.

- An increase in income will shift the budget line upward (and _____). A decrease in income will shift the budget line downward (and _____). These shifts are parallel: Changes in income do not affect the budget line's _____.

- When the _____ of a good changes, the budget line rotates: Both its slope and one of its intercepts will change.

- The consumer will always choose a point _____ _____ budget line, rather than a point _____ it.

The next three statements refer to the section, "Consumer Decisions: The Marginal Utility Approach." If you used the appendix instead, you can skip these statements.

- Marginal utility is the _____ in utility an individual enjoys from consuming an additional unit of a good. The marginal utility of a thing to anyone _____ with every increase in the amount of it he already has.

53

- A utility-maximizing consumer (choosing between two goods *x* and *y*) will choose the point on the budget line where marginal utility _____ _____ is the same for both goods (MU_x/P_x = _____). At that point, there is no further gain from reallocating expenditures in either direction.

- A rise in income, with no change in prices, leads to a new quantity demanded for each good. Whether a particular good is _____ (quantity demanded increases) or _____ (quantity demanded decreases) depends on the individual's preferences, as represented by the marginal utilities for each good, at each point along his budget line.

The next six statements refer to the section, "The Indifference Curve Approach." If you used the Marginal Utility approach instead, you can skip these statements.

- An _____ _____ represents all combinations of two goods that make the consumer equally well off.

- The marginal rate of substitution of good y for good x ($MRS_{Y,X}$) along any segment of an indifference curve is the absolute value of the _____ along that segment. The MRS tells us the _____ amount of y a consumer would willingly trade for one more unit of x.

- Any point on a _____ indifference curve is preferred to any point on a _____ one.

- The optimal combination of goods for a consumer is the point on the budget line where an indifference curve is _____ to the budget line.

- The optimal combination of two goods X and Y is that combination on the budget line for which $MRS_{Y,X}$ = _____.

- A rise in income, with no change in prices, leads to a new quantity demanded for each good. Whether a particular good is _____ (quantity demanded increases) or _____ (quantity demanded decreases) depends on the individual's preferences, as represented by his indifference map.

Chapter 5 Consumer Choice   55

The remaining statements apply to both approaches to consumer decision making.

- The _____ effect of a price change arises from a change in the relative price of a good, and it always moves quantity demanded in the opposite direction to the price change. When price decreases, the _____ effect works to increase quantity demanded; when price increases, the _____ effect works to decrease quantity demanded.

- The _____ effect of a price change arises from a change in purchasing power over both goods. A drop in price _____ purchasing power, while a rise in price _____ purchasing power.

- For _____ goods, the _____ and _____ effects work together, causing quantity demanded to move in the opposite direction of the price. _____ goods, therefore, must always obey the law of demand.

- For inferior goods, the _____ and _____ effects of a price change work against each other. The _____ effect moves quantity demanded in the opposite direction of the price, while the _____ effect moves it in the same direction as the price. But since the _____ effect virtually always dominates, consumption of inferior goods—like _____ goods—will virtually always obey the law of demand.

- The _____ demand curve is found by horizontally summing the individual demand curves of every consumer in the market.

LEARN THE LINGO

Fill in each blank with the appropriate word or phrase from the list provided in the word bank. (For a challenge, fill in as many blanks as you can *without* using the word bank.)

_____ 1. The different combinations of goods a consumer can afford with a limited budget, at given prices.

_____ 2. The graphical representation of a budget constraint, showing the maximum affordable quantity of one good for given amounts of another good.

_____ 3. The price of one good relative to the price of another.

_____ 4. Preferences that satisfy two conditions: (1) Any two alternatives can be compared, and one is preferred or else the two are valued equally, and (2) the comparisons are logically consistent.

_____ 5. A curve showing the quantity of a good or service demanded by a particular individual at each different price.

_____ 6. As the price of a good falls, the consumer substitutes that good in place of other goods whose prices have not changed.

_____ 7. As the price of a good decreases, the consumer's purchasing power increases, causing a change in quantity demanded for the good.

_____ 8. A subfield of economics focusing on behavior that deviates from the standard assumptions of economic models.

For Marginal Utility Approach Only:

_____ 9. Pleasure or satisfaction obtained from consuming goods and services.

_____ 10. The change in total utility an individual obtains from consuming an additional unit of a good or service.

_____ 11. As consumption of a good or service increases, marginal utility decreases.

For Indifference Curve Approach Only:

_____ 12. A curve representing all combinations of two goods that make the consumer equally well off.

_____ 13. A set of indfference curves that represent an individual's preferences.

_____ 14. The maximum amount of good *y* a consumer would willingly trade for one more unit of good *x*. Also, the slope of a segment of an indifference curve.

Word Bank

behavioral economics
budget constraint
budget line
income effect

individual demand curve
rational preferences
relative price
substitution effect

For the marginal utility approach only:
law of diminishing marginal utility
marginal utility
utility

For the indifference curve approach only:
indifference curve
indifference map
marginal rate of substitution ($MRS_{y,x}$)

Chapter 5 Consumer Choice

BUILD YOUR SKILLS

For each of the following items, write the correct answer in the blank or circle the correct answer.

1. Joan has $20 to spend on novels and videos each month. Every video costs $4 to rent, and every novel costs $2 to buy. Complete the table describing different combinations of videos and novels Joan can afford.

	Videos at $4 each Quantity	Total Expenditure on Videos	Novels at $2 each Quantity	Total Expenditure on Novels
A	0	_____	10	_____
B	1	_____	8	_____
C	2	_____	6	_____
D	3	_____	4	_____
E	4	_____	2	_____
F	5	_____	0	_____

2. Using data from the previous question, plot along the horizontal axis the quantity of videos, and along the vertical axis the quantity of novels. Now plot as points each combination of videos and novels that Joan can just afford with her $20 budget each month. Label the points A through F as indicated in the table above, and connect the points with the straight line giving Joan's monthly **budget line**.

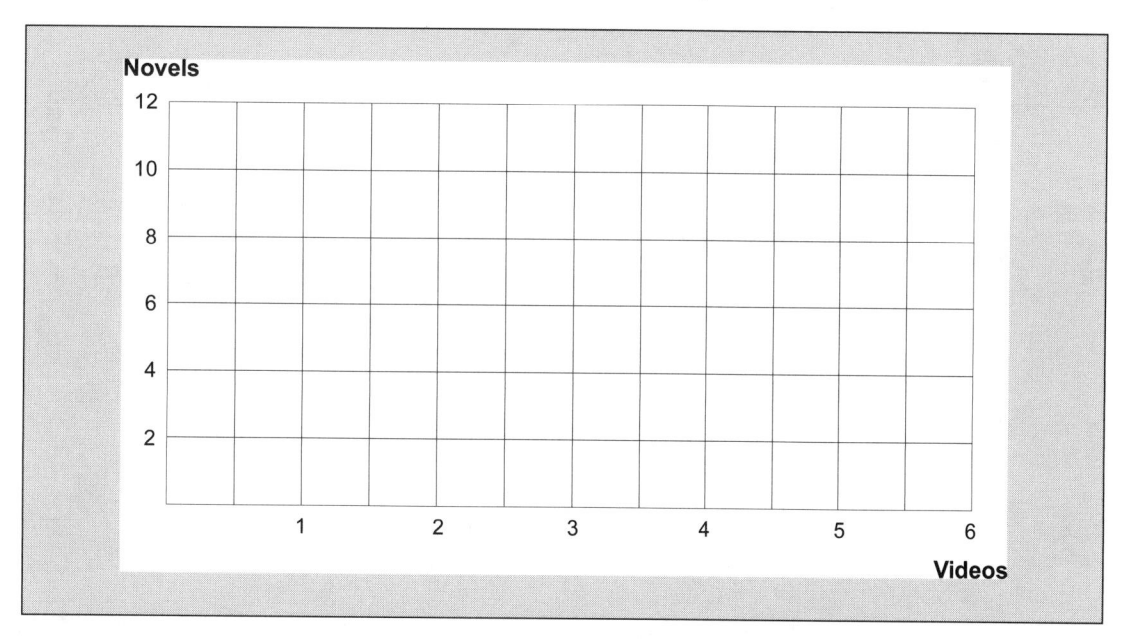

3. Jeeves is in charge of buying food and clothing for the staff at Lordly Manor. Food costs $25 per pound, and clothing costs $10 per pound. Jeeves is allowed to spend no

more than $4000 per month. Alternative combinations of food and clothing Jeeves can afford within his budget are listed in the first two columns below.

Food	Clothing	B
0	400	__
20	350	__
40	300	__
60	250	__
80	200	__
100	150	__
120	100	__
140	50	__
160	0	__

a. On the grid below, plot Jeeves' budget line using the data in the first two columns. Label the budget line "A".

b. Lord Lordly decides to increase the staff's allowance. He now gives Jeeves $5,000 to spend each month on food and clothing. In the column labeled "B" above, calculate the maximum amount of clothing Jeeves can now afford with each alternative amount of food listed in the first column. Plot Jeeves' new budget line using the data from the first and third columns. Label the new budget line "B".

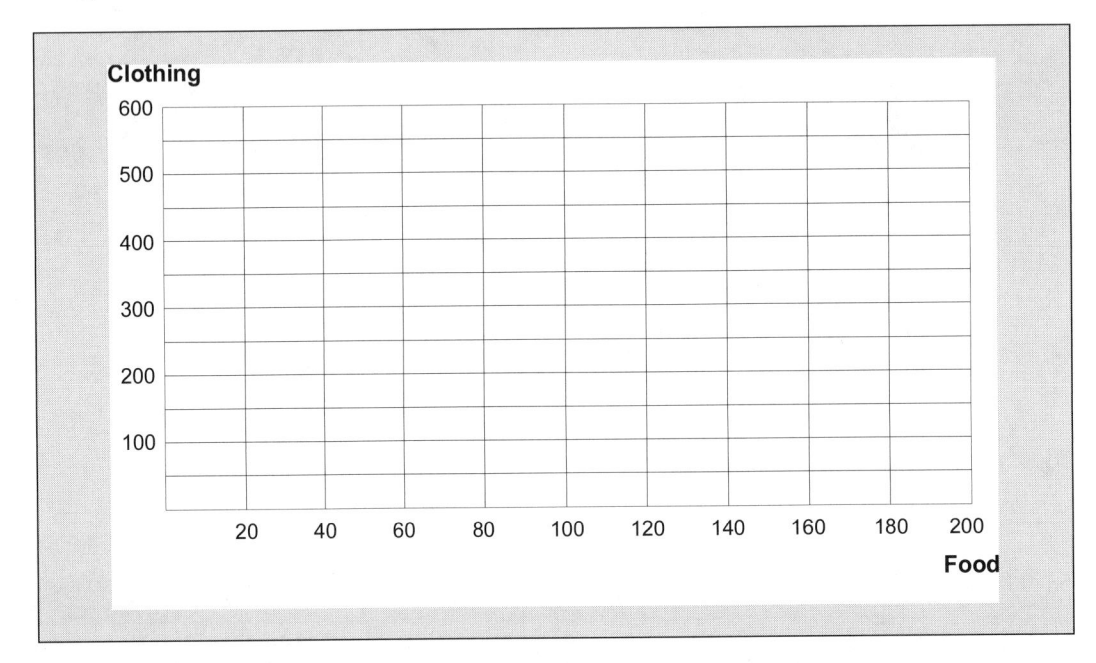

4. Carla eats only two things: artichokes and brown rice. Carla has $400 per month to spend on food. The first column below indicates different numbers of bags of rice Carla might buy.

Rice	Artichokes at $40	Artichokes at $20
400	_____	_____
320	_____	_____
240	_____	_____
160	_____	_____
80	_____	_____
0	_____	_____

a. If she pays $1 per bag of rice, and $40 per bushel of artichokes, how can Carla combine rice and artichokes in her diet? Fill in the second column of the table with the greatest number of bushels of artichokes Carla can afford given the number of bags of rice in the first column.

b. Suppose Carla moves to California where artichokes are cheap. If she still pays $1 per bag of rice, but now only pays $20 per bushel of artichokes, how can Carla now combine rice and artichokes in her diet? Fill in the third column of the table with the greatest number of bushels of artichokes Carla can now afford.

c. On the axes below, use the data in the table to plot Carla's budget lines at the two different prices for artichokes. Label with "A" the budget line when the price of artichokes is $40. Label with "B" the budget line when the price of artichokes is $20.

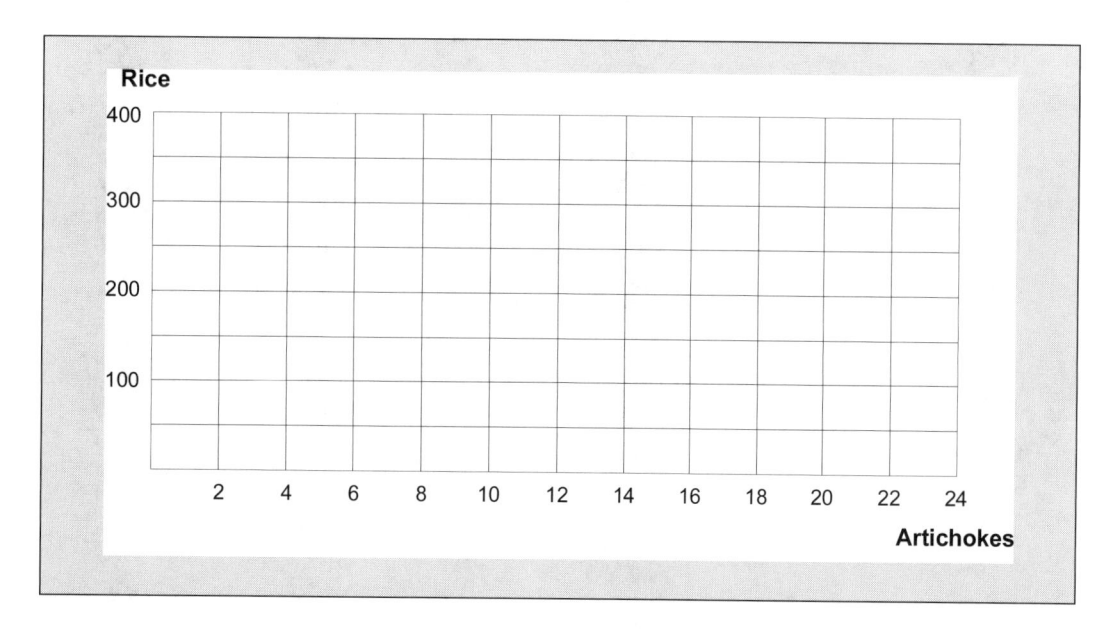

Questions 5 and 6 refer to the section, "Consumer Decisions: The Marginal Utility Approach." If you used the Indifference Curve approach instead, you can skip these and go directly to question 8.

5. Marshall loves crumpets. The more he gets of them, the happier he feels. The following table shows the level of total utility Marshall enjoys when he consumes increasing numbers of crumpets per day. Compute the marginal utility Marshall enjoys from each successive pair of crumpets he consumes. Do Marshall's preferences obey the law of diminishing marginal utility? _____

Crumpets Consumed	Total Utility	Marginal Utility
0	0	_____
2	31	_____
4	45	_____
6	55	_____
8	63	_____
10	70	_____
12	76	_____
14	81	_____
16	85	_____
18	88	_____

Chapter 5 Consumer Choice

6. Johnny loves two goods, X and Y. Interestingly, the marginal utility Johnny gets from consuming an additional unit of either good depends only on the number of units of that good he consumes, and not on his consumption of the other good. The following table tells us the relationship between different amounts of X and Y that Johnny consumes and the marginal utility he enjoys from the last unit consumed.

Units of X Consumed	Marginal Utility from Last unit of X	Units of Y Consumed	Marginal Utility from Last unit of Y
1	96	1	190
2	92	2	180
3	88	3	170
4	84	4	160
5	80	5	150
6	76	6	140
7	72	7	130
8	68	8	120
9	64	9	110
10	60	10	100
11	56	11	90
12	52	12	80
13	48	13	70
14	44		
15	40		
16	36		
17	32		
18	28		
19	24		
20	20		
21	16		
22	12		

a. Currently, the price of X is $4 per unit and the price of Y is $10 per unit. On the graph below, carefully draw Johnny's budget line when he has an income of $90 per month. (Hint: At these prices and income, Johnny can just afford 9 units of Y if he buys no X, or he can afford 20 units of X if he buys just 1 unit of Y, among other combination he can afford.)

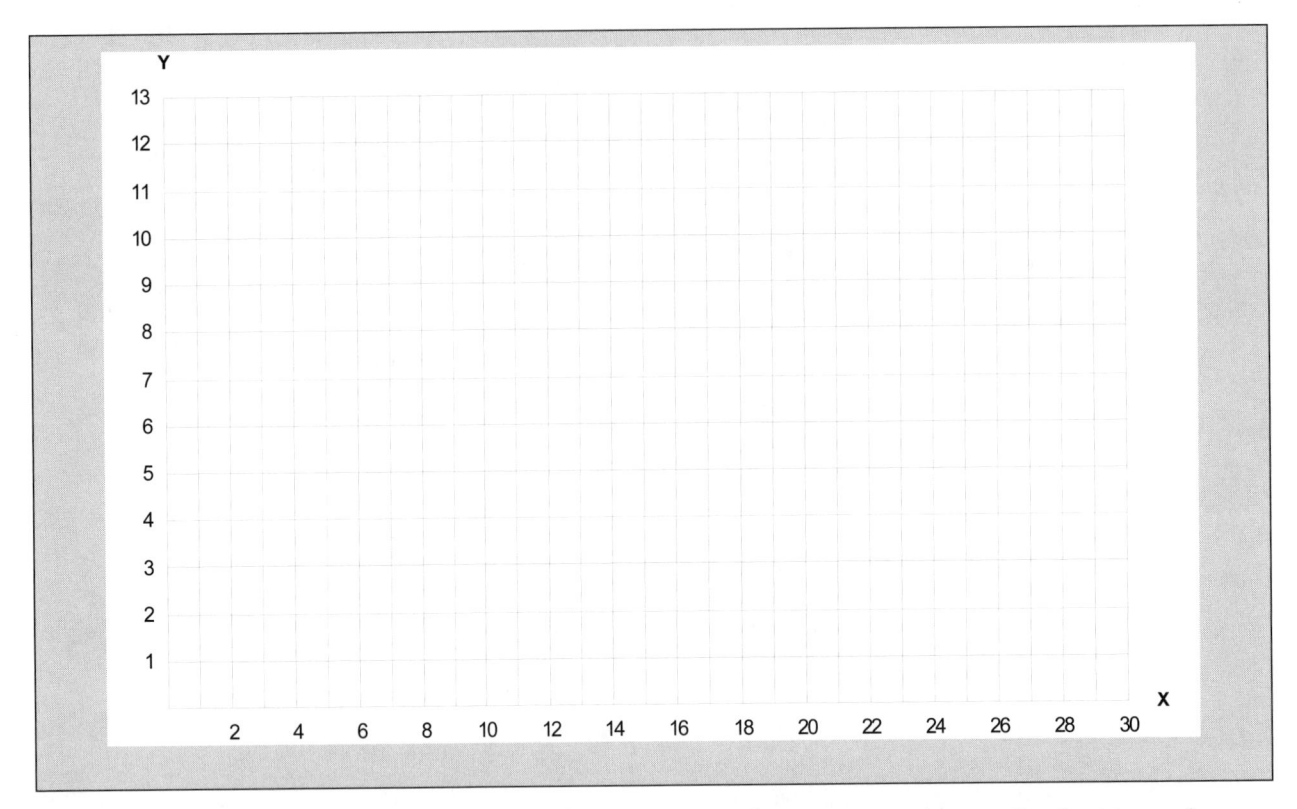

b. Using data on Johnny's preferences from the previous table, and referring to the graph above as necessary, complete the following table. Be sure to label the points A through D on Johnny's budget line.

Income = $90 per month

Point on Budget Line	Units of X Consumed	Marginal Utility from Last Unit of X	Marginal Utility per Dollar Spent on Last Unit of X	Units of Y Consumed	Marginal Utility From Last Unit of Y	Marginal Utility per Dollar Spent on Last Unit of Y
A	0	___	___	9	___	___
B	5	___	___	7	___	___
C	10	___	___	5	___	___
D	15	___	___	3	___	___
E	20	___	___	1	___	___

c. From your computations in the previous table, we can see that at point A on Johnny's budget constraint, the marginal utility per dollar Johnny spends on his last unit of X is (greater than/equal to/less than) the marginal utility per dollar he spends on his last unit of Y. To increase his utility, Johnny should buy more (units of X / units of Y) and buy fewer (units of X / units of Y).

d. At point E on Johnny's budget constraint, the marginal utility per dollar Johnny spends on his last unit of X is (greater than/equal to/less than) the marginal utility per dollar he spends on his last unit of Y. To increase his utility, Johnny should buy more (units of X / units of Y) and buy fewer (units of X / units of Y).

e. To maximize his utility, Johnny should allocate his expenditure between units of X and units of Y along his budget line until the marginal utility per dollar spent on his last unit of X is (greater than/equal to/less than) the marginal utility per dollar spent on his last unit of Y. If he follows this rule for maximizing utility, Johnny will select the point (A/B/C/D/E/F) on his budget line and he will consume _____ units of X and _____ units of Y.

f. Johnny just got a raise at work. His income will now be $118 per month. If the price of X remains at $4 and the price of Y remains at $10, carefully draw Johnny's new budget line on the same grid as the other one, above. (Hint: With his new income, Johnny can just afford 2 units of X and 11 units of Y, or 27 units of X and 1 unit of Y, among other combinations he can afford.)

g. Using data on Johnny's preferences from the first table, above, and referring to the graph above as necessary, complete the following table. Be sure to label the points F through J on Johnny's new budget line.

Income = $118 per month

Point on Budget Line	Units of X Consumed	Marginal Utility from Last Unit of X	Marginal Utility per Dollar Spent on Last Unit of X	Units of Y Consumed	Marginal Utility From Last Unit of Y	Marginal Utility per Dollar Spent on Last Unit of Y
F	2	___	___	11	___	___
G	7	___	___	9	___	___
H	12	___	___	7	___	___
I	17	___	___	5	___	___
J	22	___	___	3	___	___

h. Once again, to maximize his utility, Johnny should allocate his expenditure between units of X and units of Y along his new budget line until the marginal utility per dollar spent on his last unit of X is (greater than/equal to/less than) the marginal utility per dollar spent on his last unit of Y. If he follows this rule for maximizing utility, Johnny will select the point (F/G/H/I/J) on his new budget line and he will consume _____ units of X and _____ units of Y.

i. We've seen that a rise in Johnny's income, with no change in prices, has lead to an (increase/decrease) in the quantity of X demanded, and to an (increase/decrease) in the quantity of Y demanded. From this we can see that X is a(n) (normal/inferior) good and Y is a(n) (normal/inferior) good for Johnny.

Questions 7 and 8 refer to the appendix, "The Indifference Curve Approach." If you used the Marginal Utility approach instead, you can skip these and go directly to question 9.

7. Little Miss Muffet loves her Curds and Whey. One of her indifference curves is illustrated below, with pints of Curds on the horizontal axis and ounces of Whey on the vertical.

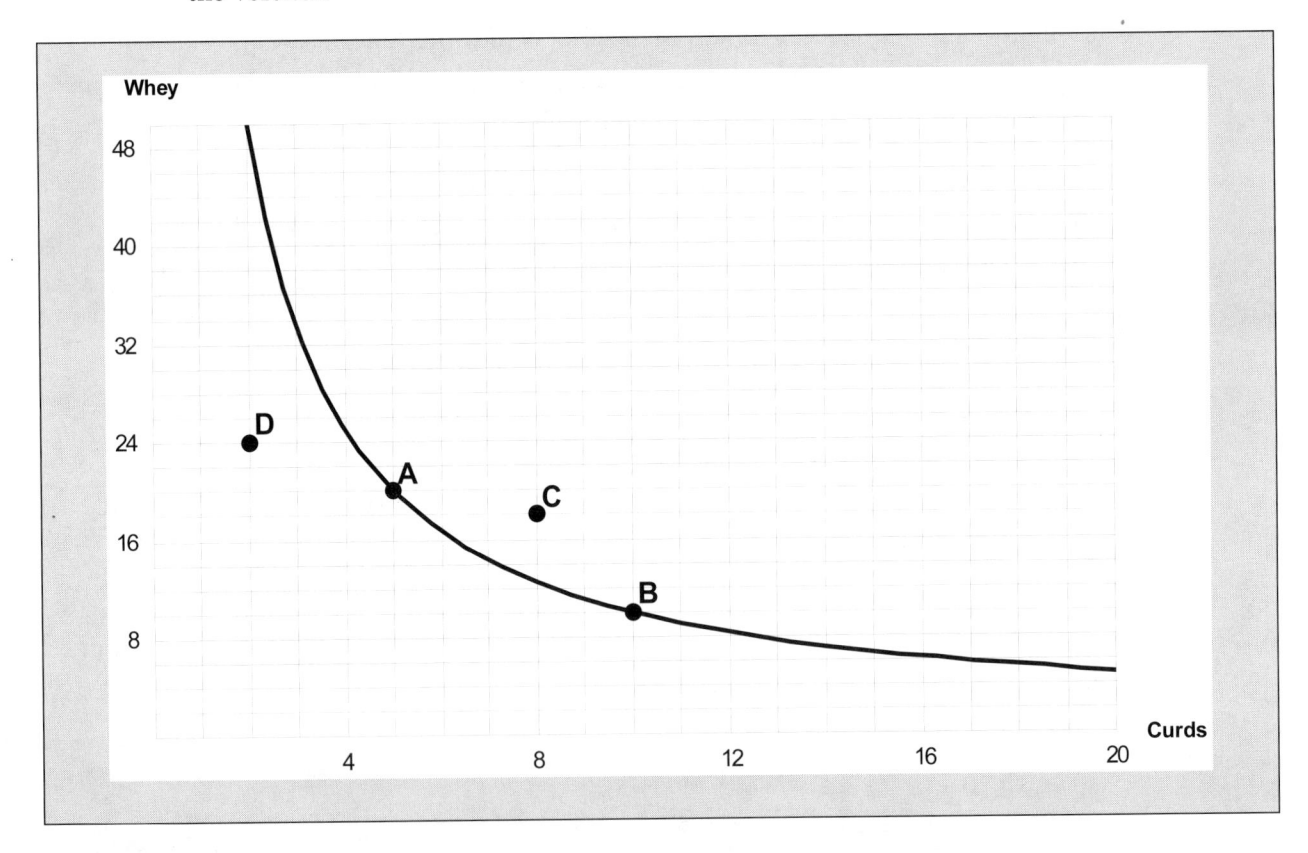

Chapter 5 Consumer Choice

a. We can tell quite alot about Miss Muffet's preferences from this one indifference curve. For example, because point C lies above the indifference curve through point A, we know she (prefers A to C/ prefers C to A/ is indifferent between A and C). Similarly, because point D lies below the indifference curve through point A, we know Miss Muffet (prefers A to D/ prefers D to A/ is indifferent between A and D). Since Miss Muffet is rational, and her preferences are logically consistent, we may in turn deduce that, if asked to compare points D and C, she would tell us that she (prefers D to C/ prefers C to D/ is indifferent between C and D).

b. The $MRS_{Y,X}$ is the (absolute value of/reciprocal of /square root of) the slope of the indifference curve. It tells us the maximum amount of (X/Y) the consumer would willingly trade for one more unit of (X/Y).

c. In the appendix to Chapter 1 of the text you learned to measure the slope of a curve at a point by the slope of a tangent to the curve at that point. (You practiced doing this in Chapter 1 of this Study Guide). Using that technique, Miss Muffet's $MRS_{Y,X}$ at point A is (approximately) equal to _____, while at point B her $MRS_{Y,X}$ is (approximately) equal to _____. Like that of most people, for most goods, Miss Muffet's $MRS_{Y,X}$ tends to (decline/increase/remain unchanged) as we move southeasterly down her indifference curve through A and B.

8. Johnny loves two goods, X and Y. A few of his indifference curves between them are plotted on the grid below.

   a. Currently, the price of X is $4 per unit and the price of Y is $10 per unit. On the graph below, carefully draw Johnny's budget line when he has an income of $90 per month. (Hint: At these prices and income, Johnny can just afford 9 units of Y if he buys no X, or he can afford 20 units of X if he buys just 1 unit of Y, among other combination he can afford.)

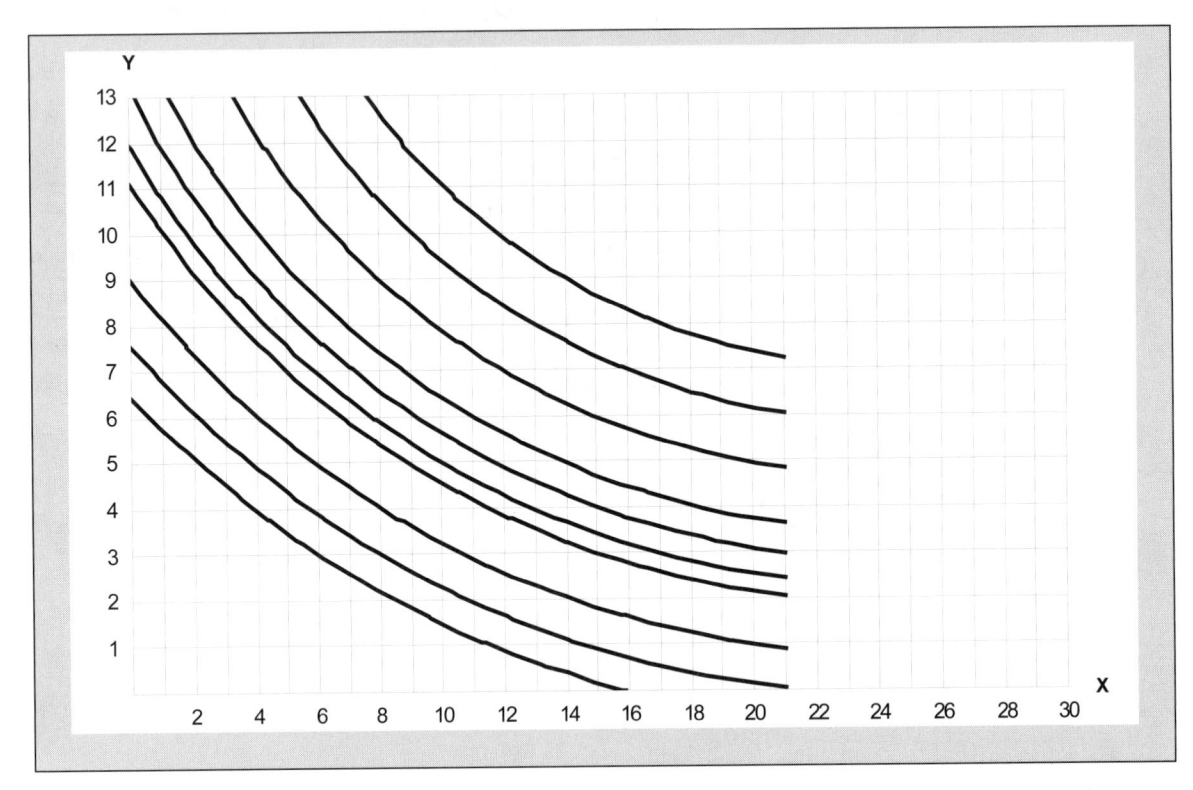

   b. By looking at Johnny's indifference curves and budget line, we can see that when he consumes 5 units of X and 7 units of Y his $MR_{Y,X}$ is (greater than/less than/equal to) P_X/P_Y. To obtain a combination of X and Y that he prefers to 5 units of X and 7 units of Y, Johnny should (spend less on both goods/spend less on X and more on Y/spend more on X and less on Y/ spend more on both goods).

   c. When he consumes 15 units of X and 3 units of Y Johnny's $MRS_{Y,X}$ is (greater than/less than/equal to) P_X/P_Y. To obtain a combination of X and Y that he prefers to 15 units of X and 3 units of Y, Johnny should (spend less on both goods/spend less on X and more on Y/spend more on X and less on Y/ spend more on both goods).

   d. The optimal combination of X and Y for Johnny to consume is _____ units of X and _____ units of Y. When he consumes this combination, Johnny's $MRS_{Y,X}$ is (greater than/less than/equal to)

P_X/P_Y, and his indifference curve is (flatter than / tangent to / steeper than) his budget line. Specifically, we know that at the optimal combination of X and Y for Johnny to consume, the value of his $MRS_{Y,X}$ is _____. (Hint: Remember that $P_X=\$4$ and $P_Y=\$10$).

e. Johnny just got a raise at work. His income will now be $118 per month. If the price of X remains at $4 and the price of Y remains at $10, carefully draw Johnny's new budget line on the same grid as the other one, above. (Hint: With his new income, Johnny can just afford 2 units of X and 11 units of Y, or 27 units of X and 1 unit of Y, among other combinations he can afford.)

f. Once again, to find his new optimal combination of X and Y, Johnny should allocate his expenditure along the new budget line until his $MRS_{Y,X}$ is (greater than/equal to/less than) P_X/P_Y, and his indifference curve is (flatter than / tangent to / steeper than) his budget line. In his new optimal combination, there will be _____ units of X and _____ units of Y.

g. We've seen that a rise in Johnny's income, with no change in prices, has lead to an (increase/decrease) in the quantity of X demanded, and to an (increase/decrease) in the quantity of Y demanded. From this we can see that X is a(n) (normal/inferior) good and Y is a(n) (normal/inferior) good for Johnny.

The remaining questions apply to both approaches to consumer decision making.

9. Sarah loves apples and oranges. She knows her preferences pretty well, too. She can look down along any budget line and tell you exactly which combination of X and Y is the one she most prefers among all those she can afford[*]. In the graph below, Sarah has identified points A, B and C as three such point on three separate budget lines. Sarah would like to plot her demand curve for apples in the lower panel of that graph, but there's a problem----she's forgotten what the price per apple was when she drew each of those budget lines! You'll need to help her.

   a. Sarah remembers that the price per orange was $1, and her weekly allowance was $14, each time she drew a budget line. She also remembers that the slope of the budget line is always equal to $-P_{apple}/P_{orange}$. Sarah figures, therefore, that when she drew the budget line through point A, the price per apple must have been _____ dollars. When she drew the budget line through point B it must have been _____ dollars and when she drew the one through C it must have been _____ dollars.

---

[*] If you studied the marginal utility approach, this will be the combination where marginal utility per dollar spent on the last apple is equal to marginal utility per dollar spent on the last orange. If you studied the indifference curve approach, this will be the combination where the marginal rate of substitution of Y for X is equal to the price of X relative to the price of Y.

b. Knowing what we know now about Sarah's preferences and the choices she makes at different prices per apple, construct Sarah's demand curve for apples on the grid below, assuming the price of oranges is $1 and her allowance is $14 per week.

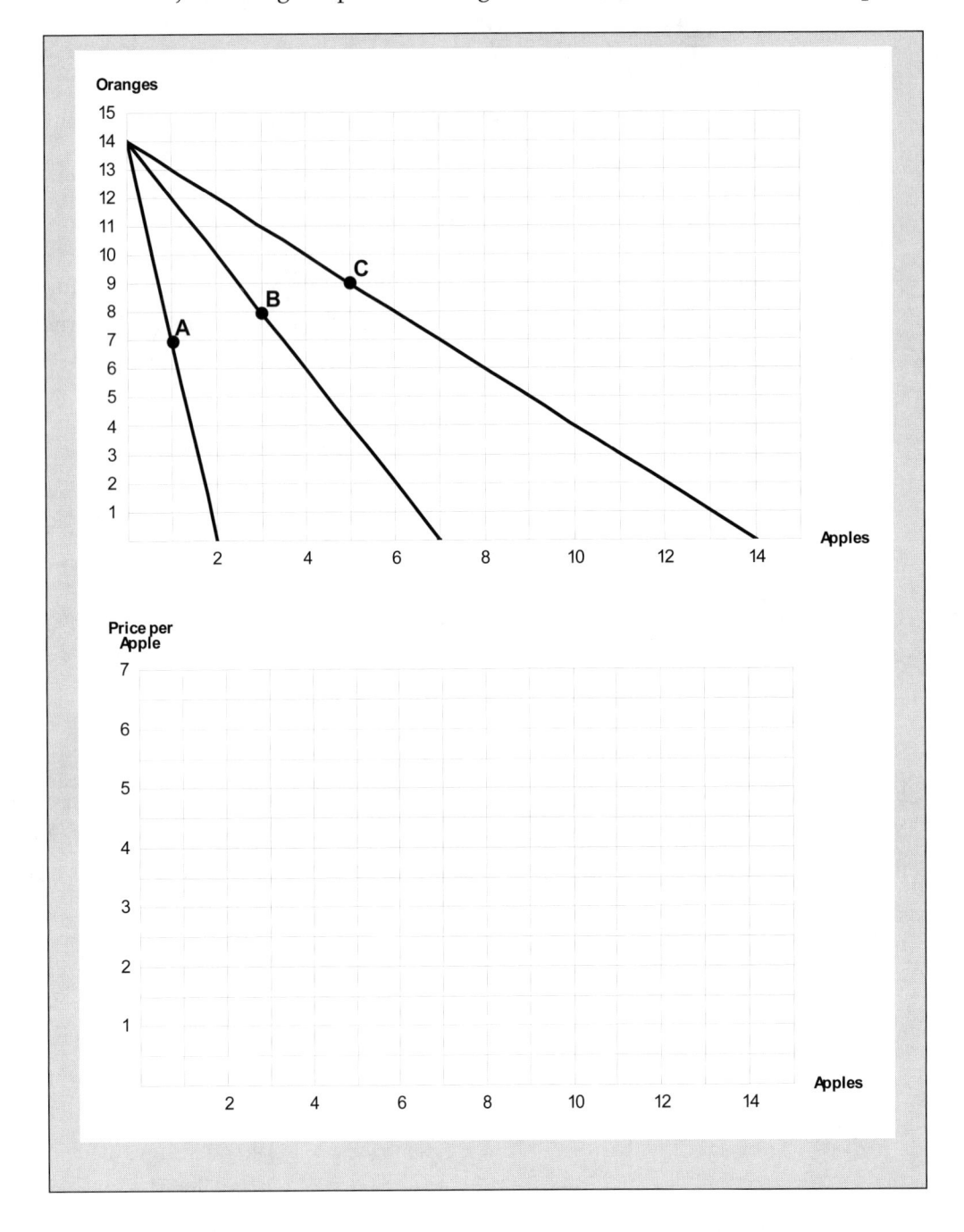

Chapter 5 Consumer Choice

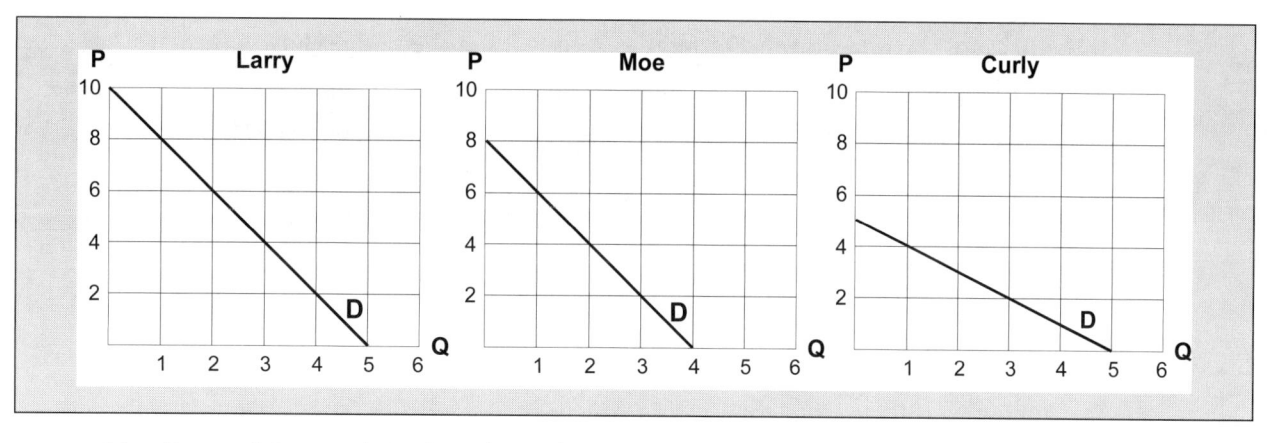

10. Larry, Moe, and Curly, whose demand curves are drawn above, are the only three buyers in the market for castor oil. In the table below, complete **the market demand schedule** for castor oil. Then plot the market demand curve on the grid provided.

Price	Quantity Demanded
$10	_____
9	_____
8	_____
7	_____
6	_____
5	_____
4	_____
3	_____
2	_____
1	_____

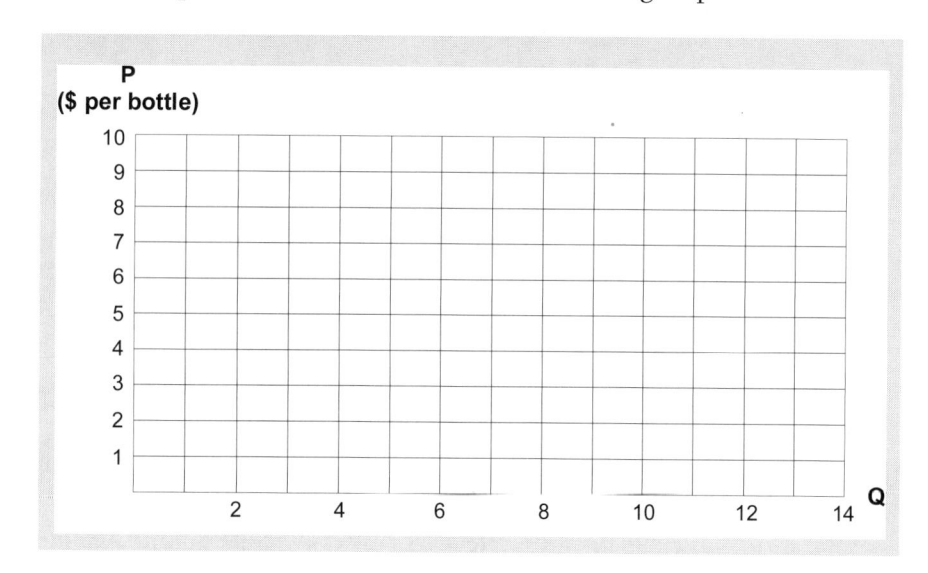

TEST YOURSELF

To see what you *really* know and remember, take this test at least a day *after* you've read the chapter in the text and completed the exercises in this study guide.

Multiple Choice: Circle the letter in front of the single best answer.

1. Which of the following statements about the budget line is true?
    a. The consumer can afford every combination of goods on the budget line.
    b. The consumer can afford every combination of goods below the budget line, but not those on the line.
    c. The consumer can afford only those combinations of goods along the upper-half of the budget line.
    d. The consumer can afford only those combinations of goods along the lower-half of the budget line.
    e. The budget line does not tell us anything about which combinations of goods the consumer can afford.

2. If the price of the good on the vertical axis rises, then the budget line will
   a. rotate upward, with its horizontal intercept remaining unchanged.
   b. rotate downward, with its horizontal intercept remaining unchanged.
   c. rotate upward, with its vertical intercept remaining unchanged.
   d. rotate downward, with is vertical intercept remaining unchanged.
   e. shift, with no change in its slope.

3. When the price of the good on the horizontal axis rises,
   a. the budget line becomes steeper.
   b. the budget line becomes flatter.
   c. the budget line shifts rightward, with no change in slope.
   d. the budget line shifts leftward, with no change in slope.
   e. the budget line may shift in either direction, or become steeper or flatter, depending on the consumer's tastes.

4. A rise in income will
   a. shift the budget line rightward, and increase its slope.
   b. shift the budget line leftward, and decrease its slope.
   c. shift the budget line rightward, but leave its slope unchanged.
   d. shift the budget line leftward, but leave its slope unchanged.
   e. none of the above.

5. When the price of a normal good decreases,
   a. the substitution effect works to increase quantity demanded, but the income effect works to decrease quantity demanded.
   b. the substitution effect works to decrease quantity demanded, but the income effect works to increase quantity demanded.
   c. the substitution effect works to increase quantity demanded, but the income effect works to leave quantity demanded unchanged.
   d. both the substitution effect and the income effect work to increase quantity demanded.
   e. both the substitution effect and the income effect work to decrease quantity demanded.

6. Which of the following is most likely to be an inferior good?
   a. Air travel
   b. Steak
   c. Starbucks coffee
   d. Ground beef
   e. Fresh squeezed orange juice

Chapter 5 Consumer Choice

Questions 7 through 10 refer to the marginal utility approach

7. Suppose that tomatoes cost $2 per pound, while apples cost $1 per pound. When someone is consuming the utility-maximizing quantities of tomatoes and apples,
   a. the total utility of tomatoes is twice the total utility of apples.
   b. the total utility of apples is twice the total utility of tomatoes.
   c. the additional utility from one more tomato would equal the additional utility from one more apple.
   d. the additional utility of one more apple would be twice the additional utility from one more tomato.
   e. the additional utility from one more tomato would be twice the additional utility from one more apple.

8. Someone who wishes to maximize total utility should consume the combination of goods for which
   a. total utility is equal for all goods.
   b. total utility per dollar is equal for all goods.
   c. marginal utility is equal for all goods.
   d. marginal utility per dollar is equal for all goods.
   e. total utility divided by marginal utility is equal for all goods.

9. Suppose that a consumer likes both orange juice and cola, but likes cola much more. When she is consuming the optimal quantities of both drinks, it must be true that
   a. the marginal utility of cola is greater than that for orange juice.
   b. the marginal utility of orange juice is greater than that for cola.
   c. the marginal utility per dollar for more cola is greater than the marginal utility per dollar for more orange juice.
   d. the marginal utility per dollar for more orange juice is greater than the marginal utility per dollar for more cola.
   e. none of the above.

10. The law of diminishing marginal utility tells us that each time we increase the quantity of a good consumed by one unit,
    a. total utility decreases, but by less and less each time.
    b. total utility increases, but by less and less each time.
    c. total utility decreases by more and more each time.
    d. total utility increases by more and more each time.
    e. total utility first decreases and then, beyond a certain point, increases.

Questions 11 through 14 refer to the appendix to Chapter 5

11. Which of the following statements is correct?
    a. As a consumer moves rightward along an indifference curve, he is better off.
    b. A consumer prefers higher indifference curves to lower ones.
    c. The $MRS_{y,x}$ is the rate at which a consumer can substitute good y for good x along his budget line.
    d. All of the above.
    e. None of the above.

12. The optimal combinations of goods x and y will satisfy the condition that:
    a. $p_x / p_y = p_y / p_x$
    b. $MRS_{y,x} = p_x / p_y$
    c. $MRS_{y,x} = (p_x) \times (p_y)$
    d. $MRS_{y,x} = p_x$
    e. $MRS_{y,x} = p_y$

13. As we move leftward along an indifference curve (with good y on the vertical axis and good x on the horizontal axis),
    a. the consumer is made worse off.
    b. the consumer's income decreases.
    c. $MRS_{y,x}$ increases.
    d. the ratio p_y / p_x decreases.
    e. the ratio p_x / p_y decreases.

14. If burgers cost $3 each and bananas cost $1 each, then an individual is consuming the optimal combination of these two goods when
    a. the quantities of burgers and bananas are equal.
    b. the quantity of bananas is 3 times the quantity of burgers.
    c. the quantity of burgers is 3 times the quantity of bananas.
    d. the individual could trade 1 burger for 3 bananas and remain indifferent.
    e. the individual could trade 1 banana for 3 burgers and remain indifferent.

True/False: For each of the following statements, circle T if the statement is true or F if the statement is false.

T   F   1. When good Y is plotted on the vertical axis, and good X is plotted on the horizontal axis, then the slope of the budget line will equal the negative of the price of good Y divided by the price of good X.

T   F   2. A consumer who likes odd combinations of goods—like ice cream with ketchup or maple syrup on spaghetti—would be considered "irrational" by economists.

Chapter 5 Consumer Choice

T F 3. A consumer can afford to buy all combinations of goods on or below the budget line.

T F 4. When the price of an inferior good decreases, both the substitution effect and the income effect work to increase quantity demanded.

T F 5. The substitution effect always works to move quantity demanded in the opposite direction of a price change.

T F 6. Consumers who judge quality by price, as with jewelry or designer clothing, would be considered "irrational" by economists.

T F 7. When instruction in one subject becomes more effective, a rational student will always choose to score higher on tests in that subject.

T F 8. The market demand curve is found by vertically summing all the individual demand curves in the market.

Short Answer: Fill in the blanks with brief answers

For each of the following, write the word "increase" or "decrease" to indicate whether the *substitution* effect increases or decreases quantity demanded, and whether the *income* effect increases or decreases quantity demanded.

1. The price of a normal good increases.

   substitution effect _____   income effect _____

2. The price of an inferior good decreases.

   substitution effect _____   income effect _____

3. The price of a normal good decreases.

   substitution effect _____   income effect _____

CHAPTER 6
PRODUCTION AND COST

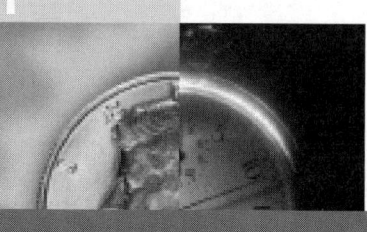

SUMMARIZE THE CHAPTER

Construct your own chapter summary by filling in the blanks. If you have difficulty, review the highlighted points in the chapter, then try again.

- A business firm is an organization, owned and operated by private individuals, that specializes in _____.

- _____ is the process of combining inputs to make outputs.

- For each different combination of inputs, the _____ _____ tells us the maximum quantity of output a firm can produce over some period of time.

- The _____ _____ is a time horizon long enough for a firm to vary all of its inputs.

- The _____ _____ refers to any time horizon over which at least one of the firm's inputs cannot be varied.

- _____ product is the maximum quantity of output that can be produced from a given combination of inputs.

- The _____ _____ of labor is the change in total product divided by the change in the number of workers hired. It tells us the rise in output produced when one more worker is hired. In equation form, MPL = $\Delta Q\ /$ _____.

- The law of _____ (marginal) returns states that as we continue to add more of any one input (holding the other inputs constant), its marginal product will eventually decline.

- A firm's total cost of producing a given level of output is the _____ cost of the owners—everything they must give up in order to produce that amount of output.

75

- A _____ cost is one that already has been paid, or must be paid, regardless of any future action being considered. _____ costs should not be considered when making decisions.

- Total cost (TC) is the sum of all fixed and _____ costs:

  TC = TFC + _____.

- The firm's average fixed cost (AFC) is its total _____ cost divided by the quantity of output:

  AFC = TFC / _____.

- Average variable cost (AVC) is the cost of the variable inputs per unit of output:

  AVC = TVC / _____.

- Average _____ cost (ATC) is the total cost per unit of output:

  ATC = TC / _____.

- _____ cost (MC) is the change in total cost divided by the change in output:

  MC = Δ TC / _____.

- It tells us how much cost rises per unit increase in output.

- The marginal cost for any change in output is equal to the _____ of the total cost curve along that interval of output.

- When the marginal product of labor (MPL) rises, marginal cost (MC) _____. When MPL falls, MC _____. Since MPL ordinarily rises and then falls, MC will do the opposite: It will _____ and then _____. Thus, the MC curve is U-shaped.

- At low levels of output, the MC curve lies below the AVC and ATC curves, so these curves will slope _____. At higher levels of output, the MC curve will rise above the AVC and ATC curves, so these curves will slope _____. Thus, as output increases, the average curves will first slope _____ and then slope _____. That is, they will have a U shape.

- The MC curve will intersect the _____ points of the AVC and ATC curves.

Chapter 6 Production and Cost

- In the long run, there are no _____ inputs or _____ costs; all inputs and all costs are _____. The firm must decide what combination of inputs to use in producing any level of output.

- To produce any given level of output, the firm will choose the input mix with the _____ cost.

- The _____ total cost of producing a given level of output can be less than or equal to, but never greater than the _____ total cost.

- The _____ average cost of producing a given level of output can be less than or equal to, but never greater than, the _____ average total cost.

- In the short run, a firm can only move along its current ATC curve. In the long run, however, it can move from one ATC curve to another by varying the size of its plant. As it does so, it will also be moving along its _____ curve.

- When long-run total cost rises proportionately less than output, production is characterized by _____ of scale, and the LRATC curve slopes downward.

- When long-run total cost rises more than in proportion to output, there are _____ of scale, and the LRATC curve slopes upward.

- When both output and long-run total cost rise by the same proportion, production is characterized by _____ _____ to scale, and the LRATC curve is flat.

LEARN THE LINGO

Fill in each blank with the appropriate word or phrase from the list provided in the word bank. (For a challenge, fill in as many blanks as you can *without* using the word bank.)

_____ 1. An organization owned and operated by private individuals, that specializes in production.

_____ 2. Total revenue minus total cost.

_____ 3. A firm owned by a single individual.

_____ 4. A firm owned and usually operated by several individuals who share in the profits and bear personal responsibility for any losses.

_____ 5. A firm owned by those who buy shares of stock and whose liability is limited to the amount of their investment in the firm.

_____ 6. The time costs and other costs required to carry out market exchanges.

_____ 7. The process of reducing risk by spreading sources of income among different alternatives.

_____ 8. A method by which inputs are combined to produce a good or service.

_____ 9. A function that indicates the maximum amount of output a firm can produce over some period of time from each combination of inputs.

_____ 10. A time horizon long enough for a firm to vary all of its inputs.

_____ 11. An input whose quantity remains constant, regardless of how much output is produced.

_____ 12. An input whose usage can change as the level of output changes.

_____ 13. A time horizon during which at least one of the firm's inputs cannot be varied.

_____ 14. The maximum quantity of output that can be produced from a given combination of inputs.

_____ 15. The additional output produced when one more worker is hired.

_____ 16. The marginal product of labor increases as more labor is hired.

_____ 17. The marginal product of labor decreases as more labor is hired.

_____ 18. As more and more of any input is added to a fixed amount of other inputs, its marginal product will eventually decline.

_____ 19. A cost that has been paid or must be paid, regardless of any future action being considered.

_____ 20. Money actually paid out for the use of inputs.

_____ 21. The cost of inputs for which there is no direct money payment.

_____ 22. Costs of fixed inputs.

Chapter 6 Production and Cost 79

_____ 23. Costs of variable inputs.

_____ 24. The cost of *all* inputs that are fixed in the short run.

_____ 25. The cost of *all* variable inputs used in producing a particular level of output.

_____ 26. The costs of *all* inputs—fixed and variable.

_____ 27. Total fixed cost divided by the quantity of output produced.

_____ 28. Total variable cost divided by the quantity of output produced.

_____ 29. Total cost divided by the quantity of output produced.

_____ 30. The increase in total cost from producing one more unit of output.

_____ 31. The cost of producing each quantity of output when the least-cost input mix is chosen in the long run.

_____ 32. The cost per unit of output in the long run, when all inputs are variable.

_____ 33. The collection of fixed inputs at a firm's disposal.

_____ 34. Long-run average total cost decreases as output increases.

_____ 35. An input whose quantity cannot be increased gradually as output increases, but must instead be adjusted in large jumps.

_____ 36. Long-run average total cost increases as output increases.

_____ 37. Long-run average total cost is unchanged as output increases.

_____ 38. The lowest output level at which the firm's LRATC curve hits bottom.

_____ 39. A market in which a single firm's production is characterized by economies of scale, even when its output expands to serve the entire market.

Word Bank

average fixed cost
average total cost
average variable cost
business firm
constant returns to scale
corporation
diminishing marginal returns to labor
diseconomies of scale
diversification
economies of scale
explicit costs
fixed costs
fixed input
implicit costs
increasing marginal returns to labor
law of diminishing marginal returns
long run
long-run average total cost
long-run total cost
lumpy input

marginal cost
marginal product of labor
minimum efficient scale
natural monopoly
partnership
plant
production function
profit
short run
sole proprietorship
sunk costs
technology
transaction costs
total cost
total fixed cost
total product
total variable cost
variable costs
variable input

Chapter 6 Production and Cost

BUILD YOUR SKILLS

For each of the following items, write the correct answer in the blank or circle the correct answer.

1. Golden Acres wheat farm can produce different amounts of wheat per season depending on the amount of labor it uses. The following is the farm's total product (TP) for different numbers of workers employed.

Number of Workers	TP	MPL
0	0	
1	100	____
2	300	____
3	700	____
4	1,000	____
5	1,200	____
6	1,300	____
7	1,350	____

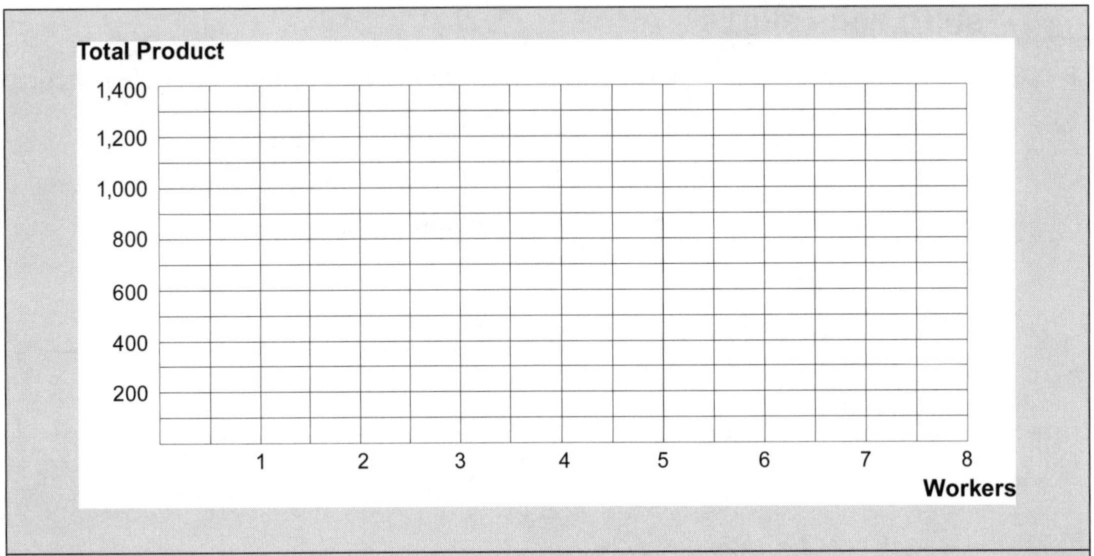

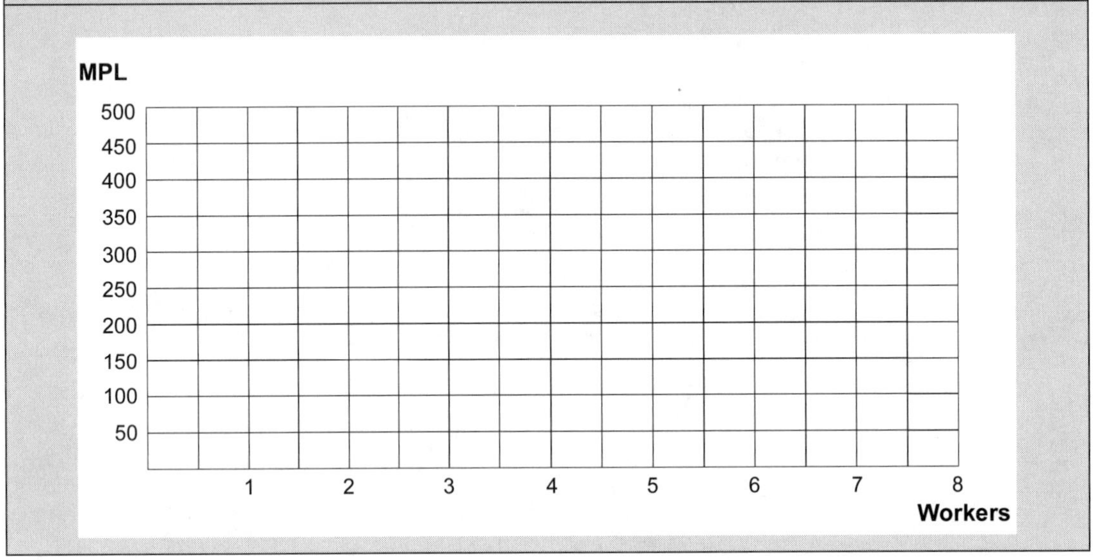

a. In the topmost grid, plot Golden Acres' total product curve.

b. Calculate the farm's marginal product of labor (MPL) for each one-worker increase in employment. Enter your calculations in the table.

c. Plot the firm's MPL curve on the lower grid. Since MPL refers to a *change* in employment, be sure to plot it *betweeen* the levels of employment for which you calculate it.

d. Looking at this graph, we can see that production of wheat at Golden Acres (does/does not) obey the law of diminishing marginal returns. The marginal product of labor is (always positive/sometimes negative), and as more workers are hired it (stays constant/ declines/increases).

Chapter 6 Production and Cost

2. Golden Acres, the farm from the previous question, has fixed costs of $20,000 per season. It can hire workers for $2,000 per season each. Complete the following table of Golden Acres' costs.

Number of Workers	TP	TFC $	TVC $	TC $	AFC $	AVC $	ATC $	MC $
0	0	___	___	___	___	___	___	
1	100	___	___	___	___	___	___	___
2	300	___	___	___	___	___	___	___
3	700	___	___	___	___	___	___	___
4	1000	___	___	___	___	___	___	___
5	1200	___	___	___	___	___	___	___
6	1300	___	___	___	___	___	___	___
7	1350	___	___	___	___	___	___	___

3. Using data from the previous question, plot ATC and MC curves for Golden Acres on the grid below. (Don't bother to plot ATC at output of 100 or 300 and remember to plot MC at the midpoint of the range over which you compute it.)

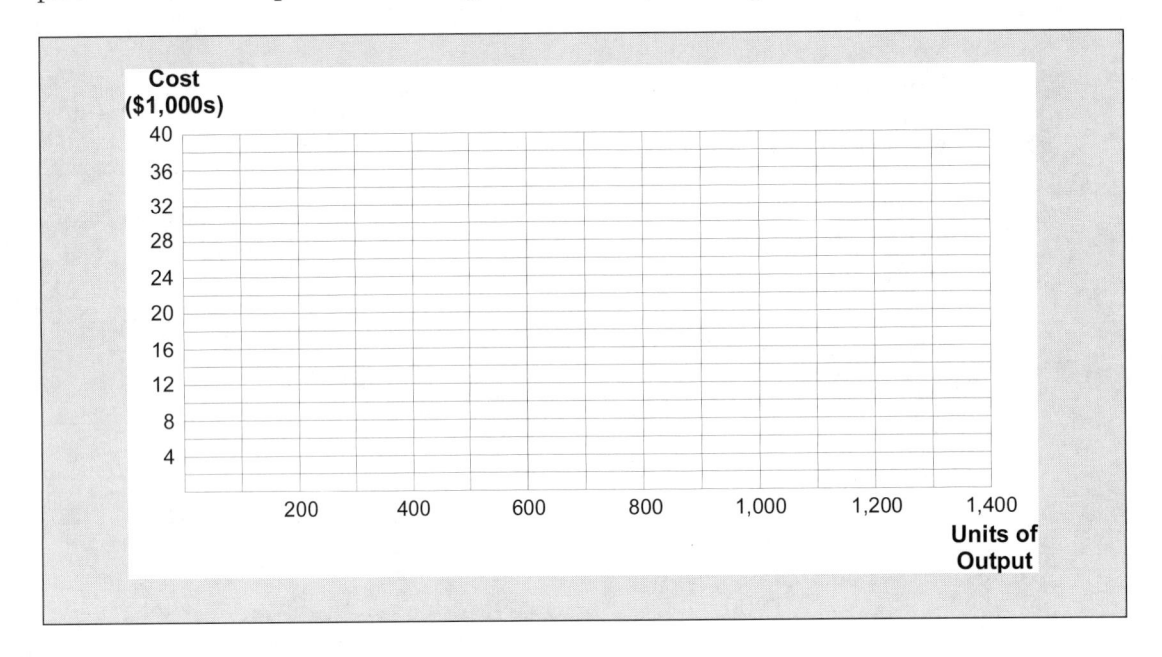

Chapter 6 Production and Cost

4. Blaze Busters, a producer of chemical fire retardant, had its records destroyed in a fire last week. Help the owners get back on their feet by reconstructing their cost data from these fragments they managed to save.

Weekly Output	TFC	TVC	TC	AFC	AVC	ATC	MC
0	$100	$ 0	___	---	---	---	
							___
1	___	150	___	___	___	___	
							___
2	___	280	___	___	___	___	
							___
3	___	380	___	33.3	___	___	
							___
4	___	___	$ 500	___	100	___	
							___
5	___	___	630	___	___	126	
							___
6	___	___	760	___	___	___	
							250
7	___	___	1,010	___	___	___	
							___
8	___	___	1,700	___	___	___	

5. Leo Knell produces electric trains, and his weekly cost curves are drawn below. Leo knows his trains, but he can't read graphs very well. Let's help him out.

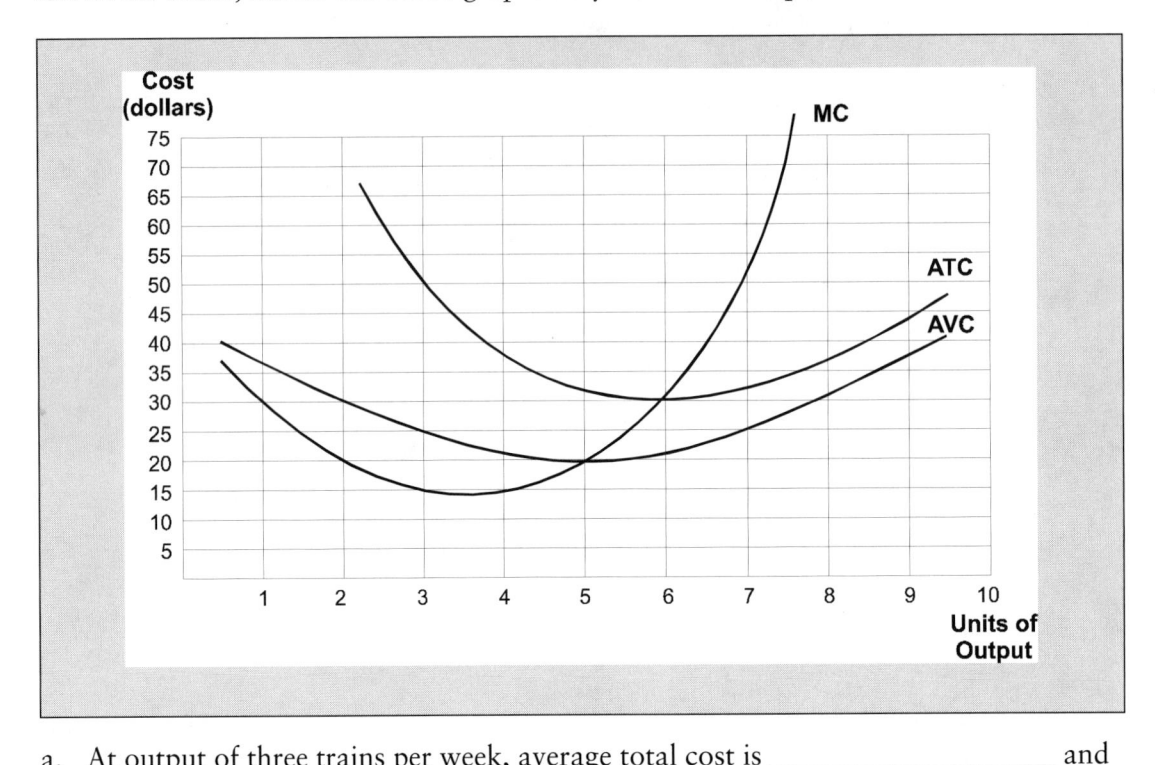

a. At output of three trains per week, average total cost is _____ and average variable cost is _____. At output of seven trains per week, average total cost is (approx.) _____; average variable cost is _____. Over the range from four to seven trains, marginal cost is (increasing/constant/decreasing).

b. Average variable cost achieves its minimum value of _____ when output is _____ trains. Average total cost achieves its minimum value when output is (approx.) _____ trains.

c. If Leo wants his average total cost to be $50, he should produce (approx.) _____ trains per week. If he wants his marginal cost to be $40 he should produce an output of (approx.) _____ trains per week. Marginal cost and average total cost are equal to each other when output is (approx.) _____ trains. Marginal cost and average variable cost are equal to each other when output is _____ trains.

d. Because ATC = AVC + AFC, we know that average fixed cost will be equal to (choose one: AVC + ATC or ATC × AVC or ATC − AVC). On the preceding graph, this means that average fixed cost can be read as the (vertical distance/horizontal distance) between the (ATC curve and the AVC curve/MC curve and the ATC curve/MC curve and the AVC curve). For instance, at an output of five trains per week, average fixed cost is (approx.) _____; at an output of 7 trains per week, average fixed cost is (approx.) _____.

6. *What's Wrong with This Picture?* Find four things wrong in the graph below.

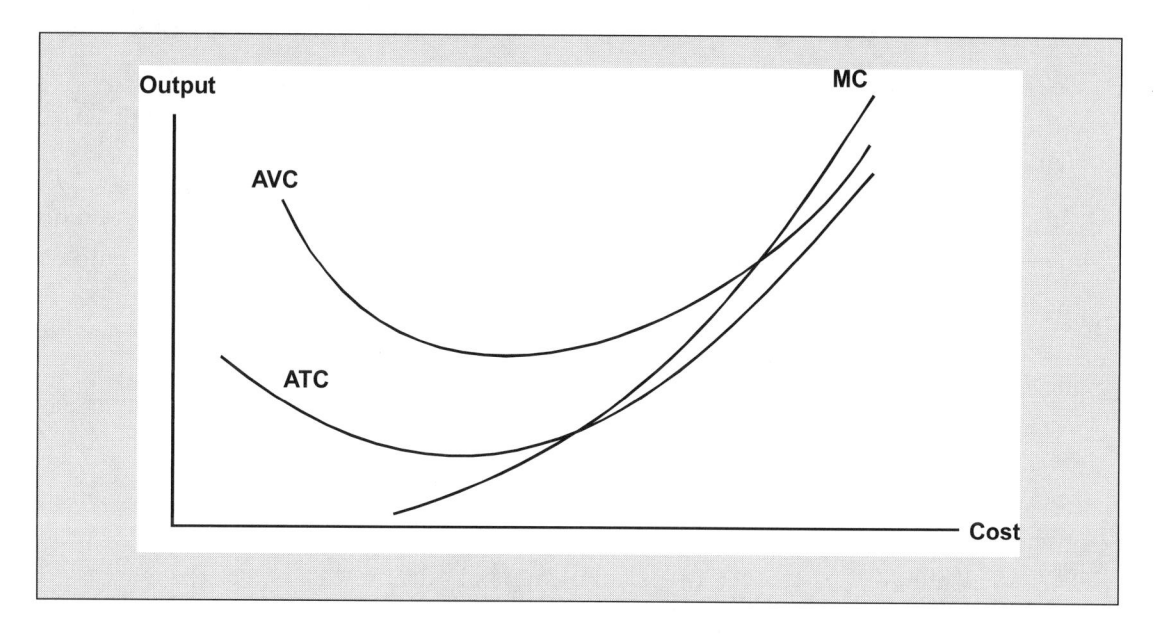

   a. _____.
   b. _____.
   c. _____.
   d. _____.

TEST YOURSELF

To see what you *really* know and remember, take this test at least a day *after* you've read the chapter in the text and completed the exercises in this study guide.

Multiple Choice: Circle the letter in front of the single best answer.

1. A partnership is defined as
   a. a firm that is owned by two or fewer private individuals.
   b. the same as a corporation.
   c. a business firm owned by highly-trained professionals, e.g. lawyers or doctors.
   d. a business firm that is co-owned by private individuals and government agencies.
   e. none of the above.

2. A plywood firm uses three inputs—labor, lumber, and saws. Although it can vary its labor each week, it must order its lumber six months in advance. Further, it would take the firm a year to sell its saws, or acquire new saws. For this firm, the long run is
   a. any time period longer than one week.
   b. any time period longer than one week and shorter than six months.
   c. any time period longer than six months.
   d. any time period longer than six months and shorter than one year.
   e. any time period longer than one year.

3. When a firm increases its employment from four to five workers, with no other change, its total output rises from 1,000 to 1,500. For this change in employment, the marginal product of labor is
   a. 100.
   b. 200.
   c. 250.
   d. 300.
   e. 500.

4. If the MPL rises over a particular range of output, then—over that range—
   a. MC rises.
   b. MC falls.
   c. ATC rises.
   d. ATC falls.
   e. both MC and ATC rise.

Chapter 6 Production and Cost

5. Whenever the marginal cost curve lies above the average total cost curve, an increase in output will cause
   a. the marginal cost curve to shift upward.
   b. the marginal cost curve to shift downward.
   c. the average total cost curve to shift upward.
   d. the average total cost curve to shift downward.
   e. none of the above.

6. Which of the following is an example of an implicit cost to a farmer?
   a. The wages and salaries of the farm's workers
   b. The rent that the farmer pays to a landowner
   c. The interest the farmer must pay on bank loans
   d. The monthly payments for seeds, fertilizer, and other raw materials
   e. None of the above

7. In the short run, as output rises, the distance between the firm's TC and TVC curve
   a. increases.
   b. remains constant.
   c. decreases.
   d. first increases, then decreases.
   e. first decreases, then increases.

8. Which of the following might describe the behavior of a firm's costs in the *short run*?
   a. Economies of scale
   b. Diseconomies of scale
   c. Constant returns to scale
   d. All of the above
   e. None of the above

9. The firm's marginal cost curve
   a. intersects the minimum point of the ATC curve only.
   b. intersects the minimum point of the AVC curve only.
   c. intersects the minimum points of both the AVC and ATC curves.
   d. intersects the maximum points of both the AVC and ATC curves.
   e. none of the above.

10. If a firm doubles its output, but finds that its LRTC *less than doubles*, the firm is experiencing
    a. economies of scale.
    b. constant returns to scale.
    c. diseconomies of scale.
    d. increasing returns to labor.
    e. diminishing returns to labor.

True/False: For each of the following statements, circle T if the statement is true or F if the statement is false.

T F 1. The three major types of business firms are: sole proprietorship, public agency, and partnership.

T F 2. The law of diminishing (marginal) returns tells us that as the firm increases its output by varying all of its inputs together, the average cost of production will rise.

T F 3. In making a decision, all costs—whether sunk or not—should be considered.

T F 4. The *long run* for a business firm is a time period during which at least one of its inputs is variable.

T F 5. The *short run* for a business firm is a time period during which at least one of its inputs is variable.

T F 6. At any level of output, a firm's ATC can be greater than or equal to, but not less than, its LRATC.

T F 7. As output increases in the short run, average fixed cost always declines.

T F 8. As output rises in the short run, ATC always rises.

Numerical Word Problem: An ice manufacturer produces ice blocks using just two inputs that it must pay for: freezers and labor. The freezers each cost $200 per month in foregone interest and maintenance. Workers are paid $2,000 per month. The firm currently has 5 freezers. With three workers, the firm can produce 1,000 ice blocks per month. With four workers, it can produce 1,200 ice blocks per month.

Calculate each of the following:

1. TC per month with 3 workers = _____;
   TC per month with 4 workers = _____

2. TFC per month with 3 workers = _____;
   TFC per month with 4 workers = _____

3. TVC per month with 3 workers = _____;
   TVC per month with 4 workers = _____

4. ATC with 3 workers = _____;
   ATC with 4 workers = _____

5. AFC with 3 workers = _____;
   AFC with 4 workers = _____

6. AVC with 3 workers = _____;
   AVC with 4 workers = _____

7. MPL when labor increases from 3 to 4 workers = _____

8. MC when labor increases from 3 to 4 workers = _____

Formulas: Identify each of the following (use abbreviations, e.g. "TC" for total cost):

1. $\Delta Q/\Delta L$ = _____

2. TFC/Q = _____

3. TVC/Q = _____

4. TFC + TVC = _____

5. ATC − AFC = _____

6. $\Delta TC/\Delta Q$ = _____

7. LRTC /Q = _____

CHAPTER 7
HOW FIRMS MAKE DECISIONS: PROFIT MAXIMIZATION

SUMMARIZE THE CHAPTER

Construct your own chapter summary by filling in the blanks. If you have difficulty, review the highlighted points in the chapter, then try again. (Note: the shorter blanks should be filled in with mathematical symbols such as "<" or "=", or with abbreviations such as "Q" or "ΔTC")

- In this chapter, we view the firm as a single economic decision maker whose goal is to maximize its owners' _____.

- The proper measure of profit for understanding and predicting the behavior of firms is _____ profit. Unlike accounting profit, _____ profit recognizes all the opportunity costs of production, both explicit costs and _____ costs.

- The _____ _____ facing the firm tells us, for different prices, the quantity of output that customers will choose to purchase from that firm. It also tells us the maximum price the firm can charge to sell any given amount of output.

- The firm uses its production function, and the prices it must pay for its inputs, to determine the _____ _____ method of producing any given output level. Therefore, for any level of output the firm might want to produce, it must pay the cost of the "_____ _____ method" of production.

- In the total revenue and total cost approach, the firm calculates economic _____ = TR - TC at each output level and selects the output level where economic _____ is greatest.

- _____ revenue is the change in the firm's total revenue divided by the change in its output: MR = $\Delta TR/$____. It tells us how much _____ rises per unit increase in output.

- When a firm faces a downward-sloping _____ curve, each increase in output causes a revenue gain, from selling additional output at the new price, and a revenue loss, from having to lower the price on all previous units of output. _____ revenue is therefore less than the price of the last unit of output.

- An increase in output will always raise profit as long as marginal revenue is _____ than marginal cost (MR ____ MC).

- An increase in output will always lower profit whenever marginal revenue is _____ than marginal cost (MR ____ MC).

- To find the profit-maximizing output level, the firm should _____ output whenever MR > MC, and _____ output when MR < MC.

- The marginal revenue for any change in output is equal to the slope of the _____ revenue curve along that interval.

- To maximize profit, the firm should produce the quantity of output where the vertical distance between the TR and TC curves is _____ and the TR curve lies above the TC curve.

- Equivalently, to maximize profit, the firm should produce the level of output closest to the point where MC ____ MR, that is, the level of output at which the MC and MR curves _____.

- The marginal approach to profit states that a firm should take any action that adds more to its _____ than to its _____.

- Let Q* be the output level at which MR = MC. Then, in the short run:
    If TR ____ TVC at Q*, the firm should keep producing.
    If TR ____ TVC at Q*, the firm should shut down.
    If TR ____ TVC at Q*, the firm should be indifferent between shutting down and producing.

- A firm should _____ the industry in the long run when, at its best possible output level, it has any loss at all.

Chapter 7 How Firms Make Decisions: Profit Maximization 95

■ LEARN THE LINGO

Fill in each blank with the appropriate word or phrase from the list provided in the word bank. (For a challenge, fill in as many blanks as you can *without* using the word bank.)

_____ 1. Total revenue minus accounting costs.

_____ 2. Total revenue minus all costs of production, explicit and implicit.

_____ 3. A curve that indicates, for different prices, the quantity of output that customers will purchase from a particular firm.

_____ 4. The total inflow of receipts from selling a given amount of output.

_____ 5. The difference between total cost (TC) and total revenue (TR) when TC > TR.

_____ 6. The change in total revenue from producing one more unit of output.

_____ 7. A firm maximizes its profit by taking any action that adds more to its revenue than to its cost.

_____ 8. In the short run, the firm should continue to produce if total revenue exceeds total variable costs; otherwise, it should shut down.

_____ 9. A permanent cessation of production when a firm leaves an industry.

Word Bank

accounting profit
demand curve facing the firm
economic profit
exit
loss

marginal approach to profit
marginal revenue (MR)
shutdown rule
total revenue

■ BUILD YOUR SKILLS

For each of the following items, write the correct answer in the blank or circle the correct answer.

1. Last summer, Paula hired an economics student from Big U. to determine the demand curve facing her firm, Paula's Pickled Peppers. The student presented Paula with the

demand curve in the figure below. Data on the horizontal axis are pecks of peppers per period. The vertical axis measures price in dollars.

a. Complete the following table using information from the demand curve.

Price	Output	Total Revenue
$10	_____	_____
9	_____	_____
8	_____	_____
7	_____	_____
6	_____	_____
5	_____	_____
4	_____	_____
3	_____	_____
2	_____	_____
1	_____	_____
0	_____	_____

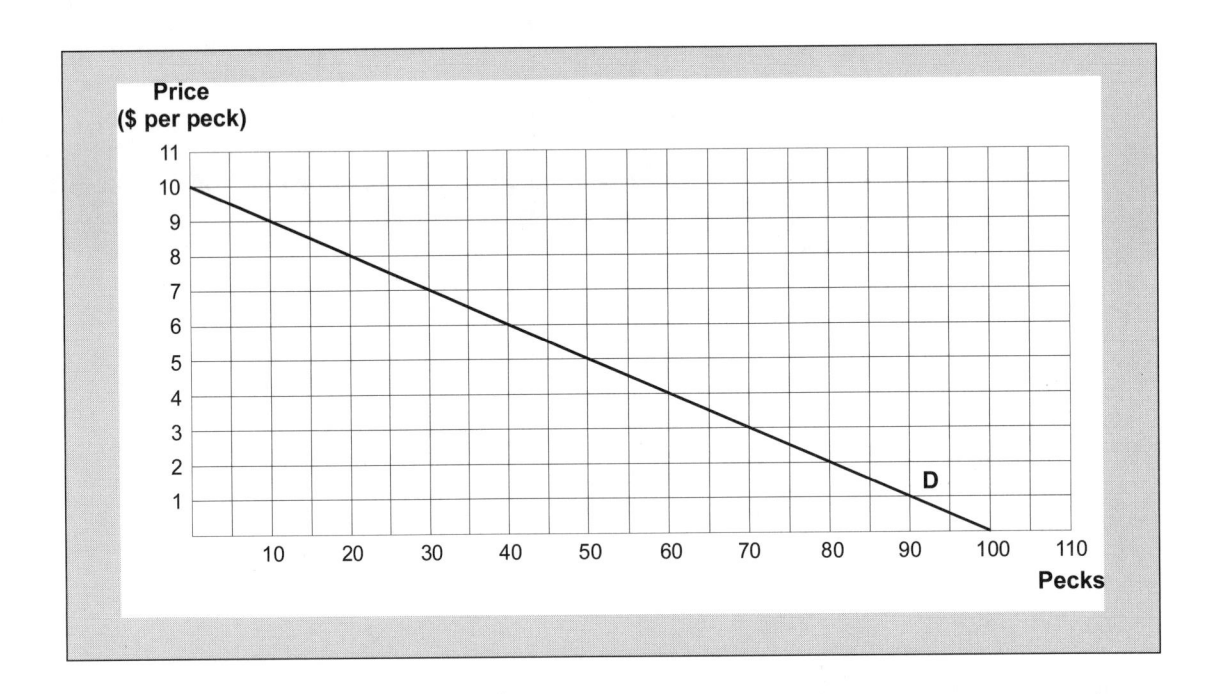

Chapter 7 How Firms Make Decisions: Profit Maximization

b. On the grid provided, plot the total revenue (TR) curve for Paula's Pickled Peppers.

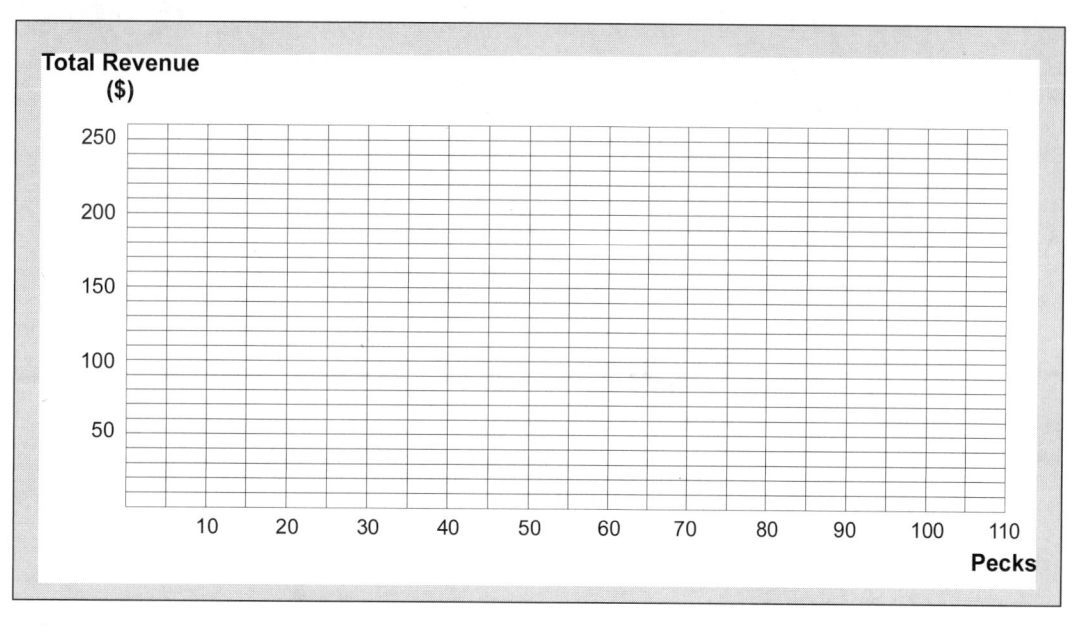

c. If Paula wants to maximize her revenue from selling peppers, how many pecks of peppers should she push each period? _____ What price should she charge? _____ How much revenue will she earn? _____

2. Paula may not be perfect, but she is nobody's patsy. She knows that revenue is only half of the story in business. What she cares *most* about is profit. After all, profit is what she gets to keep for herself, and she picked this particular profession for one reason only—its potential pecuniary rewards. Paula's peppers cost her $4 per peck to pick and pack. She has no fixed costs, so her total costs are given by the equation

$$TC = \$4q$$

where q is the number of pecks of peppers produced.

a. Carefully plot Paula's total cost curve on the grid provided in part (b) of the previous question. You will now have Paula's TR and TC curves on the same graph.

b. Reading from those two graphs, we can see that when Paula produces:
an output of 10 her profit will be _____
an output of 20 her profit will be _____
an output of 30 her profit will be _____
an output of 40 her profit will be _____
an output of 50 her profit will be _____
an output of 60 her profit will be _____

c. From the graph, we can see that if Paula wants to maximize her profit, she should produce an output of _____ pecks per period. From the demand curve in problem (1), this will mean Paula must charge a price of _____. Paula will then earn total revenue of _____ per period. Her total cost will be _____. That will leave Paula with a profit of _____ per period.

3. The following data on total revenue and total cost have been reported by your Vice President for Planning.

Output	Total Revenue	Marginal Revenue	Total Cost	Marginal Cost
0	$ 0		$50	
1	50	_____	60	_____
2	90	_____	75	_____
3	120	_____	95	_____
4	140	_____	120	_____
5	150	_____	150	_____
6	150	_____	185	_____

a. Your VP does not know how to compute marginal revenue and marginal cost, so you will have to fill in the table yourself.

b. In trying to decide how much to produce, you first compare MR and MC for the change from zero to one unit of output. Because you find that (MR>MC / MR=MC / MR<MC) you decide that you (should/should not) make that change because doing so adds (less/the same/more) to the firm's total revenue than it does to the firm's total cost.

c. Next you compare MR and MC for the move from 1 to 2 units of output. Because you find that (MR>MC / MR=MC / MR<MC) you decide that you (should/should not) make that move because doing so adds (less/more) to the firm's total revenue than it does to the firm's total cost.

d. Then you compare MR and MC for the move from 2 to 3 units of output. Because you find that (MR>MC / MR=MC / MR<MC) you decide that you (should/should not) make that move because doing so adds (less/more) to the firm's total revenue than it does to the firm's total cost.

e. Now you compare MR and MC for the move from 3 to 4 units of output. Because you find that (MR>MC / MR=MC / MR<MC) you decide that you (should/should not) make that move because doing so adds (less/more) to the firm's total revenue than it does to the firm's total cost.

f. Next you compare MR and MC for the move from 4 to 5 units of output. Because you find that (MR>MC / MR=MC / MR<MC) you decide that you (should/should not) make that move because doing so adds (less/more) to the firm's total revenue than it does to the firm's total cost.

g. Finally you compare MR and MC for the move from 5 to 6 units of output. Because you find that (MR>MC / MR=MC / MR<MC) you decide that you (should/should not) make that move because doing so adds (less/more) to the firm's total revenue than it does to the firm's total cost.

h. Having completed your analysis, you decide that in order to maximize profit you should produce _____ units of output. By doing so, you earn profit of _____. You can tell that you've chosen the best output, because had you decided to produce one unit less than that, your profit would have been _____; while if you had decided to produce one unit more than that your profit would have been _____.

4. Paula, who already produces pickled peppers, decides she'd like to branch into peaches, too. Her new venture, Paula's Prime Peaches, faces the following demand schedule

Quantity Demanded	Price	TR	MR
1	$28	___	
			___
2	26	___	
			___
3	24	___	
			___
4	22	___	
			___
5	20	___	
			___
6	18	___	
			___
7	16	___	
			___
8	14	___	
			___
9	12	___	
			___
10	10	___	

a. Complete the table.

b. If the marginal cost to Paula of each bushel of peaches is a constant $10, how many peaches should Paula pick and package in order to maximize her profit? _____

c. If the weather is good, the marginal cost of picking and packing peaches falls to $6 per bushel. If she gets good weather, how many peaches should Paula pick and pack in order to maximize her profit? _____

d. If the weather is good, and some of her neighbors help out for free, the marginal cost of picking and packing peaches will fall to $2 per bushel. If her neighbors help her out and the weather is good, how many peaches should Paula pick and pack?

Chapter 7 How Firms Make Decisions: Profit Maximization

5. Roger bought a Bed & Breakfast Inn (B & B) in Annapolis, Maryland. It's a good location, but he borrowed heavily to bankroll the business. Mortgage interest, interest on his renovation loan, taxes insurance and other fixed charges total $10,200 per month. At $150 per night, Roger's eight rooms can yield revenue of $33,600 per month, assuming 100% occupancy. Roger contracts out for cleaning, cooking and waitstaff at $4,200 per month. These contracts are for one month's service, and can be renewed each month if Roger chooses to do so. He therefore considers these latter expenses variable from month to month.

Month	Occupancy Rate	TR	TVC	TFC	Profit
January	10%				
February	10%				
March	20%				
April	25%				
May	60%				
June	85%				
July	95%				
August	95%				
September	80%				
October	50%				
November	20%				
December	10%				

a. The previous owners kept excellent records, and the monthly occupancy rates recorded in the table above are time-tested and highly accurate. Use that information to calculate the total revenue Roger can anticipate each month, and enter your results in the table.

b. Assuming that Roger is open for business every month, complete the remainder of the table using the information provided above.

c. According to the **shutdown rule**, Roger's B & B should stay open in a given month only if total revenue from operations that month (exceeds/equals/falls short of) the firm's (total variable cost/total fixed cost/total cost) for the month. Otherwise, the B & B should be shut down.

d. Roger has figured out he really should shut down part of the year. According to the shutdown rule, Roger maximizes his profit if he shuts down the B & B for the months of _____. He should remain open during the months of _____.

e. If Roger follows the guidelines in part (d) and shuts down part of the year, his total profit will be _____. If, instead, he stays open year round his total profit will be only _____.

TEST YOURSELF

To see what you *really* know and remember, take this test at least a day *after* you've read the chapter in the text and completed the exercises in this study guide.

Multiple Choice: Circle the letter in front of the single best answer.

1. Economic profit is
   a. the same as accounting profit.
   b. the difference between the firm's total revenue and its explicit costs.
   c. the difference between the firm's marginal revenue and marginal cost.
   d. all of the above.
   e. none of the above.

2. The demand curve facing the firm shows us, for any given output level,
   a. total revenue.
   b. total cost.
   c. the minimum price the firm can charge.
   d. the maximum price the firm can charge.
   e. none of the above.

3. The firm maximizes profit by producing the output level at which
   a. total revenue equals total cost.
   b. total revenue minus total cost is greatest.
   c. marginal revenue minus marginal cost is greatest.
   d. total revenue is as high as possible.
   e. price is as high as possible.

4. According to the marginal approach to profit, a firm should take any action that
   a. increases marginal revenue.
   b. increases total revenue.
   c. decreases total cost.
   d. decreases marginal cost.
   e. adds more to revenue than to cost.

Chapter 7 How Firms Make Decisions: Profit Maximization

Questions 5–8 refer to the following data, derived from the demand curve facing the firm

P	Q	TC
$100	4	$350
$ 90	5	$375
$ 80	6	$425
$ 70	7	$500

5. For this firm, the marginal revenue when price is lowered from $100 to $90 is
   a. $50.
   b. $90.
   c. $100.
   d. $400.
   e. $450.

6. At which output level or levels could this firm make a positive economic profit?
   a. 4
   b. 5
   c. 6
   d. All of the above.
   e. None of the above.

7. For this firm, as output increases from 4 to 5 to 6 to 7,
   a. marginal cost increases.
   b. marginal cost decreases.
   c. marginal revenue increases.
   d. total revenue decreases.
   e. total revenue remains unchanged.

8. For this firm, the profit maximizing output level is
   a. 4.
   b. 5.
   c. 6.
   d. 7.
   e. none of the above—the firm should shut down.

9. According to the shut-down rule, a firm should shut down in the short run whenever—at the output level where MR = MC—
   a. total cost exceeds total revenue.
   b. total cost exceeds marginal cost.
   c. total fixed cost exceeds total revenue.
   d. total variable cost exceeds total revenue.
   e. total fixed cost exceeds total variable cost.

10. At a particular output level, a firm's total revenue would be $40 million, its total explicit costs would be $30 million, and its economic profit would be zero. Which of the following must be true at that output level?
    a. The firm's total implicit costs would equal $40 million.
    b. The firm's total implicit costs equal $10 million.
    c. The firm's accounting profit would be zero.
    d. The firm's implicit costs would be negative.
    e. The firm's marginal revenue exceeds its marginal cost.

True/False: For each of the following statements, circle T if the statement is true or F if the statement is false.

T F 1. While economists can explain why there are payments for land, labor and capital, they have not been able to explain why there are profits.

T F 2. Economic profit can be defined as total revenue minus all explicit and implicit costs to the firm.

T F 3. In the short run, if a firm's total revenue is less than its total variable cost at all levels of output, the firm should exit the industry.

T F 4. Whenever marginal revenue is positive, increasing output by one unit will increase total revenue.

T F 5. The output level that maximizes profit is the same as the output level that maximizes total revenue.

T F 6. When MR and MC cross at two places, the profit-maximizing output level is the one at which the MC curve crosses the MR curve from above.

T F 7. A useful rule for deciding whether to increase output is to compare the gain in revenue with the average cost of production.

T F 8. No matter how large the loss, a firm should always stay open in the short run if its total revenue is sufficient to cover the total variable cost of production.

Short Answers: Organize the following information in a way that will help you answer the associated questions:

A firm must choose whether to produce an output level of 1, 2, 3, 4, or 5 units per day. The maximum price it can charge to sell each of these output levels,

Chapter 7 How Firms Make Decisions: Profit Maximization

respectively, is $100, $90, $80, $70, $60 and $50. The firm's total variable cost of producing each level of output is, respectively, $30, $60, $90, $120 and $150. Finally, in the short run, the firm has fixed costs of $200 per day.

1. For this firm, marginal cost for any change in output is equal to _____.

2. If this firm decides to produce any output level greater than zero, the best output level would be _____ units per day.

3. All things considered, the best decision for this firm in the short run would be to _____ (keep producing / shut down).

4. When this firm makes the best decision for the short run, it will earn an economic profit of _____ per day.

5. If the firm's fixed cost rises to $1,000 per day, with no other change in the data, the best decision for the firm in the short run would be to _____ (keep producing / shut down).

CHAPTER 8

PERFECT COMPETITION

SUMMARIZE THE CHAPTER

Construct your own chapter summary by filling in the blanks. If you have difficulty, review the highlighted points in the chapter, then try again. (Note: the shorter blanks should be filled in with mathematical symbols such as "<" or "=", or with abbreviations such as "Q" or "ΔTC")

- Market _____ means all the characteristics of a market that influence the behavior of buyers and sellers when they come together to trade.

- Perfect competition is a market _____ with three important characteristics:

    1. There are a _____ number of buyers and sellers, and each buys or sells only a tiny fraction of the total quantity in the market.

    2. Sellers offer a _____ product.

    3. Sellers can easily enter into or exit from the market.

- In a perfectly competitive market, the number of buyers and sellers is so _____ that no individual decision maker can significantly affect the _____ of the product by changing the quantity it buys or sells.

- A perfectly competitive firm faces a cost _____ like any other firm. The cost of producing any given level of output depends on the firm's production technology and the prices it must pay for its inputs.

- In perfect competition, the firm is a _____ taker: It treats the _____ of its output as given.

- For a competitive firm, _____ _____ at each quantity is the same as the market price. For this reason, the _____ _____ curve and the demand curve facing the firm are the same, a horizontal line at the market price.

107

- A firm earns a profit whenever P _____ ATC. Its total profit at the best output level equals the area of a _____ with height equal to the distance between P and ATC, and width equal to the level of output.

- A firm suffers a loss whenever P _____ ATC at the best level of output. Its total loss equals the area of a _____ with height equal to the distance between P and ATC, and width equal to the level of output.

- As the price of output changes, the firm will slide along its _____ curve in deciding how much to produce.

- The competitive firm's supply curve has two parts. For all prices above the minimum point on its _____ curve, the supply curve coincides with the MC curve. For all prices below the minimum point on the _____ curve, the firm will shut down, so its supply curve is a vertical line segment at _____ units of output.

- In the short run, the number of firms in the industry is _____.

- To obtain the _____ supply curve, we add up the quantities of output supplied by all firms in the market at each _____.

- In perfect competition, the market sums up the buying and selling preferences of individual consumers and producers, and determines the market _____. Each buyer and seller then takes the market _____ as given, and each is able to buy or sell the desired quantity.

- In a competitive market, economic _____ and _____ are the forces driving long-run change. The expectation of continued economic _____ causes outsiders to enter the market; the expectation of continued economic _____ causes firms in the market to exit.

- In a competitive market, positive economic _____ continues to attract new entrants until economic _____ is reduced to _____.

- In a competitive market, economic _____ continues to cause exit until the economic _____ is reduced to _____.

- In the long run, every competitive firm will earn normal profit—that is, _____ economic profit.

- In long-run equilibrium, every competitive firm will select its plant size and output level so that it operates at the _____ point of its LRATC curve.

Chapter 8   Perfect Competition

- At each competitive firm in long-run equilibrium, P = _____ = minimum ATC = minimum LRATC.

- The long-run _____ curve shows the relationship between market price and market quantity produced after all long-run adjustments have taken place.

- In a (an) _____ cost industry, entry causes input prices to rise, which shifts up the typical firm's _____ curve, and raises the market price at which firms earn zero economic profit. As a result, the long-run supply curve slopes _____.

- In a (an) _____ cost industry, entry has no effect on input prices, so the typical firm's _____ curve stays put and the market price at which firms earn zero economic profit does not change. As a result, the long-run supply curve is _____.

- In a (an) _____ cost industry, entry causes input prices to fall, which causes the typical firm's _____ curve to shift downward, and lowers the market price at which firms earn zero economic profit. As a result, the long-run supply curve slopes _____.

- In a market economy, price changes act as *market signals,* ensuring that the pattern of production matches the pattern of consumer demands. When demand increases, a _____ in price signals firms to _____ the market, increasing industry output. When demand decreases, a _____ in price signals firms to _____ the market, decreasing industry output.

- Under perfect competition, a technological advance leads to a rightward shift of the market supply curve, causing the market price to _____. In the short run, early adopters may earn positive economic profit. In the long run, all adopters will earn _____ economic profit. Firms that refuse to use the new technology will not survive.

■ LEARN THE LINGO

Fill in each blank with the appropriate word or phrase from the list provided in the word bank. (For a challenge, fill in as many blanks as you can *without* using the word bank.)

_____ 1. The characteristics of a market that influence how trading takes place.

_____ 2. A market in which there are many buyers and sellers, the product is standardized, and sellers can easily enter or exit the market.

_____ 3. Any firm that treats the price of its product as given and beyond its control.

_____ 3. Any firm that treats the price of its product as given and beyond its control.

_____ 4. The price at which a firm is indifferent between producing and shutting down.

_____ 5. A curve that shows the quantity of output a competitive firm will produce at different prices.

_____ 6. A curve indicating the quantity of output that all sellers in a market will produce at different prices.

_____ 7. Another name for zero economic profit.

_____ 8. A curve indicating the quantity of output that all sellers in a market will produce at different prices, after all long-run adjustments have taken place.

_____ 9. An industry in which the long-run supply curve slopes upward because each firm's ATC curve shifts upward as industry output increases.

_____ 10. An industry in which the long-run supply curve is horizontal because each firm's ATC curve is unaffected by changes in industry output.

_____ 11. An industry in which the long-run supply curve slopes downward because each firm's ATC curve shifts downward as industry output increases.

_____ 12. Price changes that cause firms to change their production to more closely match consumer demand.

Word Bank

constant cost industry
decreasing cost industry
firm's supply curve
increasing cost industry
long-run supply curve
market signals

market structure
market supply curve
normal profit
price taker
perfect competition
shutdown price

Chapter 8   Perfect Competition

BUILD YOUR SKILLS

For each of the following items, write the correct answer in the blank or circle the correct answer.

1. Wired is one of many small producers in the perfectly competitive copper wire market. The table below provides data on Wired's output in coils of wire per week, and its total costs in dollars.

Output	TR	TC	MR	MC	Profit
0	____	6			____
1	____	7	____	____	____
2	____	10	____	____	____
3	____	15	____	____	____
4	____	22	____	____	____
5	____	31	____	____	____
6	____	42	____	____	____
7	____	55	____	____	____
8	____	70	____	____	____
9	____	87	____	____	____
10	____	106	____	____	____

a. If the market price of wire is currently $12 per coil, compute marginal revenue, marginal cost and total profit at each level of output. Fill in the table.

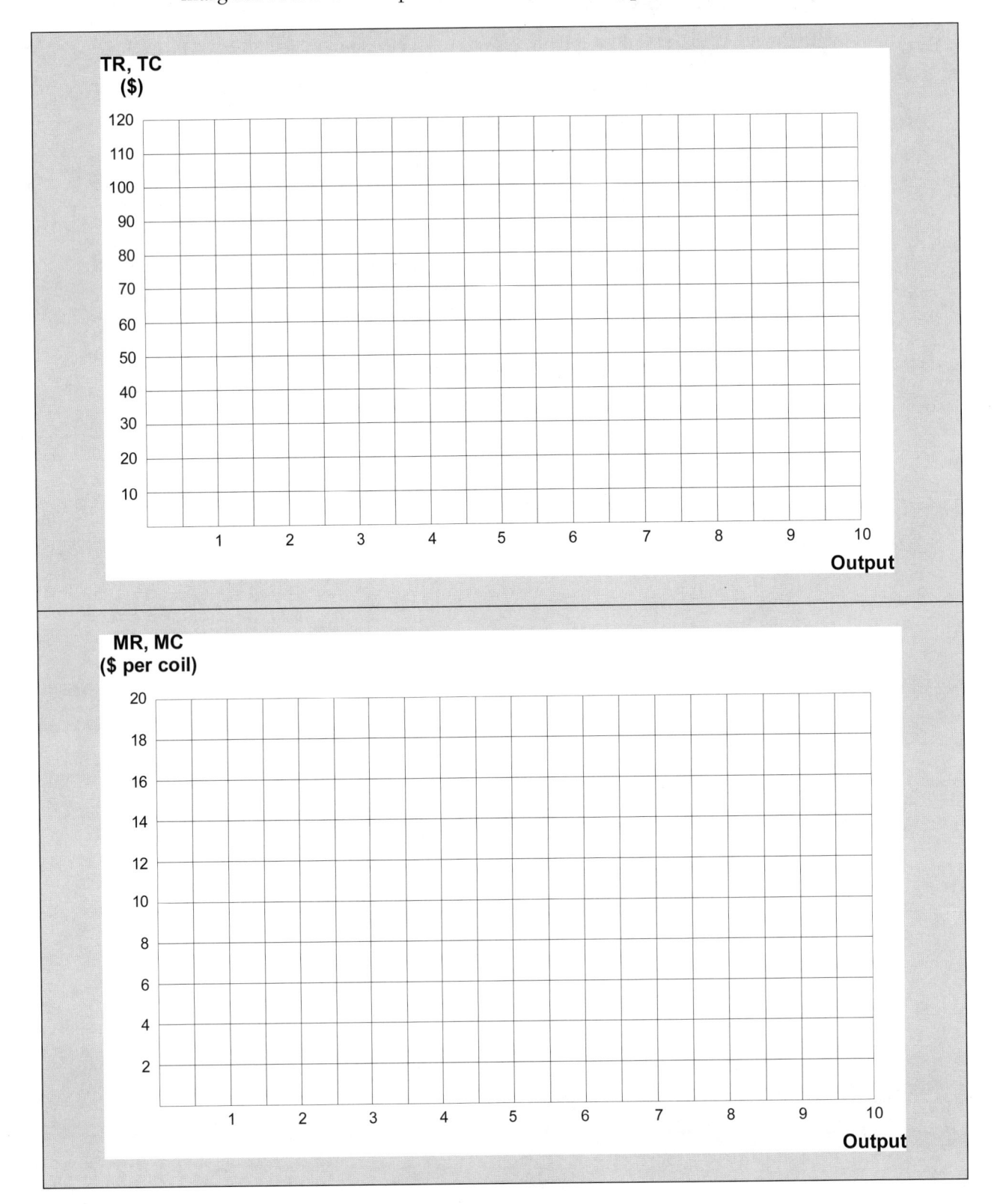

TR, TC ($)

MR, MC ($ per coil)

b. In the topmost grid, plot Wired's total revenue and total cost curves. Plot Wired's marginal revenue and marginal cost curves in the bottom grid. (Remember to observe the convention of plotting marginal values at the midpoint of the range over which you calculate them.)

c. To maximize profit, Wired should produce _____ coils per week. When it does, it will realize maximum total profit of _____ dollars per week. In the topmost grid, this amount of profit corresponds to the (horizontal/vertical) distance between the TR and the TC curves at an output of _____ coils per week. In the bottom grid, we can see that when output is less than the profit-maximizing level, marginal cost is (greater than/equal to/less than) marginal revenue. When output is greater than the profit-maximizing level, marginal cost is (greater than/equal to/less than) marginal revenue. When Wired is producing the profit-maximizing output of _____ coils per week, marginal revenue is (greater than/equal to/less than) marginal cost.

2. A firm sells its output in a perfectly competitive market. Its ATC, AVC, and MC curves are drawn below.

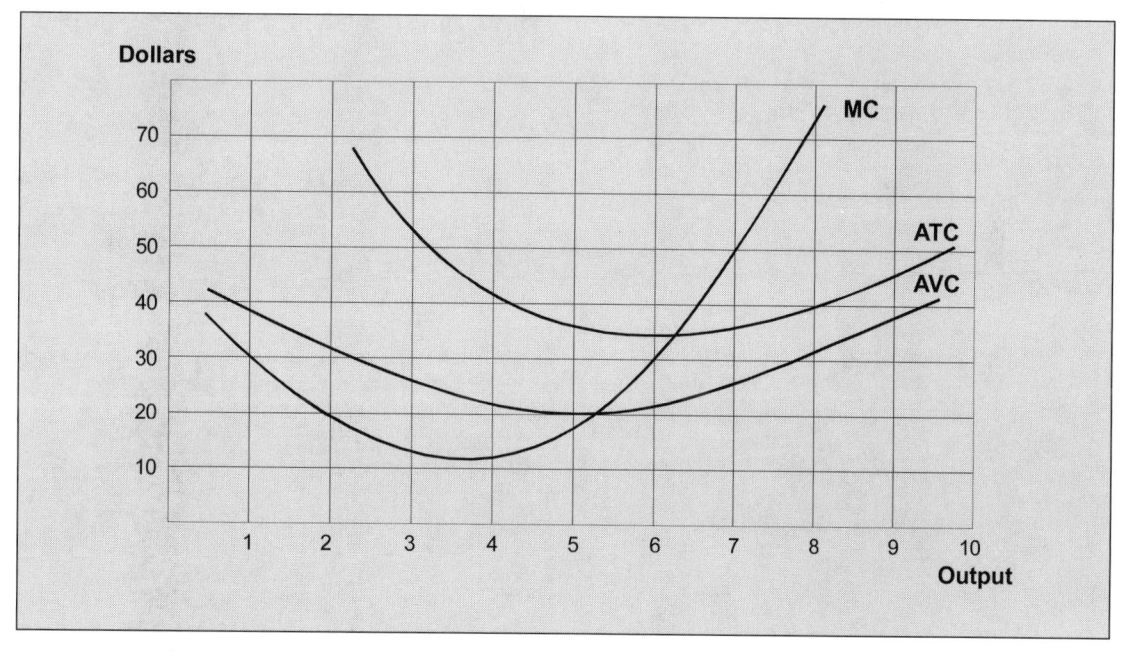

a. When the market price of output is $50 per unit, this firm will maximize its profit by producing approximately _____ units. At that level of output, profit per unit will be approximately (5/15/25) dollars. Total profit will be approximately (35/105/175) dollars.

b. If the market price of output rises to $60, the firm will maximize profit by (decreasing/ increasing) its output to approximately _____ units. Its profit per unit will (rise/fall) to between (30 and 35 / 20 and 25 / 10 and 15) dollars, and its total profit will (rise/fall) to between (225 and 263 / 150 and 188 / 75 and 113) dollars

c. If the market price should fall to $30, the firm's best course of action in the short run is to (keep producing/shut down) because its total revenue (exceeds/equals/falls below) its total variable cost. The firm will maximize profit by producing approximately _____ units of output. At a price of $30, producing this output, the firm will earn (negative/positive/zero) profits in the short run.

d. If the market price should fall to $15, it (is/is not) possible for the firm to earn positive profit. To maximize profit, the firm should (shut down/produce what it can) in the short run.

3. For the firm in the previous question, complete the following short-run supply schedule, indicating the quantity this firm would supply to the market at different market prices. Then plot the firm's short-run supply curve in the grid provided.

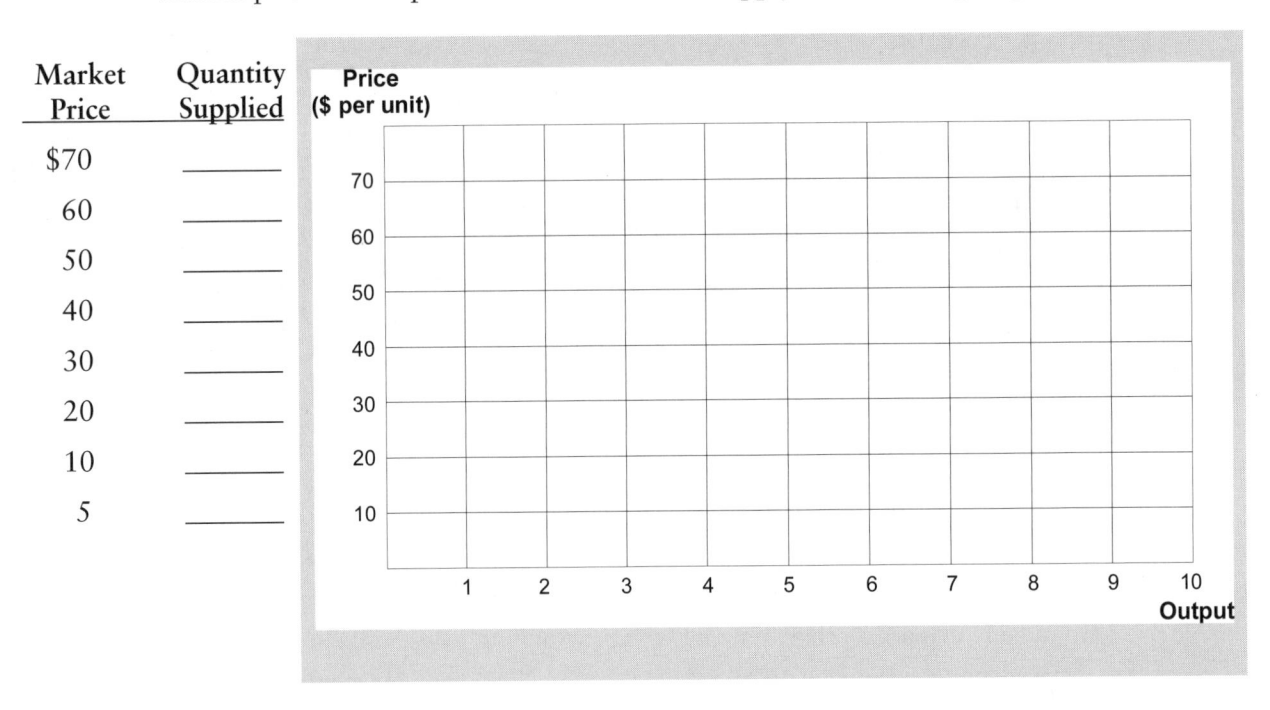

Market Price	Quantity Supplied
$70	_____
60	_____
50	_____
40	_____
30	_____
20	_____
10	_____
5	_____

Chapter 8 Perfect Competition

4. Regional monthly market demand for alfalfa sprouts is depicted in the panel on the left below. The marginal cost curve for a typical sprout producer is depicted in the panel on the right. The minimum level of average variable cost is zero. We know that the regional market for alfalfa sprouts is perfectly competitive.

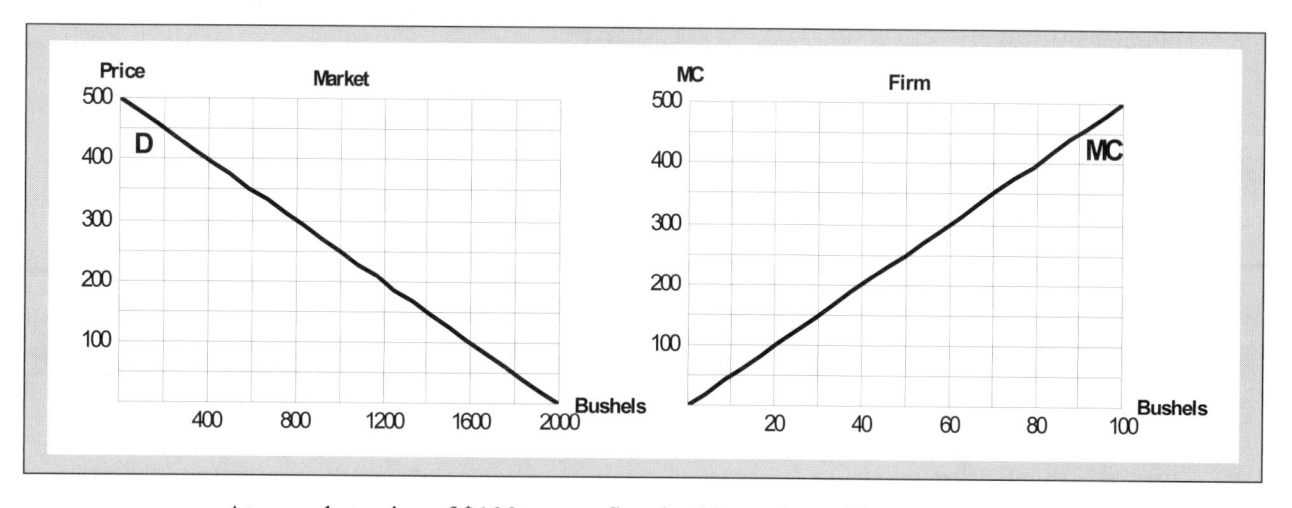

a. At a market price of $100, every firm in this market will supply _____ bushels to the market. At a price of $200, every firm will supply _____ bushels. At a price of $300, every firm will supply _____ bushels. At a market price of $0, every firm will supply _____ bushels.

b. Suppose there are 20 firms in the market. Then, at a price of $100, _____ bushels will be supplied to the market. At a price of $200, _____ bushels will be supplied to the market. At a price of $300, _____ bushels will be supplied to the market. On the left grid, plot the short-run market supply curve with 20 firms in the market. What is the short-run equilibrium price when there are 20 firms in this market? _____

c. Suppose there are 30 firms in the market. Then at a price of $100, _____ bushels will be supplied to the market. At a price of $200, _____ bushels will be supplied to the market. At a price of $300, _____ bushels will be supplied to the market. On the left grid, plot the short-run market supply curve with 30 firms in the market. What is the short-run equilibrium price when there are 30 firms in this market? _____

d. Suppose there are 80 firms in the market. Then, at a price of $0, _____ bushels will be supplied to the market. At a price of $50, _____ bushels will be supplied to the market. At a price of $100, _____ bushels will be supplied to the market. On the left grid, plot the short-run market supply curve with 80 firms in the market. What is the short-run equilibrium price when there are 80 firms in this market? _____

5. Consider the perfectly competitive market and firm depicted below.

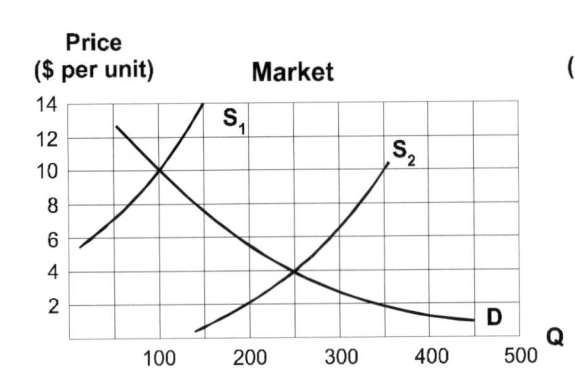

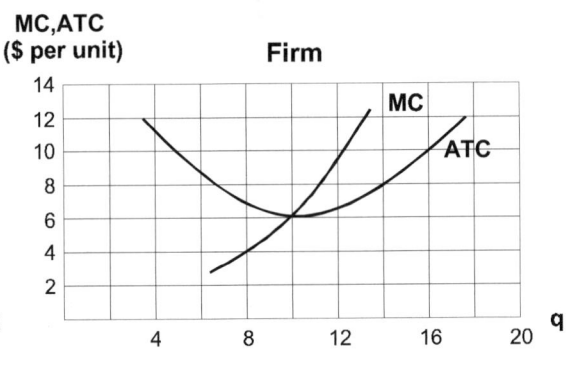

a. When the short-run market supply curve is S₁, the short-run equilibrium price in this market will be _____ dollars. At this price, the market (is/is not) in long-run equilibrium. When market supply is S₁, firms earn (positive profit/negative profit/zero profit). This will cause other firms to (enter this market/exit this market/ neither enter nor exit this market). This will (shift market supply to the right/shift market supply to the left/leave the market supply curve unchanged), causing market price to (fall/rise/remain unchanged) in the long run.

b. When the short-run market supply curve is S₂, the short-run equilibrium price in this market will be _____ dollars. At this price, the market (is/is not) in long-run equilibrium. When market supply is S₂, firms earn (positive profit/negative profit/zero profit). This will cause other firms to (enter this market/exit this market/neither enter nor exit this market). This will (shift market supply to the right/shift market supply to the left/leave the market supply curve unchanged), causing market price to (fall/rise/ remain unchanged) in the long run.

c. In the long run, entry and exit will occur until market supply intersects market demand at a price of _____. When equilibrium price is this level, firms will (earn positive profit/make losses/earn zero economic profit). Firms will then (enter/exit/neither enter nor exit) this market, and the market (will/will not) be in long run equilibrium.

Chapter 8   Perfect Competition

TEST YOURSELF

To see what you *really* know and remember, take this test at least a day *after* you've read the chapter in the text and completed the exercises in this study guide.

Multiple Choice: Circle the letter in front of the single best answer.

1. Which of the following is a characteristic of perfect competition?
    a. There are many buyers and sellers.
    b. The firm faces a downward sloping demand curve.
    c. Every seller offers a different product from other sellers.
    d. All of the above.
    e. None of the above.

2. Which of the following is a condition for short-run profit-maximization in a perfectly competitive firm?
    a. TR = TC
    b. P = MC
    c. P = AVC
    d. All of the above.
    e. None of the above.

3. A perfectly competitive firm earns positive economic profit whenever
    a. P > MC.
    b. P > MR.
    c. MR > P.
    d. P > ATC.
    e. ATC > MC.

4. For a competitive firm, profit per unit of output is equal to
    a. P − ATC.
    b. MC − ATC.
    c. TR − TC.
    d. P − AVC.
    e. MR − MC.

5. Which of the following statements about perfect competition is *false*?
    a. In the short run, the number of firms in the industry is fixed.
    b. All firms in the industry produce a standardized product.
    c. Each firm chooses the price at which it will sell its output.
    d. For each firm, marginal revenue is the same as market price.
    e. There are no significant barriers to entry or exit.

6. In a perfectly competitive, increasing-cost industry, an increase in demand will, in the long run, cause:
   a. an increase in price.
   b. an increase in market output.
   c. an increase in the number of firms.
   d. all of the above.
   e. none of the above.

7. A perfectly competitive firm should shut down in the short run whenever, at the best possible output,
   a. P < ATC
   b. P < AVC
   c. P < MR
   d. P < ATC + AVC
   e. none of the above

8. A technological advance in a perfectly competitive market will, in the long run, lead to
   a. greater profit at each firm.
   b. higher prices charged by each firm.
   c. a leftward shift of the market supply curve.
   d. all of the above.
   e. none of the above.

9. In a perfectly competitive market, an increase in the price of a variable input will cause an upward shift in each firm's
   a. MC curve.
   b. ATC curve.
   c. AVC curve.
   d. All of the above.
   e. None of the above.

10. In a competitive industry, a rightward shift of the demand curve will cause
    a. economic profit for each firm in the long run.
    b. economic loss for each firm in the long run.
    c. economic profit for each firm in the short run, and entry in the long run.
    d. economic profit for each firm in the short run, and exit in the long run.
    e. economic loss for each firm in the short run, and exit in the long run.

True/False: For each of the following statements, circle T if the statement is true or F if the statement is false.

T F 1. Since the assumptions of perfect competition are rarely completely satisfied in practice, the perfectly competitive model is rarely used by economists.

Chapter 8   Perfect Competition

T   F   2. Under perfect competition, the firm's supply curve is horizontal.

T   F   3. Under perfect competition, in long run equilibrium, accounting profit may be greater than zero.

T   F   4. Under perfect competition, an increase in the market price will increase each firm's marginal revenue.

T   F   5. In a perfectly competitive, increasing cost industry, a *leftward* shift of the demand curve will—in the long run—cause the market price to rise.

T   F   6. Under perfect competition, in long-run equilibrium, P = MC = AVC.

T   F   7. Under perfect competition, a technological advance enabling firms to produce the same output at lower cost will cause the market supply curve to shift rightward.

T   F   8. A perfectly competitive firm should shut down whenever the market price is lower than the minimum point on the AVC curve.

Short Answer: Write a brief answer below each of the following questions.

1. List the three characteristics that define a perfectly competitive market.

    a.

    b.

    c.

2. Which of the three characteristics of perfect competition ensures that economic profit is driven to zero in the long run?

3. Fill in the following table by writing the word "increase," "decrease," or "no change" in each of the 12 blank cells. Pay attention to the wording. (Hint: drawing graphs might help.)

Type of Industry	Short-run effect of an increase in demand on:		Long-run effect of a decrease in demand on:	
	Quantity:	Price:	Quantity:	Price:
Increasing cost industry				
Decreasing cost industry				
Constant cost industry				

CHAPTER 9
MONOPOLY

SUMMARIZE THE CHAPTER

Construct your own chapter summary by filling in the blanks. If you have difficulty, review the highlighted points in the chapter, then try again. (Note: the shorter blanks should be filled in with mathematical symbols such as "<" or "=", or with abbreviations such as "Q" or "ΔTC")

- A monopoly firm is the only seller of a good or service with no close _____. The market in which the monopoly firm operates is called a monopoly market.

- A _____ monopoly exists when, due to economies of scale, one firm can produce at a lower cost per unit than can two or more firms.

- In dealing with _____ property, government strikes a compromise: It allows the creators to enjoy a monopoly and earn economic profit, but only for a limited period of time. Once the time is up, other sellers are allowed to enter the market, and it is hoped that competition among them will cause the market price to _____.

- Network _____ exist when an increase in the network's membership (more users of the product) increase its value to current and potential members.

- A monopolist, like any firm, strives to maximize profit. And, like any firm, it faces constraints. For any level of output it might produce, total _____ is determined by (1) its technology of production and (2) the prices it must pay for its inputs. And for any level of output it might produce, the maximum price it can charge is determined by the market _____ curve for its product.

- When any firm, including a monopoly, faces a downward-sloping demand curve, marginal revenue is _____ than the price of output. Therefore, the marginal revenue curve will lie _____ the demand curve.

- A monopoly will always produce at an output level where marginal revenue is _____.

- To maximize profit, a monopoly—like any firm—should produce the quantity where MC _____ MR and the MC curve crosses the MR curve from _____.

- A monopoly earns a profit whenever P _____ ATC. Its total profit at the best output level equals the area of a _____ with height equal to the distance between P and ATC and width equal to the level of output.

- A monopoly suffers a loss whenever P _____ ATC. Its total loss at the best output level equals the area of a _____ with height equal to the distance between ATC and P and width equal to the level of output.

- Any firm—including a monopoly—should shut down if P < _____ at the output level where MR = MC.

- Unlike _____ _____ firms, monopolies may earn economic profit in the long run.

- A privately owned monopoly suffering an economic loss in the _____ run will exit the industry, just as would any other business firm. In the _____ run, therefore, we should not find privately owned monopolies suffering economic losses.

- We can expect a monopoly market to have a _____ price and _____ output than an otherwise similar perfectly competitive market.

- The monopolization of a competitive industry leads to two opposing effects. First, for any given technology of production, monopolization leads to _____ prices and _____ output. Second, changes in the technology of production made possible under monopoly may lead to _____ prices and _____ output. The ultimate effect on price and quantity depends on the relative strengths of these two effects.

- Any costly action a firm undertakes to establish or maintain its monopoly status is called _____ - _____ activity.

- _____ - _____ that helps establish or maintain a firm's monopoly position is part of the firm's costs. As a result, it can reduce the economic profit of a monopoly and may even reduce it to zero.

- A monopolist will react to an increase in demand by producing more output, charging a _____ price, and earning a _____ profit. It will react to a decrease in demand by reducing output, _____ price, and earning a _____ profit.

- In general, a monopoly will pass to consumers only part of the benefits from a cost-saving technological change. After the change in technology, the monopoly's profits will be _____.

- In general, a monopoly will pass only part of a cost increase onto consumers in the form of a _____ price. After the cost increase, the monopoly's profits will be _____.

- Price discrimination occurs when a firm charges different prices to different customers for reasons other than differences in _____.

- When price discrimination raises the price for some consumers above the price they would pay under a single-price policy, it harms consumers. The additional _____ for the firm is equal to the monetary loss of consumers. When price discrimination lowers the price for some consumers below what they would pay under a single-price policy, it benefits consumers as well as the firm.

- Under _____ price discrimination, a firm charges each customer the most the customer would be willing to pay for each unit he or she buys.

- For a _____ price discriminator, marginal revenue revenue is equal to the price of the additional unit sold. Thus, the firm's MR curve is the same as its _____ curve.

- A _____ price discriminator increases profit at the expense of consumers, charging each customer the most he or she would willingly pay for the product.

LEARN THE LINGO

Fill in each blank with the appropriate word or phrase from the list provided in the word bank. (For a challenge, fill in as many blanks as you can *without* using the word bank.)

_____ 1. The only seller of a good or service that has no close substitutes.

_____ 2. The market in which a monopoly firm operates.

_____ 3. A market in which, due to economies of scale, one firm can operate at lower average cost than can two or more firms.

_____ 4. A temporary grant of monopoly rights over a new product or scientific discovery.

_____ 5. A grant of exclusive rights to sell a literary, musical, or artistic work.

_____ 6. A government-granted right to be the sole seller of a product or service.

_____ 7. A situation in which the value of a good or service to each user increases as more people use it.

_____ 8. Any costly action a firm undertakes to establish or maintain its monopoly status.

_____ 9. A monopoly firm that is limited to charging the same price for each unit of output sold.

_____ 10. Charging different prices to different customers for reasons other than differences in costs.

_____ 11. Charging each customer the most he or she would be willing to pay for each unit purchased.

Word Bank

copyright
government franchise
monopoly firm
monopoly market
natural monopoly
network externalities

patent
perfect price discrimination
price discrimination
rent-seeking activity
single-price monopoly

Chapter 9 Monopoly

BUILD YOUR SKILLS

For each of the following items, write the correct answer in the blank or circle the correct answer.

1. Margaret manages a monopoly in the market for mailbox magnets in metropolitan Muskegon. Monthly market demand is graphed below.

P	Q^D	TR	MR
$20	___	___	
			___
18	___	___	
			___
16	___	___	
			___
14	___	___	
			___
12	___	___	
			___
10	___	___	
			___
8	___	___	
			___
6	___	___	
			___
4	___	___	
			___
2	___	___	
			___
0	___	___	

a. Read Margaret's demand curve, and complete the first column in the table. Then complete the rest of the table.

b. Plot Margaret's marginal revenue curve. (Remember to plot the marginal value at the midpoint of the range over which you've calculated it.)

c. When Margaret is selling two mailbox magnets per month, marginal revenue is (positive/ negative/zero). This tells us that her revenue will (increase/decrease remain unchanged) if she sells an additional magnet.

d. When Margaret is selling seven mailbox magnets per month, marginal revenue is (positive/negative/zero). This tells us that her revenue will (increase/decrease/remain unchanged) if she sells an additional magnet.

e. Margaret is a profit maximizer, and she will always pick a level of output that maximizes her profit. Even though we know nothing about Margaret's costs, we know she will never produce an output where marginal revenue is (positive/negative/zero). Thus, no matter what her costs are, we can be sure Margaret will never produce more that _____ magnets per month.

2. Margaret's mother, Molly, sells antique movie magazines. Molly knows her marginal cost curve and it is plotted below. She does not know what her demand curve looks like, although she has collected the bits of evidence on price, quantity demanded, and total revenue per month reported in the table below.

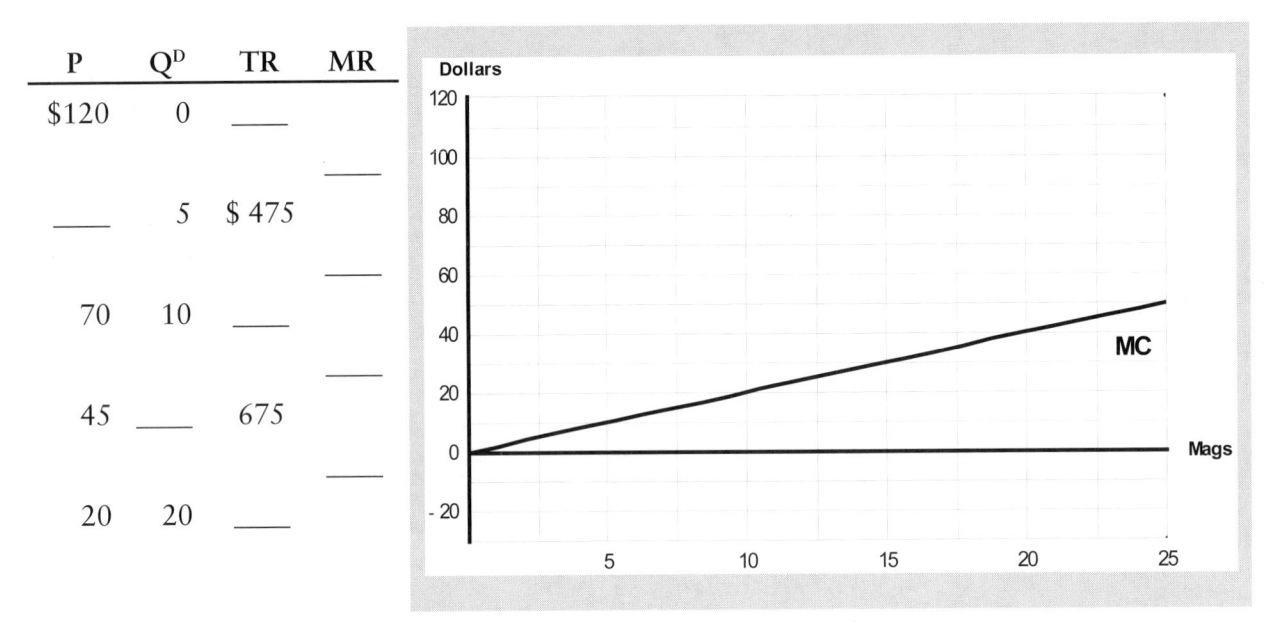

P	Q^D	TR	MR
$120	0	____	
			____
____	5	$ 475	
			____
70	10	____	
			____
45	____	675	
			____
20	20	____	

a. Complete the table.

b. Plot Molly's demand curve and marginal revenue curve. (Remember to plot the marginal values at the midpoint of the range over which you calculate them).

c. To maximize her profit, how many movie mags should Molly sell each month? _____ At that level of output, marginal revenue will equal approximately _____ dollars, and marginal cost will equal approximately _____ dollars. Molly should sell these magazines at a price of approximately _____ dollars.

d. If Molly were to sell one more movie mag beyond the profit maximizing output you found, marginal revenue would (be greater than/less than/equal to) marginal cost, and her profit would (rise/fall/remain unchanged).

Chapter 9 Monopoly

3. A monopolist has the cost, demand and marginal revenue curves depicted below.

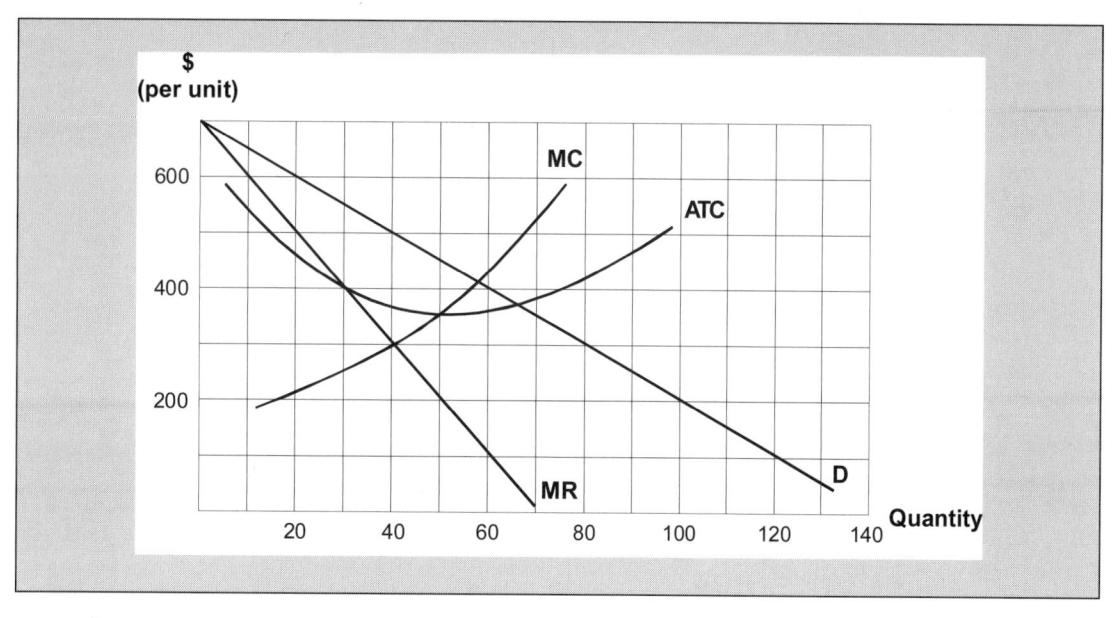

   a. What output maximizes the monopolist's profit? _____

   b. What is marginal revenue at the profit-maximizing output? _____ What is marginal cost at the profit maximizing output? _____ At the profit maximizing output, marginal revenue (is greater than/equal to/less than) marginal cost.

   c. What price does the monopolist charge? _____

   d. What is average total cost at the monopoly equilibrium? _____

   e. What is profit per unit in the monopoly equilibrium? _____

   f. What is the monopolist's total profit in equilibrium? _____

4. Monty just invented a new board game—he calls it "Slopes and 'Cepts." Market research indicates that demand for this game is given by

   $$P = 56 - 0.25Q,$$

   and Monty's marginal revenue is given by the equation:

   $$MR = 56 - 0.5Q$$

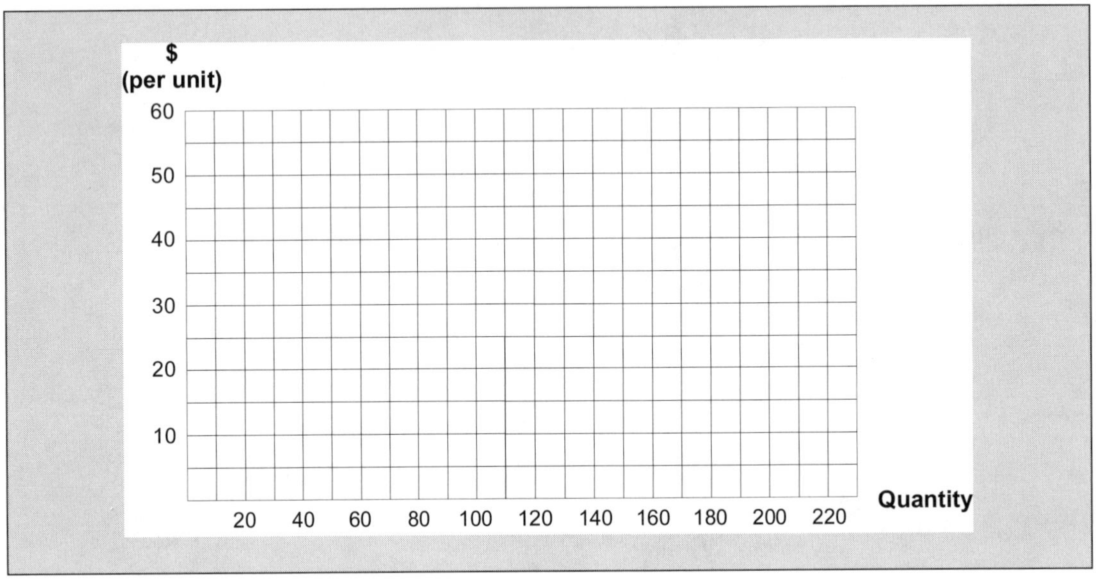

a. Plot Monty's demand curve and marginal revenue curves on the grid above. Label each one clearly.

b. Right now, the marginal cost of producing each game is constant and equal to \$30 no matter how many games Monty produces. Plot the corresponding marginal cost curve on the grid.

c. How many games should Monty produce to maximize his profit? ______________ How much should he charge for each game? ______________

d. One day, the price of the cardboard used in producing board games rises. Monty now finds that the marginal cost of producing a game has increased to \$40. Plot Monty's new marginal cost curve on the grid above. How many games should Monty produce now? ______________ How much should he charge? ______________

e. Looking back over (c) and (d), we can see that when marginal cost rose by \$10, the price Monty charges rose by only ______________ dollars. In this situation, Monty's best course of action was (to/to not) pass along to his customers the entire increase in his costs.

5. You may have noticed a curious fact while you were working on the last problem: Monty's demand curve and marginal revenue curve share the same vertical intercept, and the marginal revenue curve is exactly twice as steep as the demand curve.

   This is no coincidence. In fact, it is the result of a general rule that governs the relationship between the marginal revenue and demand curves when the demand curve is a straight line. Specifically, it can be shown that when a firm's demand curve is linear and can be written in the form:

$$\text{Demand: } P = a - bQ$$

the firm's associated marginal revenue curve will have the form:

$$MR = a - 2bQ$$

a. If we were to graph the equation for demand displayed above, the demand curve would intercept the vertical (dollars) axis at _____ . The slope of the demand curve would be _____ . The demand curve would cross the horizontal quantity axis at a quantity of _____. (Hint: What is the value of P when the demand curve hits the horizontal axis?)

b. If we were to graph the marginal revenue equation displayed above, the marginal revenue curve would intercept the vertical (dollars) axis at _____ . The slope of the marginal revenue curve would be _____ . The marginal revenue curve would intercept the horizontal (quantity) axis at a quantity of _____.

c. Making use of the rule we just described, fill in the blanks

Demand	Marginal Revenue
P = 34 − 4Q	MR = ____ − 8Q
P = ____ − 15Q	MR = 28 − 30Q
P = 72 − 12Q	MR = 72 − ____Q
P = 12 − 8Q	MR = ____ − ____Q
P = ____ − ____Q	MR = 105 − 50Q

6. When old Doc rode into town on the stage last month, he was the first and only surgeon to set foot in this part of the country. It didn't take him long to learn that if he charged $1,000 for a hernia operation, no one would have the procedure. If, however, he cut the price to $750, the banker would have his done right away. If he charged only $500, both the banker and the grocer would have the procedure, while if he went as low as $250, the ranch hand would get one, too. Of course, if he repaired hernias for free, even the schoolteacher would get one done, but let's be realistic—Doc can't just give these things away. In fact, he figures that the average total cost he incurs for each hernia he repairs is constant and equal to $125.

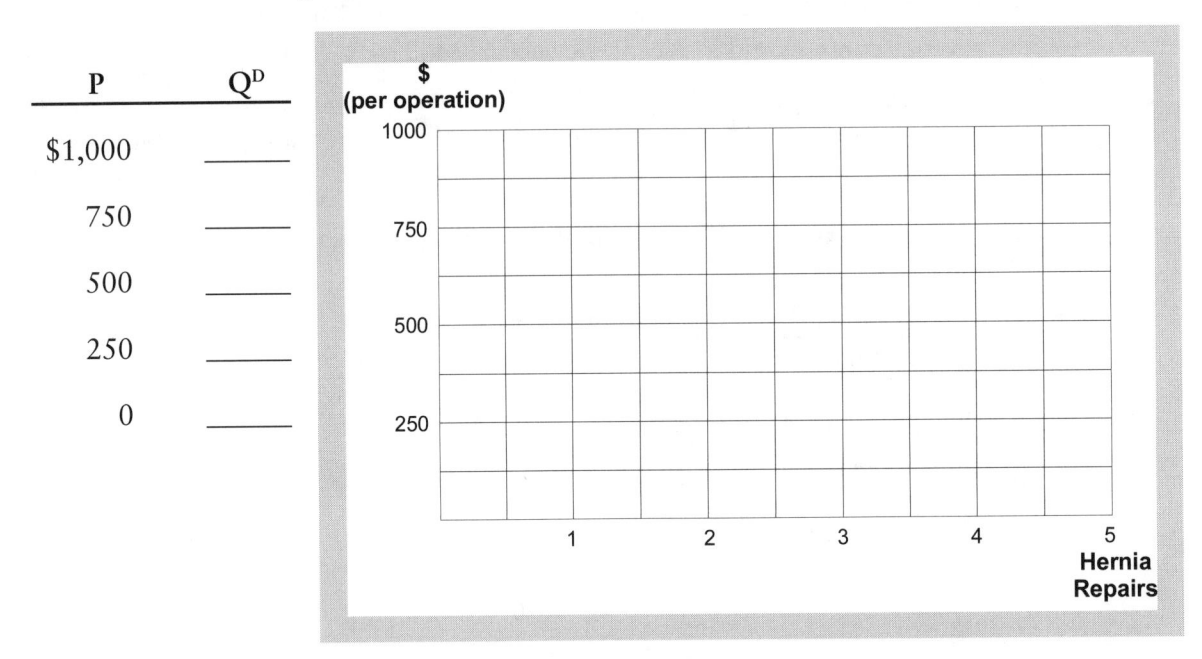

P	Q^D
$1,000	____
750	____
500	____
250	____
0	____

a. If Doc were to charge everyone the same price for an operation, complete the table telling how many operations would be demanded at each listed price. Using the information in this table, plot the demand curve Doc faces.

b. Plot Doc's average total cost (ATC) curve.

c. If Doc decides to charge everyone the same price of $250 for a hernia repair:

How many repairs will he perform? _____

How much revenue will he earn? _____

What will be Doc's total cost? _____

How much profit will he earn? _____

One day, when the fog cleared, Doc had a realization: Since he knows who will pay what, he thought he might be able to make *more* money by price discriminating among his buyers.

d. If, for otherwise indistinguishable hernia repairs, Doc charges the banker $750, the grocer $500, and the ranch hand $250:

How many repairs will he perform? _____.

How much revenue will he earn? _____

What will be Doc's total cost? _____

How much profit will he earn? _____

e. Does Doc make more profit when he price discriminates or when he charges everyone the same price? _____

TEST YOURSELF

To see what you *really* know and remember, take this test at least a day *after* you've read the chapter in the text and completed the exercises in this study guide.

Multiple Choice: Circle the letter in front of the single best answer.

1. A monopoly firm is the only seller of a good or service with
   a. no barriers to entry.
   b. no close substitutes.
   c. no close complements.
   d. no government involvement.
   e. none of the above.

2. Which of the following can explain why a market becomes a monopoly rather than a purely competitive market?
   a. Economies of scale
   b. Easy entry and exit
   c. Standardized product
   d. horizontal demand curve
   e. Horizontal demand curve

3. For a single-price monopoly, the marginal revenue curve
   a. is horizontal.
   b. is vertical.
   c. lies below the demand curve.
   d. lies above the demand curve.
   e. is the same as the demand curve.

4. A single-price monopoly will never produce a level of output where
    a. profit is negative.
    b. marginal revenue is negative.
    c. marginal cost is positive.
    d. marginal cost exceeds average total cost.
    e. average total cost exceeds marginal cost.

5. A single-price monopoly should shut down when, at the output level where MR = MC,
    a. MC > ATC.
    b. ATC > MC.
    c. P < ATC.
    d. P < AVC.
    e. ATC < AVC.

6. When a competitive market is monopolized, the result must be
    a. higher prices.
    b. a lower level of output.
    c. the end of rent-seeking activity.
    d. all of the above.
    e. none of the above.

7. When demand for a single-price monopoly's output increases, the monopolist will
    a. raise its price.
    b. increase its output.
    c. earn greater profit.
    d. All of the above.
    e. None of the above.

8. Which of the following is a requirement for successful price discrimination?
    a. perfectly inelastic demand for the firm's output
    b. The ability to know exactly how much each consumer is willing to pay
    c. The ability to prevent low-price customers from reselling to high-price customers
    d. All of the above
    e. None of the above

9. When the conditions for price discrimination are satisfied, price discrimination
    a. always harms consumers and benefits the firm.
    b. always benefits the firm, and may help or harm consumers.
    c. always benefits both consumers and the firm.
    d. always harms both consumers and the firm.
    e. always harms the firm, and may help or harm consumers.

10. For a perfect price discriminator, the MR curve
    a. is vertical.
    b. is horizontal.
    c. lies above the demand curve.
    d. lies below the demand curve.
    e. is the same as the demand curve.

True/False: For each of the following statements, circle T if the statement is true or F if the statement is false.

T F 1. In dealing with intellectual property, government grants patents and copyrights, knowing that this will permanently raise the price above the competitive price and create an unending stream of profits for the creator.

T F 2. Just like perfectly competitive firms, monopoly firms can earn economic profit in the long run.

T F 3. For a single-price monopoly, the marginal revenue of producing another unit of output is equal to the price at which that unit of output will be sold.

T F 4. To maximize profit, a single-price monopoly should produce the output level at which P = MC.

T F 5. A monopoly firm's supply curve is upward sloping.

T F 6. A (single price) monopoly firm should shut down in the short run whenever P < ATC at the best level of output.

T F 7. Lobbying government officials to preserve barriers to entry is an example of rent-seeking activity.

T F 8. Price discrimination always benefits the firm and harms consumers.

Short Answer: Write a brief answer below each of the following questions.

1. Other than patents and copyrights, list three distinct types of barriers to entry that can explain the existence of a monopoly.

    a.

    b.

    c.

2. List two reasons why monopolies—in spite of barriers to entry—often earn zero economic profit over the long run.

    a.

    b.

3. List the three conditions that must be satisfied for successful price discrimination.

    a.

    b.

    c.

CHAPTER 10

MONOPOLISTIC COMPETITION AND OLIGOPOLY

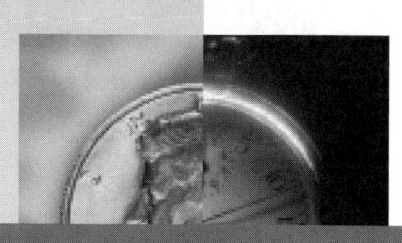

SUMMARIZE THE CHAPTER

Construct your own chapter summary by filling in the blanks. If you have difficulty, review the highlighted points in the chapter, then try again.

- Imperfect competition refers to market structures between _____ _____ and monopoly. In imperfectly competitive markets, there is more than one seller, but too few to create a perfectly competitive market. In addition, imperfectly competitive markets often violate other conditions of perfect competition, such as the requirement of a _____ product or free entry and exit.

- A monopolistically competitive market has three fundamental characteristics:
    1. many buyers and sellers;
    2. sellers offer a _____ product; and
    3. sellers can easily enter or exit the market.

- Because it produces a differentiated product, a monopolistic competitor faces a downward-sloping _____ curve: When it _____ its price a modest amount, quantity demanded will decline (but not all the way to zero).

- Under monopolistic competition, firms can earn positive or negative economic profit in the _____ run. But in the _____ run, free entry and exit will ensure that each firm earns _____ economic profit, just as under perfect competition.

- In the _____ run, a monopolistic competitor will operate with excess capacity—that is, it will produce too _____ output to achieve minimum cost per unit.

135

- Any action a firm takes to increase the demand for its output—other than cutting its price—is called _____ competition.

- An oligopoly is a market dominated by a _____ number of _____ interdependent firms.

- A _____ strategy is a strategy that is best for a player regardless of the strategy of the other player.

- A _____ equilibrium exists when each player is taking the best action for herself, given the actions taken by all other players.

- A game with two players will have a _____ equilibrium as long as at least one player has a _____ strategy, whether the other has a _____ strategy or not.

- Under monopolistic competition, advertising may increase the size of the market, so that more units are sold. But in the long run, each firm earns _____ economic profit, just as it would if no firm were advertising. The price to the consumer, however, may either rise or fall.

LEARN THE LINGO

Fill in each blank with the appropriate word or phrase from the list provided in the word bank. (For a challenge, fill in as many blanks as you can *without* using the word bank.)

_____ 1. A market structure in which there are many firms selling products that are differentiated, yet are still close substitutes, and in which there is easy entry and exit.

_____ 2. Any action a firm takes to increase the demand for its product, other than cutting its price.

_____ 3. A market structure in which a small number of firms are strategically interdependent.

_____ 4. A market that is likely to be an oligopoly because the minimum efficient scale of the typical firm is a large fraction of the market.

_____ 5. An approach to modeling the strategic interaction of oligopolists in terms of moves and countermoves.

_____ 6. A table showing the payoffs to each of two players for each pair of strategies they choose.

Chapter 10 Monopolistic Competition and Oligopoly

_____ 7. A strategy that is best for a player no matter what strategy the other player chooses.

_____ 8. A situation in which every player of a game is taking the best action for themselves, given the actions taken by all other players.

_____ 9. An oligopoly market with only two sellers.

_____ 10. A situation in which strategically interdependent sellers compete over many time periods.

_____ 11. Cooperation involving direct communication between competing firms about setting prices.

_____ 12. A group of firms that selects a common price that maximizes total industry profits.

_____ 13. Any form of oligopolistic cooperation that does not involve an explicit agreement.

_____ 14. A game-theoretic strategy of doing to another player this period what he has done to you in the previous period.

_____ 15. A form of tacit collusion in which one firm sets a price that other firms copy.

Word Bank

cartel
dominant strategy
duopoly
explicit collusion
game theory
monopolistic competition
Nash equilibrium
natural oligopoly

nonprice competition
oligopoly
payoff matrix
price leadership
repeated play
tacit collusion
tit for tat

BUILD YOUR SKILLS

For each of the following items, write the correct answer in the blank or circle the correct answer.

1. Roma Deli is typical of many small delicatessen-groceries throughout the country. Its biggest business is the lunch trade, and its biggest-selling lunchtime item is the "Heart Stopper," a large sandwich stuffed with prosciutto, ham, salami, provolone, etc. There are many other delis in town, and each has its own specialty similar (but not identical) to the Heart Stopper. Roma Deli's daily cost and demand curves, depicted below, are typical of other local firms. The horizontal axis (Q) measures the number of Heart Stoppers sold daily.

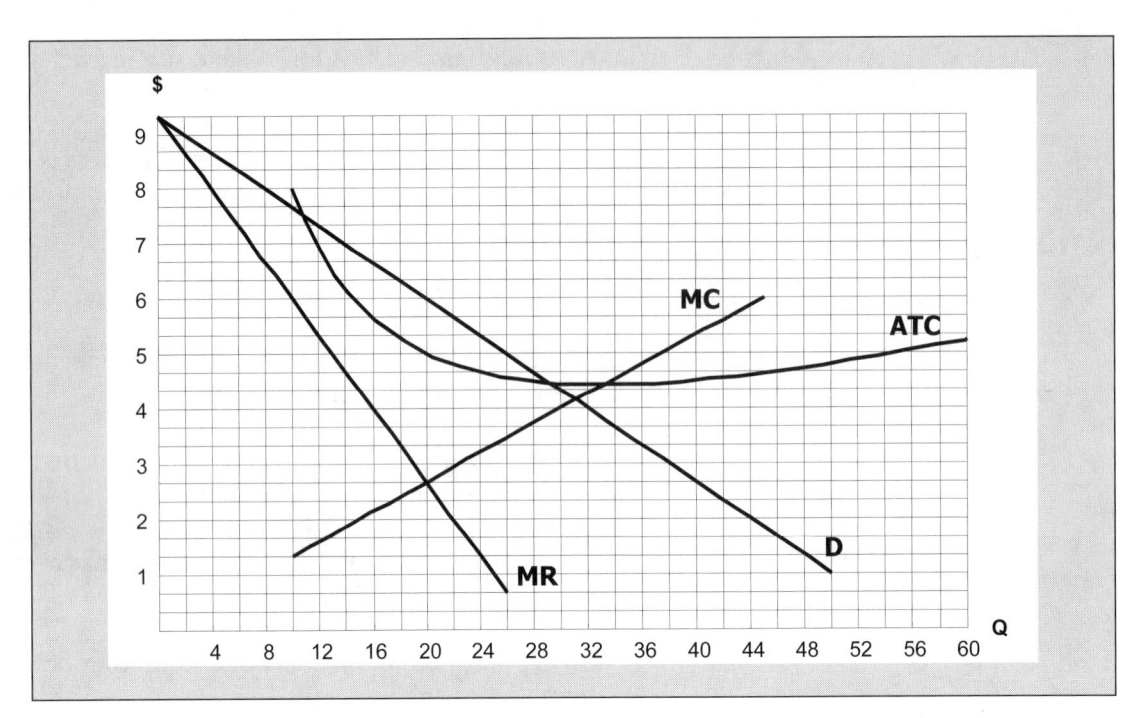

a. In the short run, Roma Deli (can/cannot) make a profit on Heart Stoppers. To (maximize profit/minimize loss), the deli should produce (no output/where marginal revenue exceeds marginal cost/where marginal revenue is equal to marginal cost/where average total cost is equal to marginal cost).

b. In the short run:
   How many Heart Stoppers should Roma Deli sell? _____
   What price should it charge? _____
   What is the average total cost of a Heart Stopper at the profit maximizing output? _____
   How much profit will Roma Deli earn each day? _____

c. In the long run, we would expect to see other delis (enter/exit) this market. As those firms (enter/exit), the demand curve facing Roma Deli will (shift leftward/shift rightward/be unaffected). After all adjustments, the deli market will be in long run equilibrium when Roma Deli, and others like it, earn (positive/negative/zero) economic profit.

2. The market demand for crispy rye crackers, recently re-discovered as a healthy snack food, has been estimated to be

$$Q^D = 16{,}000 - 1{,}000P,$$

where P is price per case in dollars, and Q is quantity demanded in the market each week.

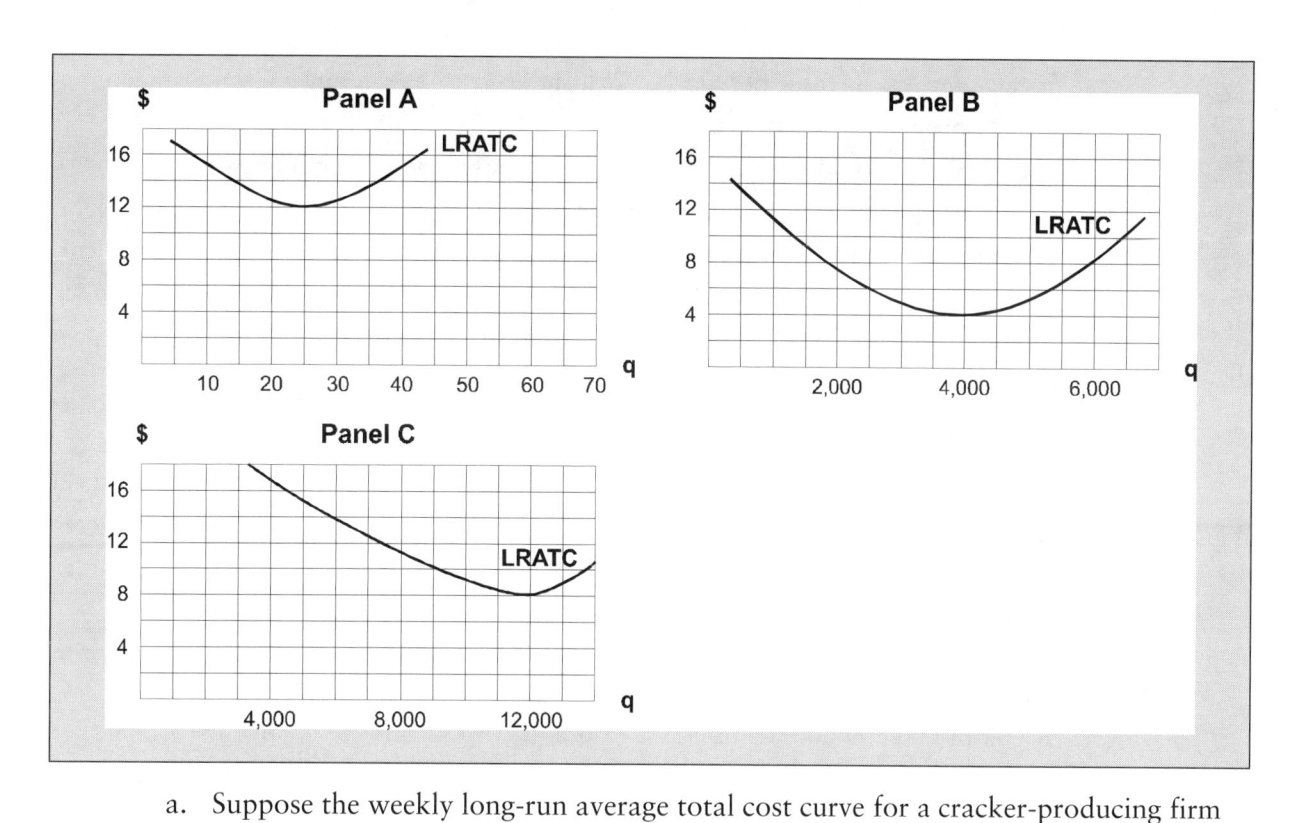

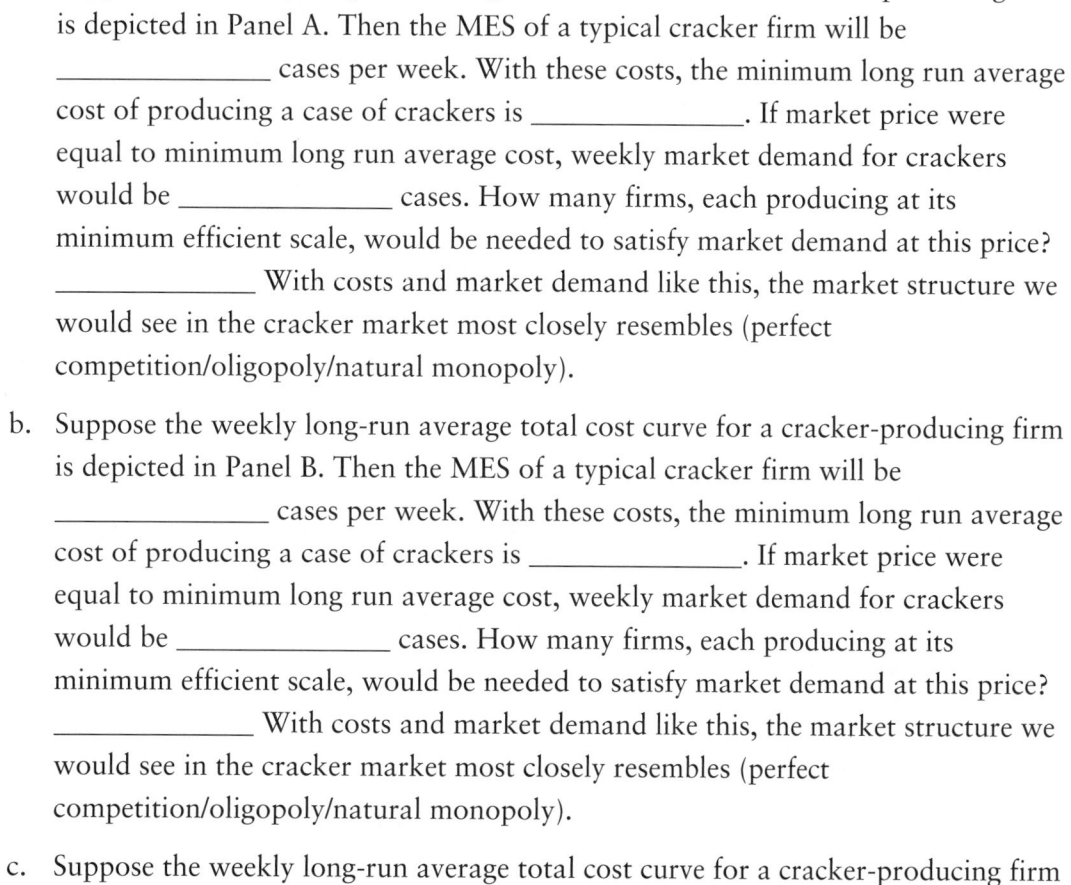

Chapter 10 Monopolistic Competition and Oligopoly

Panel A: LRATC curve, q-axis from 10 to 70, $ axis showing values around 12 minimum near q=25-30.

Panel B: LRATC curve, q-axis from 0 to 6,000, minimum around $4 near q=4,000.

Panel C: LRATC curve, q-axis from 0 to 12,000+, minimum around $8 near q=10,000-12,000.

a. Suppose the weekly long-run average total cost curve for a cracker-producing firm is depicted in Panel A. Then the MES of a typical cracker firm will be _____ cases per week. With these costs, the minimum long run average cost of producing a case of crackers is _____. If market price were equal to minimum long run average cost, weekly market demand for crackers would be _____ cases. How many firms, each producing at its minimum efficient scale, would be needed to satisfy market demand at this price? _____ With costs and market demand like this, the market structure we would see in the cracker market most closely resembles (perfect competition/oligopoly/natural monopoly).

b. Suppose the weekly long-run average total cost curve for a cracker-producing firm is depicted in Panel B. Then the MES of a typical cracker firm will be _____ cases per week. With these costs, the minimum long run average cost of producing a case of crackers is _____. If market price were equal to minimum long run average cost, weekly market demand for crackers would be _____ cases. How many firms, each producing at its minimum efficient scale, would be needed to satisfy market demand at this price? _____ With costs and market demand like this, the market structure we would see in the cracker market most closely resembles (perfect competition/oligopoly/natural monopoly).

c. Suppose the weekly long-run average total cost curve for a cracker-producing firm is depicted in Panel C. Then the MES of a typical cracker firm will be

_____ cases per week. With these costs, the minimum long run average cost of producing a case of crackers is _____. If market price were equal to minimum long run average cost, weekly market demand for crackers would be _____ cases. How many firms, each producing at its minimum efficient scale, would be needed to satisfy market demand at this price? _____ With costs and market demand like this, the market structure we would see in the cracker market most closely resembles (perfect competition/oligopoly/natural monopoly).

3. Market research shows that consumers like blue—it is a soothing color that most people find attractive. However, red gets attention on the shelf—but too much red can be jarring and turn consumers off. You and your rival must each decide upon the color for your packaging. Both of you have looked at the same research, and both are pretty much in agreement about the following facts.
   - If you both use blue, you'll have profit (in thousands) of $100 this year, and your rival will earn $90.
   - If you use blue, while she uses red, you'll make $50 but she'll earn $110.
   - If you use red and she uses blue, you'll make $120 and she'll only make $40.
   - If you both use red, you'll earn $80 and she'll earn $70.

In the following payoff matrix, each row represents one of your strategies, each column one of your rival's strategies.

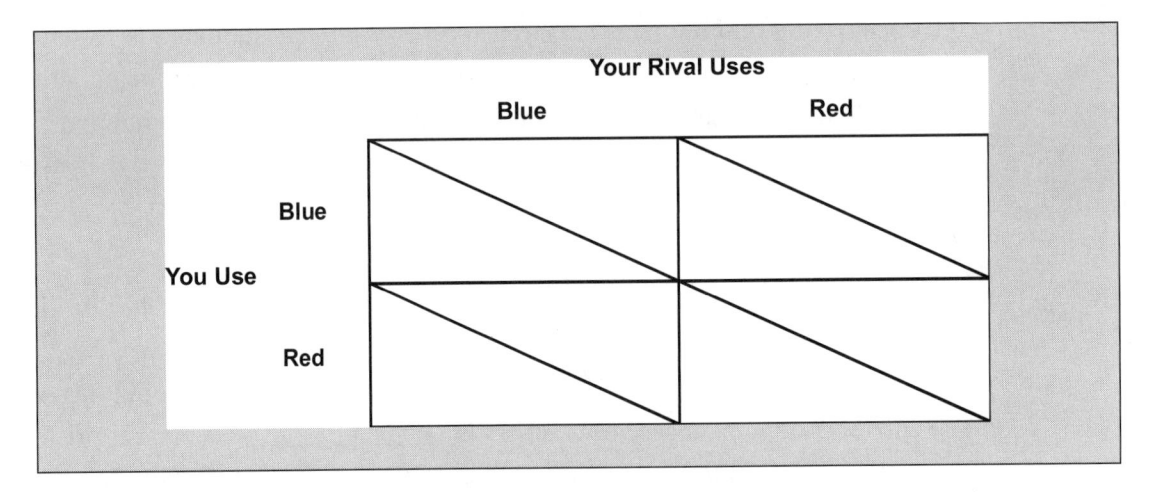

	Your Rival Uses Blue	Your Rival Uses Red
You Use Blue		
You Use Red		

a. Complete the payoff matrix using the information on profits for you and your rival. Put your payoff in the lower left of the cell, and your rival's payoff in the upper right.

b. Which of your strategies is best for you when your rival uses blue? _____ Which is best for you when your rival uses red? _____ Do you have a dominant strategy? _____

c. Now look at the game from your rival's perspective. Which of her strategies is best for her when you use blue? _____ Which is best for her when you use red? _____ Does your rival have a dominant strategy? _____

d. If you and your rival must act independently of one another—each picking your own strategy without knowing the other's choice—what strategy will you choose? _____ What strategy will your rival choose? _____

e. If you and your rival could agree to cooperate, is there a pair of strategies the two of you could agree to follow that would be better for *both of you* than the equilibrium you described in (d)? (Yes/No). To pull it off, you would have to agree to (use blue/use red) and your rival would have to agree to (use blue/use red).

f. If you can count on your rival to keep her word and pursue the strategy agreed upon for her in (e), how much profit do you make if you keep your word, too, and pursue what you agreed to in (e)? _____ How much profit do you make if you cheat, and choose your other strategy despite having agreed not to do so? _____ When do you make the most: when you play by the rules, or when you cheat? _____

g. If your rival can count on you to keep your word and pursue the strategy agreed upon for you in (e), how much profit does she make if she keeps her word, too, and pursues what you agreed to in (e)? _____ How much profit does she make if she cheats, and chooses her other strategy despite having agreed not to do so? _____ When does she make the most: when she plays by the rules, or when she cheats? _____

4. Folks in Goodgrass, ND, remember when just about anyone could get 40 acres and a mule for practically nothing. In those days, anyone could plant in the spring and get a good crop to market by fall. One year, there were 100 farms, all producing the same grade of wheat. Market demand for that wheat is graphed in the panel on the left below, and the average total cost and marginal cost of a typical farm are drawn in the panel on the right.

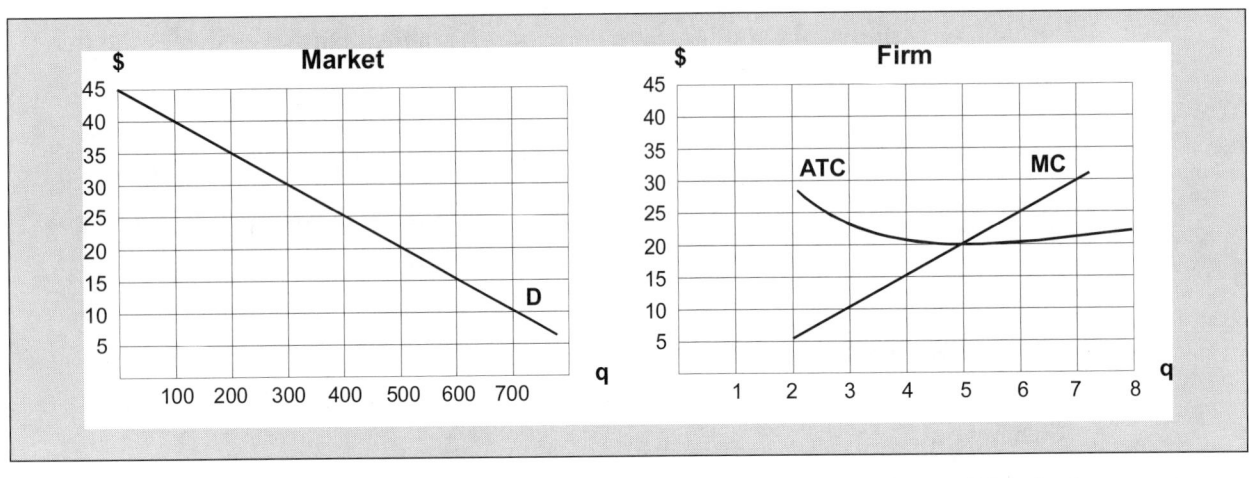

a. If the regional wheat market is perfectly competitive, what will be the long run equilibrium price of wheat? _____ How many bushels will each farm produce at that price? _____ How much economic profit will the typical farm earn? _____

One day down at the Grange Hall, they started talking about forming a regional wheat cartel. All the farmers in Goodgrass would get together and agree to cut back their production in order to raise the price of wheat for everybody. Some folks said that, if everyone pulled together, the price could go as high as $25 a bushel.

b. To get the market price to $25, total market output would have to be _____ bushels. If every one of the 100 farms in Goodgrass produced an equal share of this output, how many bushels would each farm have to produce? _____

c. Obviously, every farm would be better off with the cartel in operation. It may be hard to see in these graphs exactly how much each farm would earn, but because market price of $25 is (greater than/less than/equal to) the farm's average total cost when it produces its output in (b), we know that profit per unit, as well as total profit, will be (positive/ negative/zero) for every firm in the cartel.

d. But then Arne Killjoy just had to speak up. He pointed out that if a farm cuts output back to its share of the cartel output, its marginal cost will be _____. If the market price of wheat is $25, it is easy to see that market price will (exceed/equal/be less than) marginal cost at every farm. But then every farmer will think to himself, "If I can just increase my own output a little and sell it all at $25 per bushel, I can make even *more* profit than I'm making in the cartel. And, after all, I'm in the farming business to make money, and the other 99 will probably never notice I'm cheating, so why shouldn't I just go ahead and do it?"

e. Everyone agreed that made sense. But all of them could see that if everyone cheated on the cartel, then everyone would be competing with one another once again and, in the long run, they'd no doubt see the equilibrium market price fall back down to _____ dollars. Then they'd all be back to producing _____ bushels and earning (negative/zero/positive) economic profit once again.

One thing seemed clear to everybody: With the actions of so many farms to coordinate and monitor, collusion was likely to be impossible. That was when they all gave up on the idea and started for the door. . . .

TEST YOURSELF

To see what you *really* know and remember, take this test at least a day *after* you've read the chapter in the text and completed the exercises in this study guide.

Multiple Choice: Circle the letter in front of the single best answer.

1. The restaurant industry in a large city most closely resembles the market structure of
   a. perfect competition.
   b. monopolistic competition.
   c. monopoly.
   d. oligopoly with cooperative behavior.
   e. oligopoly without cooperative behavior.

2. Both monopoly and monopolistic competition share which of the following features?
   a. No significant barriers to entry or exit
   b. Zero economic profit in the long run
   c. Downward sloping demand curve
   d. All of the above
   e. None of the above

3. Which of the following is *not* true for monopolistically competitive firms in the *long run*?
   a. Economic profit equals zero.
   b. Price equals average total cost.
   c. Marginal revenue equals marginal cost.
   d. Average total cost is minimized.
   e. Price exceeds marginal revenue.

4. Which of the following is *always* true for monopolistically competitive firms in the *short run*?
   a. Economic profit equals zero.
   b. Price equals average total cost.
   c. Marginal revenue equals marginal cost.
   d. Average total cost is minimized.
   e. Marginal revenue equals price.

5. Under monopolistic competition, firms operate with "excess capacity" in the long run. This means that each firm produces a level of output at which
   a. marginal revenue equals marginal cost.
   b. marginal revenue is greater than marginal cost.
   c. average total cost is greater than its minimum possible value.
   d. price is greater than marginal revenue.
   e. marginal cost is greater than average cost.

6. Which of the following is an example of nonprice competition?
   a. Economic profit attracts entry by new firms.
   b. Economic loss causes exit of existing firms.
   c. A firm produces additional units for which marginal revenue exceeds marginal cost.
   d. A firm cuts back production in order to increase profit.
   e. A firm advertises to gain new customers.

7. A key feature of oligopoly is
   a. differentiated output.
   b. standardized output.
   c. no significant barriers to entry.
   d. strategic interaction.
   e. none of the above.

8. A natural oligopoly is an oligopoly that can be explained by
   a. economies of scale.
   b. zoning regulations.
   c. lobbying of government agencies.
   d. the reputation of existing firms.
   e. none of the above.

9. A dominant strategy in an oligopoly game is a strategy that is best for a player
   a. as long as its competitor follows the same strategy.
   b. as long as its competitor follows a different strategy.
   c. as long as no additional players are allowed to play.
   d. when both players cooperate.
   e. regardless of the strategy of the other player.

10. Price leadership is generally considered an example of
    a. explicit collusion.
    b. tacit collusion.
    c. a tit for tat strategy.
    d. uncooperative behavior.
    e. none of the above.

True/False: For each of the following statements, circle T if the statement is true or F if the statement is false.

T F 1. Monopolistic competition has three characteristics: a differentiated product, no significant barriers to entry, and few buyers and sellers.

T F 2. Monopolistic competitors may earn positive economic profit in the short run, but earn zero economic profit in the long run.

T F 3. Under both perfect competition and monopolistic competition, price equals minimum average total cost in the long run.

T F 4. A market in which there are 100 firms, each with a 1 percent share of the total market, would most likely be considered an oligopoly.

T F 5. A natural oligopoly occurs when a single firm would achieves its minimum efficient scale (MES) at an output level that can supply the entire market.

T F 6. Cheating on a collusive agreement is more likely when firms can easily observe other firms' prices.

T F 7. Because advertising adds to firms' costs, it always increases the price paid by the consumer.

T F 8. If airlines suddenly began advertising their safety records, it would be evidence that the airlines have begun to cooperate, tacitly or explicitly.

Short Answer: Write a brief answer below for each of the following questions.

1. List one characteristic of monopolistic competition which is completely *different* from perfect competition, and one characteristic which monopolistic competition completely *shares* with perfect competition.

   a. (Different characteristic) _____

b. (Shared characteristic) _____

2. Identify the type of market structure in which each of the following firms sells its output:

   a. One of three clothing stores in a small town.
   _____

   b. A drug company that holds a patent on the only medicine to treat a serious disease.
   _____

   c. A used car dealer in a large city with several dozen used car dealers.
   _____

   d. A small banana farm in Colombia. _____

3. Two firms, A & B, must decide whether to charge a high price or a low price.

   If A & B both charge a high price, each earns profits that are "High"

   If A charges a high price and B charges a low price, A earns "Very High" profit while B earns "Very Low" profit.

   If B charges a high price and A charges a low price, both A and B earn "Medium" profit.

   If A & B both charge a low price, A earns "Medium" profit and B earns "High" profit.

   a. Arrange the information in a payoff matrix.

   b. Which firm (or firms) have a dominant strategy?

   c. Does this game have a Nash equilibrium? If so, what is it? If not, briefly, why not?

Chapter 10 Monopolistic Competition and Oligopoly

4. Without using the table in the text, fill in the following summary table for the four market structures:

Characteristic	Perfect Competition	Monopolistic Competition	Oligopoly	Monopoly
Number of Firms (one, few, many, or very many)				
Output of Different Firms (identical/standardized vs. differentiated)				
View of Pricing (price taker or price setter)				
Barriers to Entry or Exit?				
Strategic Interdependence? (Yes or no)				
How profit-maximizing output level is found				
Possible range of values for short-run profit				
Possible range of values for long-run profit				
Is Advertising Expected? (Yes, no or maybe)				

CHAPTER 11
THE LABOR MARKET

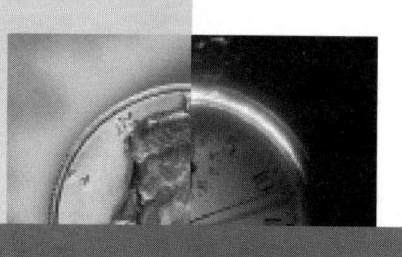

SUMMARIZE THE CHAPTER

Construct your own chapter summary by filling in the blanks. If you have difficulty, review the highlighted points in the chapter, then try again. (Note: the shorter blanks should be filled in with mathematical symbols such as "<" or "=", or with abbreviations such as "Q" or "ΔTC")

- How broadly or narrowly we define a _____ depends on the specific questions we wish to answer.

- A perfectly competitive labor market has the following three characteristics:

    There are large numbers of buyers (firms) and sellers (_____), and each individual firm or _____ is only a tiny part of the labor market.

    All workers in the labor market appear _____ _____ to firms.

    Workers can easily enter into or _____ _____ the labor market.

- The demand side of a labor market includes all firms hiring labor in that labor market. These firms may, but do not necessarily, compete in the same _____ market.

- The demand for a resource—such as labor—is a _____ demand; it arises from, and will vary with, the demand for the firm's _____ .

- The marginal approach to profit states that a firm should take any action that adds more to its _____ than it adds to its _____ .

- A firm's _____ revenue product (MRP) for any resource is the change in the firm's total _____ divided by the change in its employment of the resource: MRP = _____ / ΔQuantity of Resource. The MRP tells us the change in total _____ per unit increase in the resource.

149

- A firm's _____ factor cost (MFC) for any resource is the change in the firm's total _____ divided by the change in its employment of the resource: MFC = _____ / ΔQuantity of Resource. The MFC tells us the rise in _____ per unit increase in the resource.

- To maximize profit, the firm should increase its employment of any resource whenever MRP _____ MFC, but not when MRP _____ MFC. Thus, the profit-maximizing quantity of any resource is the quantity at which MRP _____ MFC.

- When output is sold in a competitive product market, the MRP for any change in employment will equal the price of output (P) times the marginal _____ of labor: MRP = P x _____.

- When labor is hired in a competitive labor market, the MFC for any change in employment will equal the market _____ : MFC = _____.

- For a competitive firm, the rule for maximum profit is: hire another worker when MRP _____ W, but not when MRP _____ W. Thus, to maximize profit, the firm should hire the number of workers such that MRP ___ W—that is, where the MRP curve _____ the wage line.

- When labor is the only variable input, the _____ -sloping portion of the MRP curve is the firm's labor demand curve, telling us how much labor the firm will want to employ at each wage rate.

- Whether labor is the only variable input or other inputs can be varied as well, the profit-maximizing level of employment will still satisfy MRP _____ W, and the labor demand curve will still slope _____ .

- The _____ labor demand curve tells us the total number of workers all firms in a labor market want to employ at each wage rate. It is found by horizontally summing across all firms' individual labor demand curves.

- A change in any variable that affects the quantity of labor demanded—except for the wage rate—causes the labor demand curve to _____ .

- The effect of a change in product demand on labor demand depends on whether many firms in the same product market also share the same _____ market. When they do, a rise in product demand will shift the market labor demand curve _____ ; a fall in product demand will shift the market labor demand curve _____ .

Chapter 11 The Labor Market

- A complementary input is one that _____ the marginal product of a certain type of labor. Usually, the input is used *by* this type of labor, making it _____ productive.

- A substitutable input is one that _____ the marginal product of a certain type of labor. Usually, the input can be used instead of this type of labor, _____ its marginal product.

- When many firms in a labor market acquire a new technology, the market labor demand curve will shift _____ if the technology is complementary with labor and _____ if the technology is substitutable for labor.

- When the price of some other input (besides labor) *decreases*, the market labor demand curve may shift rightward or leftward. It will shift rightward if that other input is _____ with labor and leftward if the other input is _____ for labor.

- In a competitive labor market, each seller is a "wage _____ "; he or she takes the market wage rate as given.

- The _____ the wage rate in a labor market, the greater the quantity of labor supplied in that market.

- A market labor supply curve will _____ when something other than a change in the wage rate causes a change in the number of people who want to work in a particular market.

- As long as some individuals can choose to supply their labor in two different markets, a rise in the wage rate in one market will cause a _____ shift in the labor supply curve in the other market.

- An increase in the cost of acquiring human capital needed to enter a labor market—say, due to an increase in school fees, fewer scholarships, or longer schooling requirements—will shift the labor supply curve _____ ; a decrease in the cost of acquiring human capital will shift the labor supply curve _____ .

- The long-run labor supply curve tells us how many (qualified) people will want to work in a labor market at each wage rate, after all adjustments have taken place. Specifically, all those who want to acquire new _____ or who want to move to another location have done so. The _____ -run labor supply response is more wage elastic than the _____ -run labor supply response.

- The forces of supply and demand drive a competitive labor market to its equilibrium point—the point where the labor supply and labor demand curves _____ .

- In the short run, a rightward shift in the labor demand curve moves us upward along a short-run labor supply curve, _____ the wage rate. Over the long run, this _____ in the wage rate entices qualified people to enter the labor market, and then the short-run labor supply curve shifts _____ .

- Wage rates, like the prices of goods and services, act as market signals—leading workers to move to areas where their work is most valued. When the labor demand curve _____ , the wage rate will overshoot its long-run equilibrium value. But as the signal begins to work, the temporary overshooting of the wage rate subsides.

- Surpluses and shortages in a labor market are not the natural consequence of shifts in supply and demand curves. A labor _____ will occur only when the wage rate fails to rise to its equilibrium value. Similarly, a labor _____ will occur only when the wage rate fails to fall to its equilibrium value.

The following statements refer to the appendix to Chapter 11.

- A pure _____ labor market is one in which a single firm is the only employer.

- For a monopsonist, MFC at any level of employment is _____ than the wage rate.

- Since MFC for a monopsonist is _____ than the wage rate, the MFC curve lies _____ the labor supply curve.

- When all else is the same, firms in monopsony labor markets (1) employ _____ workers, (2) produce _____ output, and (3) pay _____ wages than firms in perfectly competitive labor markets.

LEARN THE LINGO

Fill in each blank with the appropriate word or phrase from the list provided in the word bank. (For a challenge, fill in as many blanks as you can *without* using the word bank.)

_____ 1. Markets in which firms sell goods and services to households or other firms.

_____ 2. Markets in which resources—labor, capital, land and natural resources and entrepreneurship—are sold to firms.

_____ 3. A market with many indistinguishable sellers of labor and many buyers, and with easy entry and exit of workers.

Chapter 11 The Labor Market

_____ 4. The demand for a resource that arises from, and varies with, the demand for the product it helps to produce.

_____ 5. The change in the firm's total revenue divided by the change in its employment of a resource.

_____ 6. The change in a firm's total cost divided by the change in its employment of a resource.

_____ 7. A firm that takes the market wage rate as a given when making employment decisions.

_____ 8. A curve indicating the total number of workers all firms in a labor market want to employ at each wage rate.

_____ 9. An input whose utilization increases the marginal product of another input.

_____ 10. An input whose utilization decreases the marginal product of another input.

_____ 11. The lowest wage rate at which an individual would supply labor to a particular labor market.

_____ 12. A curve indicating the number of people who want jobs in a labor market at each wage rate.

_____ 13. A curve indicating how many people will want to work in a labor market after full adjustment to a change in the wage rate.

_____ 14. The quantity of labor demanded exceeds the quantity supplied for some period of time.

_____ 15. The quantity of labor supplied exceeds the quantity demanded for some period of time.

_____ 16. (Appendix term) A labor market in which a single firm is the only employer.

Word Bank

complementary input
derived demand
factor markets
labor shortage
labor supply curve
labor surplus
long-run labor supply curve
marginal revenue product (MRP)

marginal factor cost (MFC)
market labor demand curve
perfectly competitive labor market
product markets
pure monopsony
reservation wage
substitute input
wage taker

BUILD YOUR SKILLS

For each of the following items, write the correct answer in the blank or circle the correct answer.

1. The owners of Collegeview Sandwich Shop are trying to decide how many student workers to employ in the short run. They have not been able to put together all the information they need, so the table below is incomplete.

Quantity of Labor	Total Product	Marginal Product of Labor (MPL)	Price per Sandwich	Total Revenue	Marginal Revenue Product (MRP)	Wage (W)
0	0		$4	$0		$50
		30			_____	
1	_____		4	_____		50
		_____			_____	
2	_____		4	_____		50
		30			_____	
3	100		4	_____		50
		20			_____	
4	_____		4	_____		50
		_____			$40	
5	_____		4	_____		50
		_____			_____	
6	120		4	_____		50

a. Complete the table for Collegeview's owners.

b. If these owners follow the marginal approach to profits when deciding whether to hire an additional worker, they will compare the (MPL/MRP) of the additional worker to the (price of a sandwich/wage/quantity of labor employed). If the former exceeds the latter, the firm will increase its profit by (hiring the additional worker/refusing to hire the additional worker/dismissing the last worker hired). If we apply this test to the data in the preceding table, will the owners of Collegeview hire the first worker? (Yes/No) Will they hire the second worker? (Yes/No) Will they hire the third worker? (Yes/No) How many workers will Collegeview employ? _____

2. It seems that the owners of the Collegeview Sandwich Shop have trouble interpreting data from tables—they prefer to use graphs instead.

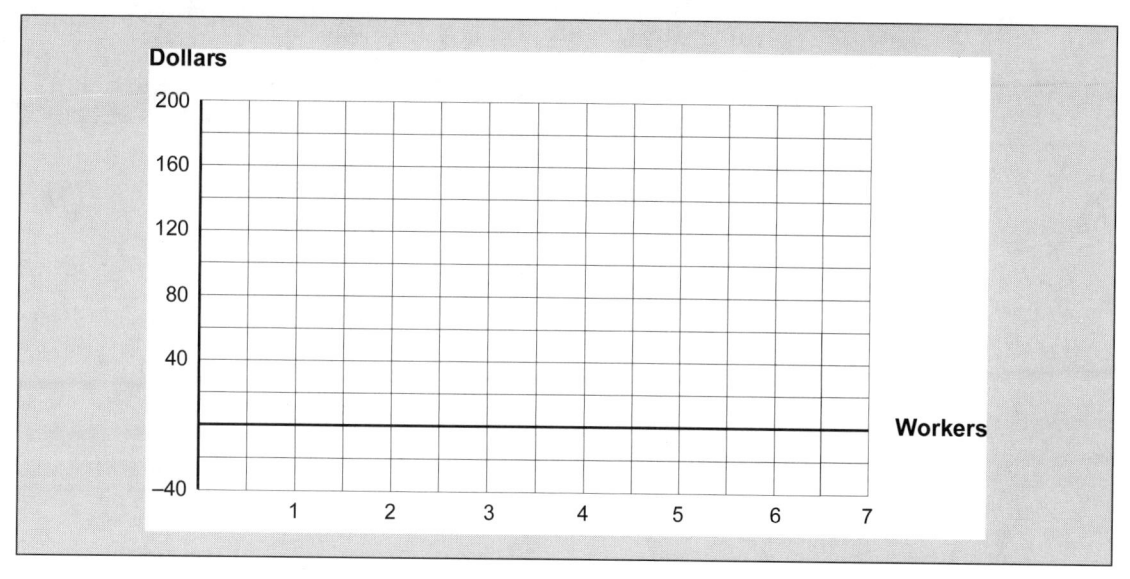

a. In the space provided, plot Collegeview's marginal revenue product (MRP) curve. (Remember to observe the convention of plotting values at the midpoint of the range over which they are computed.)

b. Using the graph, how many workers should Collegeview hire if
the wage is $100? _____
the wage is $60? _____

3. Only three firms produce oil lamps in the local market: Northern Lights, Major Electric, and Bright Lights. If you want to be an oil-lamp worker, you'll have to work for one of these firms, whose respective labor demand schedules are given below.

   a. Plot each firm's labor demand curve in the space provided to the right of its demand schedule.

Northern Lights

Wage (W)	Number of Workers Demanded
$13	2
11	4
9	6
7	8
5	10
3	12
1	14

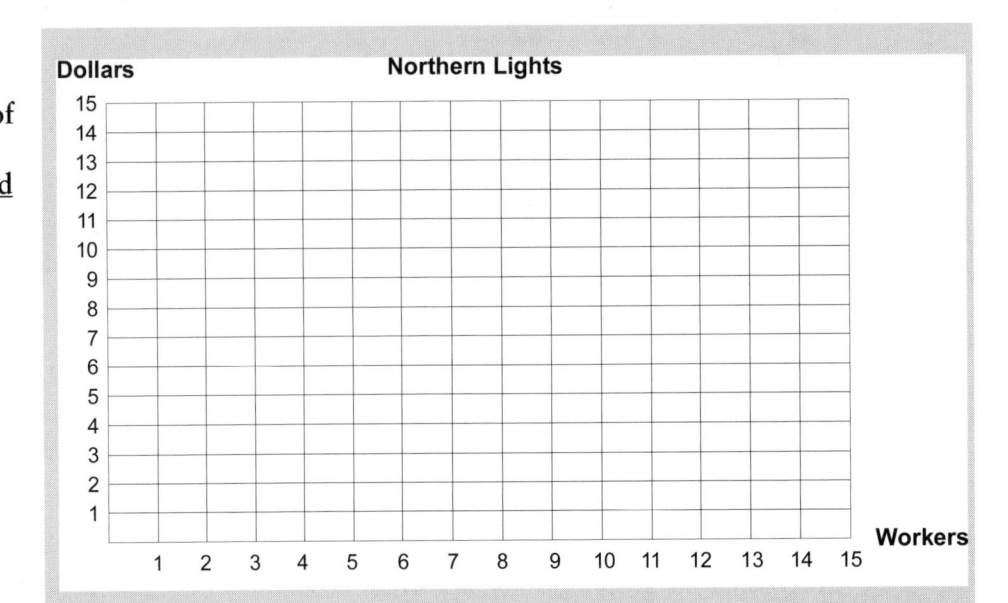

Major Electric

Wage (W)	Number of Workers Demanded
$13	1
11	2
9	3
7	4
5	5
3	6
1	7

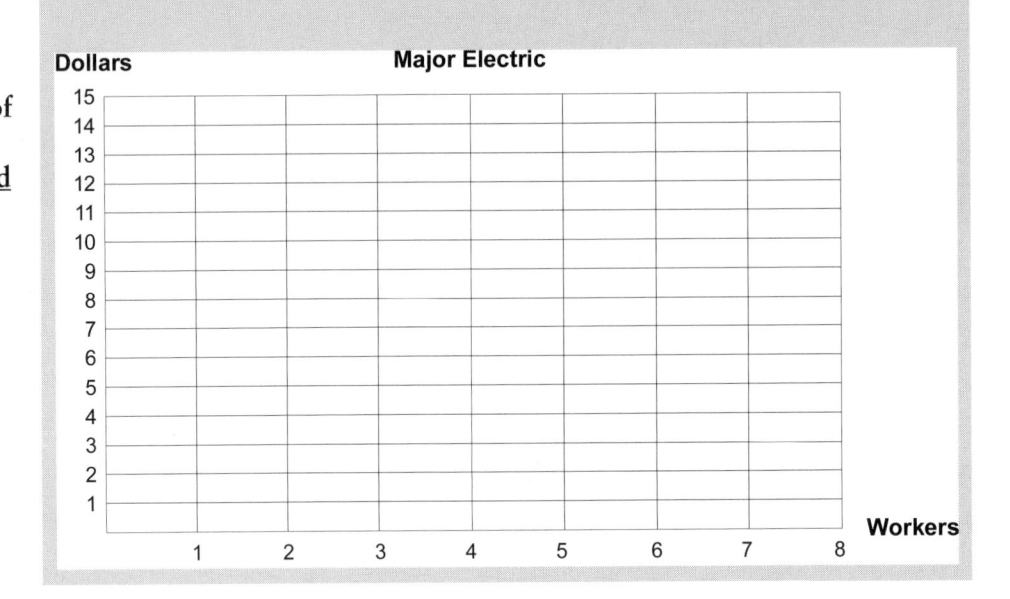

Chapter 11 The Labor Market

Bright Lights

Wage (W)	Number of Workers Demanded
$13	4
11	8
9	12
7	16
5	20
3	24
1	28

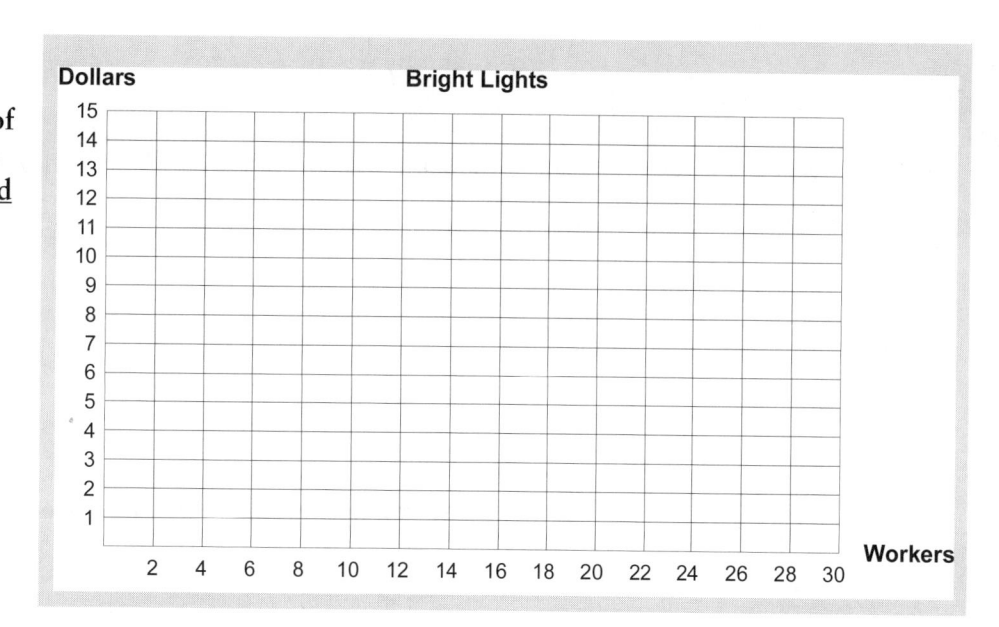

b. The United Lamp Workers' Union would like to determine the *market* demand for lamp workers. Using the information above, graph that market labor demand curve on the grid below.

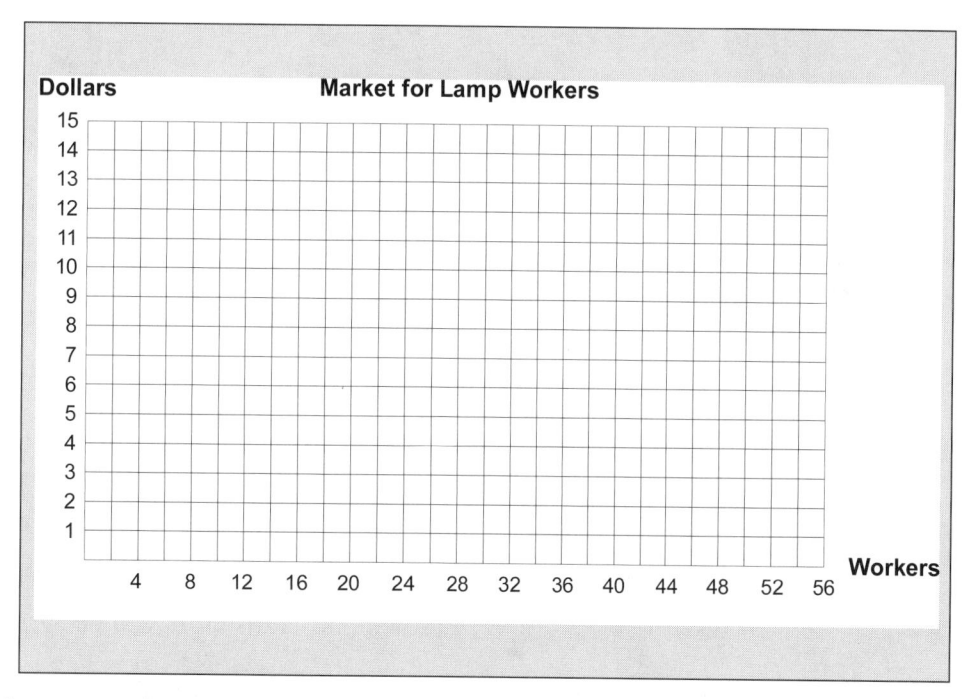

c. When the wage is $11, how many workers will be demanded in this labor market? _____ How many of these will be demanded by Northern Lights? _____ How many by Major Electric? _____ How many by Bright Lights? _____

d. When the wage is $3, how many workers will be demanded in this labor market? _____ How many of these will be demanded by Northern Lights?

_____ How many by Major Electric? _____ How many by Bright Lights? _____

4. When financial research firms sell information abroad, they ordinarily translate the information into the buyer's language. To perform that work, these firms routinely hire translators. The following is the market labor supply curve for workers who can translate English to Japanese.

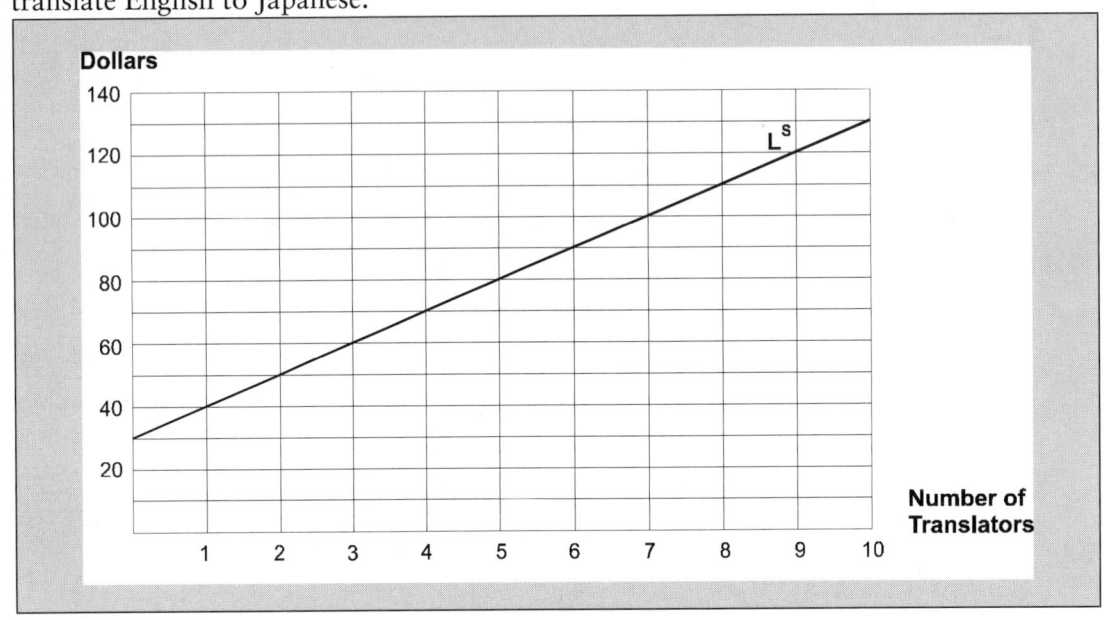

a. How many translators are willing to work at a wage of $50 per hour? _____ How many at a wage of $70? _____ An increase in the wage to as much as $100 per hour will (cause the labor supply curve to shift leftward/cause the labor supply curve to shift rightward/cause a movement along the labor supply curve).

b. Suppose the market demand curve for English/Japanese translators is given by:

$$L^D = 7 - W/40,$$

where W is the hourly wage and L^D is the number of translators demanded.

Plot the labor demand curve on the grid above. What is the equilibrium wage for translators? _____ How many translators will be employed? _____

5. Every spring, economic and management consulting firms across the United States hire thousands of new college graduates as economic analysts (EAs) and research assistants (RAs). Assume the labor market for EAs and RAs is perfectly competitive.

a. If market labor demand is given by the equation

$$L^D = 7,500 - 100W,$$

and market labor supply is given by the equation

$$L^S = 1000 + 160W,$$

what is the equilibrium market wage for EAs and RAs? _____ How many EAs and RAs will be hired this year? _____

b. Hoopers/Skybrand, a well-known consulting firm, has an office in Atlanta that hires new RAs and EAs every spring. The office has determined that the MRP for new EAs/RAs is given by the equation

$$MRP = 40 - L,$$

where L denotes the number of RAs and EAs it hires. If Hoopers/Skybrand must pay the market wage you determined in part (a), how many new EAs/RAs will the office hire this year? _____

6. Just about every farm in Titanic Valley grows iceberg lettuce—conditions there just seem perfect for it. Of course, many other farms outside the valley also grow lettuce, so Titanic's growers compete on the perfectly competitive national lettuce market.

At the current market price for iceberg lettuce, market labor demand for farm workers in the Valley is

$$L^D = 500 - 10W$$

where L^D is the number of workers hired per day and W is the daily wage.

In the short run, market labor supply in the Valley is

$$L^S = 20W - 100,$$

where L^S is the number of workers who offer their labor and W is the daily wage.

a. Plot market labor demand and short run market labor supply on the grid provided.

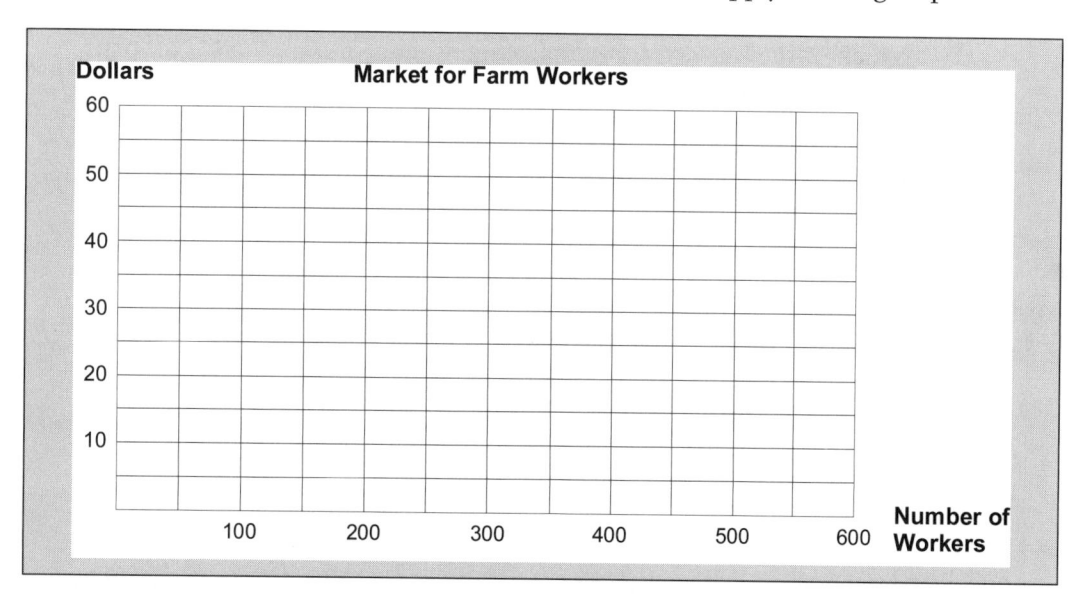

b. What is the equilibrium market wage for farm workers in the Valley? _____ What is the equilibrium level of employment in the short run? _____

c. Suppose the Lettuce Board's new promotional slogan, *Lettuce Alone!*, takes the country by storm, permanently increasing the demand for lettuce. In the short run, we would expect the market price of lettuce to (increase/decrease) as a result. Because the demand for farm workers in Titanic Valley is a derived demand, this (increase/decrease) in the price of lettuce will cause the market labor (demand curve/supply curve) for farm workers to shift (leftward/rightward).

d. Let us suppose that the shift in part (c) is in the amount of exactly 150 workers per day at every wage rate. Carefully draw in the new labor market (demand curve/supply curve) on the grid. What is the new short run equilibrium wage earned by farm workers in Titanic Valley? _____ What is the new short run equilibrium level of employment? _____

e. In the long run, we would expect the new (higher/lower) wages for farm workers in Titanic Valley to cause some workers to (move to/move away from) Titanic Valley and (seek employment/quit their employment). In the long run, after all adjustments have taken place, we would therefore expect the wage farm workers earn to be (higher/lower) than the wage we found in part (d), and we would expect the level of employment to be (higher/lower) than we found in part (d).

TEST YOURSELF

To see what you *really* know and remember, take this test at least a day *after* you've read the chapter in the text and completed the exercises in this study guide.

Multiple Choice: Circle the letter in front of the single best answer.

1. Which of the following is *not* a requirement for a perfectly competitive labor market?
   a. All workers in the market have the same reservation wage.
   b. There are many buyers and sellers of labor.
   c. All workers in the market appear the same to firms.
   d. There are no barriers to entering the labor market.
   e. There are no barriers to leaving the labor market.

2. When labor is the only variable input for a firm in a competitive labor market, the firm should continue to hire additional workers as long as
   a. total revenue is greater than total cost.
   b. the marginal product of labor is greater than the price of output.
   c. the marginal revenue product of labor is greater than the marginal revenue cost.
   d. the market wage rate is greater than the reservation wage.
   e. the marginal revenue product of labor is greater than the wage rate.

3. When labor is the only variable input, the firm's labor demand curve is
   a. the entire MRP curve.
   b. the downward sloping portion of the MRP curve.
   c. the upward sloping portion of the MRP curve.
   d. a horizontal line at the market wage rate.
   e. a vertical line at the market wage rate.

4. An increase in demand for a product made by many firms that hire their labor in the same labor market will cause
   a. the market labor supply curve to shift rightward.
   b. the market labor supply curve to shift leftward.
   c. the market labor demand curve to shift rightward.
   d. the market labor demand curve to shift leftward.
   e. no shift in either the market labor demand curve or the market labor supply curve.

5. When many firms in a labor market begin using a new input which is substitutable for labor,
   a. the market labor supply curve will shift rightward.
   b. the market labor supply curve will shift leftward.
   c. the market labor demand curve will shift rightward.
   d. the market labor demand curve will shift leftward.
   e. neither the market labor demand curve nor the market labor supply curve will shift rightward.

6. In a competitive labor market,
   a. firms are wage takers, but workers are not.
   b. firms are sometimes wage takers, but workers are not.
   c. workers are wage takers, but firms are not.
   d. both firms and workers are wage takers.
   e. neither firms nor workers are wage takers.

7. Which of the following will shift the market labor supply curve leftward?
   a. A rise in the wage rate in some other labor market
   b. A rise in the cost of acquiring human capital needed in that labor market
   c. A decrease in the number of qualified people in that labor market
   d. All of the above
   e. None of the above

8. Which of the following would cause a firm's MRP curve to shift rightward?
   a. A decrease in the price of the firm's output
   b. A rise in the wage rate
   c. A fall in the wage rate
   d. An increase in the number of qualified people.
   e. None of the above

9. In the long run, after a rightward shift in a market labor demand curve, we expect
   a. the market wage to be higher.
   b. the short-run labor supply curve to have shifted rightward.
   c. an increase in employment in the labor market.
   d. all of the above.
   e. none of the above.

10. If the market labor demand curve shifts *rightward*, then a
    a. labor shortage will generally occur.
    b. labor surplus will generally occur.
    c. labor shortage will occur only if the wage rate fails to rise to its new equilibrium value.
    d. labor shortage will occur only if the wage rate fails to drop to its new equilibrium value.
    e. labor surplus will occur only if the wage rate fails to drop to its new equilibrium value.

The following two questions refer to the appendix to chapter 11:

11. Which of the following is true of a monopsony labor market, but *not* true of a perfectly competitive labor market?
    a. The marginal factor cost of labor (MFC) is the same as the wage rate.
    b. A firm will increasing hiring until MRP = MFC.
    c. The MFC curve is higher than the labor supply curve.
    d. The firm must lower the price of its product in order to sell more output.
    e. The firm can sell all the output it wants at the market price.

12. Which of the following is true of *both* a monopsony labor market *and* a perfectly competitive labor market?
    a. The marginal factor cost of labor (MFC) is the same as the wage rate.
    b. A firm will increasing hiring until MRP = MFC.
    c. The MFC curve is higher than the labor supply curve.
    d. The firm must lower the price of its product in order to sell more output.
    e. The firm can sell all the output it wants at the market price.

Chapter 11 The Labor Market

True/False: For each of the following statements, circle T if the statement is true or F if the statement is false.

T F 1. The market labor demand curve is obtained by adding up the labor demand curves of all firms in the same output market.

T F 2. If an individual's reservation wage for a particular labor market is $15 per hour, then firms will hire that individual only if they can pay a wage rate less than $15 per hour.

T F 3. The long-run labor supply curve tells us the number of workers who want to work in a labor market at each wage rate after all those who want to move to a new location or acquire new job skills have done so.

T F 4. For any firm that operates in a competitive labor market, its MRP is given by the formula MRP = P × MPL.

T F 5. In a competitive labor market, the optimal level of employment will satisfy the MRP = W rule, even if the firm can vary other inputs besides labor.

T F 6. A government subsidy that lowers the cost of going to college will cause a rightward shift in the market demand curve for college-educated labor.

T F 7. The long-run labor supply response is more wage elastic than the short-run labor supply response.

T F 8. A change in tastes that decreases most peoples' reservation wages for working in a particular labor market will cause a rightward shift in the labor supply curve, and a decrease in the market wage.

The following two questions refer to the appendix to chapter 11:

T F 9. In a a graph of a monopsony firm's employment decision, the wage rate the firm will pay is equal to the vertical height of the point where the firm's MRP and MFC curves intersect.

T F 10. All else equal, a monopsony labor market results in a lower wage and greater employment than a perfectly competitive labor market.

Short Answer: Write a brief answer below for each of the following questions.

1. List the three requirements of a perfectly competitive labor market.

   a.

   b.

   c.

2. When a firm's output is sold in a competitive market, there is a special formula for the calculation of the marginal revenue product. What is this formula?

3. List three changes that would likely cause a market labor demand curve to shift *leftward*. (There are five such changes discussed in your textbook. For a challenge, try to list all of them.)

   a.

   b.

   c.

4. List four changes that would likely cause a market labor supply curve to shift *rightward*.

   a.

   b.

   c.

   d.

5. Suppose a new law were passed preventing people from moving from one location to another. Briefly, how would the *long-run* labor supply curve be affected for a local labor market?

CHAPTER 12
ECONOMIC INEQUALITY

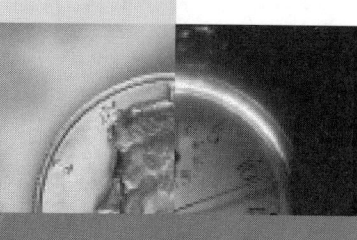

SUMMARIZE THE CHAPTER

Construct your own chapter summary by filling in the blanks. If you have difficulty, review the highlighted points in the chapter, then try again.

- A _____ wage differential is the difference in wage rates that makes two jobs equally attractive to workers.

- The nonmonetary characteristics of different jobs give rise to _____ wage differentials. Jobs considered intrinsically less attractive will tend to pay _____ wages, other things being equal.

- Differences in living costs can cause _____ wage differentials. Areas where living costs are higher than average will tend to have _____ -than-average wages.

- Differences in _____ capital requirements can give rise to _____ wage differentials. Jobs that require more costly training will tend to pay _____ wages, other things equal.

- In general, those with greater ability to do a job well—based on their talent, intelligence, motivation, or perseverance—will be more valuable to firms. As a result, firms will be willing to pay them a higher wage rate, beyond any _____ differential for their _____ capital investment.

- In a competitive labor market, a union—by _____ the wage firms must pay—_____ total employment in the union sector. This, in turn, causes wages in the nonunion sector to _____ . The result is a wage differential between union and nonunion wages.

- In a competitive labor market, a minimum wage—by _____ wage rates in covered industries, and _____ them in uncovered industries—creates a wage differential among the least-skilled workers, depending on the industry in which they work.

165

- In a competitive labor market, a minimum wage—by causing firms to substitute away from unskilled labor toward skilled labor and _____ produced by skilled labor—can _____ the wage differential between skilled and unskilled workers.

- When prejudice originates with _____, competitive labor markets work to discourage discrimination and reduce or eliminate any wage gap between the favored and the unfavored group.

- When prejudice originates with the firm's _____ or its cusomters, market forces may encourage, rather than discourage, discrimination and can lead to a permanent wage gap between the favored and unfavored groups.

- In measuring the impact of job market discrimination on earnings, the wage gap between two groups gives an _____ -estimate, since it fails to account for differences in skills and experience. However, comparing only workers with similar skills and experience leads to an _____ -estimate, since skill and experience are themselves influenced by discrimination—both in the job market and outside of it.

- The larger the Gini coefficient—up to a maximum of _____ —the _____ is the degree of income inequality.

- The U.S. income distribution exhibits significant mobility between the extremes and the middle. Lorenz curves, poverty rates, Gini ratios, and other measures of income inequality—because they provide only a snapshot of the income distribution at a moment in time—may _____ -estimate long-run income inequality.

- Inequality that results from equal _____ , but different choices, is generally regarded as fair.

The following statements refer to the appendix to Chapter 12.

- For a firm with monopsony power, a minimum wage law can not only _____ the wage rate a firm pays, but also _____ employment at the firm.

- In a monopsony labor market, a union that wins a higher wage rate for its members can not only increase their pay, but may be able to increase _____ at the firm as well.

LEARN THE LINGO

Fill in each blank with the appropriate word or phrase from the list provided in the word bank. (For a challenge, fill in as many blanks as you can *without* using the word bank.)

_____ 1. A difference in wage rates that makes two job equally attractive to a worker.

_____ 2. Any aspect of a job—other than the wage rate—that matters to a potential or current employee.

Chapter 12 Economic Inequality

_____ 3. When a group of people have different opportunities because of personal characteristics that have nothing to do with their abilities.

_____ 4. When individuals are excluded from an activity based on the statistical probability of behavior in their group, rather than their personal characteristics.

_____ 5. Income derived from supplying capital, land and natural resources, or entrepreneurship.

_____ 6. Any payment that is not compensation for supplying goods, services, or resources.

_____ 7. The percent of families whose incomes fall below a certain minimum.

_____ 8. The income level below which a family is considered in poverty.

_____ 9. When households are arrayed according to their incomes, a line showing the cumulative percent of income received by each cumulative percent of households.

_____ 10. A measure of income inequality; the ratio of the area above the Lorenz curve and under the complete equality line to the area under the diagonal.

_____ 11. A tax that collects a higher percentage of total income from higher income households.

_____ 12. A situation in which an agent maximizes his own well being at the expense of the principal who hired him.

Word Bank

compensating wage differential
discrimination
Gini coefficient
Lorenz curve
nonmonetary job characteristic
poverty line

poverty rate
principal-agent problem
progressive income tax
property income
statistical discrimination
transfer payment

BUILD YOUR SKILLS

For each of the following items, follow the instructions, write the correct answer in the blank, or circle the correct answer.

1. Residents on the island of Harmony are either Reds or Greens. There are only two industries on the island—Hunting and Gathering. It is well known that Greens and Reds are equally qualified to work in Hunting or Gathering. There are 15 Reds on the island, and no matter what the wage is all 15 will want to work. There are 40 Greens on the island, and no matter what the wage is all 40 will want to work. Letting L^D and L^S stand for the number of workers demanded and supplied at wage W, respectively, we know the following additional facts about labor supply and labor demand on the island:

   Market Labor Demand in the Hunting Industry: $L^D_H = 30 - W$

   Market Labor Demand in the Gathering Industry: $L^D_G = 50 - W$

   Labor Supply of all Reds combined: $L^S_R = 15$

   Labor Supply of all Greens combined: $L^S_G = 40$

   a. Suppose that because of employer prejudice, Hunter firms will hire only Reds, and Gatherer firms will hire only Greens. What is the equilibrium wage earned by Red workers? _____ What is the equilibrium wage earned by Green workers? _____

   b. Suppose that attitudes change overnight and employers stop discriminating: Firms in either industry are now equally willing to hire Greens and Reds to work for them. Once the labor market in Harmony reaches its new equilibrium, we know that the wage paid to any Red working in the Hunter industry will be (higher than/the same as/lower than) the wage paid to any Green working in the Hunter industry. Similarly, the wage paid to any Red working in the Gatherer industry will be (higher than/the same as/lower than) the wage paid to any Green working in the Gatherer industry. Moreover, we know that the wage paid in the Hunter industry must be (higher than/the same as/less than) the wage paid in the Gatherer industry. If this were not so, workers would move from the (higher wage industry/lower wage industry) to the (higher wage industry/lower wage industry). Then is the following statement true or false? "In the new equilibrium, every worker—Red or Green—must earn the same wage, no matter which industry employs that worker." (True/False)

   c. If, as in (b), employers no longer discriminate between Reds and Greens, what wage will a Green earn in the final labor market equilibrium?_____ What wage will a Red earn? _____ (Try to work this out on your own, but if you get stuck, there is a hint in the answers section.)

Chapter 12 Economic Inequality

d. Most people think we'd all be better off if no one were prejudiced against anyone else. To see if that is true in Harmony, compare your answers in (a) to your answers in (c). The typical Red worker is (better off/worse off) when there is employer prejudice. The typical Green worker is (better off/worse off) when there is employer prejudice. Does everyone gain from eliminating employer prejudice? (Yes/No)

2. Your text reports the following data on the distribution of income in the United States from the *Historical Income Tables, 1970-2001*:

Percent of Total Household Income Earned by Each Fifth of U.S. Households

	Lowest Fifth	Second Fifth	Third Fifth	Fourth Fifth	Highest Fifth
1970	4.1%	10.8%	17.4%	24.5%	43.3%
2001	3.5%	8.7%	14.6%	23.0%	50.1%

a. Using this data, plot the U.S. Lorenz curves in each of the two years 1970 and 2001. Be sure to label the axes properly, and draw in the line of complete equality.

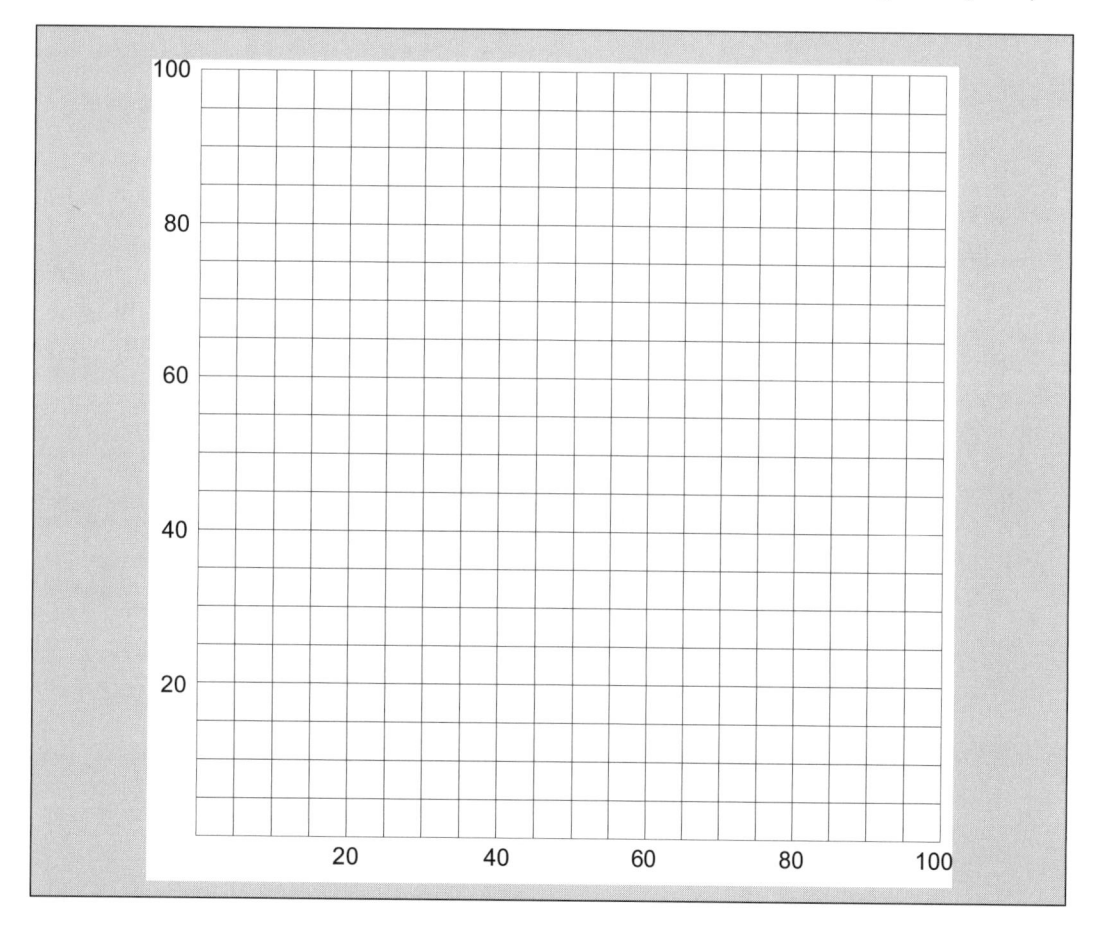

b. We can see that the Lorenz curve for 2001 is (more/less) bowed out in the middle than the Lorenz curve for 1970. From this we conclude that income inequality in the United States (increased/decreased) over the thirty-one years between 1970 and 2001.

3. In this problem, you will construct a Lorenz curve from scratch to get a better feel for how it is done. Suppose there are just ten families in society, Families A through J. Their annual family incomes are reported in the following table.

Family	Income
A	$40,000
B	27,000
C	40,000
D	18,000
E	6,000
F	13,000
G	4,000
H	8,000
I	27,000
J	27,000
Total Income	_____

a. Compute total annual income in this society and report it in the blank provided in the table at left.

b. Make the necessary computations and complete the entries in the table below.

Hints: (1) With ten families in all, each family is 10% of the total number of families. (2) "Percent of income" is the family's income as a percent of the total income in society.

Family	Percent of Population	Cumulative Percent of Population	Ordered Income (Lowest to Highest)	Percent of Income	Cumulative Percent of Income
___	10%	10%	___	2%	___
___	___	___	___	___	5%
___	___	___	___	___	___
___	___	___	$13,000	___	___
D	___	___	___	___	___
___	___	60%	___	13%	___
___	___	___	___	13%	49%
___	___	___	___	___	___
___	___	___	___	___	___
___	___	100%	___	___	100%

c. Suppose it costs $3,000 per year to feed a person in this society, and suppose there are exactly *three* people in every family. Using the definition in the text, what is the poverty line in this society? _____ How many families live below the poverty line? _____ What is the poverty rate? _____

d. Plot the Lorenz curve for this society in the grid provided.

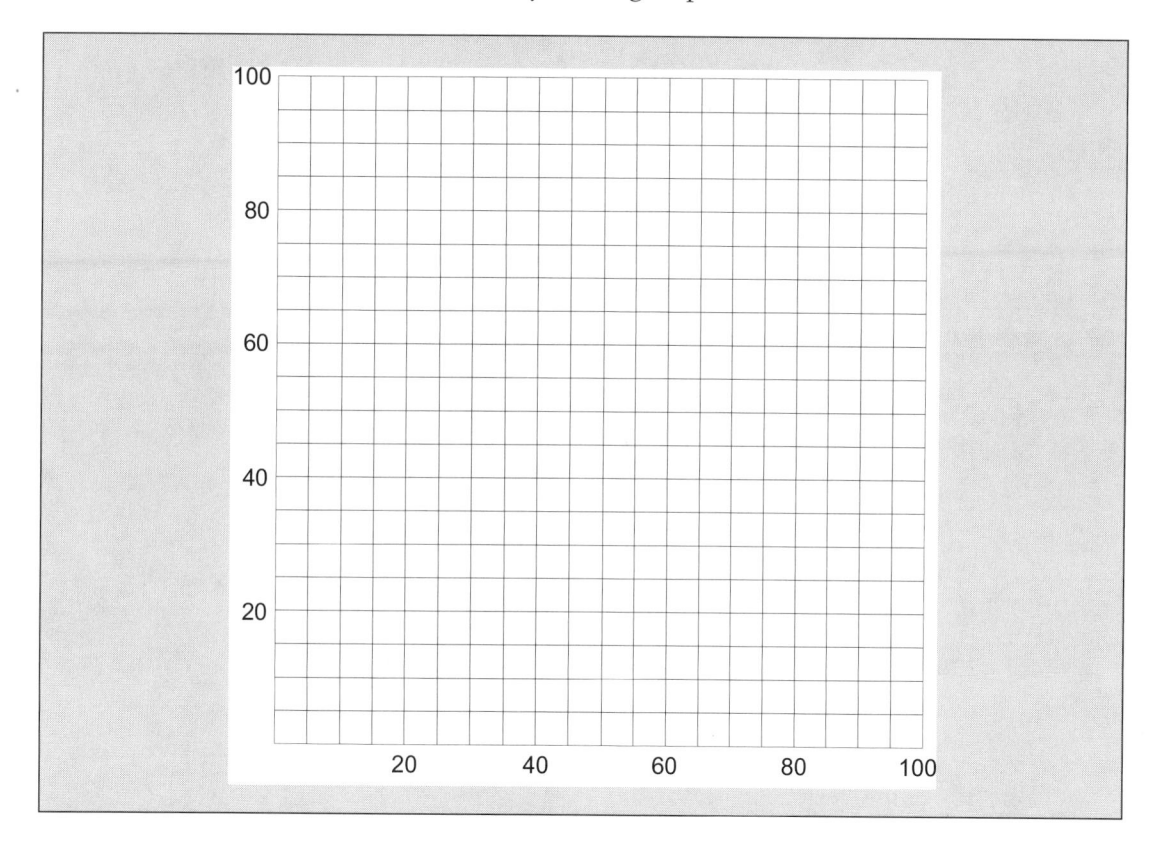

TEST YOURSELF

To see what you *really* know and remember, take this test at least a day *after* you've read the chapter in the text and completed the exercises in this study guide.

Multiple Choice: Circle the letter in front of the single best answer.

1. Under three assumptions, all workers would earn *identical* wages in the long run. Which of the following is one of these assumptions?
   a. All workers are properly compensated for human capital investments.
   b. Except for differences in wages, all jobs are equally attractive to all workers.
   c. All jobs pay an appropriate compensating differential.
   d. All of the above.
   e. None of the above.

2. Which of the following typically results in a compensating wage differential?
   a. Nonmonetary job characteristics
   b. Barriers to entry
   c. Statistical discrimination
   d. All of the above
   e. None of the above

3. Cost-of-living differences that lead to differences in wages in different cities are an example of
   a. labor shortages.
   b. compensating wage differentials.
   c. barriers to entry.
   d. statistical discrimination.
   e. none of the above.

4. Discrimination occurs when a difference in wages is due to
   a. compensating wage differentials.
   b. non-monetary job characteristics.
   c. differences in ability.
   d. all of the above.
   e. none of the above.

5. Market forces work to discourage discrimination and reduce any wage gap when the discrimination arises from prejudice by
   a. employers.
   b. employees.
   c. customers.
   d. all of the above.
   e. none of the above.

6. The poverty line for a U.S. family of a certain size is equal to
   a. what it would cost to feed that family.
   b. what it would cost to feed and clothe that family.
   c. about triple what it would cost to feed that family.
   d. the income needed to reach the bottom 10 percent of the U.S. income distribution.
   e. what the average income level for that family was twenty years earlier.

7. A Gini coefficient is a measure of income inequality derived from
   a. the poverty rate.
   b. income mobility studies.
   c. the Lorenz curve.
   d. all of the above.
   e. none of the above.

Chapter 12 Economic Inequality   173

8. When income changes over time are taken into account,
   a. income inequality increases substantially.
   b. income inequality is unchanged.
   c. income inequality is lessened.
   d. almost all of the income inequality in the United States disappears.
   e. we discover that the poverty line is a better measure of income inequality than the Lorenz curve.

9. Most people seem to agree that income inequality due to _____ is entirely fair.
   a. statistical discrimination
   b. inherited wealth
   c. difference in wages
   d. differences in property income
   e. compensating wage differentials

10. In a competitive labor market, a higher minimum wage can be expected to cause
    a. higher wages for skilled workers.
    b. higher employment for skilled workers.
    c. lower wages for unskilled workers not covered by the minimum wage.
    d. all of the above.
    e. none of the above.

The following two questions refer to the appendix to chapter 11:

11. Which of the following is true of a monopsony labor market, but *not* true of a perfectly competitive labor market?
    a. An increase in the minimum wage always decreases employment of workers covered by the minimum wage law.
    b. An increase in the minimum wage always increases employment of workers covered by the minimum wage law.
    c. A union always faces a tradeoff: the higher the wage rate it wins for its workers, the lower the level of employment.
    d. A union never faces a tradeoff between the wage rate its workers will earn and the number of its workers who will be employed.
    e. none of the above.

12. Which of the following is true of a *both* a monopsony labor market *and* a perfectly competitive labor market?
   a. Faced with an increase in the minimum wage, and all else equal, an employer covered by the law will sometimes decide to increase employment, and sometimes decide to decrease employment.
   b. Faced with a higher union wage, and all else equal, an employer of union workers will sometimes decide to increase employment, and sometimes decide to decrease employment.
   c. Faced with a union wage or a minimum wage, an affected employer will compare MRP and MFC, and only employ additional workers for which MRP > MFC.
   d. all of the above.
   e. none of the above.

True/False: For each of the following statements, circle T if the statement is true or F if the statement is false.

T F 1. The most obvious explanation for the higher salaries of college professors compared to high school teachers is "barriers to entry."

T F 2. If we compare the wages of two groups, such as men and women, and we limit ourselves to workers with similar skills and experience, the measured wage gap will underestimate the total effect of discrimination on wages.

T F 3. The Lorenz curve for U.S. *wealth* shows greater inequality than the Lorenz curve for U.S. *income*.

T F 4. According to a simple supply and demand model, unions not only raise the wages of union members, they also cause the wages of non-union members to decrease.

T F 5. Statistical discrimination occurs when an employer refuses to hire members of a certain group because of prejudice against that group.

T F 6. The larger the Gini coefficient, the greater the degree of income inequality.

T F 7. From year to year, most countries experience large changes in their Gini coefficients.

T F 8. In perfectly competitive labor markets, unskilled workers who are *not* covered by minimum wage legislation benefit when the minimum wage is increased.

T F 9. In a monopsony labor market, an increase in the minimum wage can sometimes cause an increase in employment, and sometimes cause a decrease in employment.

Short Answer: Write a brief answer below for each of the following questions.

1. When labor markets are perfectly competitive, the minimum wage affects three different groups of workers. List the three groups, and, for each group, identify the

impact of an increase in the minimum wage on the wage rate and on employment (increase, decrease, or no effect).

Group of Workers	Effect on wage rate	Effect on employment

2. List three different groups whose prejudice could cause wage discrimination. In each case, do perfectly competitive markets work to increase or decrease any resulting discrimination?

Prejudiced Group	Effect of Perfectly Competitive Market Forces on Discrimination

CHAPTER 13

CAPITAL AND FINANCIAL MARKETS

SUMMARIZE THE CHAPTER

Construct your own chapter summary by filling in the blanks. If you have difficulty, review the highlighted points in the chapter, then try again. (Note: the shorter blanks should be filled in with mathematical symbols or expressions.)

- The marginal approach to profit states that a firm should take any action that adds more to its _____ per period than it adds to its _____ per period.

- When firms rent capital, or the capital they buy lasts forever, we can apply the marginal approach to profits just as we apply it for the firm's labor decision: The firm should buy another unit of capital whenever its marginal _____ product is _____ than its marginal factor cost.

- Because present dollars can earn _____ , and because borrowing dollars requires payment of _____ , it is always preferable to receive a given sum of money earlier rather than later. Therefore, a dollar received later has _____ value than a dollar received now.

- The present value (PV) of a _____ payment is the value of that payment in today's dollars. Alternatively, it is the most anyone would pay today for the right to receive that payment.

- The present value of $Y to be received n years in the future is: PV = Y / _____, where r is the interest rate.

- The present value of a future payment is smaller if (1) the size of the payment is smaller, (2) the interest rate is _____ , or (3) the payment is received _____ .

- The principle of asset valuation says that the value of any asset is the _____ of the present values of all the future benefits it generates.

- As the interest rate rises, the value of additional capital to each business firm in the economy—using the principle of asset valuation—will _____ , and the firm will decide to purchase _____ of it. Therefore, in the economy as whole, a rise in the interest rate causes a _____ in investment expenditures.

- Lower interest rates _____ firms' investment in physical capital, causing the capital stock to be _____ , and our overall standard of living to be _____ .

- Employers have limited incentives to provide _____ human capital, since it increases the worker's value to many firms, and the worker will capture the benefits in the form of a higher wage. Therefore, workers must acquire _____ human capital on their own—or with the help of government subsidies.

- Individuals have little incentive to pay for _____ human capital, since it increases their value to only one firm, and that firm will capture the benefits. Therefore, firms provide their workers with _____ human capital at the firms' expense.

- To the worker that possesses it, human capital is an asset that generates higher income in the future. Therefore, the benefit of any given human capital investment is equal to the total _____ value of the additional future income.

- Investment in human capital, like investment in physical capital, is _____ related to the interest rate. The _____ the interest rate, the greater the benefits of any human capital investment, and the more human capital workers will want to acquire.

- Since _____ interest rates encourage individuals to invest in general human capital, the total amount of human capital—and our overall standard of living—will be higher if interest rates are _____ .

- There is a (an) _____ relationship between bond prices and bond yields. The higher the price of any given bond, the _____ the yield on that bond.

- While bond issuers are not directly participants in _____ market trading, they are affected by what happens in that market. More specifically, if a bond's price rises in the _____ market, the price one can charge for similar, newly issued bonds in the primary market will rise as well.

- If a bond's yield falls in the _____ market, the yield of similar, newly issued bonds in the primary market will _____ .

- To put a value on riskier bonds, market participants use a _____ discount rate than on safe bonds. This leads to _____ total present values and

Chapter 13   Capital and Financial Markets

_____ prices for the riskier bonds. With _____ prices, riskier bonds have _____ yields.

- If a firm will earn a constant $Y in profit after taxes each year forever, then the total present value of these future profits is _____ / _____, where r is the discount rate.

- The value of a share of stock in a firm is equal to the total present value of the firm's after-tax _____, divided by the number of _____ outstanding.

- An increase in current profits increases the value of a share of stock. An increase in the anticipated growth rate of profits increases the value of a share of stock. A (an) _____ in interest rates—or even an anticipated _____ in interest rates—decreases the value of a share of stock. An increase in the perceived riskiness of future profits _____ the value of a share of stock.

- According to the efficient markets view of the stock market, any _____ that can be used to predict a stock's future earnings will be incorporated into a stock's price as soon it becomes publicly available. Therefore, by the time a fundamental analyst predicts that a stock's price will rise or fall, it has already risen or fallen. Fundamental analysis _____ help you outperform the market.

- According to the efficient markets view of the stock market, any patterns in stock price movements that can be observed by a good technical analyst will be incorporated into stock prices as soon as they are discernable. Therefore, stock market patterns disappear as soon as anyone can discover them. Technical analysis _____ help you outperform the market.

LEARN THE LINGO

Fill in each blank with the appropriate word or phrase from the list provided in the word bank. (For a challenge, fill in as many blanks as you can *without* using the word bank.)

_____ 1. The increase in revenue due to a one-unit increase in capital.

_____ 2. The value, in today's dollars, of a sum of money to be received or paid at a specific date in the future.

_____ 3. The act of converting a future value into its present-day equivalent.

_____ 4. The interest rate used in computing present values.

_____ 5. The idea that the value of an asset is equal to the total present value of all the future benefits it generates.

_____ 6. Firms' purchases of new capital over some period of time.

_____ 7. Knowledge, education, or training that is valuable at many different firms.

_____ 8. Knowledge, education or training that is valuable only at a specific firm.

_____ 9. A promise to pay future income in some form, such as future dividends or future interest payments.

_____ 10. A promise to pay a specific sum of money at some future date.

_____ 11. The amount of money a bond promises to pay when it matures.

_____ 12. The date at which a bond's principal will be paid to the bond's owner.

_____ 13. A bond that promises no payments except for what it pays at maturity.

_____ 14. A series of periodic payments that a bond promises before maturity.

_____ 15. The rate of return a bond earns for its owner.

_____ 16. The market in which newly issued financial assets are sold for the first time.

_____ 17. The market in which previously issued financial assets are sold.

_____ 18. A share of ownership in a corporation.

_____ 19. A corporation that specializes in owning shares of stock in other corporations.

_____ 20. Part of a firm's current profit that is distributed to shareholders.

_____ 21. The return someone gets by selling a financial asset at a price higher than they paid for it.

_____ 22. An index of the prices of stocks of 30 large U.S. firms.

_____ 23. An index of the prices of stocks of 500 large corporations.

Chapter 13   Capital and Financial Markets

_____ 24. A method of predicting a stock's price based on the fundamental forces driving the firm's future earnings.

_____ 25. A method of predicting a stock's price based on that stock's past behavior.

_____ 26. A market that instantaneously incorporates all available information relevant to a stock's price.

Word Bank

bond	maturity date
capital gain	mutual fund
coupon payment	present value
discount rate	primary markets
discounting	principal (face value)
dividend	principle of asset valuation
Dow Jones industrial average	pure discount bond
efficient markets	secondary market
financial asset	share of stock
fundamental analysis	specific human capital
general human capital	Standard & Poor's 500
investment	technical analysis
marginal revenue product of capital	yield

BUILD YOUR SKILLS

For each of the following items, write the correct answer in the blank or circle the correct answer.

1. Your text explains how to compute present value. For practice, and because it will be useful for reference in subsequent problems, complete the table below, which reports the present value of $1 to be received at different points in the future, given various prevailing rates of interest (Remember to check your answers in the back of the book before you go on to the next question.)

PV of $1 received *n* years in the future, given interest rate *r*

	Years (*n*)					
Interest Rate (*r*)	1	2	3	4	5	20
5%	____	____	____	0.82	0.78	0.38
10%	____	0.83	____	0.68	0.62	0.15
15%	____	____	0.66	0.57	0.50	0.06
20%	____	____	____	0.48	____	0.03

2. Most state lotteries advertise the Big Jackpot with great fanfare. Who wouldn't want a chance to win millions of dollars? But just how much is a million-dollar jackpot worth? The answer can depend very much on two things: (1) the rate of interest and, (2) just how the jackpot is to be paid out.

   a. Assume the interest rate at which you can borrow or lend is 5% per annum. What is the present value of a $2 million jackpot if it is paid in one single payment on the following dates:
   today _____
   one year from today _____
   two years from today _____
   five years from today _____
   twenty years from today _____

   b. Assume the interest rate at which you can borrow or lend is 15% per annum. What is the present value of a $2 million jackpot if it is paid in one single payment on the following dates:
   today _____
   one year from today _____
   two years from today _____
   five years from today _____
   twenty years from today _____

   c. Lotteries usually do not pay out the jackpot all at once. Instead, they normally spread the payments over a number of years. If the interest rate is 15% per annum, what is the present value of a $2 million jackpot if it is paid out in five equal annual payments starting today? _____

   Challenge: What is the present value of this $2 million jackpot if the interest rate is 15%, but the payout (as is typical) is in twenty equal annual payments starting today? _____ (Note: You *cannot* use the preceding table to solve this one. Use your calculator, a spreadsheet or look up a more extensive present value table in a finance text.)

3. Four web-savvy friends—Azfar, Rashida, Mike and Zoey—have a great deal of free time now that they are in college. As a result, they've decided to open a student travel agency on the Internet and run it out of the dorm part-time. They've got the Internet access for free (until the computer center catches on), but they'll need some computers. They all agree they will set up their first computer as a server—the core of their whole business—where they'll mount their web site, booking and billing software, etc.. If they get a second one, they could use it to search the web for special travel deals and to book the tours and airline reservations for their call-in clients. They know that customer support can be critical, so if they got a third machine they would

devote it to customer support, using it to process client e-mail, log phone messages and generally build the client database. They don't want to forget about advertising, so if they get a fourth machine, they would devote that one to spamming the campus with their ads on a regular basis.

With technology changing so quickly, they know that any machine they buy today will have to be junked and replaced in three (3) years time. The friends have estimated the additional revenue each successive machine would contribute to their business each year, and recorded it in the table below.

Computer	Additional Annual Revenue	Total Present Value with a discount rate of: 5%	10%
1	$8,000	_____	_____
2	$5,000	_____	_____
3	$2,000	_____	_____
4	$1,000	_____	_____

a. Using the present value table you computed in question (1), and assuming a discount rate of 5%, we can see that the additional annual revenue (MRP) generated by the *first* machine in the *first* year of its useful life has a present value of _____ dollars. The MRP of the first machine in the *second* year of its useful life has a (greater/smaller) present value of _____ dollars. The MRP of the first machine in the *third* (and final) year of its useful life has an even (greater/smaller) present value of _____ dollars. With a three-year useful life, and using a discount rate of 5%, the total present value of the additional revenue generated by the first computer these friends buy is _____ dollars.

b. The friends are not so sure 5% is the best discount rate for them to use. If, instead, they decide to use a discount rate of **10%**, we can see that the additional annual revenue (MRP) generated by the *first* machine in the *first* year of its useful life has a present value of _____ dollars. The MRP of the first machine in the *second* year of its useful life has a (greater/smaller) present value of _____ dollars. The MRP of the first machine in the *third* (and final) year of its useful life has an even (greater/smaller) present value of _____ dollars. With a three-year useful life, and using a discount rate of 10%, the total present value of the additional revenue generated by the first computer purchased is _____ dollars.

c. Record the total present values you calculated in parts (a) and (b) in the table above. Then complete the table.

d. The computers they want cost $5,000 each, fully loaded. If these friends decide to use a discount rate of 5%, they should (definitely/definitely not) buy the first machine, because the present value of the additional revenue it will generate over its useful life (exceeds/falls short of) its cost. They should (definitely/definitely not) buy the second machine, because the present value of the additional revenue it will generate over its useful life (exceeds/falls short of) its cost. They should (definitely/definitely not) buy the third machine, because the present value of the additional revenue it will generate over its useful life (exceeds/falls short of) its cost. They should (definitely/definitely not) buy the fourth machine, because the present value of the additional revenue it will generate over its useful life (exceeds/falls short of) its cost. Thus, with a discount rate of 5%, and at a cost of $5,000 per machine, a total of _____ should be purchased.

e. If they decide to use a discount rate of 10%, instead, then at a price of $5,000 per computer, these friends should (buy/ not buy) the first machine; they should (buy/ not buy) the second machine; they should (buy/ not buy) the third machine; and they should (buy/ not buy) the fourth machine. Thus, with a discount rate of 10%, a total of _____ computers should be purchased.

f. Comparing the results in parts (d) and (e), we can see that, other things equal, the higher the discount rate applied, the (fewer/more) machines that should be purchased.

4. Thanks to hard work and smart investment spending, the student travel business in the previous problem is booming. So much so that our friends are planning to sell some bonds to raise money so they can expand. They've decided they need to raise about $20,000. So that other students can afford them, they want to issue bonds with a face value of only $1,000, and no coupon payments. They plan to pay off their bonds in a single payment just before they graduate, so they've set the maturity date for each bond to be exactly four (4) years from now. Use the present value table in question (1) to answer the following questions.

a. If the interest rate is 5%, each $1,000 bond has a present value of _____ dollars. The highest price anyone would pay for this bond is therefore _____ dollars. Thus, in order to raise about $20,000, they would have to sell approximately _____ bonds at this price.

b. If the interest rate is 10%, each $1,000 bond has a present value of _____ dollars. The highest price anyone would pay for this bond is therefore _____ dollars. Thus, in order to raise about $20,000, they would have to sell approximately _____ bonds at this price.

5. Well, its been an amazing four years—the student travel business just took off and kept going. Azfar, Rashida, Mike and Zoey not only learned a lot in their classes, they're set to become millionaires, too—that is, if all goes well in the initial public offering (IPO) of stock in their Internet start-up. In their final meeting with the investment bankers they just want to go over the figures one more time.

   a. The Wall Street "suits" estimate that the firm will earn after-tax profits of $2 million each year, forever, no sweat. If the discount rate is 5%, the present value of those future profits is _____ dollars. Since the bankers have recommended that 500,000 shares in all be issued, each share will have a value of _____ dollars.

   b. Azfar's not so sure, though. He thinks the profit forecasts are too high. If he's right, and the market agrees with him, the value of the stock will be (higher than /the same as/lower than) what the bankers have estimated in part (a).

   c. Rashida's not worried about the forecasts—she thinks they are right on target. She's worried about interest rates. She thinks that interest rates are going to rise and—more importantly—she thinks everyone in the market thinks so, too. If Rashida is right, the value of the stock will be (higher than /the same as/lower than) what the bankers have estimated in part (a).

   d. Zoey thinks the other two are crazy. She sees nothing but good times ahead—in fact, she expects profits to actually grow year after year, easily beating the bankers' $2 million dollar per year estimate. If she is right, and if the market thinks the same way she does, the value of the stock will be (higher than /the same as/lower than) what the bankers have estimated in part (a).

TEST YOURSELF

To see what you *really* know and remember, take this test at least a day *after* you've read the chapter in the text and completed the exercises in this study guide.

Multiple Choice: Circle the letter in front of the single best answer.

1. A firm's additional revenue per period from hiring one more unit of capital is called
   a. marginal revenue.
   b. marginal cost.
   c. the marginal product of capital.
   d. the marginal revenue product of capital.
   e. discounted capital.

2. Which of the following changes will *decrease* the present value of a given future payment?
   a. The payment will be received earlier.
   b. The interest rate rises.
   c. The payment will be received with greater certainty.
   d. All of the above
   e. None of the above

3. If the interest rate is 12%, then the present value of $100 to be received two years in the future is
   a. $144.
   b. $112.
   c. $89.29.
   d. $79.72.
   e. $69.44.

4. Consider the following three income streams A, B and C, each with three payments to be received at the end of 2006, 2007 and 2008, respectively:

Year	Stream A	Stream B	Stream C
2006	$1,100	$900	$1,000
2007	$1,000	$1,000	$1,000
2008	$900	$1,100	$1,000

   For any interest rate larger than zero, if we rank the total present value of these streams from *lowest* to *highest*, we find:
   a. A < B < C.
   b. B < A < C.
   c. C < B < A.
   d. C < A < B
   e. B < C < A.

5. In general, if you expect interest rates to decrease, you should also expect
   a. stock prices to decrease.
   b. bond prices to increase.
   c. investment in physical capital to decrease.
   d. investment in human capital to decrease.
   e. all of the above.

6. Which of the following is an example of general human capital?
   a. a pilot's knowledge of how to fly a jet plane.
   b. a waiter's knowledge of which of a restaurant's customers are temperamental and which are not.
   c. a college professor's knowledge of different classrooms at the college, and knowledge of where in the college bureaucracy to request a good classroom.
   d. all of the above.
   e. none of the above.

7. A pure discount bond is one that
   a. is sold for less than its market price.
   b. has no coupon payments.
   c. has no maturity date.
   d. has no principal (face value).
   e. has a yield less than the yield on other, similar bonds.

8. The primary bond market is where
   a. the bonds of large corporations are bought and sold.
   b. the bonds of large corporations or the government are bought and sold.
   c. the bonds of small corporations only are bought and sold.
   d. newly issued bonds are sold for the first time.
   e. most of the day to day trading in previously issued bonds takes place.

9. According to the principal of asset valuation, the value of a share of stock in a corporation is equal to
   a. the value of one of its bonds.
   b. the total present value of its after-tax profits.
   c. the total present value of its after tax profits divided by the number of shares outstanding.
   d. the total present value of its retained earnings divided by the number of shares outstanding.
   e. the total present value of its retained earnings divided by the total present value of its dividends.

10. "You should buy XYZ stock right away. It's gone up at least 3 percent every week for the last 10 weeks, and it's *hot!*" This statement would most likely be made by a believer in
    a. fundamental analysis.
    b. technical analysis.
    c. efficient markets theory.
    d. the principle of asset valuation.
    e. the marginal revenue product of capital

True/False: For each of the following statements, circle T if the statement is true or F if the statement is false.

T F 1. The higher the interest rate, the greater the present value of any given future payment.

T F 2. The principal of asset valuation says that the value of any asset is the simple sum of all the future benefits (e.g. future payments) that it generates.

T F 3. In general, higher interest rates lead to lower levels of investment in both physical and human capital.

T F 4. Specific human capital is typically paid for by the firm, while general human capital is typically paid for by workers themselves.

T F 5. A rise in the interest rate will decrease bond prices in the primary market, but not in the secondary market.

T F 6. All else equal, a riskier bond will earn a higher interest rate (yield) than a bond with less risk.

T F 7. If a public offering of shares shifts the supply curve for a stock significantly rightward, we can expect the price of the stock to rise.

T F 8. Economists who believe in efficient markets theory believe that only those with a high level of training in economics can predict stock prices well enough to outperform the general market.

Short Answer: Write a numerical answer below for each of the following questions. (You'll need a calculator.) In all cases, assume that the interest rate in the economy is 5%, and that you are making your decisions on Jan 1, 2006.

1. What is the most you would pay for a bond that promises to pay $1,000 on January 1, 2008?

2. What is the most you would pay for a bond with a face value (principal) of $1,000, that matures on January 1, 2009, and that provides a coupon payment of $200 on each of the following dates: January 1, 2007, January 1, 2008, and January 1, 2009?

3. What is the most you would pay for a share of stock in a firm that is expected to earn $100 million in after-tax profits each year forever, and that has an (unchanging) 10 million shares of stock outstanding?

4. What is the most you would pay for a unit of capital equipment that will increase your revenue by $20,000 in 2006, $30,000 and 2007, and would be sold for $50,000 at the end of 2007? (For simplicity, assume that all additional revenue for a year is earned all at once, at the very end of the year.)

CHAPTER 14

ECONOMIC EFFICIENCY AND THE ROLE OF GOVERNMENT

SUMMARIZE THE CHAPTER

Construct your own chapter summary by filling in the blanks. If you have difficulty, review the highlighted points in the chapter, then try again.

- Economic efficiency is achieved when we cannot rearrange the production or allocation of goods to make one person _____ off without making anybody else _____ off.

- An efficient economy is not necessarily a _____ economy.

- A Pareto _____ is any action that makes at least one person better off, and harms no one.

- Economic efficiency is achieved when every possible Pareto _____ is exploited.

- If an action creates total benefits for gainers that are _____ than total harm to losers, then a _____ payment exists which, if transferred from gainers to losers, would make the action a Pareto _____ .

- The height of the market _____ curve at any quantity shows us the value— to someone—of the last unit of the good consumed.

- The height of the market _____ curve at any quantity shows us the additional cost—to some producer—of each unit of the good supplied.

- Whenever—at some quantity—the demand curve is higher than the supply curve, the value of one more unit to some consumer is _____ than its additional cost to some producer.

- The efficient quantity of a good is the quantity at which the market demand curve and market supply curves _____ .

- In a well-functioning, _____ _____ market, the equilibrium quantity is also the efficient quantity.

- A buyer's consumer surplus on a unit of a good is the difference between its value to the buyer and what the buyer actually _____ for that unit.

- Market consumer surplus at any price, measured in dollars, is the total area _____ the market demand curve and _____ the market price.

- An individual seller's producer surplus on a unit of a good is the difference between what the seller actually gets and the additional _____ of providing it.

- Market producer surplus at any price, measured in dollars, is the total area _____ the market supply curve and _____ the market price.

- We measure the total net _____ gained in a market as the sum of consumer and producer surplus in that market.

- A market is _____ when the sum of producer and consumer surplus is maximized in that market.

- In a well-functioning, perfectly competitive market, the equilibrium quantity provides the _____ possible benefit to buyers and sellers combined, and is thus the efficient quantity.

- The welfare _____ in a market is the dollar value of potential benefits not achieved due to inefficiency in that market.

- A price _____ or a price _____ imposed on a perfectly competitive market—by reducing quantity below the efficient level—reduces the total net benefits in the market (causes a welfare _____).

- By making most involuntary exchanges illegal, _____ law helps to channel our energies into exchanges and productive activities that benefit all parties involved: Pareto improvements. In this way, _____ law contributes to economic efficiency.

- _____ law—by reducing disputes about property, and channeling resources into production rather than the capture of property belonging to others—contributes to economic efficiency by increasing total production, thus raising the total net benefits that markets can provide.

- Contracts enable us to make exchanges that take place over time and in which one person must act first. In this way, contracts help society enjoy the full benefits of _____ and exchange.

Chapter 14 Economic Efficiency and the Role of Government

- A legal and regulatory system that ensured the complete elimination of crime, unsafe products, and other unwelcome activities would be less _____ than a system that tolerated some amount of these activities. An efficient infrastructure must consider the _____ , as well as the benefits, of achieving our legal and regulatory goals.

- A market failure occurs when a market—even with the proper institutional support—is economically _____ .

- Monopoly and imperfectly competitive markets—in which firms charge a single price greater than marginal _____—are generally inefficient. Price is too _____ , and output is too _____ , to maximize the net benefits in the market.

- Average cost pricing is sometimes used to regulate a _____ monopoly. Regulators strive to set the price equal to cost per unit where the _____ curve crosses the demand curve. At this price, the monopoly makes _____ economic profit, which provides its owners with a fair rate of return and keeps the monopoly in business.

- An _____ is a by-product of a good or activity that affects someone not immediately involved in the transaction.

- The Coase theorem states that—when side payments can be negotiated and arranged without cost—the private market will solve the _____ problem on its own, always arriving at the _____ outcome. While the initial distribution of legal rights will determine the allocation of gains and losses among the parties, it will not affect the action taken.

- The _____ _____ problem occurs when the efficient outcome requires a side payment but individual gainers—each obligated to pay a small share of the side payment—will not contribute.

- A market with a negative externality associated with producing or consuming a good will produce _____ than the efficient quantity, creating a welfare _____ .

- A _____ on each unit of a good, equal to the external harm it causes, can correct a negative externality and bring the market to a (an) _____ output level. Other methods of reducing output to the _____ level are regulation and _____ permits.

- A market with a positive externality associated with producing or consuming a good will produce _____ than the efficient quantity, creating a welfare _____ .

- A _____ on each unit of a good, equal to the external benefits it creates, can correct a positive externality and bring the market to a (an) _____ output level.

- If a good is _____ , efficiency requires that people pay a price for its use. In the absence of any market failure, _____ provision will lead to the efficient level of production.

- If a good is excludable, it *can* be provided by the _____ market.

- A good that is both rivalrous and excludable is a pure _____ good. In the absence of any significant market failure, private firms will provide these goods at close to efficient levels.

- When a good is nonexcludable, the _____ sector will generally be unable to provide it. In most cases, if we want such a good, _____ must provide it.

- When a good or service is nonrival, the market cannot provide it efficiently: to achieve economic efficiency, the good or service would have to be provided at a price equal to _____ .

- A good that is both nonrival and nonexcludable is a pure _____ good.

- The tragedy of the commons occurs when a good that is both _____ and _____ is overused, to the detriment of all.

LEARN THE LINGO

Fill in each blank with the appropriate word or phrase from the list provided in the word bank. (For a challenge, fill in as many blanks as you can *without* using the word bank.)

_____ 1. An action that makes at least one person better off, and harms no one.

_____ 2. The difference between the value of a unit of a good to the buyer and what the buyer actually pays for it.

_____ 3. The total consumer surplus enjoyed by all consumers in a market.

_____ 4. The difference between what the seller actually gets for a unit of a good and the cost of providing it.

_____ 5. The total producer surplus gained by all sellers in a market.

_____ 6. The sum of consumer and producer surplus in a particular market.

_____ 7. The dollar value of potential benefits not achieved due to inefficiency in a particular market.

_____ 8. A wrongful act that harms someone.

Chapter 14 Economic Efficiency and the Role of Government   195

_____ 9. A market that fails to take advantage of every Pareto improvement.

_____ 10. A by-product of a good or activity that affects someone not immediately involved in the transaction.

_____ 11. When a side payment can be arranged without cost, the market will solve an externality problem—and create the efficient outcome—on its own.

_____ 12. Occurs when the efficient outcome requires a side payment but individual gainers will not contribute.

_____ 13. The full cost of producing another unit of a good, including the marginal cost to the producer *and* any harm done to third parties.

_____ 14. A license that allows a company to release a unit of pollution into the environment over some period of time.

_____ 15. The full benefit of producing another unit of a good, including the benefit to the consumer *and* any benefits enjoyed by third parties.

_____ 16. A situation in which one person's consumption of a unit of a good or service means that no one else can consume that unit.

_____ 17. The ability to exclude those who do not pay for a good from consuming it.

_____ 18. A good that is both rivalrous and excludable.

_____ 19. A good that is both nonrivalrous and nonexcludable.

_____ 20. The problem of overuse when a good is rivalrous but nonexcludable.

Word Bank

Coase theorem
consumer surplus
excludability
externality
free rider problem
marginal social benefit (MSB)
marginal social cost (MSC)
market consumer surplus
market failure
market producer surplus

Pareto improvement
producer surplus
pure private good
pure public good
rivalry
total net benefits
tort
tradable permit
tragedy of the commons
welfare loss

BUILD YOUR SKILLS

For each of the following items, write the correct answer in the blank or circle the correct answer.

1. The New Orleans wholesale market for frozen medium shrimp is perfectly competitive. The weekly market supply curve and market demand curve are displayed below.

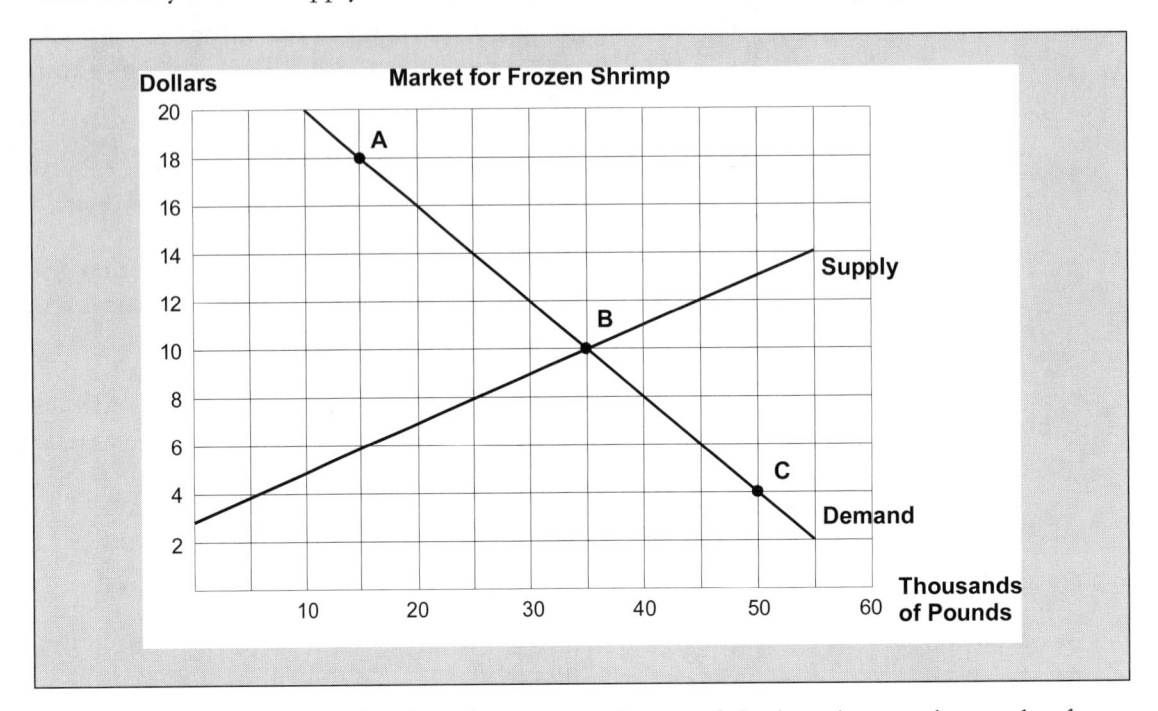

    Market for Frozen Shrimp

    a. At 15 thousand pounds, the value to some buyer of the last thousand pounds of shrimp purchased is _____. The cost of producing this last thousand pounds at some firm is _____. Because the value is (greater than/equal to/less than) the cost, we can deduce that 15 thousand pounds (is/is not) the economically efficient level of production for this good. Were production at 15 thousand pounds, Pareto improvements (could/could not) be achieved by increasing output and Pareto improvements (could/could not) be achieved by decreasing output.

    b. At 35 thousand pounds, the value to some buyer of the last thousand pounds of shrimp purchased is _____. The cost of producing this last thousand pounds at some firm is _____. Because the value is (greater than/equal to/less than) the cost, we can deduce that 35 thousand pounds (is/is not) the economically efficient level of production for this good. Were production at 35 thousand pounds, Pareto improvements (could/could not) be achieved by increasing output and Pareto improvements (could/could not) be achieved by decreasing output.

    c. At 50 thousand pounds, the value to some buyer of the last thousand pounds of shrimp purchased is _____. The cost of producing this last thousand pounds at some firm is ____________________. Because the value is (greater than/equal to/less than) the cost, we can deduce that 50 thousand pounds (is/is not) the economically efficient level of production for this good. Were production at 50 thousand pounds, Pareto improvements (could/could not) be achieved by increasing output and Pareto improvements (could/could not) be achieved by decreasing output.

d. With market demand and market supply as drawn above, the New Orleans frozen shrimp market will reach equilibrium at a market price of ____________________ dollars per pound. The equilibrium quantity supplied by firms and consumed by buyers will be ____________________ thousand pounds per week. In this market, the equilibrium quantity (is/is not) economically efficient.

2. Galveston, like New Orleans, is host to a large shrimp-fishing fleet, and the Galveston wholesale market for frozen medium shrimp is perfectly competitive. Weekly market supply and market demand are given by:

$$Q^D = 70 - (5/2)P$$

$$Q^S = 5P - 20.$$

a. Graph market demand and market supply on the grid below.

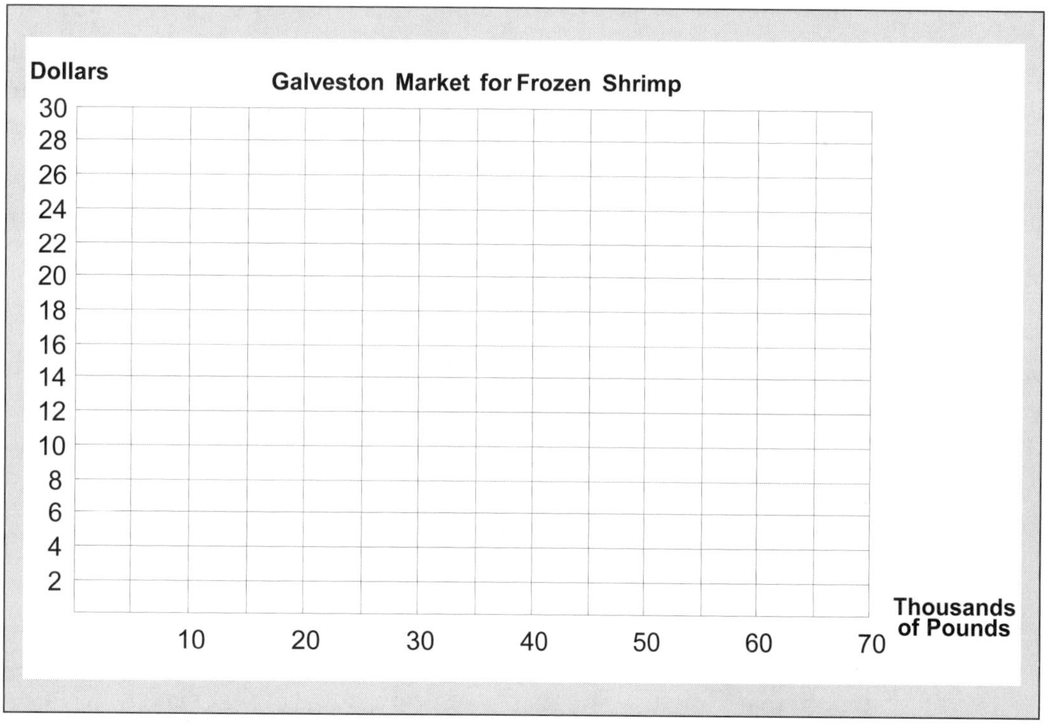

b. When the Galveston shrimp market is in equilibrium, market price is ____________________ dollars per pound and ____________________ thousand pounds are bought and sold every week. Shrimp buyers enjoy a weekly market consumer surplus of ____________________ thousand dollars, and producers enjoy a weekly market producer surplus of _____ thousand dollars. (*Hint*: Recall that the area of a triangle is one-half base times height). The total net benefits that consumers and producers gain from participating in this market is _____ thousand dollars each week.

c. Suppose, now, that the Galveston market is not allowed to reach the perfectly competitive equilibrium. Specifically, suppose that the market price of shrimp is fixed at $20 per pound. Then consumers will demand only _____ thousand pounds per week, so that is how many producers will be able to sell. If that many pounds of shrimp are bought and sold at the fixed price of $20, shrimp buyers will enjoy a weekly market consumer surplus of _____ thousand dollars, and producers will enjoy a weekly market producer surplus of _____ thousand dollars. The total net benefits that consumers and producers gain from participating in this market when the price is fixed at $20 per pound is _____ thousand dollars each week.

d. Comparing the answers in parts (b) and (c), it is easy to see that imposing a price floor of $20 in the Galveston shrimp market has had the effect of transferring surplus from (consumers/producers) to (consumers/producers). Moreover, total net benefits in the Galveston market with the price floor of $20 are (greater/smaller) than they are at the perfectly competitive market equilibrium, so total net surplus has been (increased/reduced/left unchanged) by this market intervention. Indeed, with a little experimenting at other, non-equilibrium prices and quantities, we would be able to see that total net benefits---measured by the sum of consumer and producer surplus in this market---are as (great/small) as they can be at the market equilibrium price and quantity because only there are total net benefits (maximized/minimized) in a perfectly competitive market.

3. Gillette's trademark gives it a monopoly in the market for Atra™ razor blades. Suppose that weekly market demand for 10-packs of Atra™ blades in the Southwestern market area is known to be

$$P = 10 - 0.25Q,$$

where Q is thousands of packs per week. Gillete's marginal revenue from sales in this market area will therefore be

$$MR = 10 - 0.5Q.$$

Suppose that Gillette's marginal cost of producing these blades increases with output, and is given by

$$MC = 1 + 0.25Q.$$

Chapter 14 Economic Efficiency and the Role of Government 199

Dollars Market for Atra Blades

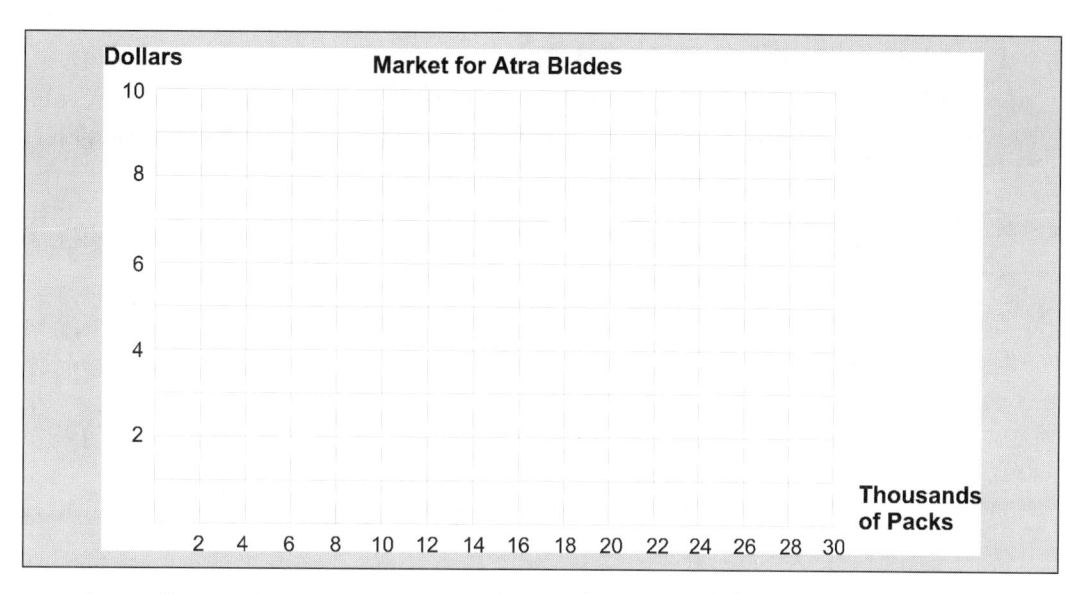

[Graph with y-axis "Dollars" marked 2, 4, 6, 8, 10 and x-axis "Thousands of Packs" marked 2, 4, 6, 8, 10, 12, 14, 16, 18, 20, 22, 24, 26, 28, 30]

a. Plot Gillette's demand curve, marginal revenue curve, and marginal cost curve on the grid provided. To maximize profit, Gillette should produce where (demand equals supply/marginal revenue equals marginal cost/demand equals marginal cost). The level of output that maximizes profit is _____ thousand packs per week. Gillette will sell this output at a price of _____ dollars per pack.

b. At the monopoly equilibrium price and output, market consumer surplus is _____ thousand dollars per week and market producer surplus is _____ thousand per week. Total net benefits in this market are therefore _____ thousand dollars per week at the monopoly equilibrium.

c. Suppose that instead of being free to choose its own price and output, Gillette were required comply with price controls under which it could charge a price no higher than $5.50 per pack. At this price, Gillette would sell _____ thousand packs per week, buyers would enjoy market consumer surplus of _____ thousand dollars per week, Gillette (the only producer) will enjoy market producer surplus of _____ thousand dollars per week, and total net benefits in this market would be _____ thousand dollars per week.

d. Comparing your answers in parts (b) and (c), we can see that total net benefits---measured by the sum of market consumer and producer surplus---are (greater/smaller) at the monopoly price and quantity than they are when the monopolist is required to produce more and charge a lower price. Hence, total net benefits in this market (are/are not) maximized at the monopoly price and output. In this way, we can see that the monopoly equilibrium (is/is not) economically efficient.

4. Cell-U was first to perfect low-power campus-wide wireless communication for university students. Using their own technology and a single centrally-located antenna on campus, the company can provide student customers with a convenient bare-bones service the company calls, "Cell-U-*Lite*."

The company's *LRATC* curve is drawn on the grid below, where Q is thousands of calls per week. It has found that the marginal cost of an additional phone call over its campus network is always constant and equal to 10 cents, so for this firm MC=10.

Demand for this service on one university campus is given by

$$P = 40 - (1/8)Q,$$

where P is cents and Q is thousands of calls per week. Cell-U's marginal revenue is therefore

$$MR = 40 - (1/4)Q.$$

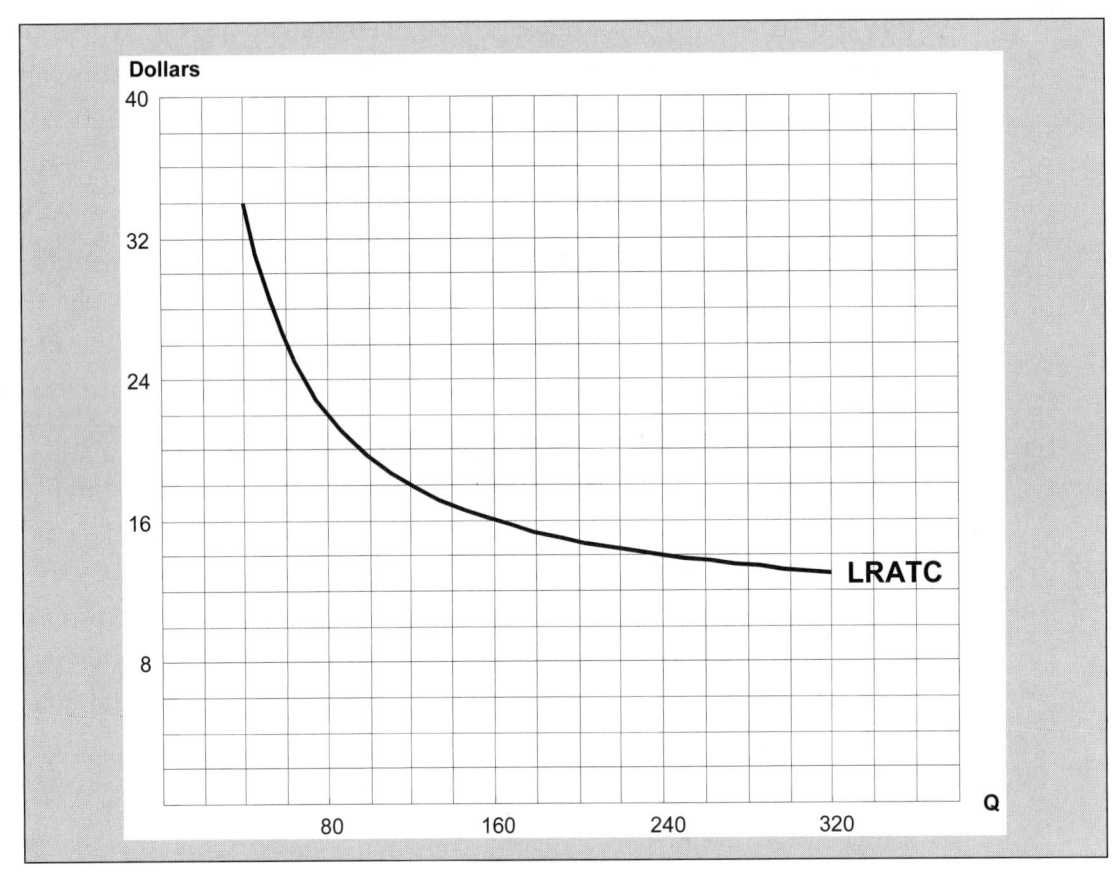

a. Because its *LRATC* curve is everywhere downward sloping, Cell-U will be a (natural disaster/natural competitor/natural monopoly) on campus.

b. Plot Cell-U's demand and marginal revenue curves on the grid provided. Plots its marginal cost curve too.

Chapter 14 Economic Efficiency and the Role of Government 201

c. If Cell-U is allowed to choose output to maximize its own profit, it will service _____ thousand calls per week, and it will charge _____ cents per call. From the graph, we can see that the long run average total cost of that many calls is _____ cents per call. Cell-U's weekly profit from this campus-wide market will therefore be _____ dollars per week.

d. The level of output that maximizes this firm's profit (is/is not) economically efficient because if an additional unit were produced and sold, it would have a value to some consumer of _____ cents, while the additional cost to produce that additional unit would be _____ cents. The government (can/can not) intervene in this market to increase efficiency.

e. If the government were to require this firm to charge a price equal to marginal cost, how much would Cell-U charge per call? _____ How many calls would it service each month? _____ Under this form of regulation, Cell-U (would/would not) produce and sell the economically efficient level of output, and the firm would (suffer a loss/reap a profit) of approximately _____ dollars each week. Thus, if required to set price equal to marginal cost, Cell-U will provide the economically efficient level of output (no matter what/only if the firm also receives a subsidy to cover its losses/and generate tax revenue for the government as well).

f. If, instead, the government were to regulate Cell-U's price so that the firm was able to earn no more than a fair rate of return, Cell-U would choose to service (approximately) _____ thousand calls per week. The firm would charge a price of (approximately) _____ cents per call, and earn a profit of _____ dollars per week under this form of regulation. The level of output Cell-U would produce under this form of regulation is therefore (higher than/equal to/lower than) the monopoly level of output and (higher than/equal to/lower than) the economically efficient level of output.

g. Under average cost pricing, this firm will still charge a price that is (greater than/equal to/ less than) marginal cost, and so produce a level of output that is (greater than/equal to/less than) the economically efficient level in this market. However, the difference between price charged and marginal cost of additional output under rate of return regulation is (lower than/equal to /greater than) the difference between price and marginal cost when the firm is completely unregulated.

5. In Manila, capital of the Philippines, a favorite form of transportation is the colorful "Jeepney," an elaborately decorated US Army surplus Jeep modified to carry passengers for hire. Because there are so many of them in the city, Jeepney traffic is a major contributor to Manila's air pollution problem.

Suppose it has been determined that the marginal social cost of Jeepney rides in Metro-Manila is given by the equation

$$MSC = 1 + 0.01Q$$

where Q is the quantity of rides per day. In addition, the daily market demand and market supply of Jeepney rides in the purely competitive Metro-Manila market are plotted below.

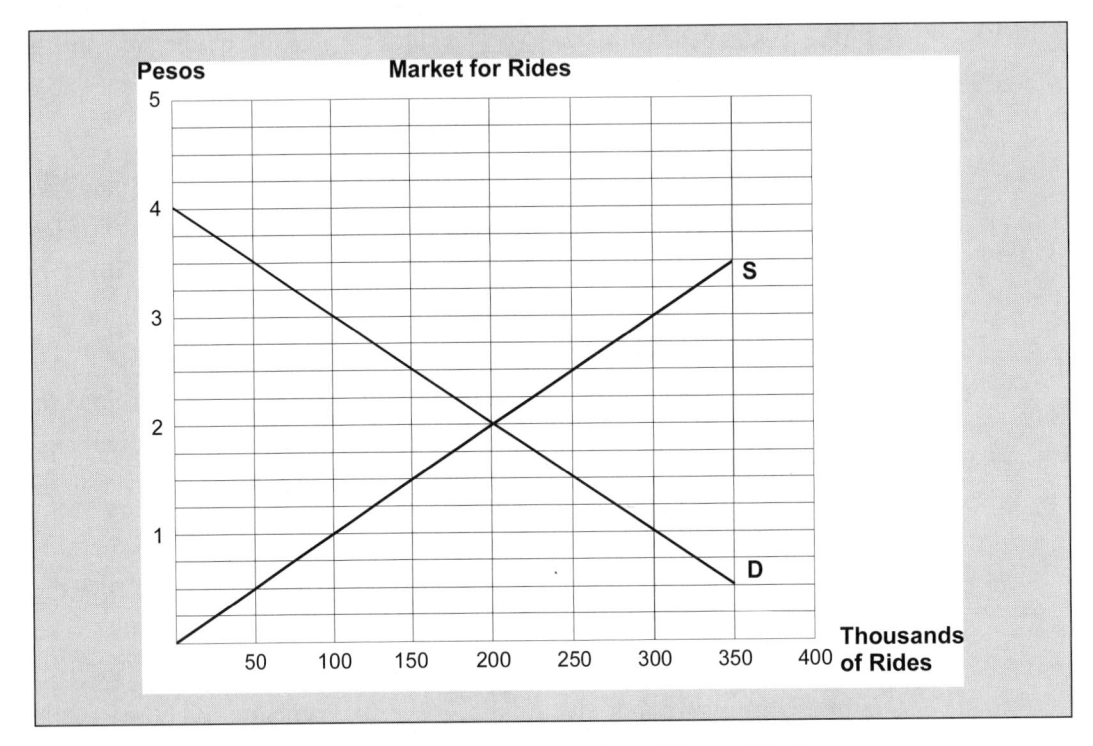

a. Plot the marginal social cost (MSC) curve on the grid provided.

b. In the absence of government involvement, the equilibrium price of a Jeepney ride will be _____ peso(s). The equilibrium quantity of Jeepney rides will be _____ thousand per day.

c. The competitive equilibrium in this market (is/is not) efficient: the equilibrium quantity of Jeepney rides produced and consumed is (too high/just right/too low). This is clear because, in equilibrium, the value of the last ride to some consumer is (greater than/equals to/less than) the marginal social cost of producing it.

d. To ensure that the efficient quantity of rides is produced and consumed each day, the government should (levy a tax of 1 peso per ride on Jeepneys/provide a subsidy of 1 peso per ride to Jeepneys). This will (raise/lower) the cost of a Jeepney ride and cause the market (demand/supply) curve to shift (rightward/leftward). The equilibrium price of rides produced will (increase/decrease) to _____ peso(s), and the quantity of rides produced and consumed will (increase/decrease) to _____ thousand rides per day.

e. The new equilibrium achieved after imposition of the 1 peso tax (will/will not) be efficient. In this new equilibrium, the value of the last ride to some consumer is (greater than/equal to/less than) the cost of producing it.

TEST YOURSELF

To see what you *really* know and remember, take this test at least a day *after* you've read the chapter in the text and completed the exercises in this study guide.

Multiple Choice: Circle the letter in front of the single best answer.

1. A Pareto improvement is best defined as any change in which
   a. at least one person gains and no one is harmed.
   b. many people gain and no one is harmed.
   c. the gains to the gainers are greater than the losses to the losers.
   d. the gainers are forced to compensate the losers for their losses.
   e. the losers are forced to compensate the gainers to prevent the change.

2. Some actions which by themselves are not Pareto improvements can be *converted* into Pareto improvements by using
   a. an imperfectly competitive market.
   b. a mixture of labor and capital.
   c. fewer resources.
   d. a side payment.
   e. a price ceiling.

3. As a rule, when a market is imperfectly competitive, economic efficiency is not achieved because the price is
   a. too high, and too little of the good is produced.
   b. too low, and too little of the good is produced.
   c. too low, and too much of the good is produced.
   d. too high, and too much of the good is produced.
   e. right and the amount produced is right, but the wrong consumers end up with the good.

4. Which of the following would *not* be a Pareto improvement?
   a. You pay $9 for a movie ticket and enjoy the movie.
   b. The economy stops producing a good that no one wants, and uses the freed-up inputs to produce a good that some people want.
   c. The government eliminates all regulations on food safety, and production of food rises dramatically.
   d. A collector of comic books buys a rare comic for $2,000.
   e. None of the above (i.e., all of the above are Pareto improvements).

5. The height of the market demand curve at any quantity tells us
   a. the cost—to some firm—of the last unit produced.
   b. the total cost—to some firm—of all units produced up to that quantity.
   c. the value—to some consumer—of the last unit consumed.
   d. the total value—to all consumers—of all units consumed up to that quantity.
   e. the sum of the cost and the value of the last unit consumed and produced.

6. Which type of law sets up incentives against injuries that result from accidents?
   a. Criminal law
   b. Property law
   c. Contract law
   d. Tort law
   e. Antitrust law

7. Which of the following activities is restricted in some way by U.S. antitrust law?
   a. Agreements among competitors
   b. Mergers
   c. Formation of a monopoly
   d. All of the above
   e. None of the above

8. An excise tax on a good is most likely to make the market more efficient if
   a. the good is beneficial to society.
   b. the good is a pure private good.
   c. the good is a pure public good.
   d. the good is provided in an imperfectly competitive market.
   e. the market is characterized by a negative externality.

9. Which of the following is *not* an example of a market failure?
   a. A imperfectly competitive market
   b. A positive externality
   c. A negative externality
   d. A good characterized by nonrivalry and nonexcludability
   e. A good that few people want

10. An efficient way to correct a *positive* externality is to impose a _____ equal to the difference between the _____ and the _____ a unit of the good.
    a. subsidy; marginal social benefit; value to consumers of
    b. subsidy; cost; revenue earned from
    c. tax; cost; marginal social cost
    d. tax; marginal social cost; marginal social benefit
    e. tax; price; cost to firms of producing

11. A pure public good is characterized by
    a. excludability and rivalry.
    b. excludability and nonrivalry.
    c. nonexcludability and rivalry.
    d. nonexcludability and nonrivalry.
    e. excludability, rivalry, and a negative or positive externality.

12. The "free rider" problem is defined as the problem that arises when
    a. a public transport worker cannot properly check for tickets because he is distracted by traffic or other conditions.
    b. fleas or other parasites travel from person to person undetected.
    c. side payments are negotiated to deal privately with an externality.
    d. externalities are solved by government, which is enable to enforce its decisions.
    e. side payments can't be negotiated because of an unclear initial distribution of legal rights.

13. Which of the following is an illustration of the "tragedy of the commons"?
    a. Too few people go to college because it is so expensive.
    b. The government makes weather reports available free of charge.
    c. Netscape and Mozilla goes out of business, leaving Microsoft as the only Internet browser available to PC users.
    d. A high quality television program is taken off the air because too few people watch it.
    e. A city park is overcrowded with sunbathers on a nice day.

14. Two campers, Smith and Jones, are at a standoff: each wants to pitch a tent on the same prime spot in a campground. The spot is worth more to Smith than Jones. According to the Coase theorem, if side payments can be easily arranged at low cost, we would expect Smith to end up with the spot as long as
    a. Smith has the initial legal rights to the spot.
    b. Jones has the initial legal rights to the spot.
    c. *either* Smith *or* Jones has the initial legal rights to the spot.
    d. *neither* Smith nor Jones has the initial legal rights to the spot.
    e. the government or similar authority becomes involved in settling the dispute.

True/False: For each of the following statements, circle T if the statement is true or F if the statement is false.

T   F   1. Economic efficiency requires that all Pareto improvements be exploited.

T   F   2. If a change occurs in which some people would lose, but the losers are given side payments from the gainers that more than compensates for their losses, then the final result is a Pareto improvement.

T F   3. Any change that is a Pareto improvement will tend to make the economy more fair.

T F   4. If you are desperately hungry, and you buy a loaf of bread from the only food store in town for $500, then you have been exploited so the purchase is *not* a Pareto improvement.

T F   5. Surprisingly, the data show only a weak or non-existent correlation between the quality of the institutional infrastructure and output per worker.

T F   6. While legal procedures tell businesses what to do, regulation typically imposes fines or other penalties if businesses do something wrong.

T F   7. The existence of even small amounts of crime, unsafe products and other activities that harm society is evidence of economic inefficiency.

T F   8. While negative externalities represent a market failure, positive externalities do not.

T F   9. Under completely accurate "average cost pricing," a natural monopoly would make positive accounting profit, but zero economic profit.

T F 10. Downloadable computer software is an example of a pure private good.

Short Answer: Write a brief answer below for each of the following questions.

1. List the five types of law that contribute to economic efficiency.
   a. _____ law
   b. _____ law
   c. _____ law
   d. _____ law
   e. _____ law

2. List the three different types of market failures discussed in this chapter
   a. _____
   b. _____
   c. _____

3. In the blanks below, state the specific type of market failure represented by each of the following situations:

   a. A noisy dance club opens in your neighborhood, causing noise and traffic at all hours of the night. _____

   b. All of the gas stations in your town except one go out of business. The remaining gas station raises its prices. _____

Chapter 14 Economic Efficiency and the Role of Government

c. If your neighbor would shovel the snow off of the sidewalk in front of her house, it would be easier for you and everyone else on the block, as well as your neighbor, to walk to the bus stop. _____

d. Everyone in a city would benefit if more trees were planted along sidewalks, but no firm will plant them because it would be impossible to charge those who benefit by walking by_____.

4. In the blanks below, list the two characteristics of a pure private good, and the two characteristics of a pure public good.

a. Pure private good: _____ and _____

b. Pure public good: _____ and _____

CHAPTER 15

COMPARATIVE ADVANTAGE AND THE GAINS FROM INTERNATIONAL TRADE

SUMMARIZE THE CHAPTER

Construct your own chapter summary by filling in the blanks. If you have difficulty, review the highlighted points in the chapter, then try again.

- A country has an _____ _____ in a good when it can produce it using fewer resources than another country.

- A nation has a _____ _____ in producing a good if it can produce it at a lower opportunity cost than some other country.

- Mutually beneficial trade between any two countries is possible whenever one country is relatively better at producing a good than the other country is. Being relatively better means having the ability to produce a good at a lower _____ cost—that is, at a lower sacrifice of other goods foregone.

- If countries specialize according to _____ advantage, a more efficient use of given resources occurs. That is, with the same resources, the world can produce more of at least one good, without decreasing production of any other good.

- As long as _____ costs differ, specialization and trade can be beneficial to all involved. This remains true regardless of whether the parties are different nations, different states, different counties, or different individuals. It remains true even if one party has an all-round _____ advantage or disadvantage in all goods.

- For the world as a whole, the gains from international trade are due to increased production as nations specialize according to _____ advantage. How those world gains are distributed among specific countries depends on the _____ of _____.

- When consumers are free to buy at the lowest prices, they will naturally buy a good from the country that has a _____ advantage in producing it. That country's industries respond by producing more of that good and less of other goods. In this way, countries naturally move toward specializing in those goods in which they have a _____ advantage.

- A country that has relatively large amounts of a particular _____ at its disposal will tend to have a comparative advantage in goods that make heavy use of that _____. But countries can also develop strong comparative advantages in the goods they have produced in the past, regardless of why they began producing those goods in the first place.

- When the opening of trade results in increased exports of a good, the _____ of the good are made better off. _____ of the good in the exporting country will be made worse off.

- When the opening of trade results in increased imports of a product, the domestic _____ of the product are made worse off. _____ of the good in the importing country are better off.

- The distribution of gains and losses creates a policy bias against free trade. Those who benefit from trade in a specific product either have little incentive to lobby for it (_____ of imports) or have limited power to influence policy (_____ of exports). But one constituency harmed by trade—domestic _____ threatened by imports—has both a powerful incentive to lobby and the ability to influence policy.

- Tariffs _____ the volume of trade and _____ the domestic prices of imported goods. In the country that imposes the tariff, producers of the good _____ and consumers of the good _____. But the world as a whole _____, because tariffs _____ the gains from trade.

- Quotas have effects similar to tariffs: They _____ the quantity of imports and _____ domestic prices. While both measures help domestic _____ of the good, they _____ the benefits of trade to the nation as a whole. However, a tariff has one saving grace (one advantage over a quota): an increase in _____ _____.

- Production is most likely to reflect the principle of _____ advantage when firms can obtain funds for investment projects and when they can freely enter industries that are profitable. Thus, free trade, without government intervention, works best when markets are working well.

Chapter 15 Comparative Advantage and the Gains from International Trade

LEARN THE LINGO

Fill in each blank with the appropriate word or phrase from the list provided in the word bank. (For a challenge, fill in as many blanks as you can *without* using the word bank.)

_____ 1. Goods and services produced domestically, but sold abroad.

_____ 2. Goods and services produced abroad, but consumed domestically.

_____ 3. The ability to produce a good using fewer resources than another country.

_____ 4. The ability to produce a good at a lower opportunity cost than another country.

_____ 5. The ratio at which a country can trade domestically produced products for foreign-produced products.

_____ 6. The amount of one currency that is traded for one unit of another currency.

_____ 7. A tax on imports.

_____ 8. A limit on the physical volume of imports.

_____ 9. The belief that a nation's industries should be protected from foreign competition.

_____ 10. The argument that a new industry in which a country has a comparative advantage might need protection from foreign competition n order to flourish.

Word Bank

absolute advantage
comparative advantage
exchange rate
exports
imports

infant industry argument
protectionism
quota
tariff
terms of trade

BUILD YOUR SKILLS

For each of the following items, write the correct answer in the blank or circle the correct answer.

1. Data on the labor requirements in producing bicycles and DVRs in Germany and the US are provided in the table. Assume that labor is the only resources in each country, that it is (and remains) fully employed, and that labor requirements per unit remain constant no matter how many units of the good are produced.

   Labor Requirements per Unit

	Germany	United States
Per Bicycle	20	15
Per DVR	40	45

   a. Suppose Germany produced one additional DVR. This would require Germany to divert _____ hours from bicycle production. Since each bike requires _____ hours to produce, producing one additional DVR requires that Germany produce _____ fewer (bicycles/DVRs). In Germany, the opportunity cost of an additional DVR is therefore _____ (bicycles/DVRs).

   b. Suppose the United States produced one additional DVR. This would require the United States to divert _____ hours from bicycle production. Since each bicycle requires _____ hours to produce, producing one additional DVR requires that the United States produce _____ fewer (bicycles/DVRs). In the United States, the opportunity cost of an additional DVR is therefore _____ (bicycles/DVRs).

   c. Carry forward your answers to (a) and (b), then compute the remaining opportunity costs to complete the table.

   Opportunity Costs

	Germany	United States
Per Bicycle	_____	_____
Per DVR	_____	_____

   d. From this table, we can see that Germany has a comparative advantage in producing _____ while the United States has a comparative advantage in producing _____. This is because the opportunity cost of _____ in Germany is less than it is in the United States, while the opportunity cost of _____ in the United States is less than it is in Germany.

Chapter 15 Comparative Advantage and the Gains from International Trade   213

2. Let's continue with the data from the previous question and consider the gains from specialization and exchange.

   a. To achieve gains from trade, Germany should produce more _____ and fewer _____, while the United States should produce more _____ and fewer _____. Germany should then export _____ to the United States and import _____ from the United States, while the United States should export _____ to Germany and import _____ from Germany.

   b. As an example of the potential for gain through specialization and trade, suppose that Germany diverts enough resources from bicycles to produce an additional 25 DVRs, while the United States diverts enough resources from DVRs to produce an additional 60 bicycles. Complete the table.

   A Change in Production

	Germany	United States	World
Bicycle Production	_____	+60	_____
DVR Production	+25	_____	_____

   c. To show that both sides can gain from trade, let us suppose that production in each country has shifted as in (b). Suppose that trade is opened between the two countries and that:

   Germany exports (and the U.S. imports) 22 DVRs

   Germany imports (and the U.S. exports) 55 bicycles.

   Complete the following table.

   The Gains from Specialization and Trade

	Germany Bicycles	Germany DVRs	United States Bicycles	United States DVRs
Change in Production	−50	_____	+60	_____
Exports (−) or Imports (+)	+55	−22	−55	+22
Net Gain	_____	_____	_____	_____

   d. In the example of part (c), the United States exports 55 bicycles in exchange for 22 DVRs. The **terms of trade** in this example are therefore _____ bicycles for 1 DVR. At these terms of trade, our example has shown that (only Germany/only the United States/both Germany and the United States) can gain from specialization and trade. This is clear from the table in part (c): the gains from trade for the United States are _____ bicycles and _____ DVRs, while the gains from trade for Germany are _____ bicycles and _____ DVRs.

3. The French and Israelis both consume oranges. France and Israel are also both capable of producing oranges. Domestic demand and domestic supply of oranges in each country are provided below.

For simplicity, P is the price per pound of oranges *measured in U.S. dollars*, and Q is thousands of kilos per month.

	Domestic Demand	Domestic Supply
France	$Q^D = \dfrac{4400}{6} - \dfrac{400P}{3}$	$Q^S = \dfrac{200P}{3} - \dfrac{200}{3}$
Israel	$Q^D = \dfrac{1100}{3} - \dfrac{200P}{3}$	$Q^S = \dfrac{500}{3} + \dfrac{400P}{3}$

a. Plot these demand and supply curves in the grids provided.

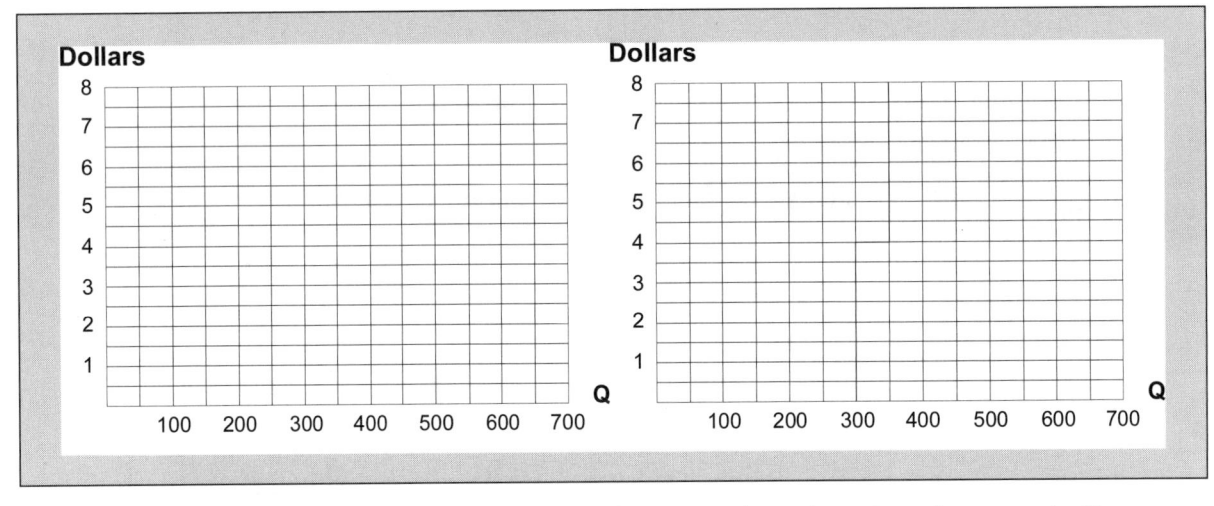

b. If France and Israel do not trade with one another, the price of oranges in France will be _____ dollars and the quantity of oranges produced and consumed will be _____ thousand kilos per month. In Israel, the price of oranges will be _____ dollars and the quantity of oranges produced and consumed will be _____ thousand kilos per month.

c. If free trade in oranges is opened between these two countries, France will (import/export/neither import nor export) oranges, while Israel will (import/export/neither import nor export) oranges.

d. With free trade, the price of oranges in France will (rise/fall/remain unchanged) while the price oranges in Israel will (rise/fall/remain unchanged). As this occurs, the quantity of oranges consumed in France will (increase/decrease/remain unchanged), while the quantity of oranges produced in France will (increase/decrease/remain unchanged). In Israel, the price of oranges will (rise/fall/remain unchanged). As this occurs, the quantity of oranges consumed in Israel will (increase/decrease/remain unchanged), while the quantity of oranges produced will (increase/decrease/remain unchanged).

e. As a result of trade, French consumers pay (higher/lower) prices for oranges, and so will be (better off/worse off) with trade. French orange producers receive (higher/lower) prices for oranges, and so will be (better off/worse off) with trade. At the same time, Israeli consumers pay (higher/lower) prices for oranges, and so will be (better off/worse off) with trade. Israeli orange producers receive (higher/lower) prices for oranges, and so will be (better off/worse off) with trade.

4. As a challenge, let's determine the exact price of oranges after free trade is opened between France and Israel.

In the text, you learned that after trade is opened, one country's imports must equal the other country's exports in the final market equilibrium. Because imports at any price are the amount by which domestic demand exceeds domestic supply, the equation for French orange imports can be found by subtracting quantity demanded from quantity supplied. Using France's demand and supply equations from question (3), compute the quantity of French orange imports. _____

Similarly, exports at any price will be the amount by which domestic production exceeds domestic consumption. The equation for Israeli orange exports can be found using the Israel's equations in question (3) by subtracting quantity supplied from quantity demanded. Thus, the quantity of Israeli orange exports is _____.

To find the post-trade equilibrium price of oranges, set French imports equal to Israeli exports, and solve for P.

We conclude that the post-trade market equilibrium price of oranges will be _____ dollars per kilo. (Sketch this onto your graphs in part (a) of the previous question and verify that French imports equal Israeli exports at this price.)

TEST YOURSELF

To see what you *really* know and remember, take this test at least a day *after* you've read the chapter in the text and completed the exercises in this study guide.

Multiple Choice: Circle the letter in front of the single best answer.

1. A nation has a comparative advantage in producing some good if
    a. its workers have a lower wage than the workers in other countries.
    b. it can produce the good with less resources than other countries.
    c. it can produce the good with a lower opportunity cost than other countries.
    d. its technology for producing the good is more advanced than in other countries.
    e. all of the above.

Questions 2–4 refer to the following information: Suppose that, in the United States, it takes 10 hours to produce a ton of corn, and 5 hours to produce a ton of wheat. In Mexico, it takes 15 hours to produce a ton of corn, and 10 hours to produce a ton of wheat.

2. In Mexico, the opportunity cost of a ton of wheat is
    a. 2/3 ton of corn.
    b. 1 ton of corn.
    c. 1.5 tons of corn.
    d. 10 tons of corn.
    e. 15 tons of corn.

3. Based on the information given, which of the following statements is true?
    a. The United States has an absolute advantage in both goods.
    b. The United States has a comparative advantage in producing corn.
    c. Mexico has a comparative advantage in producing wheat.
    d. All of the above.
    e. None of the above.

4. If trade opens up between the U.S. and Mexico, and these are the only two goods traded, then
    a. the United States will export both corn and wheat to Mexico.
    b. Mexico will export both corn and wheat to the United States.
    c. Mexico will export corn and the United States will export wheat.
    d. the United States will export corn and Mexico will export wheat.
    e. neither country will export either good; i.e., there will be no trade between these two countries.

5. The "terms of trade" refers to
   a. bilateral agreements between nations to remove tariffs and quotas.
   b. the harm that trade causes to firms, workers and consumers in certain industries.
   c. promises made to those harmed by trade, in order to weaken their support for protectionism.
   d. the additional transportation and other costs exporters and importers must pay.
   e. the exchange ratio between exported and imported goods.

6. An "infant industry" is
   a. any industry that serves newborns.
   b. any industry begun less than 10 years earlier.
   c. any industry in one country that is younger than the same industry in another country.
   d. an industry in which a country could have a comparative advantage once that industry was in place, if it were temporarily protected from foreign competition.
   e. an industry in which a firm has an absolute, but not a comparative, advantage.

7. When there are increasing, rather than constant, opportunity costs,
   a. our conclusions about which country has a comparative advantage in which good are reversed.
   b. absolute advantage, rather than comparative advantage, determines which country will produce which good.
   c. there will be no gain from trading between nations.
   d. there will be gains from trade, but complete specialization is less likely.
   e. there will be gains from trade, but only when countries completely specialize.

8. If trade opens up between Country A and Country B, and Country A exports good X while Country B exports good Y, then
   a. the price of good X to consumers in Country A will fall.
   b. the price of good Y to consumers in Country B will fall.
   c. producers of good Y in Country A will gain.
   d. all of the above.
   e. none of the above.

9. One key difference between a quota and a tariff is that
   a. tariffs reduce the volume of trade, while quotas do not.
   b. quotas reduce the volume of trade, while tariffs do not.
   c. tariffs generate revenue for the government, while quotas generally do not.
   d. quotas generate revenue for the government, while tariffs generally do not.
   e. quotas benefit domestic producers of the protected good, while tariffs do not.

10. The argument for "strategic trade policy" is strongest when
    a. the market is dominated by a few large firms.
    b. the country using the policy is very large.
    c. tariffs are already in place.
    d. quotas are already in place.
    e. the opportunity costs of production differ widely among different trading partners.

True/False: For each of the following statements, circle T if the statement is true or F if the statement is false.

T F 1. If a nation has an absolute advantage in producing some good, it will also have a comparative advantage in producing that good.

T F 2. When trade opens up between two countries, one country generally gains and the other generally loses.

T F 3. The United States has a comparative advantage in the production of computer software largely because of its endowments of natural resources.

T F 4. When trade in a good opens up between two countries, consumers in both countries generally gain while producers in both countries generally lose.

T F 5. When a country imposes a *tariff* on imports of a good, the price of that good to consumers in the *other* country will generally fall.

T F 6. When a country imposes a *quota* on imports of a good, the price of that good to consumers in the *other* country will generally fall.

T F 7. A less-advanced, low-productivity country generally does not gain when it trades with a more-advanced, high-productivity country.

T F 8. The United States is a "free trade" country: it allows foreign goods to be sold in U.S. markets with virtually no restrictions.

Chapter 15 Comparative Advantage and the Gains from International Trade

Short Answer: Write a brief answer below each of the following questions.

1. Suppose that when trade opens up between two countries, Country A exports good X and Country B exports good Y. In the table below, state how each group is affected by filling in each cell with the word "gain" or "lose." For example, in the leftmost, top cell, state whether producers of good X in Country A gain or lose when trade opens up.

	Country A		Country B	
	Producers (workers and owners of firms):	Consumers:	Producers (workers and owners of firms)	Consumers:
Good X				
Good Y				

2. Now suppose that Country A and Country B have been trading for years, and one day Country A decides to impose a tariff on imports of Good Y from Country B. In the table below, state how each group is affected by filling in each cell with the word "gain" or "lose."

	Country A		Country B	
	Producers (workers and owners of firms):	Consumers:	Producers (workers and owners of firms):	Consumers:
Good Y				

FINAL EXAM IN MICROECONOMICS

This exam is meant to test your understanding of *all* of microeconomics, rather than just the material in individual chapters. To distinguish between memorization and understanding, many of these problems require you to *apply* the theory in a new way.

Answers and explanations are provided at the end. Keep in mind that (1) your own instructor may emphasize different material—including lecture material that may differ from the book; (2) your instructor may have asked the class to skip certain sections of the book (these questions will look entirely unfamiliar to you); and (3) your instructor's exam may not include multiple choice questions. So—although this exam will give you a chance for self-assessment—it may *not* be representative of the exam your instructor will give.

Give yourself 1¼ hours to do the exam. Answer all questions you can answer easily first, then go back to the more difficult ones.

1. Nadine is considering whether to go to Italy for three months to learn Italian, at a cost of $800 for a round trip ticket, and $1,000 for the course. If she did *not* take the trip, her most preferred choice would be to quit her current job and do part-time consulting work at home, for which she would earn $3,000 per month but have more time to spend with family and friends. Finally, her third choice would be to keep her current job, for which she is paid $4,000 per month. The opportunity cost for Nadine of going to Italy and taking the course is:
   a. $1,800
   b. $10,800
   c. $13,800
   d. $10,800 plus the value of the lost time with friends and family
   e. $13,800 plus the value of the lost time with friends and family

2. Imagine a production possibilities frontier with civilian goods on one axis and military goods on the other. Which of the following would shift the PPF outward in a parallel fashion (i.e., increase both the vertical and horizontal intercepts of the PPF)?
   a. A decision to shift resources out of military and into civilian production.
   b. A technological advance in the production of military goods.
   c. An increased desire for working among the population, resulting in an increase in the labor force.
   d. The ending of a recession.
   e. All of the above.

221

3. Hernando and James are roommates. It takes Hernando one hour to clean the apartment, and two hours to shop and cook dinner, while it takes James one hour to clean the apartment and three hours to shop and cook dinner. Which of the following statements is true?
   a. Hernando has an absolute advantage in cleaning the apartment.
   b. James has an absolute advantage in cleaning the apartment.
   c. James has a comparative advantage in shopping and cooking dinner.
   d. Neither James nor Hernando has a comparative advantage in cleaning the apartment.
   e. none of the above.

4. Which of the following must cause the equilibrium price of breakfast cereal to rise, but at the same time might either increase or decrease the equilibrium quantity of breakfast cereal?
   a. An increase in the population.
   b. An increase in the population and a technological advance in cereal production.
   c. An increase in population and an increase in the price of milk.
   d. An increase in population and a decrease in the price of milk.
   e. An increase in the population and an increase in the price of grains used to make breakfast cereal.

5. Which of the following would shift the supply curve for breakfast cereal rightward, but cause no shift in the demand curve for breakfast cereal?
   a. A decrease in the price of grain used to make breakfast cereal.
   b. An increase in population.
   c. A decrease in population.
   d. An increase average income among consumers in the market.
   e. None of the above.

6. Suppose the price elasticity of demand for breakfast cereal is -0.4. Then, if the average price per box rises from $9 to $11, we can expect the quantity of breakfast cereal demanded to fall by
   a. 40%.
   b. 20%
   c. 10%
   d. 9%
   e. 8%

7. Along a straight-line demand curve, the demand for the good
   a. becomes less price-elastic as we move upward and leftward along the curve.
   b. becomes less price-elastic as we move upward and leftward along the curve, but only if we are in the upper half of the curve.
   c. becomes more price-elastic as we move upward and leftward along the curve.
   d. becomes more price-elastic as we move upward and leftward along the curve, but only if we are in the upper half of the curve.
   e. has the same price-elasticity, because the slope of a straight-line demand curve doesn't change.

8. For which of the following would demand be the most price-elastic?
   a. Fruit.
   b. Oranges.
   c. Florida oranges.
   d. Deluxe Florida oranges.
   e. Florida oranges being offered for sale at Kroger food markets.

9. In a market where the equilibrium price is $10, a price ceiling of $12 would
   a. cause a shortage of the good.
   b. cause an excess supply of the good.
   c. have no immediate effect on the market.
   d. increase supply in the short run, but decrease it in the long run.
   e. decrease supply in the short run, but increase it in the long run.

10. Lydia currently has an annual income of $18,000, and is seeing 8 rock concerts per year. Lydia claims that, for her, rock concerts are an economic necessity. If Lydia's annual income were to rise to $22,000, which *new* number of rock concerts would be consistent with Lydia's claim?
    a. 9
    b. 10
    c. 11
    d. 12

11. Canned tuna would be considered an inferior good in a market if its income elasticity in that market had the value
    a. -0.1
    b. 0.1
    c. 0.5
    d. 1.0
    e. 1.5

12. A decrease in the price of a good whose quantity is measured on the vertical axis will
    a. shift the budget line rightward, but not change its slope.
    b. shift the budget line leftward, but not change its slope.
    c. rotate the budget line from a fixed point on the horizontal axis, making the budget line steeper.
    d. rotate the budget line from a fixed point on the vertical axis, making the line steeper.
    e. rotate the budget line from a fixed point on the vertical axis, making the line flatter.

13. An increases in a consumer's income will cause
    a. the budget line to shift leftward, with an unchanged slope.
    b. the budget line to shift rightward, with an unchanged slope.
    c. the budget line to shift leftward and become steeper.
    d. the budget line to shift rightward and become steeper.
    e. none of the above.

14. [only if you read the Marginal Utility approach in Chapter 5] Kim is consuming optimal quantities of books (which cost $25 each) and movies (which cost $10 each). If her marginal utility from another movie is 5, then her marginal utility from another book must be
    a. 5
    b. 10
    c. 12.5
    d. 25
    e. 125

15. [only if you read the Marginal Utility approach in Chapter 5] Suppose books cost $25 each and movies cost $10 each. For Alfred, the marginal utility of books is 200 and the marginal utility of movies is 100. Then
    a. Alfred would be better off shifting his consumption toward books.
    b. Alfred would be better off shifting his consumption toward movies.
    c. Alfred is allocating his income between the two goods in the best possible way.
    d. for Alfred, books are inferior.
    e. Alfred's demand for movies is unitary inelastic.

16. [only if you read the Indifference Curve approach in Chapter 5] Suppose books cost $25 each, and movies cost $10 each. For Howard, the marginal rate of substitution of movies for books (MRS$_{movies,books}$) is 3. Then
    a. Howard would be better off shifting his consumption toward books.
    b. Howard would be better off shifting his consumption toward movies.
    c. Howard is allocating his income between the two goods in the best possible way.
    d. for Howard, movies are inferior.
    e. for Howard, the demand for books is elastic.

17. A rise in the price of movies causes a decrease in Sarah's quantity of movies demanded. This tells us that, for Sarah, movies
    a. must be a normal good.
    b. must be an economic necessity.
    c. must be price-elastically demanded (i.e., elastic demand).
    d. all of the above.
    e. none of the above.

18. When the price of eggs decreases, the substitution effect
    a. always works to increase the quantity of eggs demanded.
    b. always works to decrease the quantity of eggs demanded.
    c. works to increase the quantity of eggs demanded *only if* the good is normal.
    d. works to increase the quantity of eggs demanded *only if* the good is inferior.
    e. works to increase the quantity of eggs demanded *only if* the demand for the good is elastic.

19. The "short run" for a consulting firm would be
    a. about a week.
    b. about a month.
    c. about a year.
    d. any time period during which the firm is stuck with it's current quantity of at least *one* input.
    e. whatever period of time it would take for the firm to be able to adjust *all* of its inputs.

20. If a firm is experiencing "increasing returns to labor," then
    a. it is operating in the long run.
    b. equal increases in employment generate greater and greater increases in output.
    c. equal increases in output require greater and greater increases in employment.
    d. equal increases in labor and all other inputs the firm uses will generate greater and greater increases in output.
    e. equal increases in labor and all other inputs the firm uses will generate smaller and smaller increases in output.

Questions 20-22 refer to the following situation: Bob has opened up a computer repair shop. To start the shop, he invested $100,000 of his own money a few years ago, and he works in the shop himself full time. He pays *each* of his two employees $6,000 per month, pays rent of $2,000 per month on the shop, and pays $200 per month for utilities. The interest rate that he could have earned on similar investments is 1 percent per month, and Bob's next best alternative would be to work as a full time chef, earning $4,000 per month. The total monthly revenue at Bob's shop is $15,000 per month.

21. To an economist, the total monthly cost of Bob's business is:
    a. $5,000
    b. $18,200
    c. $19,200
    d. $114,200
    e. $118,200

22. Bob's monthly *accounting* profit is:
    a. -$103,200
    b. -$3,200
    c. -$4,200
    d. -$800
    e. $800

23. Bob's monthly *economic* profit is
    a. -$103,200
    b. -$3,200
    c. -$4,200
    d. -$800
    e. $800

24. Which of the following formulas is *not* correct?
    a. ATC – AVC = AFC
    b. TC / Q = ATC
    c. TVC / Q = AVC
    d. TR / Q = MR
    e. TR / Q – ATC = profit per unit.

25. When the marginal product of labor is falling, we know that
    a. profit is falling.
    b. output is falling.
    c. total revenue is falling.
    d. average total cost is rising.
    e. marginal cost is rising.

Final Exam in Microeconomics

26. At any given output level, long run average total cost *must* be
    a. greater than (short-run) average total cost.
    b. greater than or equal to (short-run) average total cost.
    c. greater than or equal to (short-run) average variable cost.
    d. less than (short-run) average total cost.
    e. less than or equal to (short-run) average total cost.

27. If a firm experiences diseconomies of scale at all output levels, then its long-run average total cost curve will
    a. slope downward.
    b. be horizontal.
    c. slope upward.
    d. slope downward at lower output levels and upward at higher output levels.
    e. slope upward at lower output levels and downward at higher output levels.

28. To maximize total profit, a firm should always produce the level of output at which
    a. the distance between the MR and MC curves is greatest.
    b. the difference between price and average total cost is greatest.
    c. the TR curve intersects the TC curve.
    d. all of the above.
    e. none of the above.

29. A firm's total *revenue* is maximized at the level of output where
    a. MR and MC cross.
    b. TR and TC cross.
    c. the MR curve crosses the horizontal axis.
    d. the MC curve crosses the demand curve.
    e. the MR curve crosses the demand curve.

30. If marginal revenue is less than marginal cost, we can be certain that a small increase in output will
    a. increase total profit.
    b. decrease total profit.
    c. increase total revenue.
    d. decrease total revenue.
    e. decrease total revenue and increase cost.

31. Suppose Q* is the output level at which MR = MC for a firm. In the short run, a firm should shut down whenever
    a. it suffers a loss at Q*.
    b. it suffers a loss or breaks even at Q*.
    c. it suffers a loss and P < TR at Q*.
    d. it suffers a loss and TR < TVC at Q*.
    e. it suffers a loss and P < ATC at Q*.

32. Suppose the minimum efficient scale (MES) for a typical firm in a market is equal to 20 percent of the maximum possible demand in that market. Then we would expect this market to most closely resemble
    a. perfect competition.
    b. monopoly.
    c. monopolistic competition.
    d. oligopoly.
    e. monopsony.

33. Which of the following markets fits best with perfect competition?
    a. The market for gasoline in a town with only two gas stations, the owners of which—because of personal dislike for one another—are constantly trying to compete with each other.
    b. The market for feature films shown in movie theaters.
    c. The market for walnuts.
    d. The market for designer clothes.
    e. The market for local telephone service.

34. In a perfectly competitive market
    a. the demand curve facing the firm is horizontal.
    b. the firm's marginal revenue curve is horizontal.
    c. the market demand curve is downward sloping.;
    d. all of the above.
    e. none of the above.

35. A perfectly competitive firm should shut down in the short run if, at the output level for which MR = MC, price is less than
    a. average total cost.
    b. average variable cost.
    c. marginal revenue.
    d. marginal cost.
    e. total cost.

36. Which of the following is true of the perfectly competitive firm in long run equilibrium?
    a. P = minimum AVC.
    b. P = minimum LRATC.
    c. The ATC curve is downward sloping at the profit-maximizing output level.
    d. all of the above.
    e. none of the above.

37. When demand decreases in a perfectly competitive market that is also an increasing cost industry, then the price will drop in the short run,
    a. but rise back up in the long run and end up at its original level.
    b. but rise in the long run and end up higher than its initial level.
    c. rise back somewhat in the long run, but end up lower than its initial level.
    d. and drop even further in the long run.
    e. and stay at its new short-run level over the long run.

38. A single price monopolist's marginal revenue curve lies below its demand curve because the monopoly
    a. can charge whatever price it wants for its output.
    b. must lower the price on all units of output to increase the quantity it can sell.
    c. need not worry about substitutes provided by competitors.
    d. is able to charge each customer a different "single price" that is the most each is willing to pay.
    e. will never shut down in the short run.

39. Comparing a monopoly market with an otherwise similar perfectly competitive market, we generally expect the monopoly market to
    a. charge a higher price and produce less output than a competitive market.
    b. charge a higher price and produce more output than a competitive market.
    c. charge a lower price and produce less output than a competitive market.
    d. charge a lower price and produce more output than a competitive market.
    e. charge a higher price than a competitive market, but produce the same output level.

40. Which of the following is an example of price discrimination?
    a. A package delivery service charges more to deliver packages to Hawaii than to cities in the continental United States.
    b. A cup of coffee costs more at Starbucks than at McDonalds.
    c. A supermarket gives discounts to those who have clipped coupons from the newspaper.
    d. It costs more to fly from Dallas to New York than from Los Angeles to San Francisco.
    e. Apartment rents are higher in big cities than in small town.

41. Which of the following is a requirement for a market to be considered an oligopoly?
    a. easy entry and exit.
    b. many firms.
    c. standardized product.
    d. all of the above.
    e. none of the above.

42. Consider the following situation: if Firm A and B both charge a high price, their profits will each be $100,000 per year. If firm A and B both charge a low price, each earns profits of $40,000 per year. If one firm charges a high price and the other charges a low price, the high-price firm earns $30,000, while the low price firm earns $60,000. Assuming there is no cooperation between firms,
    a. the dominant strategy for firm A is to charge a high price.
    b. the dominant strategy for firm A is to charge a low price.
    c. the dominant strategy for firm A is to charge a high price if firm B charges a high price, and a low price if firm B charges a low price.
    d. dominant strategy for firm A is to charge a high price if firm B charges a low price, and a low price if firm B charges a high price.
    e. Firm A has no dominant strategy.

43. Which of the following is a requirement for monopolistic competition?
    a. many buyers and sellers.
    b. easy entry and exit.
    c. differentiated product.
    d. all of the above.
    e. none of the above.

44. Which of the following characteristics does monopolistic competition share with monopoly?
    a. Long run profits are possible.
    b. The demand curve facing the firm slopes downward.
    c. Price and marginal revenue are the same.
    d. All of the above.
    e. None of the above.

45. In long run equilibrium, a monopolistic competitor
    a. can*not* produce where MR and MC intersect.
    b. can*not* produce at the minimum point of its LRATC curve.
    c. will never advertise.
    d. will earn positive economic profit.
    e. will earn negative accounting profit.

46. A firm's marginal revenue product tells us the increase in its
    a. revenue when it produces one more unit of output.
    b. output when it hires one more worker.
    c. revenue when it hires one more worker.
    d. price when it produces one less unit of output.
    e. profit when it hires one more worker.

47. Suppose a machine is *complementary* with unskilled labor in a market. Then when the price of the machine falls, we ordinarily expect
    a. the market demand curve for unskilled labor to shift rightward.
    b. the market demand curve for unskilled labor to shift leftward.
    c. the market supply curve for unskilled labor to shift rightward.
    d. the market supply curve for unskilled labor to shift leftward.
    e. the market supply curve for *skilled* labor will to shift rightward.

48. In general, the long-run labor supply curve in a labor market
    a. slopes upward, and is steeper than the short run labor supply curve.
    b. slopes upward, and is flatter than the short run labor supply curve.
    c. slopes downward, and is steeper than the short-run labor supply curve.
    d. slopes downward, and is the same steepness as the short-run labor supply curve.
    e. slopes downward, and is flatter than the short-run labor supply curve.

49. In the market for college educated labor, wages have risen in spite of the increase in the number of college educated workers because
    a. many college students are foreign, and often emigrate back to their home countries.
    b. the number of workers *without* a college education has also risen.
    c. the number of workers *without* a college education has fallen.
    d. the demand curve for college educated workers has shifted rightward even further than the supply curve.
    e. the demand curve for college educated workers is completely inelastic with respect to the wage rate.

50. The type of prejudice most likely to result in lower wages to the victimized group is prejudice
    a. against people of a certain age.
    b. against people from a certain country.
    c. among those who are educated.
    d. among potential employers.
    e. among fellow employees.

51. If everyone in a society earned the same income, the Lorenz curve for that society would be
    a. completely horizontal.
    b. completely vertical.
    c. a line that is first completely horizontal, and then completely vertical.
    d. an upward sloping diagonal line with slope equal to one.
    e. a smooth curve shaped like half of a parabola.

52. If the interest rate is 7 percent, then the present value of $100 to be received two years from today is
    a. $100.
    b. $93.45.
    c. $87.34.
    d. $86.00.
    e. $81.63.

53. Which of the following bonds would have the highest value for any positive interest rate?
    a. A bond that pays $100 each year, starting one year from today, for three years.
    b. A bond that pays $50 one year from today, $100 2 years from today, and $150 three years from today.
    c. A bond that pays $150 one year from today, $100 2 years from today, and $50 three years from today.
    d. A bond that pays $150 one year from today, $50 2 years from today, and $100 three years from today.
    e. All of these bonds would have the same value at any positive interest rate.

54. Which of the following is an example of *specific human capital* for college professors?
    a. Their knowledge of his subject area.
    b. Their ability to write.
    c. Their ability to express themselves clearly.
    d. Their understanding of how the bureaucracy works in the institutions in which they are teaching.
    e. All of the above.

55. If a company will earn profits per share of $100 per year forever, and the interest rate is 10 percent, then that share of stock should be worth
    a. $10.
    b. $100.
    c. $1,000.
    d. $10,000.
    e. an infinite amount.

56. According to efficient markets theory,
    a. only those with special natural talents can predict stock prices.
    b. only those with years of experience in the stock market can predict stock prices.
    c. fundamental analysts should be able to predict stock prices significantly better than technical analysts.
    d. technical analysts should be able to predict stock prices significantly better than fundamental analysts.
    e. no one can predict stock prices better than anyone else.

57. Which of the following is an example of a Pareto improvement?
    a. Someone who needs money more than you do steals your wallet.
    b. While stuck in a very small town, you end up buying gas at the towns only gas station—at a price of $10 per gallon.
    c. You call the police to quiet down the loud party next door, and they arrive promptly and are successful in reducing the noise.
    d. All of the above.
    e. None of the above.

58. Which of the following would increase the market consumer surplus from a good traded in a perfectly competitive market?
    a. A decrease in the price of an input used to produce the good.
    b. An increase in the price of an alternate good.
    c. A decrease in population.
    d. An increase in the price of a complement.
    e. None of the above.

59. Which of the following is likely to be economically inefficient?
    a. A monopoly producing in a market in which there are no externalities.
    b. A perfectly competitive market with a positive externality.
    c. A good is characterized by nonrivalry, but the government leaves its production to the private sector.
    d. All of the above.
    e. None of the above.

60. The Averch-Johnson effect occurs when
    a. a regulated monopoly does not minimize the cost of producing a given level of output.
    b. a perfectly competitive firm is forced to take the market price as given.
    c. a monopolistic competitor tries to price discriminate.
    d. the players in an oligopoly game have no dominant strategy.
    e. a negative externality causes a market failure.

61. One solution to a positive externality would be
    a. regulation.
    b. a subsidy.
    c. a tax.
    d. a law preventing the externality.
    e. a price ceiling.

62. Country A can produce guitars using 100 hours of labor, and bicycles using 25 hours of labor. In country B, it takes 200 hours to produce a guitar, and 40 hours to produce a bicycle. Which of the following statements is true?
    a. Country A has an absolute advantage in producing guitars.
    b. Country A has an absolute advantage in producing bicycles.
    c. Country A has a comparative advantage in producing guitars.
    d. All of the above.
    e. None of the above.

63. If the United States imposes a tariff on a good imported from Japan, it will likely
    a. increase the price of the good paid by Japanese consumers.
    b. decrease the price of the good paid by American consumers.
    c. increase the price of the good charged by American producers.
    d. all of the above.
    e. none of the above.

64. If Mexico—a relatively low-productivity country—has completely free trade with the U.S.—a relatively high-productivity country—then Mexico will
    a. likely be harmed, because it won't have a comparative advantage in most goods.
    b. likely be harmed, because it won't have an absolute advantage in most goods.
    c. likely be helped, because it *must* have an absolute advantage in some things.
    d. likely be helped, because it *must* have a comparative advantage in some things.
    e. be helped or hurt, depending on whether Americans want to buy the goods in which it has an absolute advantage.

65. Private firms *could* produce and sell a good, but would *not* produce or sell the *efficient* quantity of the good, if it is characterized by
   a. complete nonrivalry and complete excludability
   b. complete nonrivalry and complete nonexcludability.
   c. complete rivalry and complete excludability.
   d. complete rivalry and complete nonexcludability.
   e. complete inscrutability.

ANSWERS TO QUESTIONS

■ ANSWERS FOR CHAPTER 1

Summarize the Chapter

Economics is the study of choice under conditions of **scarcity**. As individuals, we face a scarcity of **time** and spending power. Given more of either, we could each have more of the goods and services that we desire. As a society, our resources—land and natural resources, labor, **capital**, and entrepreneurship—are insufficient to produce all the goods and services we might desire. In other words, society faces a scarcity of resources. A **model** is an abstract representation of reality, and should be as simple as possible to accomplish its purpose. Economic models contain two types of assumptions: simplifying assumptions and **critical** assumptions.

Mathematical Appendix:

A graph between two variables X and Y is only a picture of their relationship when all other variables affecting Y are **held constant**. Suppose Y is the dependent variable, which is measured on one of the axes in a graph. If the independent variable measured on the other axis changes, we **move along** the line. But if *any other* independent variable changes, the **(entire) line shifts**. To solve for X in any equation, rearrange the equation, following the rules of algebra, so that X appears on one side of the **equals sign** and everything else in the equation appears on the other side.

Learn the Lingo

1. economics
2. scarcity
3. resources
4. labor
5. capital
6. physical capital
7. human capital
8. capital stock
9. natural resources
10. entrepreneurship
11. input
12. microeconomics
13. macroeconomics
14. positive economics
15. normative economics
16. model
17. simplifying assumption
18. critical assumption

Build Your Skills

1. a.

US Population (millions)

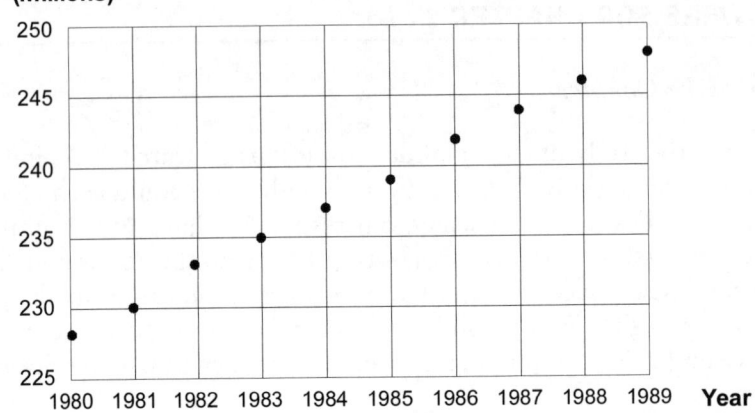

[Scatter plot showing US population from 1980 to 1989, with points rising from about 228 in 1980 to about 248 in 1989.]

   b. (iv)

   c.

US Population (millions)

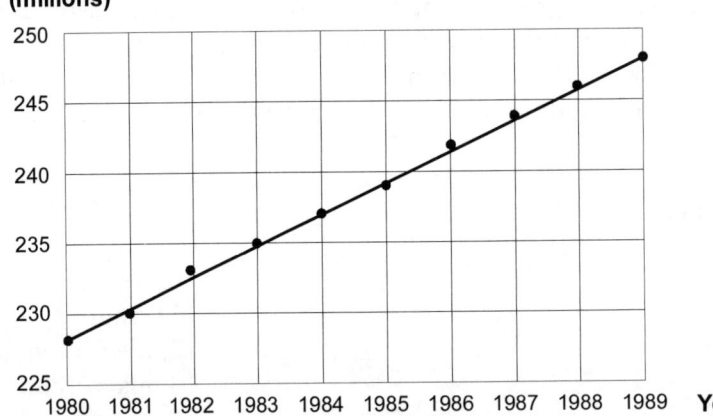

[Same scatter plot with a best-fit line drawn through the points.]

   d. Population increased by approximately 2.24 million per year. Your answer can differ from this by a bit because it will depend on how you drew your line with the ruler. To get your answer, though, calculate how much population increased along the vertical axis (the rise) as you move from any one year to the next year along the horizontal axis (the run) on the line you drew.

2. a. 30 to 60; 90 to 120; positive
   b. 0 to 30; 60 to 90; negative
   c. Maximum value of Y = 1,000 is achieved at X = 60; Minimum value of Y = 200 is achieved at X = 90.

Answers to Chapter 1 Questions

3.

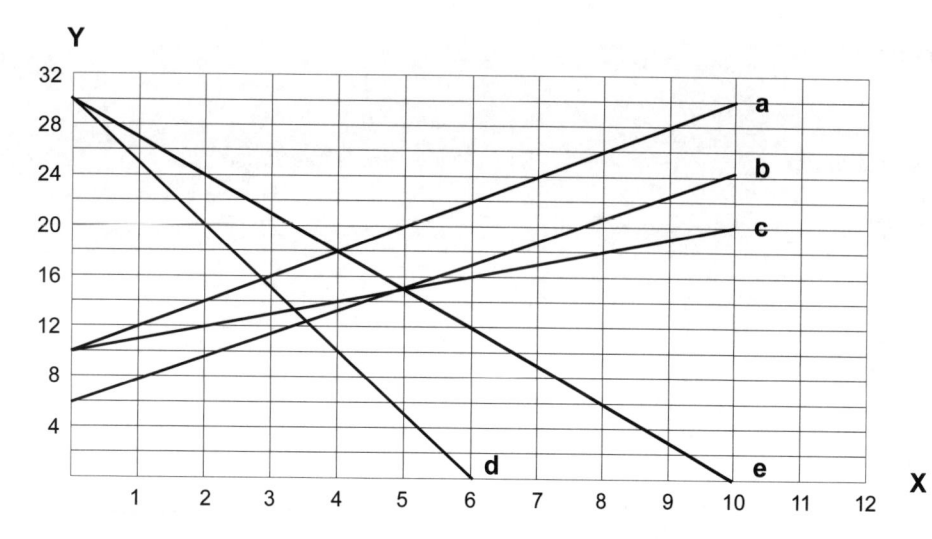

a. 10; 2; increases; constant
b. 5; 2; increases; constant
c. 10; 1; increases; constant
d. 30; −5; decreases; constant
e. 30; −3; decreases; constant

4.

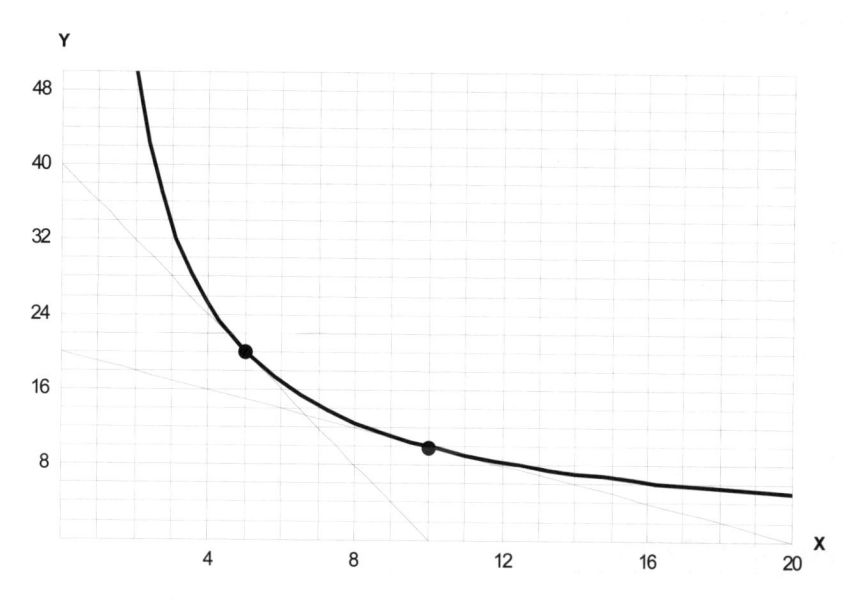

a. (See graph;) -4.
   (See graph;) -1.

5. a. independent; negative; positive.
   b. a leftward movement along the curve through A;
      an upward shift in the curve through A;
      a downward shift in the curve through A.
   c. an upward shift in the curve through B;
      a rightward movement along the curve through B;
      a leftward movement along the curve through B.

Test Yourself

Multiple Choice
1. c
2. e
3. d
4. b
5. c
6. b

True/False
1. F
2. F
3. F
4. T
5. F

Short Answer

1. a. microeconomic, positive
   b. macroeconomic, positive
   c. microeconomic, positive
   d. microeconomic, normative
   e. macroeconomic, positive
   f. microeconomic, normative
   g. macroeconomic, normative

2. a. labor
   b. capital
   c. capital
   d. natural resources
   e. labor
   f. capital
   g. labor
   h. capital
   i. entrepreneurship

■ ANSWERS FOR CHAPTER 2

Summarize the Chapter

The opportunity cost of any choice is what we must forego when we make that choice. It is the best among the available **alternatives** to that choice. The opportunity cost of a choice includes both explicit costs and **implicit** costs. The **explicit** (or direct money) cost of a choice may only be a part—and sometimes a small part—of the opportunity cost of a choice.

Virtually all production carries an opportunity cost: To produce more of one thing, society must shift **resources** away from producing something else. According to the law of **increasing opportunity cost**, the more of something we produce, the greater the opportunity cost of producing even more of it.

Answers to Chapter 2 Questions

A firm, an industry, or an entire economy is productively **inefficient** if it could produce more of at least one good without pulling resources from the production of any other good. A technological change or an increase in the **capital** stock, even when the direct impact is to increase production of just one type of good, allows us to choose greater production of all types of goods. In order to produce more goods and services in the future, we must shift **resources** toward R&D and capital production, and away from the production of things we'd enjoy right now.

Specialization and exchange enable us to enjoy greater production, and higher living standards, than would otherwise be possible. As a result, all economies exhibit high degrees of **specialization** and exchange. A person has a **comparative advantage** in producing some good if he or she can produce it with a smaller opportunity cost than some other person can. Total production of every good or service will be greatest when individuals specialize according to their **comparative advantage**. This is another reason why specialization and exchange lead to higher living standards than does self-sufficiency.

When resources are allocated by the **market,** and people must pay for their purchases, they are forced to consider the **opportunity cost** to society of their individual actions. In this way, markets are able to create a sensible allocation of resources. An **economic system** is composed of two features: a mechanism for allocating resources and a mode of resource ownership.

Learn the Lingo

1. opportunity cost
2. explicit cost
3. implicit cost
4. production possibilities frontier
5. law of increasing opportunity cost
6. productive inefficiency
7. specialization
8. exchange
9. absolute advantage
10. comparative advantage
11. resource allocation
12. traditional economy
13. command economy; centrally planned economy
14. market economy
15. market
16. price
17. communism
18. socialism
19. capitalism
20. economic system

Build Your Skills

1. a.

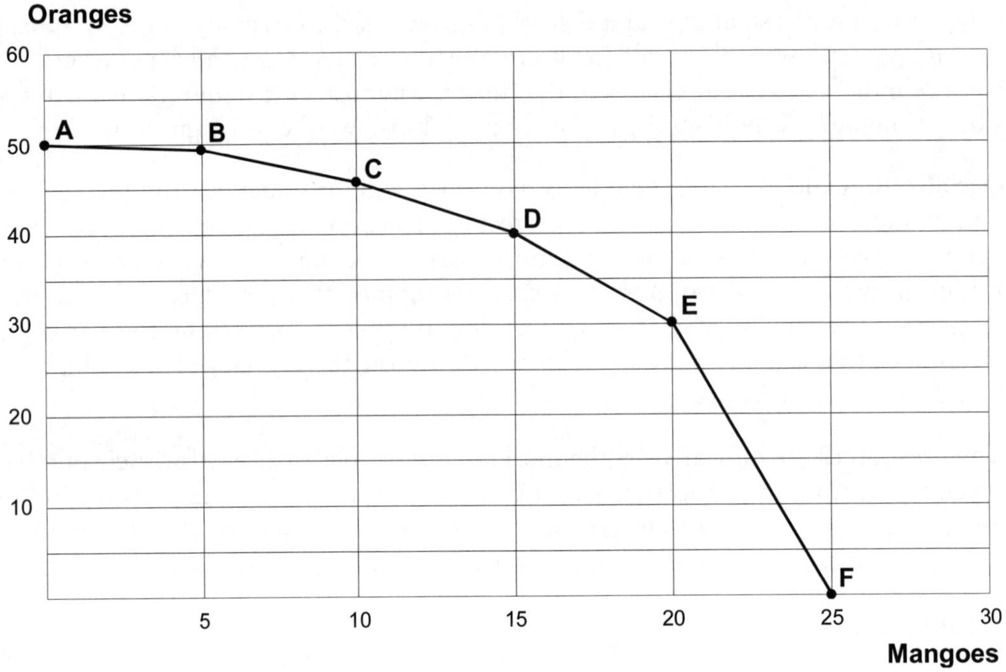

b. 1; 5; 5; 1
5; 3; 3
5; 6; 5; 10; 5; 30
increasing

c. 5; 30; 30; 5
10; 5; 5
6; 5; 3; 5
increasing

2. a. are not; zero; zero; no
b. cannot; improve; acquire more

3. Constant; 50; Y; 50; Y; 50; Y; constant

4. Increases; less than; greater than

5. a. sweaters; fish
b. 2; 1/3; fish; sweaters

Answers to Chapter 2 Questions

Test Yourself

Multiple Choice
1. c
2. d
3. a
4. b
5. b
6. e
7. d
8. c
9. a
10. e

True/False
1. F
2. F
3. T
4. T
5. F
6. T
7. F
8. F

Short Answer

1. (any order): tradition; command (or central planning); the market

2. (any order): communism; socialism; capitalism

■ ANSWERS FOR CHAPTER 3

Summarize the Chapter

A market is a group of **buyers** and **sellers** with the potential to trade with each other. In economics, markets can be defined broadly or narrowly, depending on **our purpose**. For the most part, in markets for consumer goods, we'll view business firms as the only **sellers**, and households as the only **buyers**.

In **imperfectly competitive** markets, individual buyers or sellers can influence the price of the product. In **perfectly competitive** markets (or just **competitive** markets), each buyer and seller takes the market price as a given. The supply and demand model is designed to explain how prices are determined in **perfectly competitive** markets.

A household's **quantity demanded** of a good is the specific amount the household would choose to buy over some time period, given (1) a particular price that must be paid for the good; (2) all other **constraints** on the household. Market **quantity supplied** (often just **quantity supplied**) is the specific amount of a good that all buyers in the market would choose to buy over some time period, given (1) a particular price they must pay for the good; (2) all other **constraints** on households.

The law of demand states that when the price of a good rises and everything else remains the same, the quantity of the good demanded will **fall**. The market demand curve (or just demand curve) shows the relationship between the **price** of a good and the quantity demanded, holding constant all other variables that influence demand. Each point on the curve shows the total quantity that buyers would choose to buy at a specific **price**. The law of demand tells us that demand curves virtually always slope **downward**.

A change in the price of a good causes a **movement along** the demand curve. A change in any variable that affects demand—except for the good's price— causes the demand curve to **shift**. A rise in either income or wealth will increase the demand for a **normal** good, and decrease the demand for an **inferior** good. A rise in the price of a substitute will **increase** the demand for a good, shifting the demand curve to the **right**. A rise in the price of a complement will **decrease** the demand for a good, shifting the demand curve to the **left**. In many markets, an expectation that price will **rise** in the future shifts the current demand curve rightward, while an expectation that price will **fall** shifts the current demand curve leftward.

A firm's **quantity supplied** of a good is the specific amount its managers would choose to sell over some time period, given (1) a particular price for the good; (2) all other **constraints** on the firm. Market **quantity supplied** (often just **quantity supplied**) is the specific amount of a good that all sellers in the market would choose to sell over some time period, given (1) a particular price for the good; (2) all other **constraints** on firms. The law of supply states that when the price of a good rises, and everything else remains the same, the quantity of the good supplied will **rise**. The market supply curve (or just supply curve) shows the relationship between the **price** of a good and the quantity supplied, holding constant the values of all other variables that affect supply. Each point on the curve shows the quantity that sellers would choose to sell at a specific **price**. The law of supply tells us that supply curves slope **upward**.

A change in the price of a good causes a **movement along** the supply curve. A change in any variable that affects supply—except for the good's price—causes the supply curve to **shift**. A fall in the price of an input causes a (an) **increase** in supply, shifting the supply curve to the **right**. A rise in the price of an input causes a (an) **decrease** in supply, shifting the supply curve to the **left**. When the price of an alternate good **rises**, the supply curve for the good in question shifts leftward. When the price of an alternate **falls**, the supply curve for the good in question shifts rightward. Cost-saving technological advances **increase** the supply of a good, shifting the supply curve to the **right**. An increase in the number of sellers—with no other change—shifts the supply curve **rightward**, while a decrease in the number of sellers shifts it **leftward**. In many markets, an expectation of a future price hike shifts the current supply curve **leftward**. Similarly, an expectation of a future price drop shifts the current supply curve **rightward**. Favorable weather increases crop yields, and causes a **rightward** shift of the supply curve for that crop. Unfavorable weather destroys crops and shrinks yields, and shifts the supply curve **leftward**.

The **equilibrium** price and **equilibrium** quantity are values for price and quantity in the market that, once achieved, will remain constant—unless and until the supply curve or the demand curve **shifts**. To find the **equilibrium** price and quantity in a competitive market, draw the supply and demand curves. The **equilibrium** price and **equilibrium** quantity can then be found on the vertical and horizontal axes, respectively, at the point where the supply and demand curves cross.

A rightward shift in the **demand** curve causes a rightward movement along the supply curve. Equilibrium price and equilibrium quantity both **rise**. Any change that shifts the supply curve leftward in a market will **increase** the equilibrium price and **decrease** the equilibrium quantity in that market. When just one curve shifts, and we know the direction of the shift, we can determine the direction that both equilibrium price and quantity will move. When both curves shift, and we know the directions of the shifts, we can determine the direction for either **price** or **quantity**—but not both. The direction of the other will depend on which curve shifts by more.

The next three statements concern the three step process that economists use again and again to answer questions about the economy. Step # 1 is to "**Characterize** the Market"—to decide which market or markets best suit the problem being analyzed, and identify the decision makers (buyers and sellers) who interact there. Step # 2 is to "Find the **Equilibrium**"—to describe the conditions necessary for **equilibrium** in the market, and a method for determining that **equilibrium.** Step # 3 is to determine "What Happens When **Things Change**"—to explore how events or government policies change the market **equilibrium.**

Learn the Lingo

1. aggregation
2. imperfectly competitive market
3. perfectly competitive market
4. household's quantity demanded
5. market quantity demanded
6. law of demand
7. demand schedule
8. (market) demand curve
9. income
10. normal good
11. change in quantity demanded
12. change in demand
13. inferior good
14. wealth
15. substitute
16. complement
17. firm's quantity supplied
18. market quantity supplied
19. law of supply
20. supply schedule
21. (market) supply curve
22. change in quantity supplied
23. change in supply
24. alternate good
25. equilibrium price
26. equilibrium quantity
27. excess demand
28. excess supply

Build Your Skills

1. a.

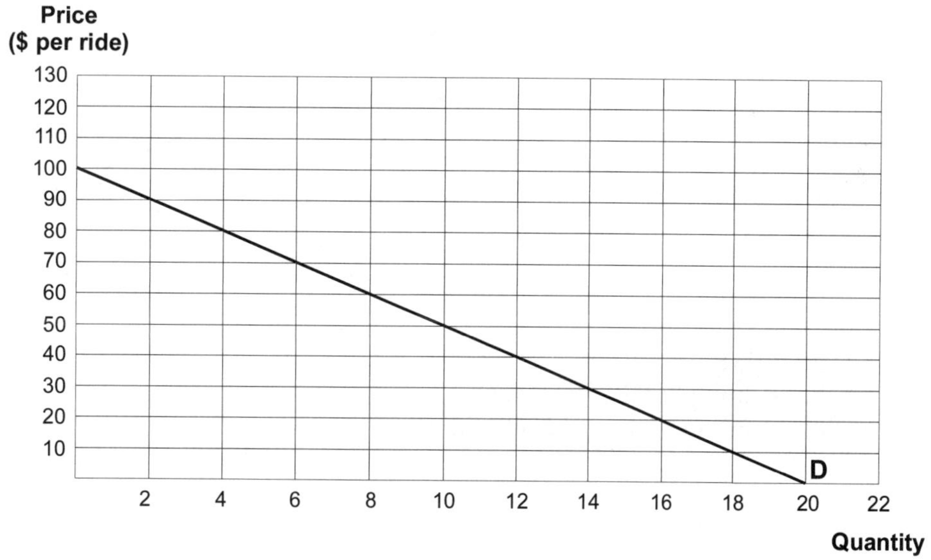

b. 10; fall; 2; rise; 18

2. a.

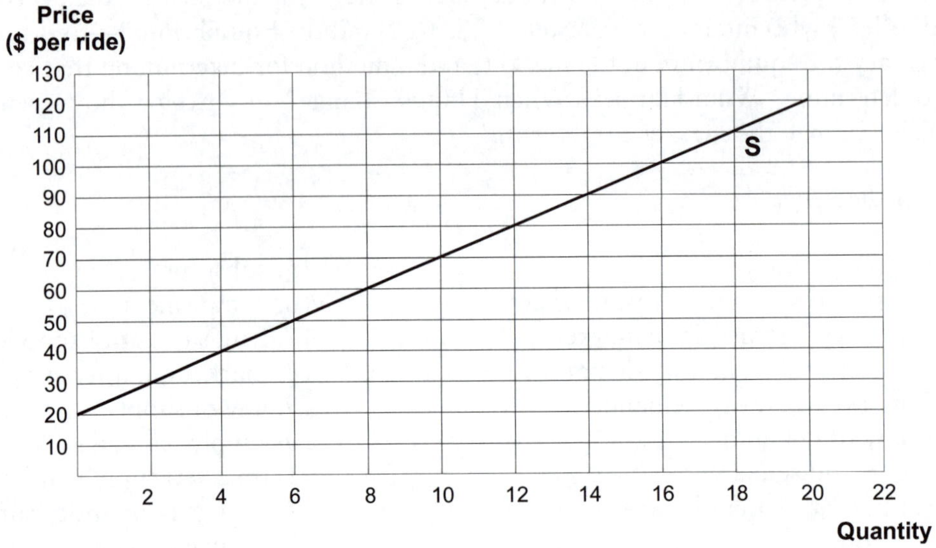

b. 6; rise; 14; fall; 2

3.

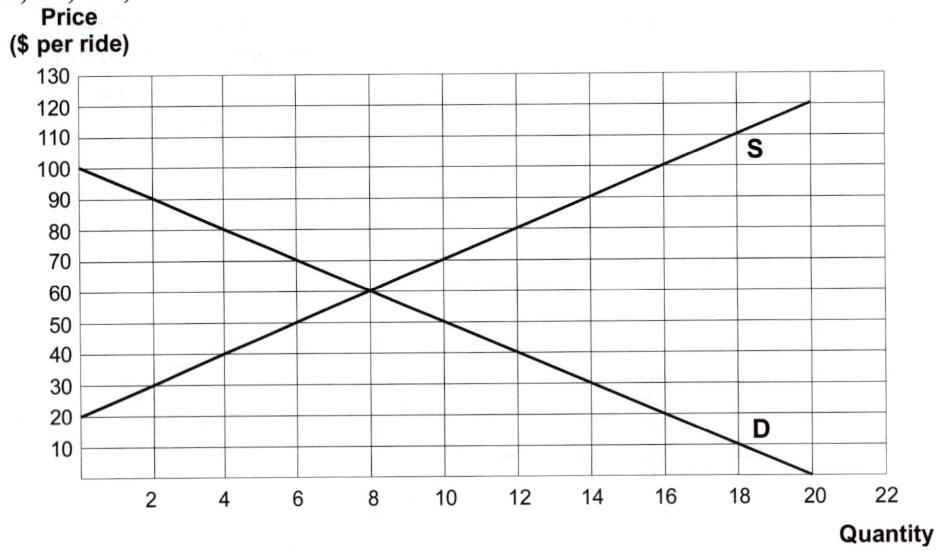

a. 60; 8
b. supply; 8; fall; sellers; sell
c. demand; 8; rise; buyers; buy

4. a. $120
b. increase; rightward

c.

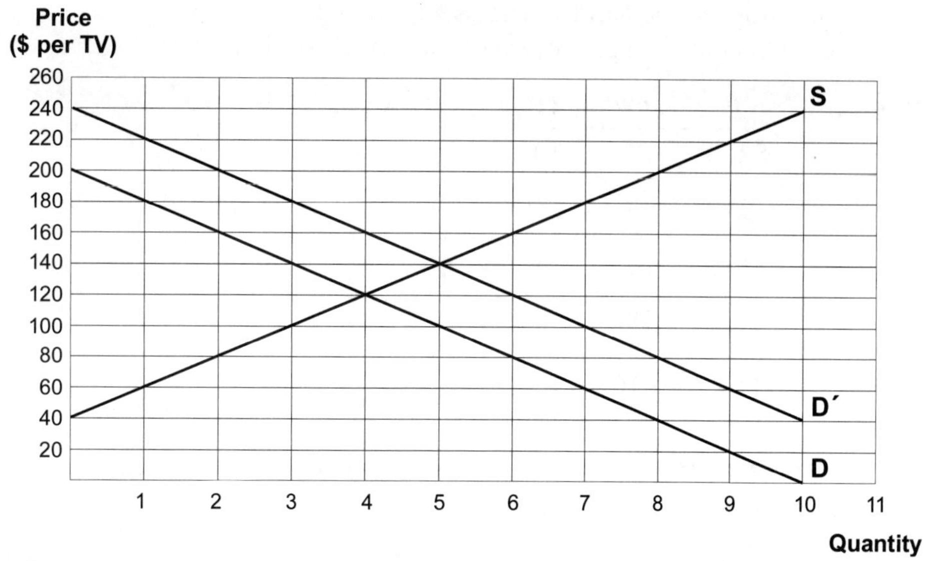

d. Equilibrium price is now $140, where D′ intersects S

e. decrease; leftward

f.

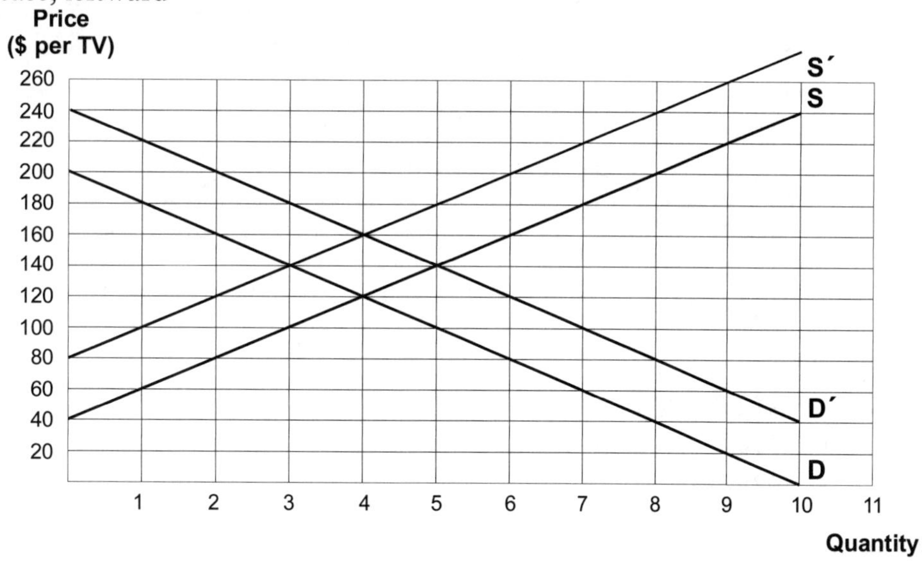

g. Equilibrium price is now $160, where S′ intersects D′

5. a.

P	Q^D	Q^S
$450	20	80
400	30	70
350	40	60
300	50	50
250	60	40
200	70	30
150	80	20

b. supplied; demanded; excess supply; 40; fall; $300
c. demanded; supplied; excess demand; 60; rise; $300

6.

P	Q^D	Q^S
$270	2	20
210	6	15
90	14	5
30	18	0

7. P_e = $150; Yes; 10; Yes

8. a. $1,600; 300
   b. 350; 100; excess demand; 250
   c. 250; 500; excess supply; 250

Test Yourself

Multiple Choice
1. e
2. b
3. d
4. a
5. d
6. b
7. b
8. c
9. b
10. c

True/False
1. F
2. F
3. T
4. F
5. T
6. F
7. F
8. T

Short Answer:

1. Answer could include any four of the following: a decrease in income; a decrease in wealth; a decrease in the price of a substitute; an increase in the price of a complement; a decrease in population; an expected decrease in price; a shift in tastes away from the good.

2. Answer could include any four of the following: an increase in the price of an input; an increase in the price of an alternate good; a decrease in the number of firms; an expected increase in price; a change to unfavorable weather for the good; a natural or man-made disaster affecting production of the good; any of a number of government policies (e.g. a tax on the good, increased regulations on producers)

■ ANSWERS FOR CHAPTER 4

Summarize the Chapter

When quantity supplied and quantity demanded differ, the short side of the market—whichever of the two quantities is **smaller**—will prevail. A price **ceiling** creates a shortage and increases the time and trouble required to buy the good. While the price decreases, the opportunity cost may **increase**. A price **floor** creates a surplus of a good. In order to maintain the price **floor**, the government must prevent the surplus from driving down the market price. In practice, the government often accomplishes this goal by purchasing the surplus itself.

The price **elasticity** of demand (E_D) for a good is the percentage change in quantity demanded divided by the percentage change in price:

$$E_D = (\% \text{ Change in Quantity Demanded}) / (\% \text{ Change in Price}).$$

A price **elasticity** of demand tells us the percentage change in quantity demanded caused by a 1 percent rise in price as we move along a **demand** curve from one point to another. When calculating elasticity, the base value for percentage changes in price or **quantity** is always midway between the initial value and the new value.

Elasticity of demand varies along a straight-line demand curve. More specifically, demand becomes **more** elastic as we move upward and leftward. Where demand is **inelastic**, total revenue moves in the same direction as price. Where demand is **elastic**, total revenue moves in the opposite direction from price. Finally, where demand is **unitary elastic**, total revenue remains the same as price changes. At any point on a demand curve, sellers' total revenue (buyers' total expenditure) is the area of a rectangle with width equal to quantity demanded and height equal to **price**.

The more narrowly we define a good, the easier it is to find substitutes, and the **more** elastic is the demand for the good. The more broadly we define a good, the harder it is to find substitutes and the **less** elastic is the demand for the good. In general, the more "necessary" we regard an item, the harder it is to find substitutes, and the **less** elastic is demand for the good.

It is usually easier to find substitutes for an item in the **long** run than in the **short** run. Therefore, demand tends to be more elastic in the **long** run than in the **short** run.

The more of their total budgets that households spend on an item, the **more** elastic is demand for that item.

The income elasticity of demand (E_Y) is the percentage change in **quantity demanded** divided by the percentage change in income, with all other influences on demand—including the price of the good—remaining constant:

$$E_Y = (\% \text{ Change in Quantity Demanded}) / (\% \text{ Change in Income}).$$

A **cross-price** elasticity of demand tells us the percentage change in quantity demanded of a good for each 1-percent increase in the price of some other good, while all other influences on demand remain unchanged. The **price elasticity** of supply (E_S) is the percentage change in the quantity of a good supplied that is caused by a 1 percent change in the price of the good, with all other influences on supply held constant:

$$E_S = (\% \text{ Change in Quantity Supplied}) / (\% \text{ Change in Price})$$

An **excise** tax shifts the market supply curve upward by the amount of the tax. For each quantity supplied, the new, higher curve tells us firms' gross price, and the original, lower curve tells us the net price. For a given supply curve, the more elastic is demand, the more of an excise tax is paid by **sellers**. The more inelastic is demand, the more of the tax is paid by **buyers**. For a given demand curve, the more elastic is supply, the more of an excise tax is paid by **buyers**. The more inelastic is supply, the more of the tax is paid by **sellers**.

Learn the Lingo

1. price ceiling
2. short side of the market
3. shortage
4. black market
5. rent controls
6. price floor
7. surplus
8. price elasticity of demand
9. inelastic demand
10. perfectly inelastic demand
11. elastic demand
12. perfectly elastic demand
13. unitary elastic demand
14. short-run elasticity
15. long-run elasticity
16. income elasticity of demand
17. economic necessity
18. economic luxury
19. cross-price elasticity of demand
20. price elasticity of supply
21. excise tax
22. incidence
23. tax shifting

Build Your Skills

1.

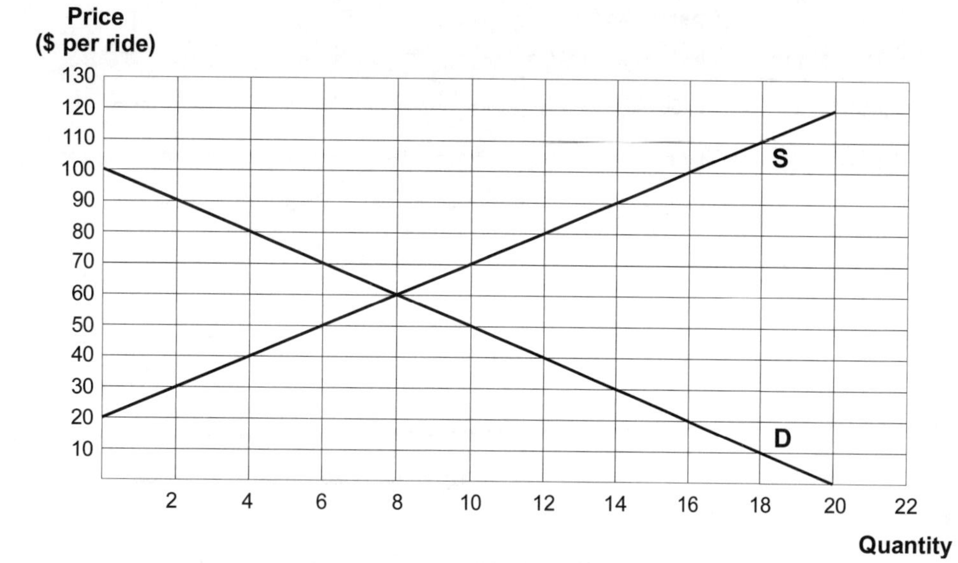

a. 60; 8
b. supply; 8
c. demand; 8
d. $80

2. a. –2/3
b. –3/4
c. –1.852
d. –1/2
e. –7/5

3. Same as (a) and (e) above.

4. a.

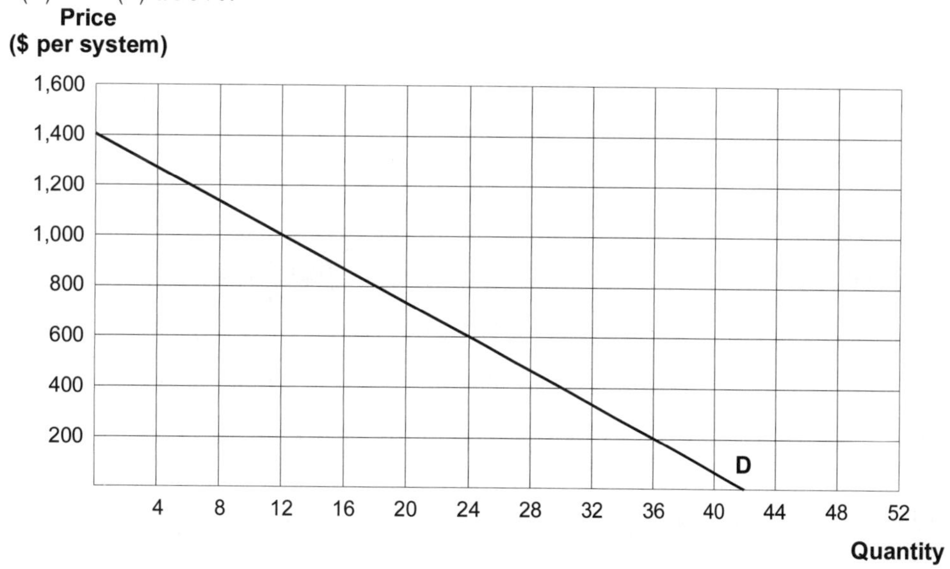

b. 0; 12; –6; elastic; increase
c. –4/3; elastic; increase
d. –2/5; inelastic; decrease

5. a.

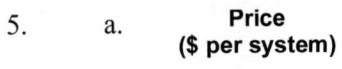

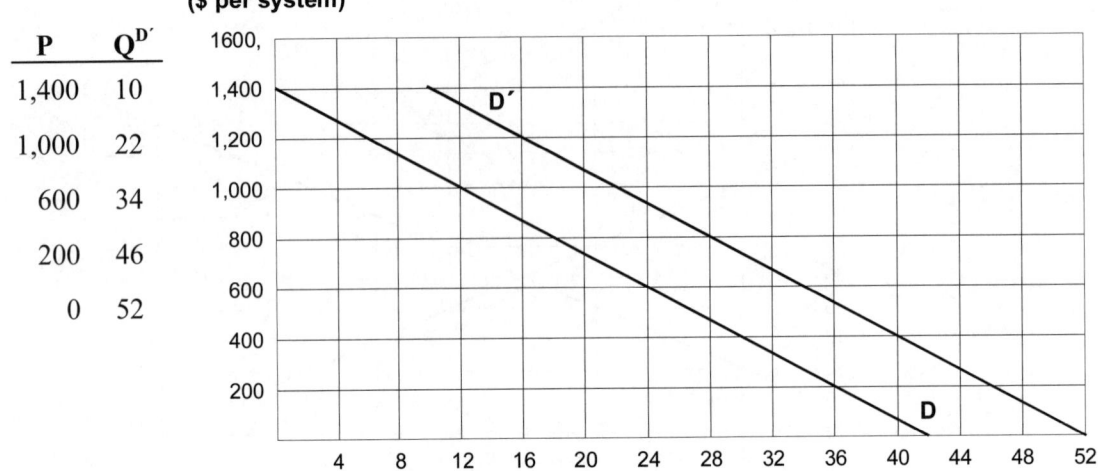

P	Q^{D'}
1,400	10
1,000	22
600	34
200	46
0	52

b. −9/4; decreased; −6/7; decreased; −3/10; decreased; decrease

6. a. −2; steeper; −5; 20; 40
    b. 10; 30; −1
    c. 16; 24; −2/5
    d. inelastic

7. a. 1/2
    b. 19/7
    c. 3/2

8. a. -1/2
    b. 0.847

9. a. 1/2
    b. 3/2
    c. 3/4
    d. 0

Test Yourself

Multiple Choice
1. b
2. d
3. c
4. e
5. b
6. e
7. d
8. e
9. d
10. b
11. a
12. e

True/False
1. T
2. F
3. T
4. T
5. T
6. F
7. T
8. F
9. F
10. F

Short Answer:

Characteristic	Type of Elasticity	Value
A rise in price increases total revenue of sellers of the good	Price elasticity of demand	Between 0 and -1
The good is an economic luxury	income elasticity of demand	>1
The good is an economic necessity	income elasticity of demand	<1
The good is a substitute for another good	cross-price elasticity of demand	>0
The good is normal	income elasticity of demand	>0
The good is inferior	income elasticity of demand	<0
The supply curve for the good is vertical	price elasticity of supply	0
The demand curve for the good is vertical	price elasticity of demand	0
The good obeys the law of demand	price elasticity of demand	>0
Demand for the good is "elastic"	Price elasticity of demand	< -1 (or abs. value > 1)

■ ANSWERS FOR CHAPTER 5

Summarize the Chapter

A consumer's budget constraint identifies which combinations of goods and services the consumer can afford with a limited budget, at given **prices**. The slope of the budget line indicates the spending trade-off between one good and another—the amount of one good that must be sacrificed in order to buy more of another good. If P_y is the price of the good on the vertical axis and P_x is the price of the good on the horizontal axis, then the slope of the budget line is $-P_x/P_y$. An increase in income will shift the budget line upward (and **rightward**). A decrease in income will shift the budget line downward (and **leftward**). These shifts are parallel: Changes in income do not affect the budget line's **slope**.

When the **price** of a good changes, the budget line rotates: Both its slope and one of its intercepts will change. The consumer will always choose a point **on the** budget line, rather than a point **below** it.

The following paragraph applies only to the section, "Consumer Decisions: The Marginal Utility Approach."

Marginal utility is the **change** in utility an individual enjoys from consuming an additional unit of a good. The marginal utility of a thing to anyone **diminishes** (or **decreases**) with every increase in the amount of it he already has. A utility-maximizing consumer (choosing between two goods x and y) will choose the point on the budget line where marginal utility **per dollar** is the same for both goods ($MU_x/P_x = MU_y/P_y$). At that point, there is no further gain from reallocating expenditures in either direction.

A rise in income, with no change in prices, leads to a new quantity demanded for each good. Whether a particular good is **normal** (quantity demanded increases) or **inferior** (quantity demanded decreases) depends on the individual's preferences, as represented by the marginal utilities for each good, at each point along his budget line.

The following paragraph applies only to the appendix, "The Indifference Curve Approach."

An **indifference curve** represents all combinations of two goods that make the consumer equally well off. The marginal rate of substitution of good y for good x ($MRS_{y,x}$) along any segment of an indifference curve is the absolute value of the **slope** along that segment. The MRS tells us the **maximum** amount of y a consumer would willingly trade for one more unit of x. Any point on a **higher** indifference curve is preferred to any point on a **lower** one. The optimal combination of goods for a consumer is the point on the budget line where an indifference curve is **tangent** to the budget line. The optimal combination of two goods x and y is that combination on the budget line for which $MRS_{y,x} = P_x / P_Y$. A rise in income, with no change in prices, leads to a new quantity demanded for each good. Whether a particular good is **normal** (quantity demanded increases) or **inferior** (quantity demanded decreases) depends on the individual's preferences, as represented by his indifference map.

The remaining paragraphs apply to both approaches to consumer decision making.

The **substitution** effect of a price change arises from a change in the relative price of a good, and it always moves quantity demanded in the opposite direction to the price change. When price decreases, the **substitution** effect works to increase quantity demanded; when price increases, the **substitution** effect works to decrease quantity demanded.

The **income** effect of a price change arises from a change in purchasing power over both goods. A drop in price **increases** purchasing power, while a rise in price **decreases** purchasing power. For **normal** goods, the **substitution** and **income** effects work together, causing quantity demanded to move in the opposite direction of the price. **Normal** goods, therefore, must always obey the law of demand.

For inferior goods, the **substitution** and **income** effects of a price change work against each other. The **substitution** effect moves quantity demanded in the opposite direction of the price, while the **income** effect moves it in the same direction as the price. But since the **substitution** effect virtually always dominates, consumption of inferior goods—like **normal** goods—will virtually always obey the law of demand.

The **market** demand curve is found by horizontally summing the individual demand curves of every consumer in the market.

Learn the Lingo

1. budget constraint
2. budget line
3. relative price
4. rational preferences
5. individual demand curve
6. substitution effect
7. income effect
8. behavioral economics
9. utility
10. marginal utility
11. law of diminishing marginal utility
12. indifference curve
13. indifference map
14. marginal rate of substitution ($MRS_{y,x}$)

Answers to Chapter 5 Questions

Build Your Skills

1.

	Videos at $4 each Quantity	Total Expenditure on Videos	Novels at $2 each Quantity	Total Expenditure on Novels
A	0	$0	10	$20
B	1	4	8	16
C	2	8	6	12
D	3	12	4	8
E	4	16	2	4
F	5	20	0	0

2.

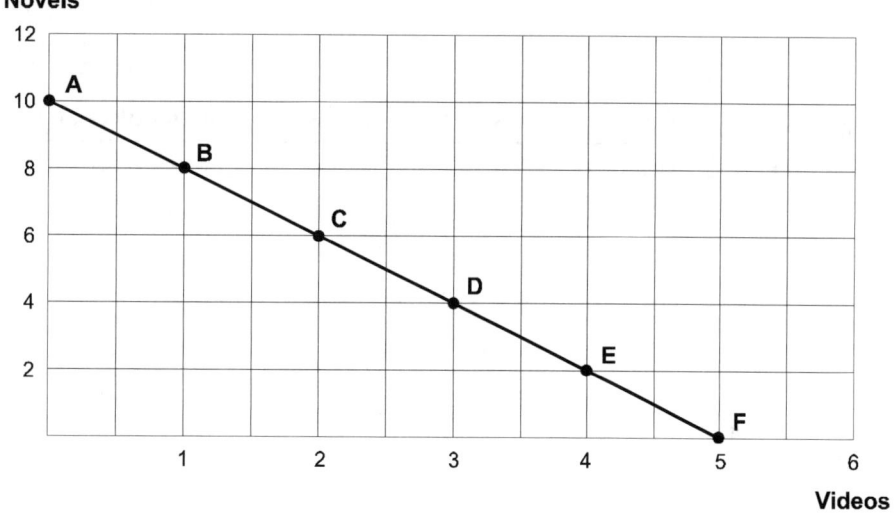

3. a. and b.

Food	Clothing	B
0	400	500
20	350	450
40	300	400
60	250	350
80	200	300
100	150	250
120	100	200
140	50	150
160	0	100

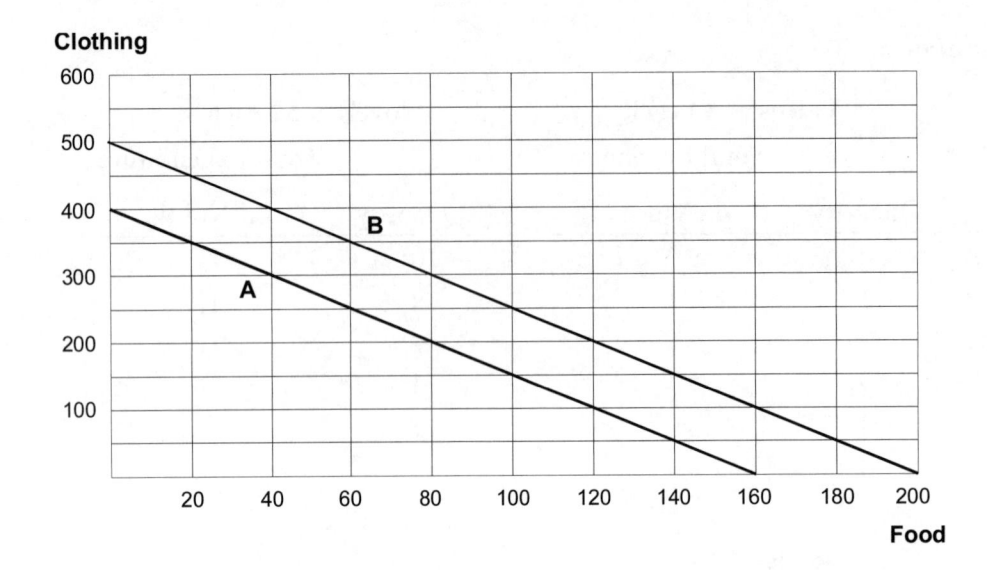

4. a and b.

Rice	Artichokes at $40	Artichokes at $20
400	0	0
320	2	4
240	4	8
160	6	12
80	8	16
0	10	20

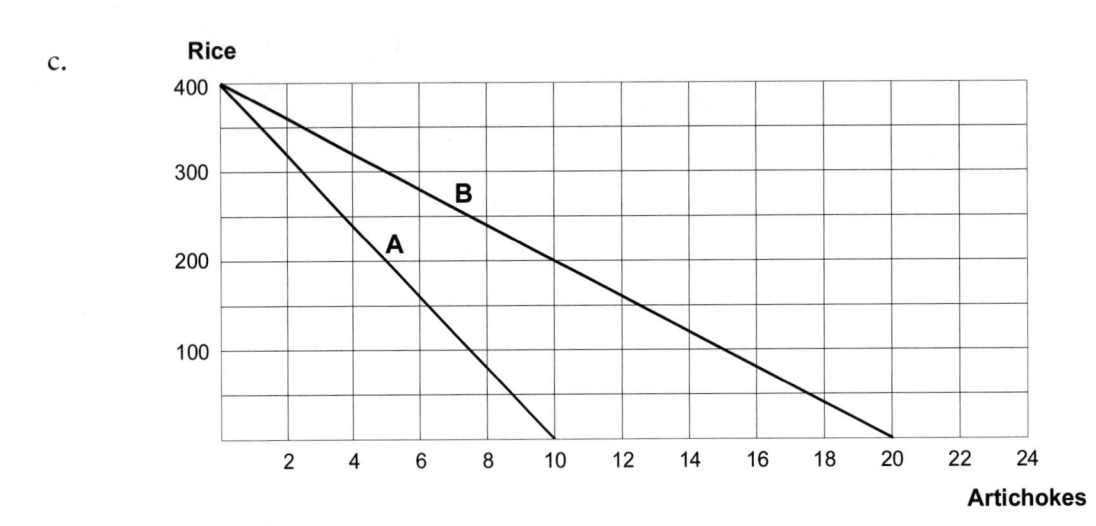

c.

Answers to Chapter 5 Questions

Questions 5 and 6 refer to the section, "Consumer Decisions: The Marginal Utility Approach." If you used the Indifference Curve approach instead, you should have skipped these and gone directly to question 8.

5. Yes, his preferences obey the law of diminishing marginal utility. Note from the table that each successive pair of crumpets gives Marshall ever-decreasing amounts of marginal utility.

Crumpets Consumed	Total Utility	Marginal Utility
0	0	
		31
2	31	
		14
4	45	
		10
6	55	
		8
8	63	
		7
10	70	
		6
12	76	
		5
14	81	
		4
16	85	
		3
18	88	

6. a.

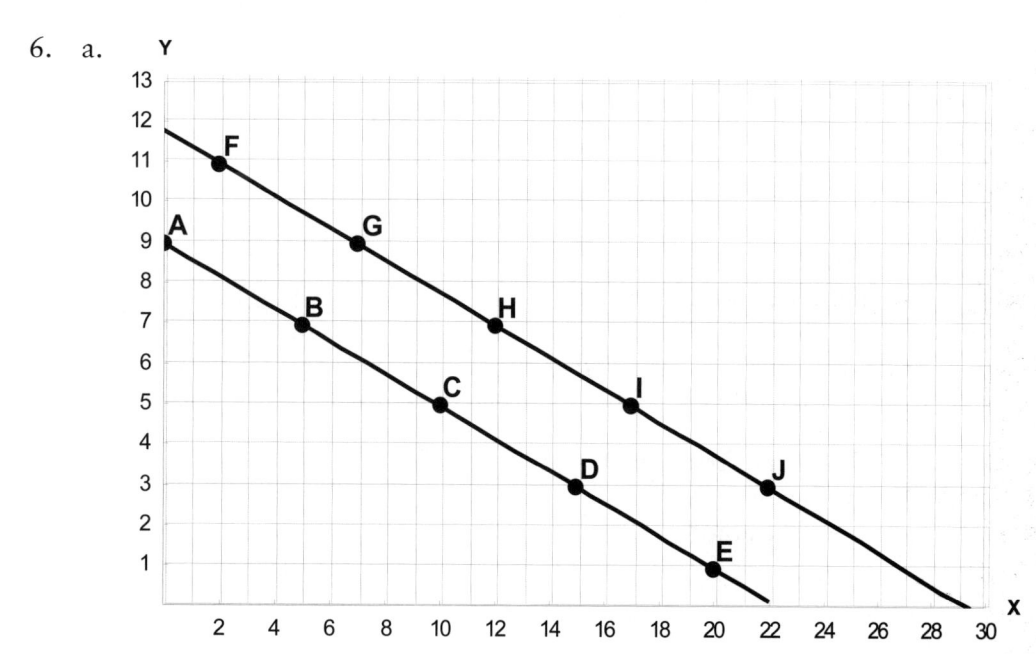

b. (See Table)

Income = $90 per month

Point on Budget Line	Units of X Consumed	Marginal Utility from Last Unit of X	Marginal Utility per Dollar Spent on Last Unit of X	Units of Y Consumed	Marginal Utility From Last Unit of Y	Marginal Utility per Dollar Spent on Last Unit of Y
A	0	100	25	9	110	11
B	5	80	20	7	130	13
C	10	60	15	5	150	15
D	15	40	10	3	170	17
E	20	20	5	1	190	19

c. greater than; units of X; units of Y
d. less than; units of Y; units of X
e. equal to; C; 10; 5
f. (See previous graph).
g. (See Table)

Income = $118 per month

Point on Budget Line	Units of X Consumed	Marginal Utility from Last Unit of X	Marginal Utility per Dollar Spent on Last Unit of X	Units of Y Consumed	Marginal Utility From Last Unit of Y	Marginal Utility per Dollar Spent on Last Unit of Y
F	2	92	23	11	90	9
G	7	72	18	9	110	11
H	12	52	13	7	130	13
I	17	32	8	5	150	15
J	22	12	3	3	170	17

h. equal to; H; 12; 7
i. increase; increase; normal; normal

Questions 7 and 8 refer to the appendix, "The Indifference Curve Approach." If you used the Marginal Utility approach instead, you should have skipped these and gone directly to question 9.

7. a. prefers C to A; prefers A to D; prefers C to D.
   b. absolute value of; Y; X
   c. 4; 1; decline (See graph)

Answers to Chapter 5 Questions

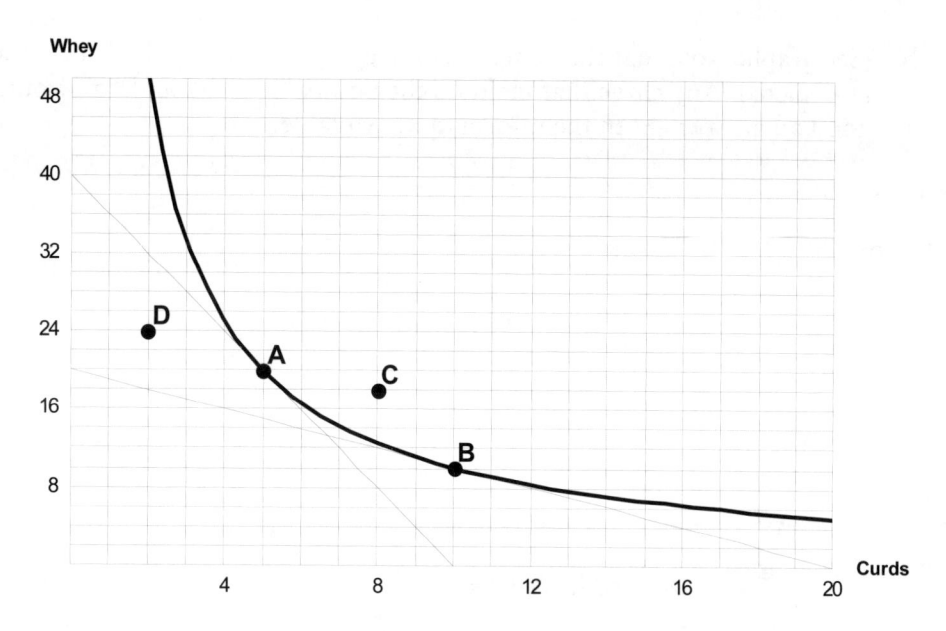

8. a. (See graph)

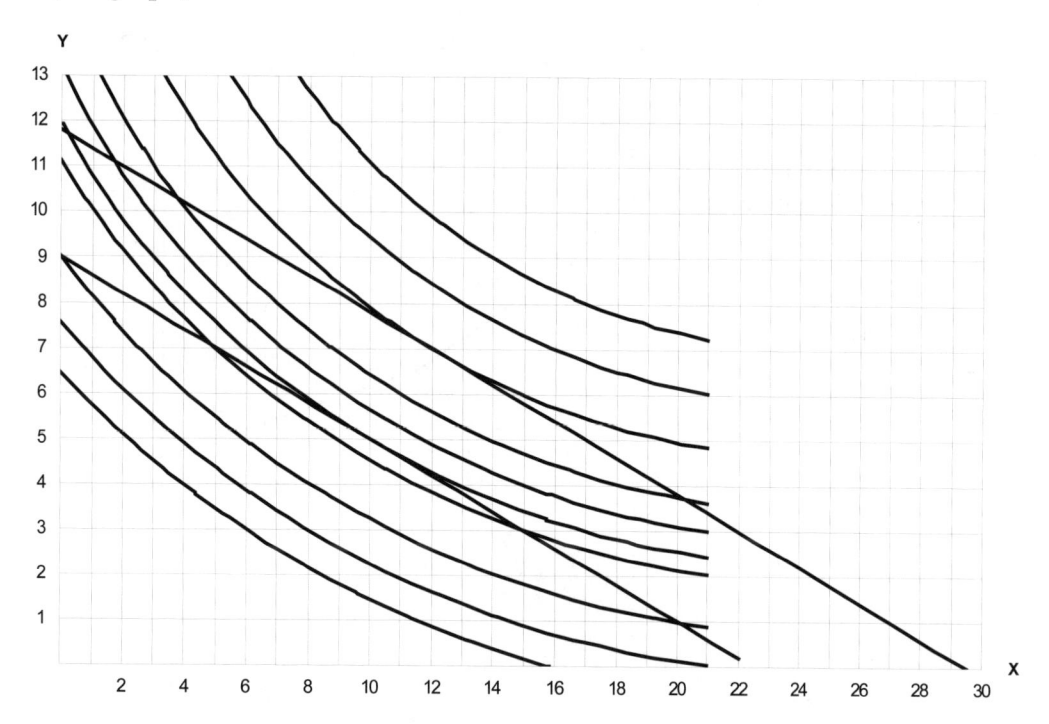

    b. greater than; spend more on X and less on Y
    c. less than; spend less on X and more on Y
    d. 10; 5; equal to; tangent to; 4/10 or 0.4
    e. (See graph)
    f. equal to; tangent to; 12; 7
    g. increase; increase; normal; normal

The remaining questions apply to both approaches to consumer decision making.

9. a. $7; $2; $1

b. (See graph. Note that the demand curve is not necessarily made of linear segments, as depicted. Any curve that includes the points "a", "b" and "c" would be just as good an answer, given the information available.)

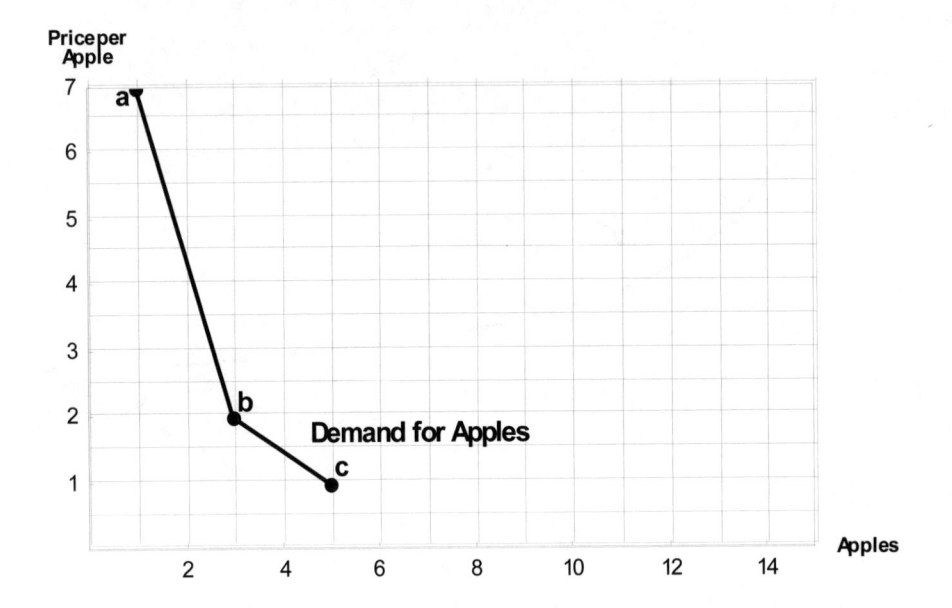

10.

Price	Quantity Demanded
$10	0
9	1/2
8	1
7	2
6	3
5	4
4	6
3	8
2	10
1	12
0	14

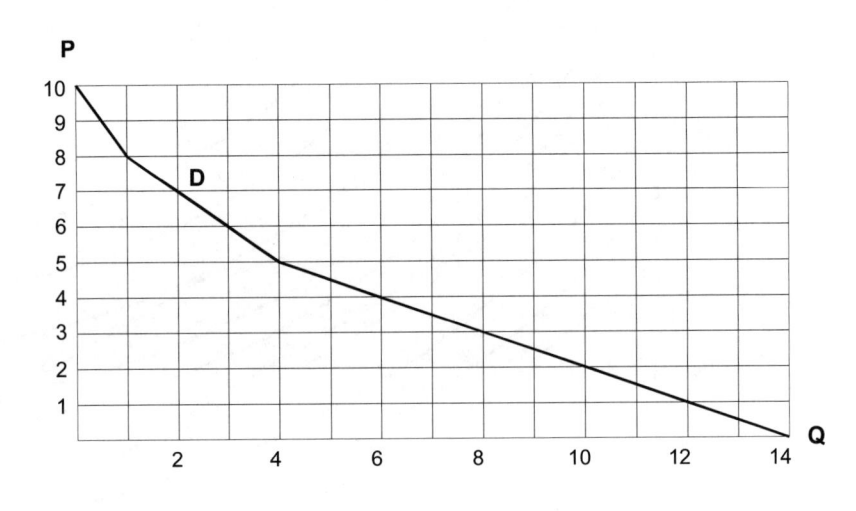

Test Yourself

Multiple Choice
1. a
2. b
3. a
4. c
5. d
6. d
7. e
8. d
9. e
10. b
11. b
12. b
13. c
14. d

True/False
1. F
2. F
3. T
4. F
5. T
6. T
7. F
8. F

Short Answer

1. substitution: **decreases** quantity demanded;
   income effect: **decreases** quantity demanded.

2. substitution: **increases** quantity demanded;
   income effect: **decreases** quantity demanded.

3. substitution: **increases** quantity demanded;
   income effect: **increases** quantity demanded.

■ ANSWERS FOR CHAPTER 6

Summarize the Chapter

A business firm is an organization, owned and operated by private individuals, that specializes in **production**. Production is the process of combining inputs to make outputs. For each different combination of inputs, the **production function** tells us the maximum quantity of output a firm can produce over some period of time.

The **long run** is a time horizon long enough for a firm to vary all of its inputs. The **short run** refers to any time horizon over which at least one of the firm's inputs cannot be varied.

Total product is the maximum quantity of output that can be produced from a given combination of inputs. The **marginal product** of labor is the change in total product divided by the change in the number of workers hired. It tells us the rise in output produced when one more worker is hired. In equation form, MPL = $\Delta Q / \Delta L$. The law of **diminishing** (marginal) returns states that as we continue to add more of any one input (holding the other inputs constant), its marginal product will eventually decline.

A firm's total cost of producing a given level of output is the **opportunity** cost of the owners—everything they must give up in order to produce that amount of output. A **sunk** cost is one that already has been paid, or must be paid, regardless of any future action being considered. **Sunk** costs should not be considered when making decisions. Total cost (TC) is the sum of all fixed and **variable** costs: TC = TFC + **TVC**. The firm's average fixed cost (AFC) is its total **variable** cost divided by the quantity of output: AFC = TFC / Q. Average variable cost (AVC) is the cost of the variable inputs per unit of output: AVC = TVC / Q. Average **total** cost (ATC) is the total cost per unit of output: ATC = TC / Q. **Marginal** cost (MC) is the change in total cost divided by the change in output: MC = Δ TC / Q. It tells us how much cost rises per unit increase in output. The marginal cost for any change in output is equal to the **slope** of the total cost curve along that interval of output.

When the marginal product of labor (MPL) rises, marginal cost (MC) **falls**. When MPL falls, MC **rises**. Since MPL ordinarily rises and then falls, MC will do the opposite: It will **fall** and then **rise**. Thus, the MC curve is U-shaped.

At low levels of output, the MC curve lies below the AVC and ATC curves, so these curves will slope **downward**. At higher levels of output, the MC curve will rise above the AVC and ATC curves, so these curves will slope **upward**. Thus, as output increases, the average curves will first slope **downward** and then slope **upward**. That is, they will have a U shape. The MC curve will intersect the **minimum** points of the AVC and ATC curves.

In the long run, there are no **fixed** inputs or **fixed** costs; all inputs and all costs are **variable**. The firm must decide what combination of inputs to use in producing any level of output. To produce any given level of output, the firm will choose the input mix with the **lowest** cost. The **long-run** total cost of producing a given level of output can be less than or equal to, but never greater than the **short-run** total cost. The **long-run** average cost of producing a given level of output can be less than or equal to, but never greater than, the **short-run** average total cost. In the short run, a firm can only move along its current ATC curve. In the long run, however, it can move from one ATC curve to another by varying the size of its plant. As it does so, it will also be moving along its **LRATC** (or **long-run average total cost**) curve.

When long-run total cost rises proportionately less than output, production is characterized by **economies** of scale, and the LRATC curve slopes downward. When long-run total cost rises more than in proportion to output, there are **diseconomies** of scale, and the LRATC curve slopes upward. When both output and long-run total cost rise by the same proportion, production is characterized by **constant returns** to scale, and the LRATC curve is flat.

Answers to Chapter 6 Questions

Learn the Lingo

1. business firm
2. profit
3. sole proprietorship
4. partnership
5. corporation
6. transaction costs
7. diversification
8. technology
9. production function
10. long run
11. fixed input
12. variable input
13. short run
14. total product
15. marginal product of labor
16. increasing marginal returns to labor
17. diminishing marginal returns to labor
18. law of diminishing marginal returns
19. sunk cost
20. explicit costs
21. implicit costs
22. fixed costs
23. variable costs
24. total fixed cost
25. total variable cost
26. total cost
27. average fixed cost
28. average variable cost
29. average total cost
30. marginal cost
31. long-run total cost
32. long-run average total cost
33. plant
34. economies of scale
35. lumpy input
36. diseconomies of scale
37. constant returns to scale
38. minimum efficient scale
39. natural monopoly

Build Your Skills

1. a, b, c

Number of Workers	TP	MPL
0	0	
		100
1	100	
		200
2	300	
		400
3	700	
		300
4	1000	
		200
5	1200	
		100
6	1300	
		50
7	1350	

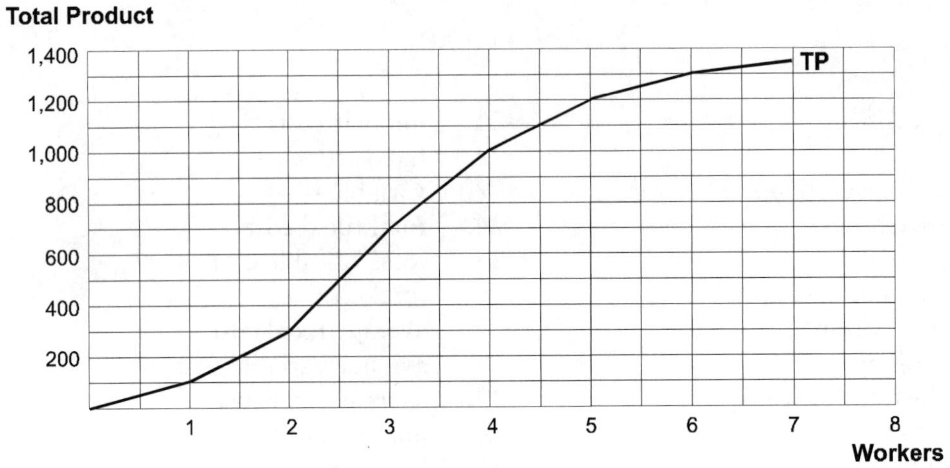

d. does; always positive; declines

2.

Number of Workers	TP	TFC $	TVC $	TC $	AFC $	AVC $	ATC $	MC $
0	0	20,000	0	20,000	---	---	---	
								20.0
1	100	20,000	2,000	22,000	200.0	20.0	220.0	
								10.0
2	300	20,000	4,000	24,000	66.7	13.3	80.0	
								5.0
3	700	20,000	6,000	26,000	28.6	8.6	37.1	
								6.7
4	1,000	20,000	8,000	28,000	20.0	8.0	28.0	
								10.0
5	1,200	20,000	10,000	30,000	16.7	8.3	25.0	
								20.0
6	1,300	20,000	12,000	32,000	15.4	9.2	24.6	
								40.0
7	1,350	20,000	14,000	34,000	14.8	10.4	25.2	

Answers to Chapter 6 Questions

3.

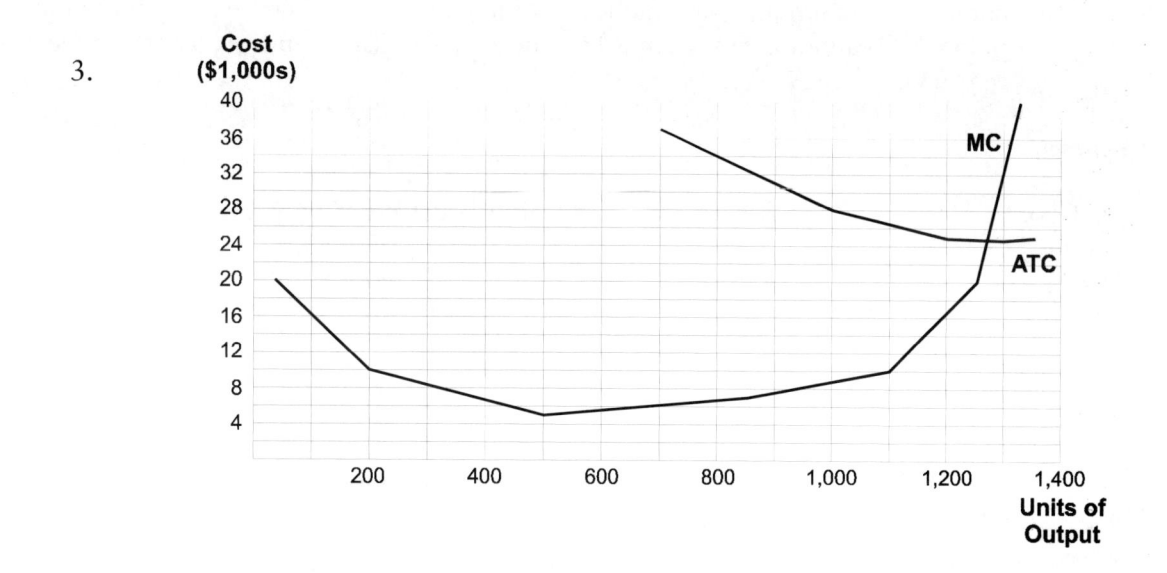

4.

Weekly Output	TFC	TVC	TC	AFC	AVC	ATC	MC
0	$100	$ 0	$ 100	---	---	---	
							$150
1	100	150	250	$100	$150	$250	
							130
2	100	280	380	50	140	190	
							100
3	100	380	480	33.3	126.7	160	
							20
4	100	400	500	25	100	125	
							130
5	100	530	630	20	106	126	
							130
6	100	660	760	16.7	110	126.7	
							250
7	100	910	1,010	14.3	130	144.3	
							690
8	100	1,600	1,700	12.5	200	212.5	

5. a. $50; $25; $32.5; $25; increasing
    b. $20; 5; 6
    c. 3; 6.5; 6; 5
    d. ATC−AVC; vertical distance; ATC curve and the AVC curve; $12.5; $7.5

6. a. Axes are labeled incorrectly—Cost should be on the vertical and output on the horizontal axis.
    b. AVC cannot exceed ATC, so the AVC and ATC curves must be labeled incorrectly.
    c. and d.   By the average-marginal relationship, the MC curve must intersect the ATC

curve at its minimum point and it must intersect the AVC curve at its minimum point: MC cannot be less than ATC when ATC is rising, and MC cannot be less that AVC when AVC is rising.

Test Yourself

Multiple Choice
1. e
2. e
3. e
4. b
5. e
6. e
7. b
8. e
9. c
10. a

True/False
1. F
2. F
3. F
4. F
5. F
6. T
7. T
8. F

Numerical Word Problem
1. $7,000; $9,000.
2. $1,000; $1,000.
3. $6,000; $8,000
4. $7; $7.50
5. $1; $0.83
6. $6; $6.67
7. 200
8. $2,000

Formulas
1. MPL
2. AFC
3. AVC
4. TC
5. AVC
6. MC
7. LRATC

■ ANSWERS FOR CHAPTER 7

Summarize the Chapter

In this chapter, we view the firm as a single economic decision maker whose goal is to maximize its owners' **profit** (or **economic profit**). The proper measure of profit for understanding and predicting the behavior of firms is **economic** profit. Unlike accounting profit, **economic** profit recognizes all the opportunity costs of production, both explicit costs and **implicit** costs.

The **demand curve** facing the firm tells us, for different prices, the quantity of output that customers will choose to purchase from that firm. It also tells us the maximum price the firm can charge to sell any given amount of output.

The firm uses its production function, and the prices it must pay for its inputs, to determine the **least cost** method of producing any given output level. Therefore, for any level of output the firm might want to produce, it must pay the cost of the "**least cost** method" of production.

In the total revenue and total cost approach, the firm calculates economic **profit** = TR - TC at each output level and selects the output level where economic **profit** is greatest. **Marginal** revenue is the change in the firm's total revenue divided by the change in its output: MR =ΔTR/ΔQ. It tells us how much **revenue** rises per unit increase in output.

Answers to Chapter 7 Questions

When a firm faces a downward-sloping **demand** curve, each increase in output causes a revenue gain, from selling additional output at the new price, and a revenue loss, from having to lower the price on all previous units of output. **Marginal** revenue is therefore less than the price of the last unit of output. An increase in output will always raise profit as long as marginal revenue is **greater** than marginal cost (MR > MC). An increase in output will always lower profit whenever marginal revenue is **less** than marginal cost (MR < MC). To find the profit-maximizing output level, the firm should **increase** output whenever MR > MC, and **decrease** output when MR < MC.

The marginal revenue for any change in output is equal to the slope of the **total** revenue curve along that interval. To maximize profit, the firm should produce the quantity of output where the vertical distance between the TR and TC curves is **greatest**, and the TR curve lies above the TC curve. Equivalently, to maximize profit, the firm should produce the level of output closest to the point where MC = MR, that is, the level of output at which the MC and MR curves **intersect**. The marginal approach to profit states that a firm should take any action that adds more to its **revenue** than to its **costs**.

Let Q* be the output level at which MR = MC. Then, in the short run. If TR > TVC at Q*, the firm should keep producing. If TR < TVC at Q*, the firm should shut down. If TR = TVC at Q*, the firm should be indifferent between shutting down and producing. A firm should **exit** the industry in the long run when, at its best possible output level, it has any loss at all.

Learn the Lingo

1. accounting profit
2. economic profit
3. demand curve facing the firm
4. total revenue
5. loss
6. marginal revenue
7. marginal approach to profit
8. shutdown rule
9. exit

Build Your Skills

1. a.

Price	Output	Total Revenue
$10	0	$ 0
9	10	90
8	20	160
7	30	210
6	40	240
5	50	250
4	60	240
3	70	210
2	80	160
1	90	90
0	100	0

b.

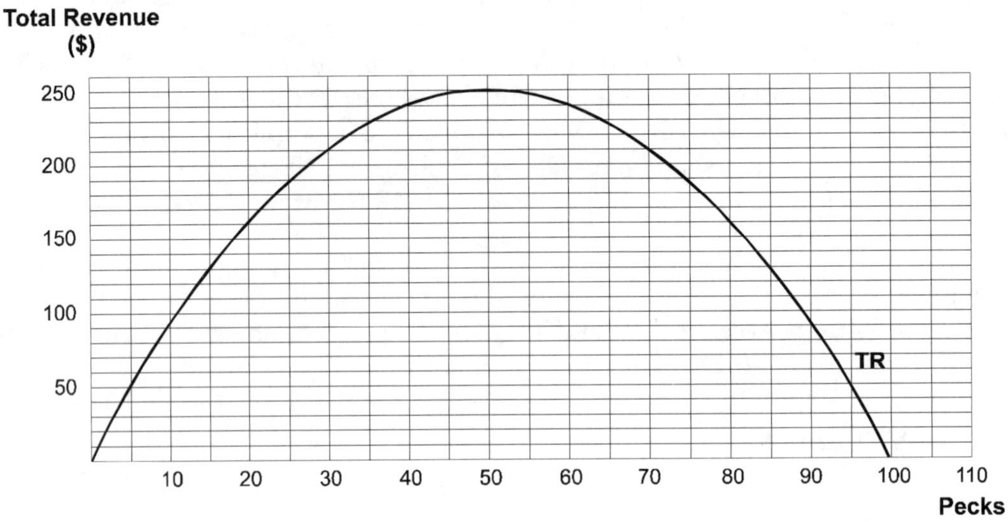

c. 50; $5; $250

2. a.

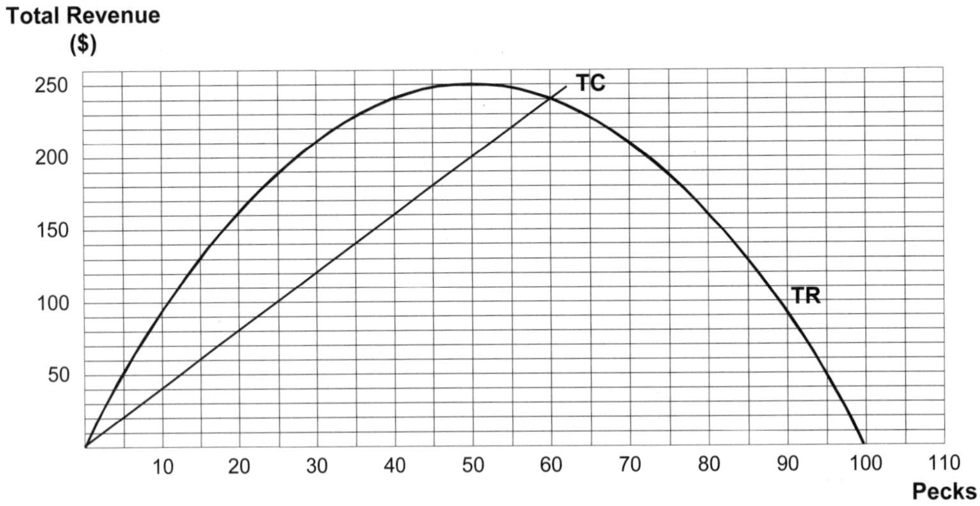

b. $50; $80; $90; $80; $50; $0
c. 30; $7; $210; $120; $90

Answers to Chapter 7 Questions

3. a.

Output	Total Revenue	Marginal Revenue	Total Cost	Marginal Cost
0	$ 0		$ 50	
		$50		10
1	50		60	
		40		15
2	90		75	
		30		20
3	120		95	
		20		25
4	140		120	
		10		30
5	150		150	
		0		35
6	150		185	

b. MR>MC; should; more
c. MR>MC; should; more
d. MR>MC; should; more
e. MR<MC; should not; less
f. MR<MC; should not; less
g. MR<MC; should not; less
h. 3; $25; $15; $20 (Note: To get the level of profit, compare total revenue and total cost)

4. a.

Quantity Demanded	Price	TR	MR
1	$28	28	
			24
2	26	52	
			20
3	24	72	
			16
4	22	88	
			12
5	20	100	
			8
6	18	108	
			4
7	16	112	
			0
8	14	112	
			−4
9	12	108	
			−8
10	10	100	

b. 5 bushels
c. 6 bushels
d. 7 bushels

5. a. See the table below. To compute the entry for monthly revenue, multiply the occupancy rate times $33,600—the revenue realized if occupancy were at 100%.
   b.

Month	Occupancy Rate	TR	TVC	TFC	Profit/Loss
January	10%	3,360	4,200	10,200	–11,040
February	10%	3,360	4,200	10,200	–11,040
March	20%	6,720	4,200	10,200	–7,680
April	25%	8,400	4,200	10,200	–6,000
May	60%	20,160	4,200	10,200	5,760
June	85%	28,560	4,200	10,200	14,160
July	95%	31,920	4,200	10,200	17,520
August	95%	31,920	4,200	10,200	17,520
September	80%	26,880	4,200	10,200	12,480
October	50%	16,800	4,200	10,200	2,400
November	20%	6,720	4,200	10,200	–7,680
December	10%	3,360	4,200	10,200	–11,040

   c. exceeds; total variable cost
   d. Shut down for December, January, February
      Stay open March, April, May, June, July, August, September, October, November
   e. $17,880; $3,360

Test Yourself

Multiple Choice
1. e
2. d
3. b
4. e
5. a
6. d
7. a
8. b
9. d
10. b

True/False
1. F
2. T
3. F
4. T
5. F
6. F
7. F
8. T

Answers to Chapter 7 Questions

Short Answer

1. $30

2. 4

3. keep producing (explanation: at 4 units, TR of $280 exceeds TVC of $120

4. -$40 (explanation: TR of $280 minus TC of $320)

5. keep producing (explanation: even with the higher fixed costs, it is still true that at 4 units of output, TR of $280 exceeds TVC of $120)

■ ANSWERS FOR CHAPTER 8

Summarize the Chapter

Market **structure** means all the characteristics of a market that influence the behavior of buyers and sellers when they come together to trade. Perfect competition is a market **structure** with three important characteristics: (1) There are a **large** number of buyers and sellers, and each buys or sells only a tiny fraction of the total quantity in the market. (2) Sellers offer a **standardized** product. (3) Sellers can easily enter into or exit from the market.

In a perfectly competitive market, the number of buyers and sellers is so **large** that no individual decision maker can significantly affect the **price** of the product by changing the quantity it buys or sells.

A perfectly competitive firm faces a cost **constraint** like any other firm. The cost of producing any given level of output depends on the firm's production technology and the prices it must pay for its inputs. In perfect competition, the firm is a **price** taker: It treats the **price** of its output as given. For a competitive firm, **marginal revenue** at each quantity is the same as the market price. For this reason, the **marginal revenue** curve and the demand curve facing the firm are the same, a horizontal line at the market price.

A firm earns a profit whenever P > ATC. Its total profit at the best output level equals the area of a **rectangle** with height equal to the distance between P and ATC, and width equal to the level of output. A firm suffers a loss whenever P < ATC at the best level of output. Its total loss equals the area of a **rectangle** with height equal to the distance between P and ATC, and width equal to the level of output.

As the price of output changes, the firm will slide along its **marginal cost** (or **MC**) curve in deciding how much to produce. The competitive firm's supply curve has two parts. For all prices above the minimum point on its **AVC** curve, the supply curve coincides with the MC curve. For all prices below the minimum point on the **AVC** curve, the firm will shut down, so its supply curve is a vertical line segment at **zero** units of output.

In the short run, the number of firms in the industry is **fixed**. To obtain the **market** supply curve, we add up the quantities of output supplied by all firms in the market at each **price**. In perfect competition, the market sums up the buying and selling preferences of individual consumers and producers, and determines the market **price**. Each buyer and seller then takes the market **price** as given, and each is able to buy or sell the desired quantity.

In a competitive market, economic **profit** and **loss** are the forces driving long-run change. The expectation of continued economic **profit** causes outsiders to enter the market; the expectation of continued economic **loss** causes firms in the market to exit. In a competitive market, positive economic **profit** continues to attract new entrants until economic **profit** is reduced to **zero**.

In a competitive market, economic **loss** continues to cause exit until the economic **loss** is reduced to **zero**. In the long run, every competitive firm will earn normal profit—that is, **zero** economic profit. In long-run equilibrium, every competitive firm will select its plant size and output level so that it operates at the **minimum** point of its LRATC curve. At each competitive firm in long-run equilibrium, P = **MC** = minimum ATC = minimum LRATC.

The long-run **supply** curve shows the relationship between market price and market quantity produced after all long-run adjustments have taken place. In a (an) **increasing** cost industry, entry causes input prices to rise, which shifts up the typical firm's **ATC** curve, and raises the market price at which firms earn zero economic profit. As a result, the long-run supply curve slopes **upward**. In a (an) **constant** cost industry, entry has no effect on input prices, so the typical firm's **ATC** curve stays put and the market price at which firms earn zero economic profit does not change. As a result, the long-run supply curve is **horizontal**. In a (an) **increasing** cost industry, entry causes input prices to fall, which causes the typical firm's **ATC** curve to shift downward, and lowers the market price at which firms earn zero economic profit. As a result, the long-run supply curve slopes **downward**.

In a market economy, price changes act as **market signals**, ensuring that the pattern of production matches the pattern of consumer demands. When demand increases, a **rise** in price signals firms to **enter** the market, increasing industry output. When demand decreases, a **fall** in price signals firms to **exit** the market, decreasing industry output. Under perfect competition, a technological advance leads to a rightward shift of the market supply curve, causing the market price to **decrease**. In the short run, early adopters may earn positive economic profit. In the long run, all adopters will earn **zero** economic profit. Firms that refuse to use the new technology will not survive.

Learn the Lingo

1. market structure
2. perfect competition
3. price taker
4. shutdown price
5. firm's supply curve
6. market supply curve
7. normal profit
8. long-run supply curve
9. increasing cost industry
10. constant cost industry
11. decreasing cost industry
12. market signals

Build Your Skills

1. a. and b.

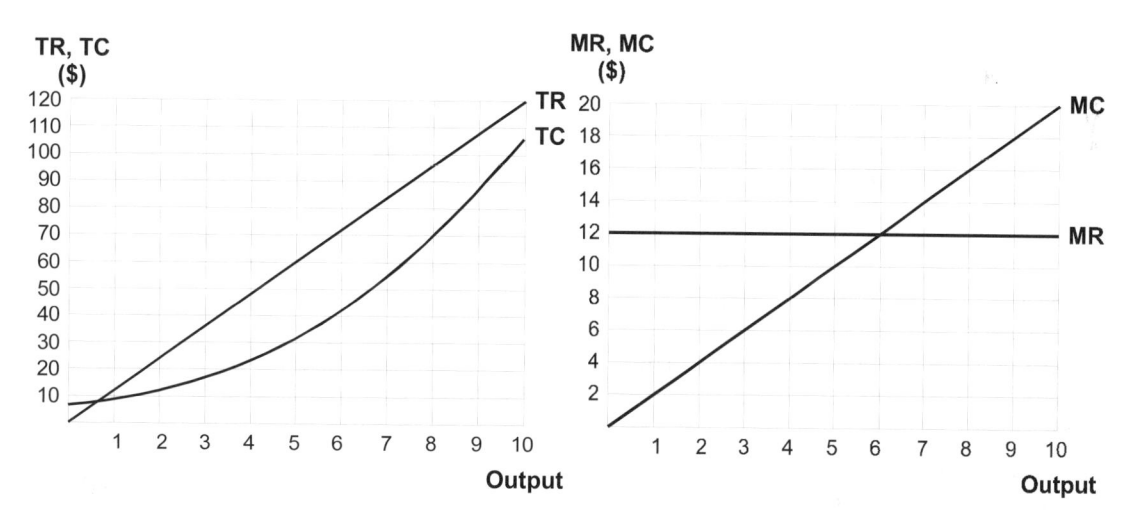

Output	TR	TC	MR	MC	Profit
0	0	6			−6
			12	1	
1	12	7			5
			12	3	
2	24	10			14
			12	5	
3	36	15			21
			12	7	
4	48	22			26
			12	9	
5	60	31			29
			12	11	
6	72	42			30
			12	13	
7	84	55			29
			12	15	
8	96	70			26
			12	17	
9	108	87			21
			12	19	
10	120	106			14

c. 6; $30; vertical; 6; less than; greater than; 6; equal to

2. a. 7; $15; $105
   b. increasing; 7.5; rise; 20 and 25; rise; 150 and 188
   c. keep producing; exceeds; 6; negative
   d. is not; shut down

3.

Market Price	Quantity Supplied
$70	7.8
60	7.5
50	7
40	6.5
30	6
20	5 or 0
10	0
5	0

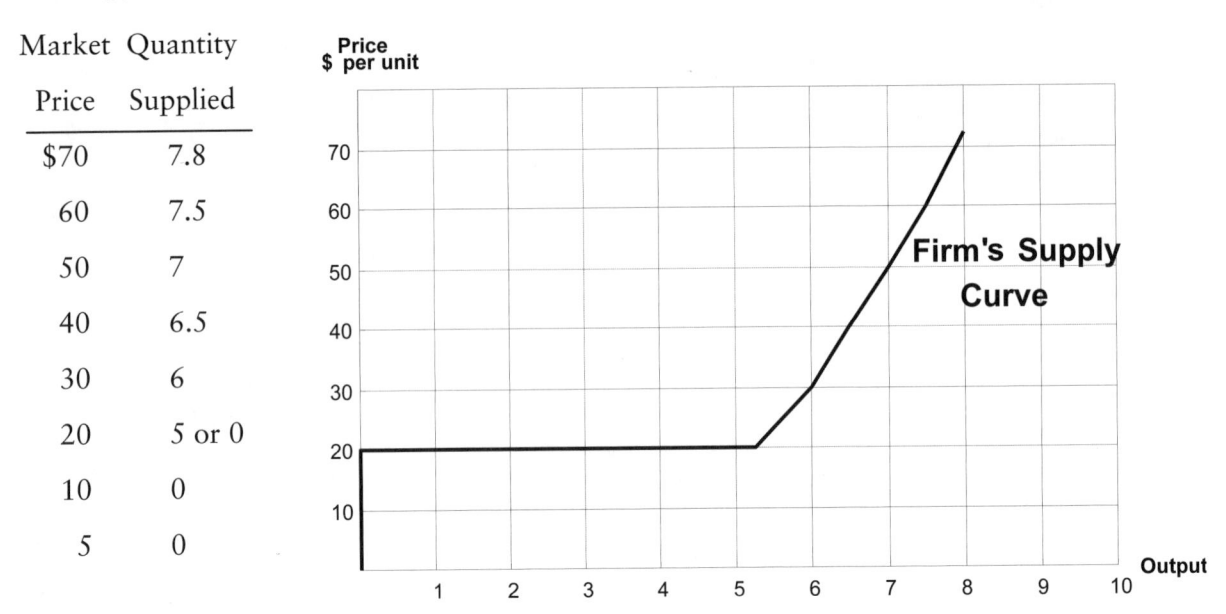

4. a. 20; 40; 60; 0
   b. 400; 800; 1,200 (See graph.) Equilibrium price is $250
   c. 600; 1,200; 1,800 (See graph.) Equilibrium price is $200
      0; 800; 1,600 (See graph.) Equilibrium price is $100

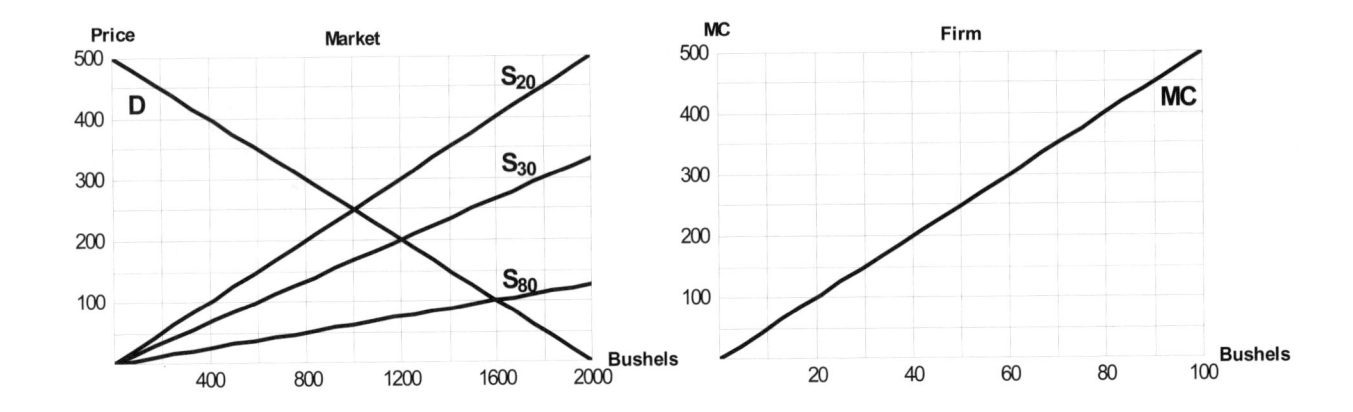

5. a. $10; is not; positive profit; enter this market; shift market supply to the right; fall
   b. $4; is not; negative profit; exit this market; shift market supply to the left; rise
   c. $6; earn zero economic profit; neither enter nor exit; will

Test Yourself

Multiple Choice
1. a
2. b
3. d
4. a
5. c
6. d
7. b
8. e
9. d
10. c

True/False
1. F
2. F
3. T
4. T
5. F
6. F
7. T
8. T

Short Answer

1. (any order): large number of firms; standardized product; easy entry into and exit from the market

2. easy entry into and exit from the market

3.

Type of Industry	Short-run effect of an increase in demand on: Quantity:	Price:	Long-run effect of a decrease in demand on: Quantity:	Price:
Increasing cost industry	increase	increase	decrease	decrease
Decreasing cost industry	increase	increase	decrease	increase
Constant cost industry	increase	increase	decrease	no change

■ ANSWERS FOR CHAPTER 9

Summarize the Chapter

A monopoly firm is the only seller of a good or service with no close **substitutes**. The market in which the monopoly firm operates is called a monopoly market.

A **natural** monopoly exists when, due to economies of scale, one firm can produce at a lower cost per unit than can two or more firms.

In dealing with **intellectual** property, government strikes a compromise: It allows the creators to enjoy a monopoly and earn economic profit, but only for a limited period of time. Once the time is up, other sellers are allowed to enter the market, and it is hoped that competition among them will cause the market price to **decrease**. Network **externalities** exist when an increase in the network's membership (more users of the product) increase its value to current and potential members.

A monopolist, like any firm, strives to maximize profit. And, like any firm, it faces constraints. For any level of output it might produce, total **cost** is determined by (1) its technology of production and (2) the prices it must pay for its inputs. And for any level of output it might produce, the maximum price it can charge is determined by the market **demand** curve for its product. When any firm, including a monopoly, faces a downward-sloping demand curve, marginal revenue is **less** than the price of output. Therefore, the marginal revenue curve will lie **below** the demand curve.

A monopoly will always produce at an output level where marginal revenue is **positive.**

To maximize profit, a monopoly—like any firm—should produce the quantity where MC = MR and the MC curve crosses the MR curve from **below**. A monopoly earns a profit whenever P > ATC. Its total profit at the best output level equals the area of a **rectangle** with height equal to the distance between P and ATC and width equal to the level of output.

A monopoly suffers a loss whenever P < ATC. Its total loss at the best output level equals the area of a **rectangle** with height equal to the distance between ATC and P and width equal to the level of output.

Any firm—including a monopoly—should shut down if P < **AVC** at the output level where MR = MC. Unlike **perfectly competitive** firms, monopolies may earn economic profit in the long run. A privately owned monopoly suffering an economic loss in the **long** run will exit the industry, just as would any other business firm. In the **long** run, therefore, we should not find privately owned monopolies suffering economic losses.

We can expect a monopoly market to have a **higher** price and **lower** output than an otherwise similar perfectly competitive market. The monopolization of a competitive industry leads to two opposing effects. First, for any given technology of production, monopolization leads to **higher** prices and **lower** output. Second, changes in the technology of production made possible under monopoly may lead to **lower** prices and **higher** output. The ultimate effect on price and quantity depends on the relative strengths of these two effects.

Any costly action a firm undertakes to establish or maintain its monopoly status is called **rent-seeking** activity. **Rent-seeking** activity that helps establish or maintain a firm's monopoly position is part of the firm's costs. As a result, it can reduce the economic profit of a monopoly and may even reduce it to zero.

A monopolist will react to an increase in demand by producing more output, charging a **higher** price, and earning a **larger** profit. It will react to a decrease in demand by reducing output, **lowering** price, and earning a **smaller** profit. In general, a monopoly will pass to consumers only part of the benefits from a cost-saving technological change. After the change in technology, the monopoly's profits will be **higher**. In general, a monopoly will pass only part of a cost increase onto consumers in the form of a **higher** price. After the cost increase, the monopoly's profits will be **lower**.

Answers to Chapter 9 Questions

Price discrimination occurs when a firm charges different prices to different customers for reasons other than differences in **costs**. When price discrimination raises the price for some consumers above the price they would pay under a single-price policy, it harms consumers. The additional **profit** for the firm is equal to the monetary loss of consumers. When price discrimination lowers the price for some consumers below what they would pay under a single-price policy, it benefits consumers as well as the firm. Under **perfect** price discrimination, a firm charges each customer the most the customer would be willing to pay for each unit he or she buys. For a **perfect** price discriminator, marginal revenue is equal to the price of the additional unit sold. Thus, the firm's MR curve is the same as its **demand** curve. A **perfect** price discriminator increases profit at the expense of consumers, charging each customer the most he or she would willingly pay for the product.

Learn the Lingo

1. monopoly firm
2. monopoly market
3. natural monopoly
4. patent
5. copyright
6. government franchise
7. network externalities
8. rent-seeking activity
9. single-price monopoly
10. price discrimination
11. perfect price discrimination

Build Your Skills

1. a. and b.

P	Q^D	TR	MR
$20	0	$ 0	
			$18
18	1	18	
			14
16	2	32	
			10
14	3	42	
			6
12	4	48	
			2
10	5	50	
			−2
8	6	48	
			−6
6	7	42	
			−10
4	8	32	
			−14
2	9	18	
			−18
0	10	0	

    c. positive; increase
    d. negative; decrease
    e. negative; 5

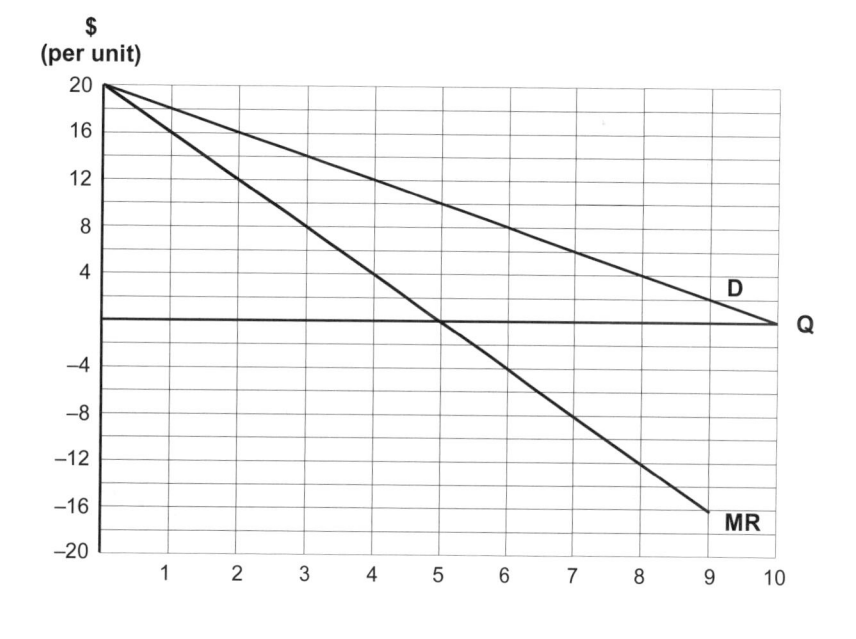

2. a. and b.

P	Q	TR	MR
$120	0	$0	
			$95
95	5	475	
			45
70	10	700	
			-5
45	15	675	
			-55
20	20	400	

c. 10; $20; $20; $70
d. less than; fall

3. a. 40
   b. $300; $300; equal to
   c. $500
   d. (approx.) $375
   e. (approx.) $125
   f. (approx.) $6,000

4. Graph for a., b., and d.

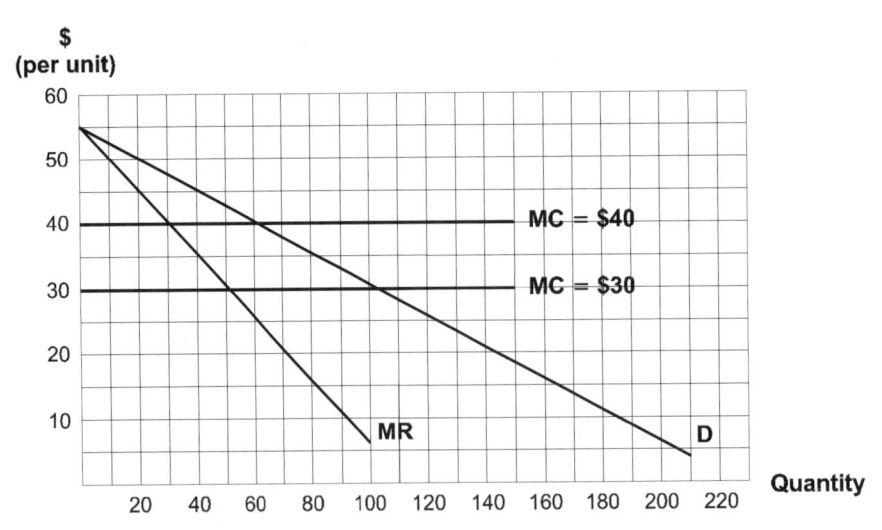

   c. 52; $43 (To get these exact, set the equation for MR equal to MC = $30. Solve for Q. Plug Q into the demand equation to get price.)
   d. 32; $48 (To get these exact, use the equation for MR equal to MC = $40. Solve for Q. Plug Q into the demand equation to get price.)
   e. $5; not to

Answers to Chapter 9 Questions

5. a. a; $-b$; a/b
    b. a; $-2b$; $a/2b$
    c.

Demand	Marginal Revenue
$P = 34 - 4Q$	$MR = 34 - 8Q$
$P = 28 - 15Q$	$MR = 28 - 30Q$
$P = 72 - 12Q$	$MR = 72 - 24Q$
$P = 12 - 8Q$	$MR = 12 - 16Q$
$P = 105 - 25Q$	$MR = 105 - 50Q$

6. a. and b.

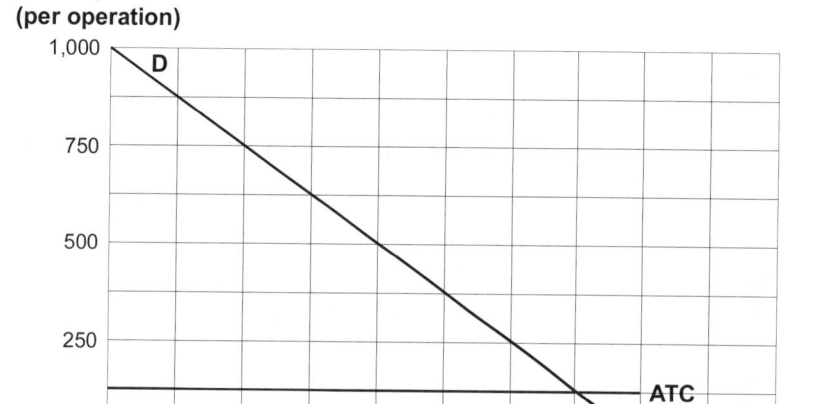

P	Q^D
$1,000	0
750	1
500	2
250	3
0	4

    c. 3; $750; $375; $375
    d. 3; $750 + $500 + $250 = $1,500; $375; $1,125
    e. He makes more profit when he price discriminates

Test Yourself

Multiple Choice
1. b
2. a
3. c
4. b
5. d
6. e
7. d
8. c
9. b
10. e

True/False
1. F
2. F
3. F
4. F
5. F
6. F
7. T
8. F

Short Answer

1. (any order): economies of scale; government franchise; network externalities

2. (any order): government regulation; rent-seeking activity

3. (any order): downward sloping demand curve; ability to identify consumers who are willing to pay more; ability to prevent low-price customers from reselling the good to high-priced customers.

■ ANSWERS FOR CHAPTER 10

Summarize the Chapter

Imperfect competition refers to market structures between **perfect competition** and monopoly. In imperfectly competitive markets, there is more than one seller, but too few to create a perfectly competitive market. In addition, imperfectly competitive markets often violate other conditions of perfect competition, such as the requirement of a **standardized** product or free entry and exit. A monopolistically competitive market has three fundamental characteristics: 1. many buyers and sellers; 2. sellers offer a **differentiated** product; and 3. sellers can easily enter or exit the market.

Because it produces a differentiated product, a monopolistic competitor faces a downward-sloping **demand** curve: When it **raises** its price a modest amount, quantity demanded will decline (but not all the way to zero). Under monopolistic competition, firms can earn positive or negative economic profit in the **short** run. But in the **long** run, free entry and exit will ensure that each firm earns **zero** economic profit, just as under perfect competition. In the **long** run, a monopolistic competitor will operate with excess capacity— that is, it will produce too **much** output to achieve minimum cost per unit.

Any action a firm takes to increase the demand for its output—other than cutting its price—is called **nonprice** competition.

An oligopoly is a market dominated by a **small** number of **strategically** interdependent firms. A **dominant** strategy is a strategy that is best for a player regardless of the strategy of the other player. A **Nash** equilibrium exists when each player is taking the best action for herself, given the actions taken by all other players. A game with two players will have a **Nash** equilibrium as long as at least one player has a **dominant** strategy, whether the other has a **dominant** strategy or not.

Under monopolistic competition, advertising may increase the size of the market, so that more units are sold. But in the long run, each firm earns **zero** economic profit, just as it would if no firm were advertising. The price to the consumer, however, may either rise or fall.

Answers to Chapter 10 Questions

Learn the Lingo

1. monopolistic competition
2. nonprice competition
3. oligopoly
4. natural oligopoly
5. game theory
6. payoff matrix
7. dominant strategy
8. Nash equilibrium
9. duopoly
10. repeated play
11. explicit collusion
12. cartel
13. tacit collusion
14. tit for tat
15. price leadership

Build Your Skills

1. a. can; maximize profit; where marginal revenue equals marginal cost
   b. 20; $6; $5; 20 × (6 − 5) = $20
   c. enter; enter; shift leftward; zero

2. a. 25; $12; 4,000; 160; perfect competition
   b. 4,000; $4; 12,000; 3; oligopoly
   c. 12,000; $8; 8,000; 1; natural monopoly

3. a.

	Your Rival Uses Blue	Your Rival Uses Red
You Use Blue	$100 / $90	$50 / $110
You Use Red	$120 / $40	$80 / $70

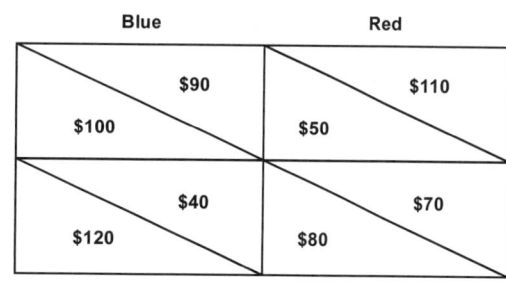

   b. Red; Red; Yes
   c. Red; Red; Yes
   d. Red; Red
   e. Yes; Blue; Blue
   f. $100; $120; When I cheat
   g. $90; $110; When she cheats

4. a. $20; 5; zero
   b. 400; 4 bushels
   c. greater than; positive
   d. $15; exceed
   e. $20; 5; zero

Test Yourself

Multiple Choice
1. b
2. c
3. d
4. c
5. c
6. e
7. d
8. a
9. e
10. b

True/False
1. F
2. T
3. F
4. F
5. F
6. F
7. F
8. F

Short Answer

1. a. differentiated product (under monopolistic competition)
   b. many firms or easy entry and exit (either answer is sufficient)

2. a. Oligopoly
   b. Monopoly
   c. Monopolistic competition
   d. Perfect competition

3. a.

	"A" charges high price	"A" charges low price
"B" charges high price	A's profit: High B's profit: High	A's profit: Medium B's profit: Medium
"B" charges low price	A's profit: Very High B's profit: Very Low	A's profit: Medium B's profit: High

b. "A" has a dominant strategy: to charge the high price. B does *not* have a dominant strategy (if A charges the high price, B should charge the high price too; if A charges the low price, B should charge the low price too.)

c. Yes, there is a Nash equilibrium: both will charge the high price. (For A, the high price is the dominant strategy; once A chooses the high price, B will choose the high price as well. Each will be doing the best it can do given the choice made by the other.

4.

Characteristic	Perfect Competition	Monopolistic Competition	Oligopoly	Monopoly
Number of Firms	Very Many	Many	Few	One
Type of Output	identical	identical	identical *or* differentiated	--
View of Pricing	price taker	price setter	price setter	price setter
Barriers to Entry or Exit?	No	No	Yes	Yes
Strategic Interdependence?	No	No	Yes	No
How profit-maximizing output level is found	MC = MR	MC = MR	Through strategic inter-dependence	MC = MR
Possible range of values for short-run profit	positive, negative or zero	positive, negative, or zero	positive, negative, or zero	positive, negative, or zero
Possible range of values for long-run profit	zero	zero	positive or zero	positive or zero
Is Advertising Expected?	No	Yes	Yes (if differentiated product)	Maybe

■ ANSWERS FOR CHAPTER 11

Summarize the Chapter

How broadly or narrowly we define a **market** depends on the specific questions we wish to answer. A perfectly competitive labor market has the following three characteristics: (1) There are large numbers of buyers (firms) and sellers (**households**), and each individual firm or **household** is only a tiny part of the labor market; (2) All workers in the labor market appear **the same** to firms; and (3) Workers can easily enter into or **exit from** the labor market.

The demand side of a labor market includes all firms hiring labor in that labor market. These firms may, but do not necessarily, compete in the same **product** market. The demand for a resource—such as labor—is a **derived** demand; it arises from, and will vary with, the demand for the firm's **output** (or **product**). The marginal approach to profit states that a firm should take any action that adds more to its **revenue** than it adds to its **costs**.

A firm's **marginal** revenue product (MRP) for any resource is the change in the firm's total **revenue** divided by the change in its employment of the resource: MRP = Δ TR/ Δ Quantity of Resource. The MRP tells us the change in total **revenue** per unit increase in the resource.

A firm's **marginal** factor cost (MFC) for any resource is the change in the firm's total **cost** divided by the change in its employment of the resource: MFC = TC/ Quantity of Resource. The MFC tells us the rise in **cost** per unit increase in the resource.

To maximize profit, the firm should increase its employment of any resource whenever MRP > MFC, but not when MRP < MFC. Thus, the profit-maximizing quantity of any resource is the quantity at which MRP = MFC.

When output is sold in a competitive product market, the MRP for any change in employment will equal the price of output (P) times the marginal **product** of labor: MRP = P x **MPL**.

When labor is hired in a competitive labor market, the MFC for any change in employment will equal the market **wage** (or **wage rate**): MFC = **W**. For a competitive firm, the rule for maximum profit is: hire another worker when MRP > W, but not when MRP < W. Thus, to maximize profit, the firm should hire the number of workers such that MRP = W—that is, where the MRP curve **intersects** the wage line.

When labor is the only variable input, the **downward**-sloping portion of the MRP curve is the firm's labor demand curve, telling us how much labor the firm will want to employ at each wage rate. Whether labor is the only variable input or other inputs can be varied as well, the profit-maximizing level of employment will still satisfy MRP = W, and the labor demand curve will still slope **downward**.

The **market** labor demand curve tells us the total number of workers all firms in a labor market want to employ at each wage rate. It is found by horizontally summing across all firms' individual labor demand curves. A change in any variable that affects the quantity of labor demanded—except for the wage rate—causes the labor demand curve to **shift**. The effect of a change in product demand on labor demand depends on whether many firms in the same product market also share the same **labor** market. When they do, a rise in product demand will shift the market labor demand curve **rightward**; a fall in product demand will shift the market labor demand curve **leftward**.

A complementary input is one that **increases** the marginal product of a certain type of labor. Usually, the input is used *by* this type of labor, making it **more** productive.
A substitutable input is one that **decreases** the marginal product of a certain type of labor. Usually, the input can be used instead of this type of labor, **decreasing** its marginal product.

When many firms in a labor market acquire a new technology, the market labor demand curve will shift **rightward** if the technology is complementary with labor and **leftward** if the technology is substitutable for labor. When the price of some other input (besides labor) *decreases*, the market labor demand curve may shift rightward or leftward. It will shift rightward if that other input is **complementary** with labor and leftward if the other input is **substitutable** for labor.

In a competitive labor market, each seller is a "wage **taker**"; he or she takes the market wage rate as given. The **higher** the wage rate in a labor market, the greater the quantity of labor supplied in that market. A market labor supply curve will **shift** when something other than a change in the wage rate causes a change in the number of people who want to work in a particular market. As long as some individuals can choose to supply their labor in two different markets, a rise in the wage rate in one market will cause a **leftward** shift in the labor supply curve in the other market. An increase in the cost of acquiring human capital needed to enter a labor market—say, due to an increase in school fees, fewer scholarships, or longer schooling requirements—will shift the labor supply curve **leftward**; a decrease in the cost of acquiring human capital will shift the labor supply curve **rightward**.

The long-run labor supply curve tells us how many (qualified) people will want to work in a labor market at each wage rate, after all adjustments have taken place. Specifically, all those who want to acquire new **skills** or who want to move to another location have done so. The **long**-run labor supply response is more wage elastic than the **short**-run labor supply response.

The forces of supply and demand drive a competitive labor market to its equilibrium point—the point where the labor supply and labor demand curves **intersect**. In the short run, a rightward shift in the labor demand curve moves us upward along a short-run labor supply curve, **raising** the wage rate. Over the long run, this **rise** in the wage rate entices qualified people to enter the labor market, and then the short-run labor supply curve shifts **rightward**. Wage rates, like the prices of goods and services, act as market signals— leading workers to move to areas where their work is most valued. When the labor demand curve **shifts**, the wage rate will overshoot its long-run equilibrium value. But as the signal begins to work, the temporary overshooting of the wage rate subsides. Surpluses and shortages in a labor market are not the natural consequence of shifts in supply and demand curves. A labor **shortage** will occur only when the wage rate fails to rise to its equilibrium value. Similarly, a labor **surplus** will occur only when the wage rate fails to fall to its equilibrium value.

The following refers to the appendix to Chapter 11:

A pure **monopsony** labor market is one in which a single firm is the only employer. For a monopsonist, MFC at any level of employment is **greater** than the wage rate. Since MFC for a monopsonist is **greater** than the wage rate, the MFC curve lies **above** the labor supply curve. When all else is the same, firms in monopsony labor markets (1) employ **fewer** workers, (2) produce **less** output, and (3) pay **lower** wages than firms in perfectly competitive labor markets.

Learn the Lingo

1. product markets
2. factor markets
3. perfectly competitive labor market
4. derived demand
5. marginal revenue product (MRP)
6. marginal factor cost (MFC)
7. wage taker
8. market labor demand curve
9. complementary input
10. substitutable input
11. reservation wage
12. labor supply curve
13. long-run labor supply curve
14. labor shortage
15. labor surplus
16. pure monopsony

Build Your Skills

1. a.

Quantity of Labor	Total Product	Marginal Product of Labor (MPL)	Price per Sandwich	Total Revenue	Marginal Revenue Product (MRP)	Wage (W)
0	0		$4	$0		$50
		30			$120	
1	30		4	120		50
		40			160	
2	70		4	280		50
		30			120	
3	100		4	400		50
		20			80	
4	120		4	480		50
		10			40	
5	130		4	520		50
		−10			−40	
6	120		4	480		50

b. MRP; wage; hiring the additional worker; yes; yes; yes; 4

2. a.

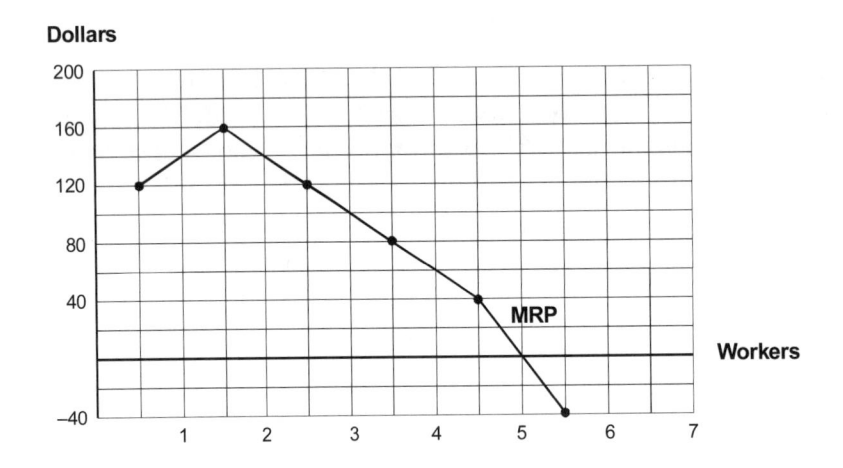

b. 3; 4

3. a.

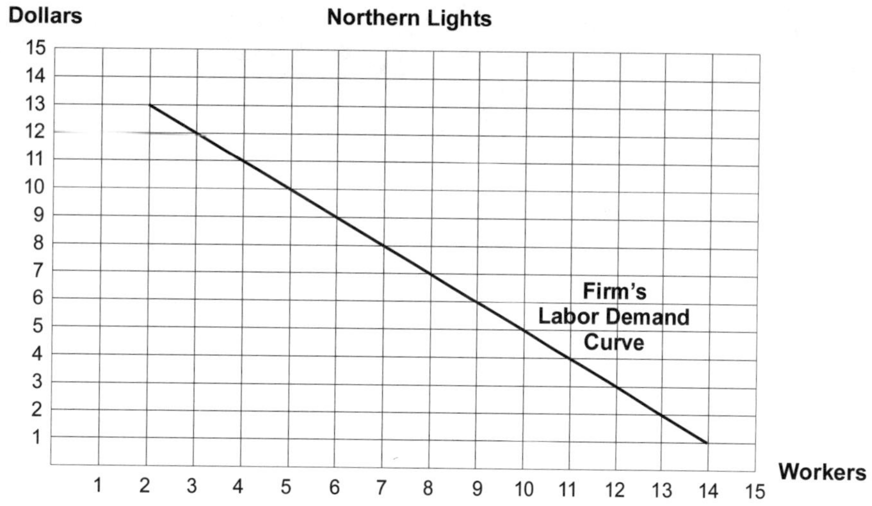
Dollars
Northern Lights
Firm's Labor Demand Curve
Workers

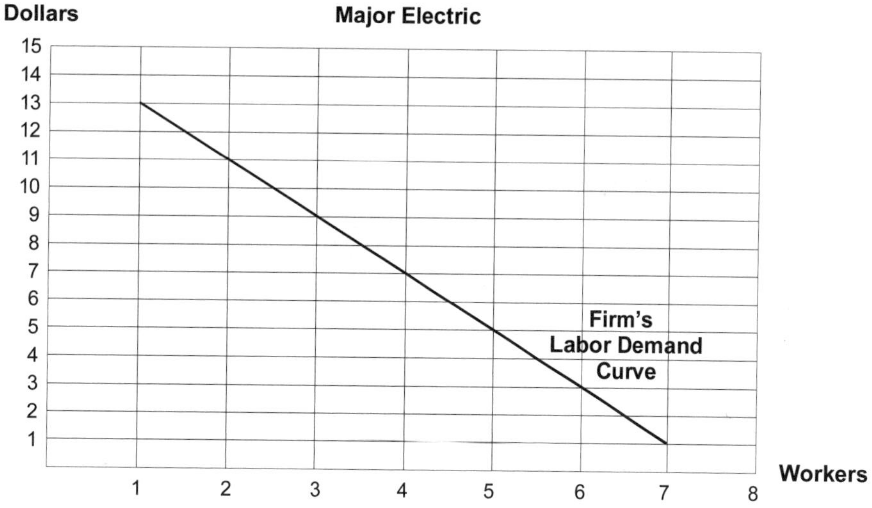
Dollars
Major Electric
Firm's Labor Demand Curve
Workers

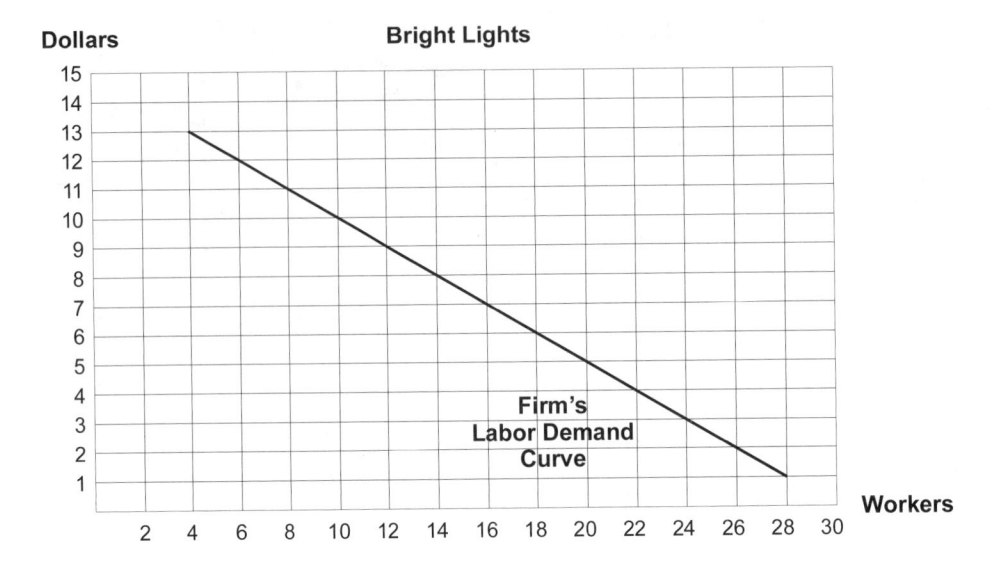

b.

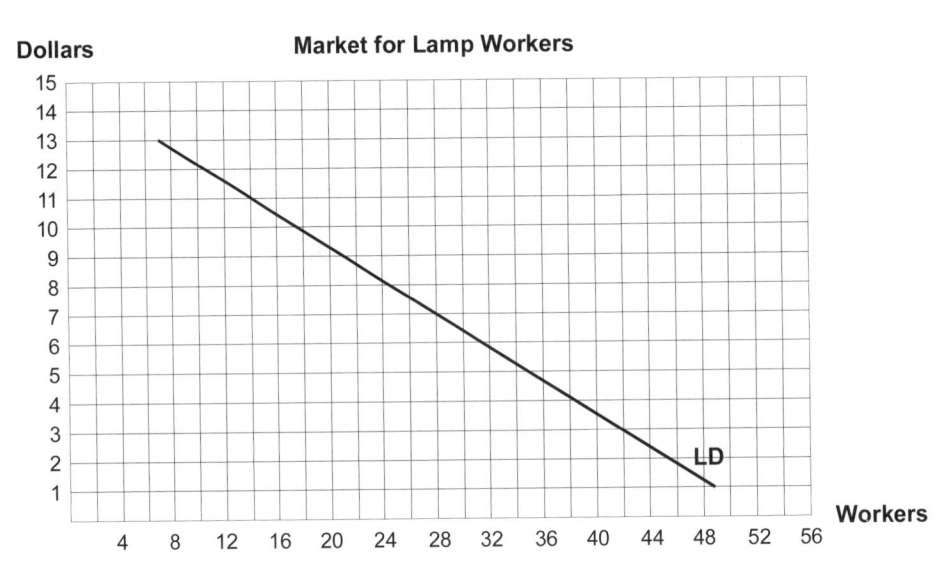

c. 14; 4; 2; 8
d. 42; 12; 6; 24

Answers to Chapter 11 Questions

4. a. 2; 4; cause a movement along the labor supply curve
   b. Equilibrium wage is $80; 5 translators employed

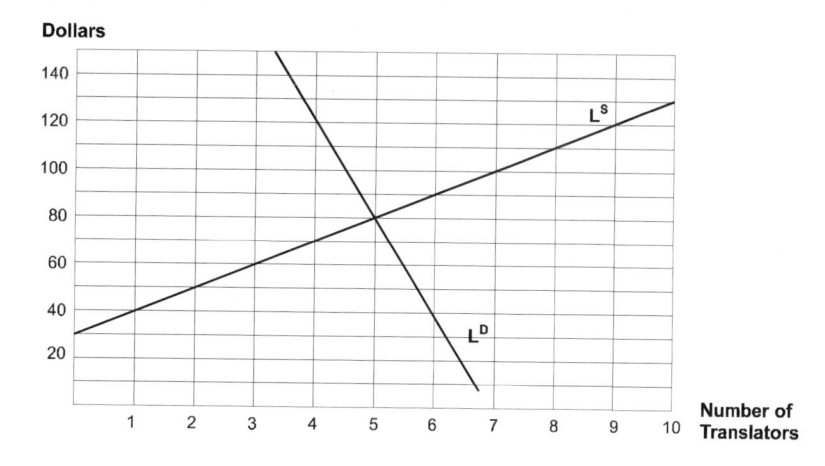

5. a. Equilibrium wage is $25; 5,000 EAs/RAs hired
   b. They hire 15 EAs/RAs this year. (Hint: They keep hiring until what equals what?)

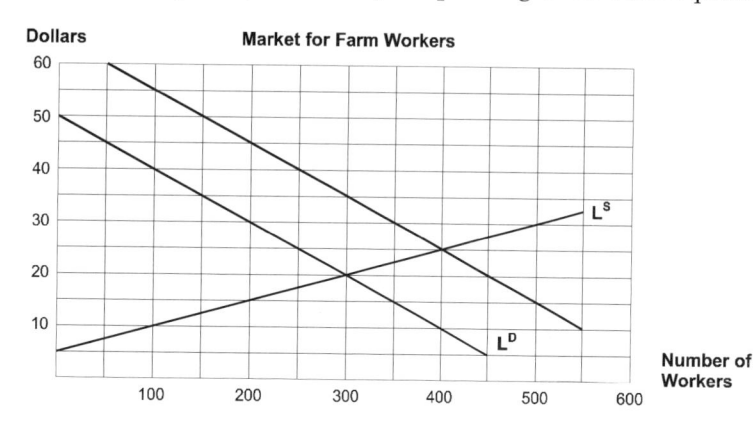

6. a.
   b. $20; 300
   c. increase; increase; demand curve; rightward
   d. (See graph;) demand curve; $25; 400
   e. higher; mover to; seek employment; lower; higher

Test Yourself

Multiple Choice
1. a
2. e
3. b
4. c
5. d
6. d
7. d
8. e
9. d
10. c
11. c
12. b

True/False
1. F
2. F
3. T
4. F
5. T
6. F
7. T
8. T
9. F
10. F

Short Answer

1. (any order): large number of buyers (firms) and sellers (households); all workers in the market appear the same to firms; workers can easily enter into or exit from the labor market.

2. MRP = P x MPL

3. (any three of the following four, in any order):
   - a *decrease* in demand for a product made by firms that hire in the same labor market
   - a technological change—specifically, a new input that is *substitutable* for labor in that market
   - an *increase* in the price of a *complementary* input to labor in that market
   - a *decrease* in the price of a *substitutable* input for labor in that market
   - a decrease in the number of firms

4. (any order):
   - a *decrease* in the market wage in a related labor market.
   - a *decrease* in the cost of acquiring human capital needed to qualify for the labor market.
   - an *increase* in the number of qualified people.
   - a change in tastes in favor of the labor market (or a change in tastes that *decreases* reservations wages for the labor market.)

5. The long-run labor supply curve would become *steeper*, since a wage change would now cause fewer people to entry into or exit from the labor market in the long run.

ANSWERS FOR CHAPTER 12

Summarize the Chapter

A **compensating** wage differential is the difference in wage rates that makes two jobs equally attractive to workers. The nonmonetary characteristics of different jobs give rise to **compensating** wage differentials. Jobs considered intrinsically less attractive will tend to pay **higher** wages, other things being equal. Differences in living costs can cause **compensating** wage differentials. Areas where living costs are higher than average will tend to have **higher**-than-average wages. Differences in **human** capital requirements can give rise to **compensating** wage differentials. Jobs that require more costly training will tend to pay **higher** wages, other things equal. In general, those with greater ability to do a job well—based on their talent, intelligence, motivation, or perseverance—will be more valuable to firms. As a result, firms will be willing to pay them a higher wage rate, beyond any **compensating** differential for their **human** capital investment.

In a competitive labor market, a union—by **raising** the wage firms must pay—**decreases** total employment in the union sector. This, in turn, causes wages in the nonunion sector to **decrease**. The result is a wage differential between union and nonunion wages. In a competitive labor market, a minimum wage—by **raising** wage rates in covered industries, and **lowering** them in uncovered industries—creates a wage differential among the least-skilled workers, depending on the industry in which they work. In a competitive labor market, a minimum wage—by causing firms to substitute away from unskilled labor toward skilled labor and **capital** produced by skilled labor—can **increase** the wage differential between skilled and unskilled workers.

When prejudice originates with **employers**, competitive labor markets work to discourage discrimination and reduce or eliminate any wage gap between the favored and the unfavored group. When prejudice originates with the firm's **employees** or its cusomters, market forces may encourage, rather than discourage, discrimination and can lead to a permanent wage gap between the favored and unfavored groups. In measuring the impact of job market discrimination on earnings, the wage gap between two groups gives an **over**-estimate, since it fails to account for differences in skills and experience. However, comparing only workers with similar skills and experience leads to an **under**-estimate, since skill and experience are themselves influenced by discrimination—both in the job market and outside of it.

The larger the Gini coefficient—up to a maximum of **1.0**—the **greater** is the degree of income inequality. The U.S. income distribution exhibits significant mobility between the extremes and the middle. Lorenz curves, poverty rates, Gini ratios, and other measures of income inequality—because they provide only a snapshot of the income distribution at a moment in time—may **over**-estimate long-run income inequality. Inequality that results from equal **opportunity**, but different choices, is generally regarded as fair.

The following refers to the appendix to Chapter 12.

For a firm with monopsony power, a minimum wage law can not only **increase** the wage rate a firm pays, but also **increase** employment at the firm. In a monopsony labor market, a union that wins a higher wage rate for its members can not only increase their pay, but may be able to increase **employment** at the firm as well

Learn the Lingo

1. compensating wage differential
2. nonmonetary job characteristic
3. discrimination
4. statistical discrimination
5. property income
6. transfer payment
7. poverty rate
8. poverty line
9. Lorenz curve
10. Gini coefficient
11. progressive income tax
12. principal-agent problem

Build Your Skills

1. a. $15; $10
   b. the same as; the same as; the same as; lower wage industry; higher wage industry; true
   c. $12.50; $12.50 (Hint: If employers view all workers the same, and if workers choose where to work only by the wage they receive, then the common equilibrium wage must equate *total* labor demand on the island to *total* labor supply on the island)
   d. better off; worse off; no

2. a.

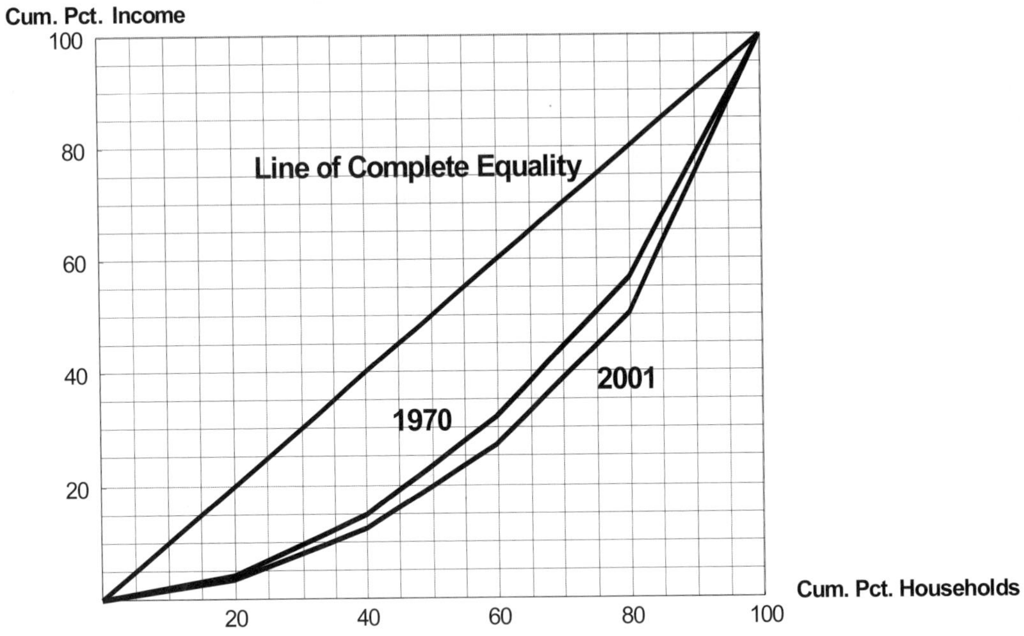
Cum. Pct. Income
100
80
60
40
20
Line of Complete Equality
1970
2001
20
40
60
80
100
Cum. Pct. Households

   b. more; increased

3. a. $210,000

b.

Family	Percent of Population	Cumulative Percent of Population	Ordered Income (Lowest to (Highest)	Percent of Income	Cumulative Percent of Income
G	10%	10%	$ 4,000	2%	2%
E	10%	20%	6,000	3%	5%
H	10%	30%	8,000	4%	9%
F	10%	40%	13,000	6%	15%
D	10%	50%	18,000	9%	23%
B*	10%	60%	27,000	13%	36%
I	10%	70%	27,000	13%	49%
J	10%	80%	27,000	13%	62%
A*	10%	90%	40,000	19%	81%
C	10%	100%	40,000	19%	100%

*Note: Families B, I, and J can appear in any order; as can families A and C.

c. $9,000; three families; 30%

d. (See graph)

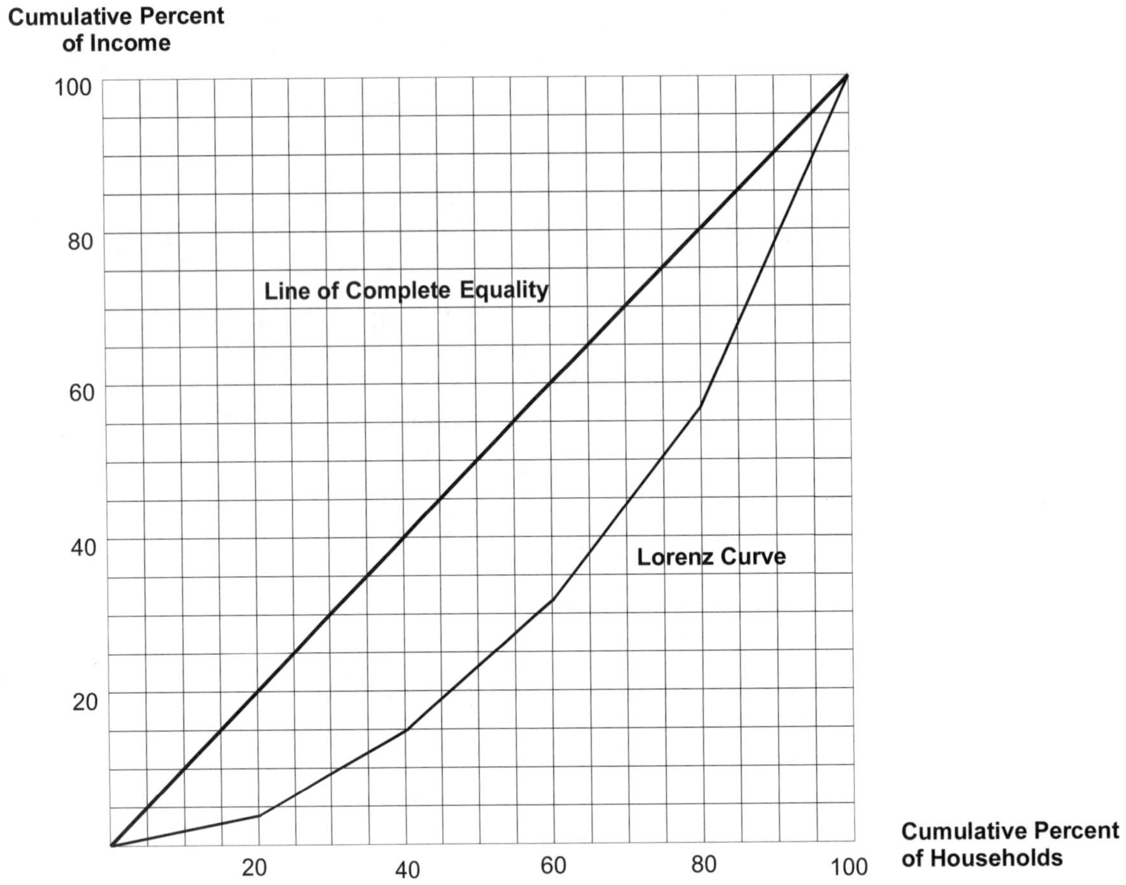
Cumulative Percent of Income
100
80
60
40
20
Line of Complete Equality
Lorenz Curve
20
40
60
80
100
Cumulative Percent of Households

Test Yourself

Multiple Choice

1. b
2. a
3. b
4. e
5. a
6. c
7. c
8. c
9. e
10. d
11. e
12. c

True/False

1. F
2. T
3. T
4. T
5. F
6. T
7. F
8. F
9. T

Answers to Chapter 13 Questions

Short Answer

1.

Group of Workers	Effect on wage rate	Effect on employment
Unskilled, covered by law	Increase	Decrease
Unskilled, not covered by law	Decrease	Increase
Skilled	Increase	Increase

2.

Prejudiced Group	Effect of Perfectly Competitive Market Forces on Discrimination
Employers	Decrease
Employees	Increase
Customers	Increase

■ ANSWERS FOR CHAPTER 13

Summarize the Chapter

The marginal approach to profit states that a firm should take any action that adds more to its **revenue** per period than it adds to its **cost** per period. When firms rent capital, or the capital they buy lasts forever, we can apply the marginal approach to profits just as we apply it for the firm's labor decision: The firm should buy another unit of capital whenever its marginal **revenue** product is **greater** than its marginal factor cost.

Because present dollars can earn **interest**, and because borrowing dollars requires payment of **interest**, it is always preferable to receive a given sum of money earlier rather than later. Therefore, a dollar received later has **less** value than a dollar received now.

The present value (PV) of a **future** payment is the value of that payment in today's dollars. Alternatively, it is the most anyone would pay today for the right to receive that payment. The present value of $Y to be received *n* years in the future is: PV = Y / (1+r)^n , where *r* is the interest rate. The present value of a future payment is smaller if (1) the size of the payment is smaller, (2) the interest rate is **larger**, or (3) the payment is received **later**. The principle of asset valuation says that the value of any asset is the **sum** of the present values of all the future benefits it generates.

As the interest rate rises, the value of additional capital to each business firm in the economy—using the principle of asset valuation—will **decrease**, and the firm will decide to purchase **less** of it. Therefore, in the economy as whole, a rise in the interest rate causes a **decrease** in investment expenditures. Lower interest rates **increase** firms' investment in physical capital, causing the capital stock to be **larger**, and our overall standard of living to be **higher**.

Employers have limited incentives to provide **general** human capital, since it increases the worker's value to many firms, and the worker will capture the benefits in the form of a higher wage. Therefore, workers must acquire **general** human capital on their own—or with the help of government subsidies. Individuals have little incentive to pay for **specific** human capital, since it increases their value to only one firm, and that firm will capture the benefits. Therefore, firms provide their workers with **specific** human capital at the firms' expense. To the worker that possesses it, human capital is an asset that generates higher income in the future. Therefore, the benefit of any given human capital investment is equal to the total **present** value of the additional future income. Investment in human capital, like investment in physical capital, is **inversely** related to the interest rate. The **lower** the interest rate, the greater the benefits of any human capital investment, and the more human capital workers will want to acquire. Since **lower** interest rates encourage individuals to invest in general human capital, the total amount of human capital—and our overall standard of living—will be higher if interest rates are **lower**.

There is a (an) **inverse** relationship between bond prices and bond yields. The higher the price of any given bond, the **lower** the yield on that bond. While bond issuers are not directly participants in **secondary** market trading, they are affected by what happens in that market. More specifically, if a bond's price rises in the **secondary** market, the price one can charge for similar, newly issued bonds in the primary market will rise as well. If a bond's yield falls in the **secondary** market, the yield of similar, newly issued bonds in the primary market will **fall**. To put a value on riskier bonds, market participants use a **higher** discount rate than on safe bonds. This leads to **lower** total present values and **lower** prices for the riskier bonds. With **lower** prices, riskier bonds have **higher** yields.

If a firm will earn a constant $Y in profit after taxes each year forever, then the total present value of these future profits is **$Y/ r**, where r is the discount rate. The value of a share of stock in a firm is equal to the total present value of the firm's after-tax **profits**, divided by the number of **shares** outstanding. An increase in current profits increases the value of a share of stock. An increase in the anticipated growth rate of profits increases the value of a share of stock. A (an) **rise** in interest rates—or even an anticipated **rise** in interest rates—decreases the value of a share of stock. An increase in the perceived riskiness of future profits **decreases** the value of a share of stock.

According to the efficient markets view of the stock market, any **information** that can be used to predict a stock's future earnings will be incorporated into a stock's price as soon it becomes publicly available. Therefore, by the time a fundamental analyst predicts that a stock's price will rise or fall, it has already risen or fallen. Fundamental analysis **cannot** help you outperform the market. According to the efficient markets view of the stock market, any patterns in stock price movements that can be observed by a good technical analyst will be incorporated into stock prices as soon as they are discernable. Therefore, stock market patterns disappear as soon as anyone can discover them. Technical analysis **cannot** help you outperform the market.

Answers to Chapter 13 Questions

Learn the Lingo

1. marginal revenue product of capital
2. present value
3. discounting
4. discount rate
5. principle of asset valuation
6. investment
7. general human capital
8. specific human capital
9. financial asset
10. bond
11. principal (face value)
12. maturity date
13. pure discount bond
14. coupon payments
15. yield
16. primary market
17. secondary market
18. share of stock
19. mutual fund
20. dividends
21. capital gain
22. Dow Jones Industrial Average
23. Standard & Poor's 500
24. fundamental analysis
25. technical analysis
26. efficient market

Build Your Skills

1. PV of $1 received n years in the future, given interest rate r

	Years (n)	1	2	3	4	5	20
Interest Rate (r)	5%	0.95	0.91	0.86	0.82	0.78	0.38
	10%	0.91	0.83	0.75	0.68	0.62	0.15
	15%	0.87	0.76	0.66	0.57	0.50	0.06
	20%	0.83	0.69	0.58	0.48	0.40	0.03

2. a. $2 million; $1.9 million; $1.82 million; $1.56 million; $0.76 million
   b. $2 million; $1.74 million; $1.52 million; $1 million; $0.12 million
   c. $1.544 million
   Challenge $0.720 million

3. a. 7,600; 7,280; 6,880; 21,760
   b. 7,280; 6,640; 6,000; 19,920
   c. (See table)
   d. definitely; exceeds; definitely; exceeds; definitely; exceeds; definitely not; fall short; 3
   e. buy; buy; not buy; 2
   f. fewer

Computer	Additional Annual Revenue	Total Present Value with a discount rate of: 5%	10%
1	$8,000	$21,760	$19,920
2	$5,000	$13,600	$12,450
3	$2,000	$5,440	$4,980
4	$1,000	$2,720	$2,490

4. a. 820; 820; 24 (or 25)
    b. 680; 680; 29 (or 30)

5. a. 40,000,000; 72.73
    b. lower than
    c. lower than
    d. higher than

Test Yourself

Multiple Choice
1. d
2. b
3. d
4. e
5. b
6. a
7. b
8. d
9. c
10. b

True/False
1. F
2. F
3. T
4. T
5. F
6. T
7. F
8. F

Short Answer

1. $1,000 / (1 + .05)^2$ = **$907.03**

2. $200 / (1.05) + $200 / (1.05)^2 + $200 / (1.05)^3 + $1,000 (1.05)^3 = **$1,408.49**

3. Annual after-tax profit *per share* = $100 million / 10 million = $10. PDV of $10 per year forever = $10 / .05 = **$200**

4. $20,000 / (1.05) + $30,000 / (1.05)^2 + $50,000 / (1.05)^2 = **$91,609.98**

■ ANSWERS FOR CHAPTER 14

Summarize the Chapter

Economic efficiency is achieved when we cannot rearrange the production or allocation of goods to make one person **better** off without making anybody else **worse** off.

An efficient economy is not necessarily a **fair** economy.

A Pareto **improvement** is any action that makes at least one person better off, and harms no one. Economic efficiency is achieved when every possible Pareto **improvement** is exploited. If an action creates total benefits for gainers that are **greater** than total harm to losers, then a **side** payment exists which, if transferred from gainers to losers, would make the action a Pareto **improvement**.

The height of the market **demand** curve at any quantity shows us the value— to someone—of the last unit of the good consumed. The height of the market **supply** curve at any quantity shows us

Answers to Chapter 14 Questions

the additional cost—to some producer—of each unit of the good supplied. Whenever—at some quantity—the demand curve is higher than the supply curve, the value of one more unit to some consumer is **greater** than its additional cost to some producer. The efficient quantity of a good is the quantity at which the market demand curve and market supply curves **intersect**. In a well-functioning, **perfectly competitive** market, the equilibrium quantity is also the efficient quantity.

A buyer's consumer surplus on a unit of a good is the difference between its value to the buyer and what the buyer actually **pays** for that unit. Market consumer surplus at any price, measured in dollars, is the total area **under** the market demand curve and **above** the market price. An individual seller's producer surplus on a unit of a good is the difference between what the seller actually gets and the additional **cost** of providing it. Market producer surplus at any price, measured in dollars, is the total area **above** the market supply curve and **under** the market price. We measure the total net **benefits** gained in a market as the sum of consumer and producer surplus in that market.

A market is **efficient** when the sum of producer and consumer surplus is maximized in that market. In a well-functioning, perfectly competitive market, the equilibrium quantity provides the **maximum** possible benefit to buyers and sellers combined, and is thus the efficient quantity. The welfare **loss** in a market is the dollar value of potential benefits not achieved due to inefficiency in that market. A price **ceiling** or a price **floor** (either order) imposed on a perfectly competitive market—by reducing quantity below the efficient level—reduces the total net benefits in the market (causes a welfare **loss**).

By making most involuntary exchanges illegal, **criminal** law helps to channel our energies into exchanges and productive activities that benefit all parties involved: Pareto improvements. In this way, **criminal** law contributes to economic efficiency. **Property** law—by reducing disputes about property, and channeling resources into production rather than the capture of property belonging to others—contributes to economic efficiency by increasing total production, thus raising the total net benefits that markets can provide.

Contracts enable us to make exchanges that take place over time and in which one person must act first. In this way, contracts help society enjoy the full benefits of **specialization** and exchange. A legal and regulatory system that ensured the complete elimination of crime, unsafe products, and other unwelcome activities would be less **efficient** than a system that tolerated some amount of these activities. An efficient infrastructure must consider the **costs**, as well as the benefits, of achieving our legal and regulatory goals.

A market failure occurs when a market—even with the proper institutional support—is economically **inefficient**. Monopoly and imperfectly competitive markets—in which firms charge a single price greater than marginal **cost**—are generally inefficient. Price is too **high**, and output is too **low**, to maximize the net benefits in the market. Average cost pricing is sometimes used to regulate a **natural** monopoly. Regulators strive to set the price equal to cost per unit where the **LRATC** curve crosses the demand curve. At this price, the monopoly makes **zero** economic profit, which provides its owners with a fair rate of return and keeps the monopoly in business.

An **externality** is a by-product of a good or activity that affects someone not immediately involved in the transaction. The Coase theorem states that—when side payments can be negotiated and arranged without cost—the private market will solve the **externality** problem on its own, always arriving at the **efficient** outcome. While the initial distribution of legal rights will determine the allocation of gains and losses among the parties, it will not affect the action taken. The **free rider** problem occurs when the efficient outcome requires a side payment but individual gainers—each obligated to pay a small share of the side payment—will not contribute.

A market with a negative externality associated with producing or consuming a good will produce **more** than the efficient quantity, creating a welfare **loss**. A **tax** on each unit of a good, equal to the external harm it causes, can correct a negative externality and bring the market to a (an) **efficient** output level. Other methods of reducing output to the **efficient** level are regulation and **tradable** permits. A market with a positive externality associated with producing or consuming a good will produce **less** than the efficient quantity, creating a welfare **loss**. A **subsidy** on each unit of a good, equal to the external benefits it creates, can correct a positive externality and bring the market to a (an) **efficient** output level.

If a good is **rivalrous**, efficiency requires that people pay a price for its use. In the absence of any market failure, **private** provision will lead to the efficient level of production.

If a good is excludable, it *can* be provided by the **private** market. A good that is both rivalrous and excludable is a pure **private** good. In the absence of any significant market failure, private firms will provide these goods at close to efficient levels.

When a good is nonexcludable, the **private** sector will generally be unable to provide it. In most cases, if we want such a good, **government** must provide it. When a good or service is nonrival, the market cannot provide it efficiently: to achieve economic efficiency, the good or service would have to be provided at a price equal to **zero**. A good that is both nonrival and nonexcludable is a pure **public** good. The tragedy of the commons occurs when a good that is both **rivalrous** and **nonexcludable** (either order) is overused, to the detriment of all.

Learn the Lingo

1. Pareto improvement
2. consumer surplus
3. market consumer surplus
4. producer surplus
5. market producer surplus
6. total net benefits
7. welfare loss
8. tort
9. market failure
10. externality
11. Coase theorem
12. free rider problem
13. marginal social cost (MSC)
14. tradable permit
15. marginal social benefit (MSB)
16. rivalry
17. excludability
18. pure private good
19. pure public good
20. tragedy of the commons

Build Your Skills

1.
   a. $18; $6; greater than; is not; could; could not
   b. $10; $10; equal to; is; could not; could not
   c. $4; $13; less than; is not; could not; could
   d. $10; 35; is

Answers to Chapter 14 Questions

2. a. (See graph.)

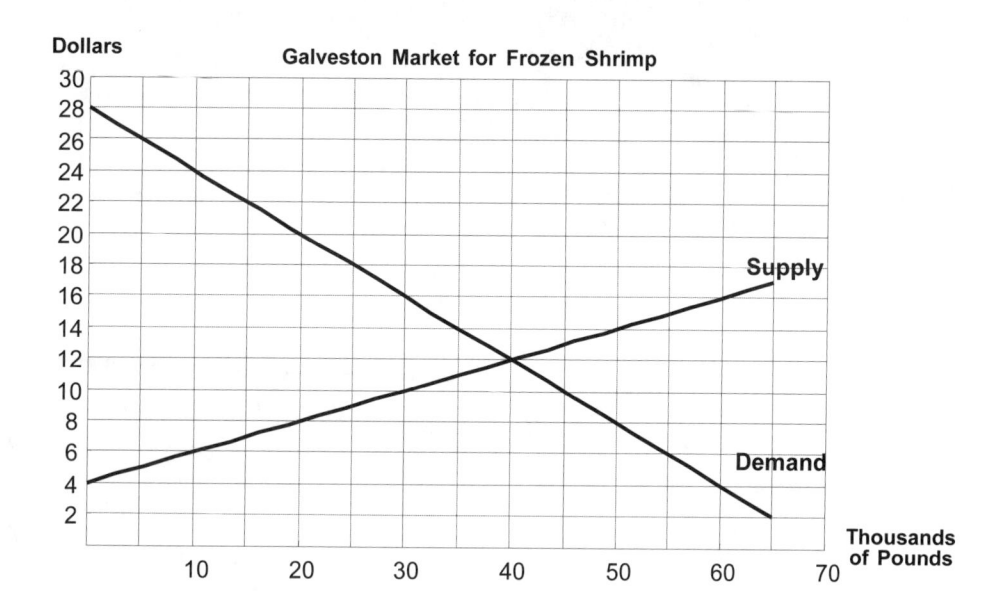

Galveston Market for Frozen Shrimp

b. 12; 40; 320; 160; 480
c. 20; 80; 280; 360
d. consumers; producers; smaller; reduced; great; maximized

3. a. (See graph); marginal revenue equals marginal cost; 12; 7

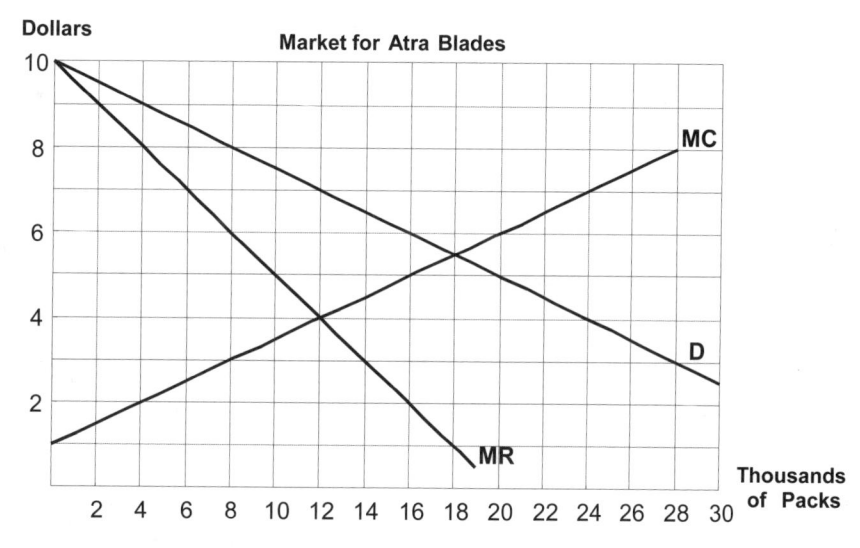

Market for Atra Blades

b. 18; 54; 72
c. 18; 40.5; 40.5; 81
d. smaller; are not; is not

4. a. natural monopoly

b. (See graph.)

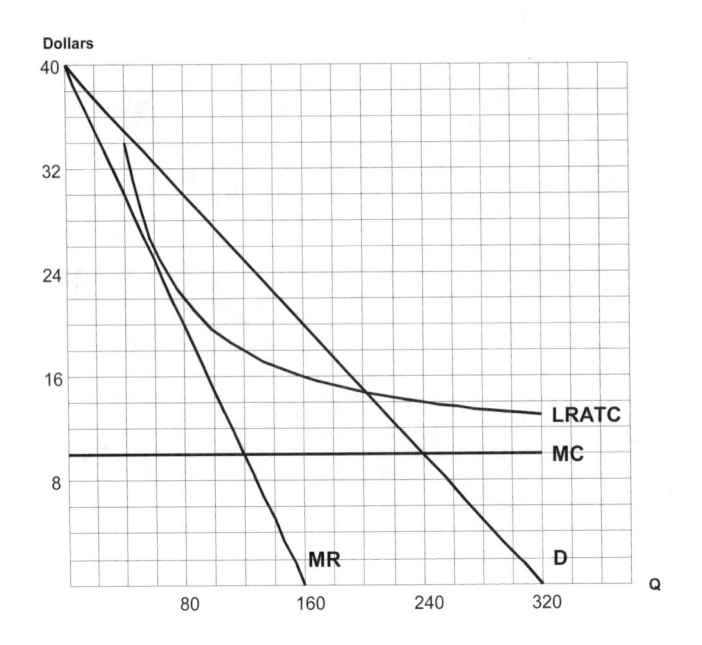

c. 120; $25; 18; $8,400
d. is not; 25; 10; can
e. 10 cents; 240 thousand; would; suffer a loss; $9,600; only if the firm also receives a subsidy to cover its losses
f. 200; 15; 0; higher than; lower than
g. greater than; less than; lower than

5. a.

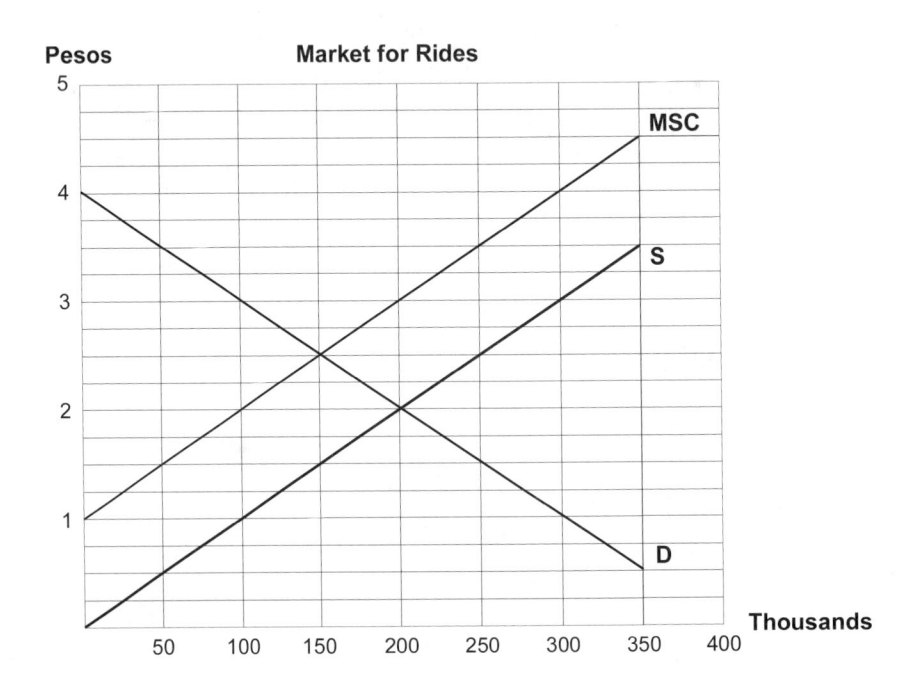

b. 2; 200
c. is not; too high; less than
d. levy a tax of 1 peso per ride on Jeeneys; raise; supply; leftward; increase; 2.5 pesos; decrease; 150

e. will; equal to

Test Yourself

Multiple Choice
1. a
2. d
3. a
4. c
5. c
6. d
7. d
8. e
9. e
10. a
11. d
12. c
13. e
14. c

True/False
1. T
2. T
3. F
4. F
5. F
6. F
7. F
8. F
9. T
10. F

Short Answer

1. (any order): criminal; tort; contract; property; antitrust

2. (any order): imperfect competition; externalities; public goods

3. a. (negative) externality
   b. imperfect competition (or monopoly)
   c. (positive) externality
   d. public good

4. a. (either order): rivalrous; excludable
   b. (either order): nonrivalrous; nonexcludable

■ ANSWERS FOR CHAPTER 15

Summarize the Chapter

A country has an **absolute advantage** in a good when it can produce it using fewer resources than another country. A nation has a **comparative advantage** in producing a good if it can produce it at a lower opportunity cost than some other country. Mutually beneficial trade between any two countries is possible whenever one country is relatively better at producing a good than the other country is. Being relatively better means having the ability to produce a good at a lower **opportunity** cost—that is, at a lower sacrifice of other goods foregone. If countries specialize according to **comparative** advantage, a more efficient use of given resources occurs. That is, with the same resources, the world can produce more of at least one good, without decreasing production of any other good.

As long as **opportunity** costs differ, specialization and trade can be beneficial to all involved. This remains true regardless of whether the parties are different nations, different states, different counties, or different individuals. It remains true even if one party has an all-round **absolute** advantage or disadvantage in all goods. For the world as a whole, the gains from international trade are due to increased production as nations specialize according to **comparative** advantage. How those world gains are distributed among specific countries depends on the **terms** of **trade**. When consumers are free to buy at the lowest prices, they will naturally buy a good from the country that has a **comparative** advantage in producing it. That country's industries respond by producing more of that good and less of other goods. In this way, countries naturally move toward specializing in those goods in which they have a **comparative** advantage.

A country that has relatively large amounts of a particular **resource** at its disposal will tend to have a comparative advantage in goods that make heavy use of that **resource**. But countries can also develop strong comparative advantages in the goods they have produced in the past, regardless of why they began producing those goods in the first place.

When the opening of trade results in increased exports of a good, the **producers** of the good are made better off. **Consumers** of the good in the exporting country will be made worse off. When the opening of trade results in increased imports of a product, the domestic **producers** of the product are made worse off. **Consumers** of the good in the importing country are better off.

The distribution of gains and losses creates a policy bias against free trade. Those who benefit from trade in a specific product either have little incentive to lobby for it (**consumers** of imports) or have limited power to influence policy (**producers** of exports). But one constituency harmed by trade—domestic **producers** threatened by imports—has both a powerful incentive to lobby and the ability to influence policy.

Tariffs **reduce** the volume of trade and **raise** the domestic prices of imported goods. In the country that imposes the tariff, producers of the good **gain** and consumers of the good **lose**. But the world as a whole **loses**, because tariffs **decrease** the gains from trade. Quotas have effects similar to tariffs: They **reduce** the quantity of imports and **raise** domestic prices. While both measures help domestic **producers** of the good, they **reduce** the benefits of trade to the nation as a whole. However, a tariff has one saving grace (i.e., one advantage over a quota): an increase in **government revenue**.

Production is most likely to reflect the principle of **comparative** advantage when firms can obtain funds for investment projects and when they can freely enter industries that are profitable. Thus, free trade, without government intervention, works best when markets are working well.

Learn the Lingo

1. exports
2. imports
3. absolute advantage
4. comparative advantage
5. terms of trade
6. exchange rate
7. tariff
8. quota
9. protectionism
10. infant industry argument

Build Your Skills

1. a. 40; 20; 2; bicycles; 2; bicycles
   b. 45; 15; 3; bicycles; 3; bicycles

Answers to Chapter 15 Questions

c.

Opportunity Costs

	Germany	United States
Per Bicycle	1/2 DVR	1/3 DVR
Per DVR	2 bicycles	3 bicycles

d. DVRs; bicycles; DVRs; bicycles

2. a. DVRs; bicycles; bicycles; DVRs; DVRs; bicycles; bicycles; DVRs

b.

A Change in Production

	Germany	United States	World
Bicycle Production	-50	+60	+10
DVR Production	+25	-20	+5

c.

The Gains from Specialization and Trade

	Germany		United States	
	Bicycles	DVRs	Bicycles	DVRs
Change in Production	-50	+25	+60	-20
Exports (-) or Imports (+)	+55	-22	-55	+22
Net Gain	+5	+3	+5	+2

d. 2.5; both Germany and the United States; 5; 2; 5; 3

3. a.

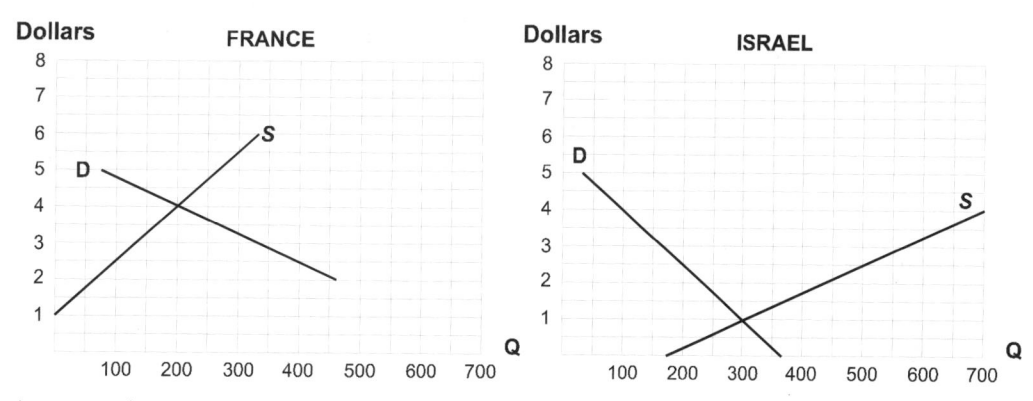

[Two supply and demand graphs: FRANCE (D downward from 5, S upward through ~6) and ISRAEL (D downward from 5, S upward to ~4 at 700)]

b. $4; 200; $1; 300
c. import; export
d. fall; rise; increase; decrease; rise; decrease; increase

e. lower; better off; lower; worse off; higher; worse off; higher; better off

4. Quantity of French orange imports = 800 − 200P
Quantity of Israeli orange exports = 200P − 200
Free trade equilibrium price is $2.5 per kilo

Test Yourself

Multiple Choice
1. c
2. a
3. a
4. c
5. e
6. d
7. d
8. e
9. c
10. a

True/False
1. F
2. F
3. F
4. F
5. T
6. T
7. F
8. F

Short Answer

1.

	Country A		Country B	
	Producers (e.g. workers and owners of firms):	Consumers:	Producers (e.g. workers and owners of firms)	Consumers:
Good X	gain	lose	lose	gain
Good Y	lose	gain	gain	lose

2.

	Country A		Country B	
	Producers (e.g. workers and owners of firms):	Consumers:	Producers (e.g. workers and owners of firms):	Consumers:
Good Y	gain	lose	lose	gain

ANSWERS TO FINAL EXAM IN MICROECONOMICS

1. d is correct. The opportunity cost is what is actually given up when making a choice—that is, what is given up by not taking the *next best alternative* course of action. This opportunity cost includes the direct cost of the trip ($1,800) plus any income lost by not pursuing her next best alternative ($3,000 x 3 = $9,000) plus anything else she would be giving up by not doing that next best alternative (time with family and friends). c. is incorrect because it ignores the time with family and friends Nadine would be giving up; e. is incorrect because it uses the income of an alternative (keeping her full time job) she would not actually choose if she didn't go to Italy.

2. c. is correct. Choice a. causes a movement along the PPF, but no shift. Choice b. causes a change in the intercept for one axis only—the axis along which military goods are plotted. Choice d. causes a movement from inside the PPF to the PPF, but no shift in the PPF itself.

3. e is correct. a. and b. are incorrect because both James and Hernando can clean the apartment using the same resources (2 hours), so neither has an absolute advantage. However, the opportunity cost to James for cleaning the apartment (a third of a dinner, including the shopping) is less than the opportunity cost to Hernando (half a dinner). Therefore, James—with the lower opportunity cost—has the comparative advantage in cleaning the apartment. Similar calculations will show that Hernando has a comparative advantage in preparing dinner.

4. e. is correct. a. shifts the demand curve rightward, causing both price and quantity to rise. b. shifts both the demand curve and the supply curve rightward, so price may rise or fall, but quantity must rise. Since milk is a complement to cereal, d. results in a rightward shift of the demand curve (both the change in population and the decrease in the price of milk contribute to the shift), causing price and quantity to rise. c. will shift the demand curve rightward or leftward depending on which influence (population or increase in price of a complement) is stronger. If the demand curve ends up shifting rightward, price and quantity will both rise; if the demand curve ends up shifting leftward, price and quantity will both fall. None of these choices are consistent with the statement in the stem of the question. e. is correct because it shifts the demand curve rightward, and the supply curve leftward. Each of these shifts causes price to rise, but depending on which shift is greater, quantity could rise or fall.

5. a. is correct. b and c. and d. shift only the demand curve (this would cause a *movement along* the supply curve, but no shift).

6. e. is correct. Using the midpoint-rule to calculate the percentage change in price, we get: $2/$10 = .20 or 20 percent. With elasticity of 0.4, each one percent rise in price causes a 0.4% decrease in quantity, so a 20 percent rise in price will cause a 20 x 0.4 = 8 percent decrease in quantity.

7. c. is correct (see Ch. 4 in your textbook). Note that while being in the "upper half" of a linear demand curve (choices b. and d.) means we are in the more elastic part of the curve, the question asks what *happens* to elasticity as we *move along* the curve. The correct answer (c) remains correct whether we are in the upper or lower portion of the curve.

8. e. is correct. The more narrowly we define the good, the more substitutes are available for it. The way the good is defined in choice e., there are the most substitutes (such as Florida oranges sold in *other* food markets). If the price of the good as defined in e. were to rise, with *all other prices held constant* (including the price of the good at other food markets), people would shift easily to other markets, and the quantity response would be relatively large.

9. c. is correct. A price ceiling is a level above which the price is not allowed to go. If the market price is already below the price ceiling, it will have no immediate effect on the market.

10. a. is correct. Rock concerts are an economic necessity for Lydia only if the income elasticity is less than one. That requires that her demand for rock concerts increase by a smaller percentage than the increase in her income. Using the midpoint rule, Lydia's income is rising by $4,000 / $20,000 = .20 or 20%. Since she is currently consuming 8 rock concerts, an increase to 9 would mean a percentage increase of 1 / 8.5 = 11%, which is less than the 20% increase in income. For all of the other choices, demand for rock concerts increases by *more* than 20%. For example, choice b gives a percentage change in rock concerts of 2 / 9 = 0.22 or 22%. For the other choices, the percentage change in rock concerts is even greater.

11. a. is correct. A good is inferior only if an *increase* in income results in a *decrease* in demand (or a *decrease* in income causes an *increase* in demand). This requires that the income elasticity have a negative sign.

12. c. is correct. A decrease in the price of the vertical axis good will increase the vertical intercept of the budget line (more of the good than before could be purchased if all income were spent on that good), but leave the horizontal intercept unchanged. The budget line will become steeper.

Answers to Final Exam in Microeconomics

13. b. is correct. Since the price of both goods has remained the same, the slope of the budget line will remain unchanged. However, with more income, more of both can be purchased, so the budget line shifts rightward.

14. c. is correct. If Kim is consuming optimal quantities, her marginal utility *per dollar* spent on each goods must be the same. Since her marginal utility per dollar spent on movies is 5 utils / $10 = 0.5, her marginal utility per dollar spent on books (MU) must be satisfy the equation: MU / $25 = 0.5. Solving for MU, we get 12.5.

15. b. is correct. The MU per dollar spent on movies is 100/10 = 10, while the MU per dollar spent on books is 200/25 = 8. Each *dollar* shifted from books to movies will decrease utility by 8 and then increase it by 10, so total utility will increase. There is no information in the problem we could use to tell if books are inferior, or if the demand for movies is inelastic.

16. a. is correct. Howard's MRS tells us that if he gave up 3 movies for one book, he would remain indifferent. However, based on the prices of these two goods, he *could* get another book by giving up only 2½ movies. If giving up 3 movies for one book keeps him indifferent, then giving up only 2½ movies for a book must make him better off. That means he should shift his consumption away from movies toward books.

17. e. is correct. The problem only tells us that, for Sarah, movies obey the law of demand (a rise in price causes a decrease in quantity demanded). All of the other choices tell us things that *might* be true, but are not *necessary* for a good to obey the law of demand. A good that is not normal (an inferior good) can (and almost always will) obey the law of demand, as long as the substitution effect dominates the inferior income effect of a price change. So will a good that is not an economic necessity (i.e., an economic luxury), or one that is *inelastically* demanded. Thus, all of the choices a throught d, because they contain the word "must," are false.

18. a. is correct. The substitution effect of a price change always moves quantity demanded in the opposite direction of the price change. This is true whether the good is normal or inferior, and whether it is elastically or inelastically demanded.

19. d. is correct. By definition, over a short-run time horizon, *at least one* of the firm's inputs is fixed (it cannot change the quantity of that input during the time period considered).

20. b. is correct. Choice c. sounds like it might be correct, but it actually is another way of defining *diminishing* returns to labor. After all, if equal increases in output require greater and greater increases in employment, then equal increases in employment will give us smaller and smaller increases in output. Choices d. and e. are incorrect because increasing returns to labor is a short run property—it concerns increases in labor when other inputs remain constant.

21. c. is the correct answer. To economists, the total cost of running a business is the economic cost or opportunity cost, which includes direct money costs and any implicit costs. For Bob, there are two implicit costs. One is the lost monthly interest income on his $100,000 investment in the business ($100,000 at 1% per month, or $1,000 per month). The other is the foregone income from not earning wages at his next best alternative ($4,000 per month). In addition, Bob has direct money costs of ($6,000 x 2) + $2,000 + $200 = $14,200. Adding the direct money costs and the implicit costs, we get $14,200 + $1,000 + $4,000 = $19,200.

22. e. is correct. Accounting profit is total revenue minus *accounting costs* (usually, explicit costs). For Bob's firm, this is $15,000 - $14,200 = $800.

23. c. is correct. Economic profit is total revenue minus total cost (total economic or opportunity cost). Since Bob's total cost is $19,200, his economic profit is $15,000 – $19,200 = -$4,200.

24. d. is the correct choice (the incorrect formula). Marginal revenue is the *change* in total revenue divided by the *change* in output. TR / Q would equal the "average revenue" from the product, which is the same as the product's price. All of the other equations are true. (e. may require a little bit of thought: TR / Q is the revenue per unit of output; ATC is the total cost per unit of output. Subtracting the latter from the former must therefore give us profit per unit of output.)

25. e. is correct. (See Ch. 6 of your textbook). When thinking about choice d., remember that ATC is not necessarily rising when MC is rising; it must also be the case that MC > ATC. So a falling marginal product of labor (which means a rising marginal cost) does not *necessarily* mean a rising ATC.

26. e. is correct. In the long run, the firm can adjust *all* of its inputs. This should enable it to produce any output level *at least* as cheaply in the long run as it could in the short run (when it is stuck with certain quantities of one or more fixed inputs).

27. c. is correct. (see Ch. 6 of your textbook).

28. e. is correct. a. is wrong because the profit maximizing output is where MR and MC *intersect* (with MC cutting MR from below). As long as MR lies above MC—even by a little—the firm can increase profit further by producing more. b. is wrong because it is where profit *per unit* is maximized, rather than *total* profit. (These two will generally *not* be maximized at the same output level). c. is wrong because when TR and TC intersect, TR = TC so total profit is zero, which will generally *not* be the maximum profit.

29. c. is correct. The MR curve tells us how much revenue rises when output increases by one unit. When the MR curve lies above the horizontal axis (so that MR is positive), an increase in output causes revenue to rise; when the curve lies below the horizontal

axis (so that MR is negative), an increase in output causes revenue to fall. Thus, when it crosses the axis, revenue stops rising and begins falling, i.e., revenue has reached a maximum.

30. b. is correct. If MR < MC, an increase in output causes revenue to rise by *less* than cost rises. Since total profit is TR – TC, total profit must fall.

31. d. is correct. (See Ch. 7, 8 and 9 of your textbook) The two forms of the shut down rule are TR < TVC and P < AVC. e. *would* be correct, except that it refers to ATC instead of AVC. a. and b. are incorrect because if the shut-down rule is not satisfied, the firm should stay open in the short run even if it suffers a loss. c. makes no sense: P is price or revenue per unit, TR is total revenue. Regardless of profit or loss, the price will automatically be less than TR except when the firm is producing only one unit.

32. d. is correct. (See the Using the Theory section of Chapter 6)

33. c. is correct. a. has only two firms, and e. has only one firm (in each local market), while perfect competition requires many firms, with each a *tiny* part of the market. b. and d. involve a highly differentiated product, violating the "standardized product" requirement of perfect competition. Walnuts, however, are highly standardized and produced by thousands of walnut farms across the country.

34. d. is correct. Choices a., b., and c. are all characteristics of perfect competition.

35. b. is correct. When price (revenue per unit) is less than average variable cost, the firm loses more by staying open because it does not even cover its "operating cost" (the cost of its variable inputs).

36. b. is correct. Choice a. *would* be correct if it said ATC instead of AVC. Choice c. is wrong because the ATC curve is flat in long run equilibrium. (see Chapter 8 of your textbook).

37. c. is correct. Chapter 8 of your textbook shows what happens when demand *increases* in an increasing cost industry. In this problem, demand decreases, so all of the movements are reversed. Do not confuse the decrease in demand, which is a change in the market, with a "decreasing cost industry," which is a *type* of market.

38. b. is correct. This is explained early in Chapter 9 of your textbook.

39. a. is correct. (See Chapter 9).

40. c. is correct. People who don't clip coupons are willing to pay more, often because the opportunity cost of their time is higher and clipping coupons is not worth it. In all of the other cases, there are either differences in costs, or the goods being sold at different prices are different goods. Price discrimination is when different units *of the same good* are sold at different prices for reasons other than differences in costs.

41. e. is correct. None of the choices are requirements for an oligopoly, which is a market of few firms in which there is strategic interaction among firms.

42. e. is correct. In this situation, firm A's best decision depends on what firm B does. If B charges a high price, it is best for A to charge a high price. But if firm B charges a low price, it is best for A to charge a low price. Although these are the actions described in choice c., they do not meet the definition of a dominant strategy, which is a single choice that is best *regardless* of the choice of the other player.

43. d. is correct—all are requirements of monopolistic competition (see Ch. 10 of your text.)

44. b. is correct. Long run profit is possible under monopoly, but not under monopolistic competition, because entry will erode any long-run profit. Price and marginal revenue are generally *not* equal to each other in *either* market structure, where marginal revenue is less than price. (The exception is when firms can perfectly price discriminate.) However, both firms face a downward sloping demand curve.

45. b. is correct. Chapter 10 of your text shows that in the long run, a monopolistic competitor will always end up producing output on the downward sloping portion of its ATC curve. The LRATC curve is tangent to the ATC curve at that output level, so the LRATC curve must be sloping downward as well (add the LRATC to the figure in the chapter illustrating long-run equilibrium to convince yourself of this). The other choices are all false—a monopolistic competitor *will* produce where MR = MC; it will *often* advertise; it will *never* earn positive economic profit in the long run, but rather zero economic profit; and if economic profit is zero, accounting profit—which is greater than or equal to economic profit—may be positive or zero, but never negative.

46. c. is correct. Choice a is marginal revenue, not marginal revenue product. Choice b. is the marginal product of labor, not the marginal revenue product of labor.

47. a. is correct. Firms will acquire more machines, and need more (complementary) unskilled labor to work with them. The labor supply curve is unaffected (although the shift in labor demand will move us *along* the labor supply curve.)

48. b. is correct (see Chapter 11)

49. d. is correct (see Chapter 11)

50. e. is correct. In choice d., prejudice by employers has more potential for a market solution, since non-prejudiced employers can take advantage of the opportunity to increase profit, driving up the market wage of the victimized group. But when employees are prejudiced, the market won't necessarily work to eliminate the damage.

Answers to Final Exam in Microeconomics

51. d. is correct. The slope of the diagonal line will be one because any fraction of the population on the horizontal axis will have the same fraction of total income. (See Chapter 12)

52. c. is correct. The formula is $100 / [(1.07)(1.07)] = $87.34

53. c. is correct. The value of a bond is the present value of its future payments. Each of the bonds could be created from the bond in choice c. by shifting money delivered in choice c. to a later year. For example, choice d. can be obtained from choice c. by taking $50 from the second year's payment and providing it at the end of the third year instead. The same type of payment postponement would result in each of the bonds in choices a., b. and d. At any interest rate, the later a sum of money is delayed, the less its present value, so the lower will be the value of the bond.

54. d. is correct. All of the other choices are skills that would be valuable at *any* institution at which a professor might teach.

55. c. is correct. (The formula is $100 / 0.1) = $1,000. (See Chapter 13 of your text).

56. e. is correct. Efficient markets theory states that stock prices already embody all information that would enable anyone to determine their value.

57. b. is correct. In all of the other examples, someone is harmed. While the price in choice b. may not seem "fair," neither the buyer nor the seller are made worse off by making the purchase or one of them wouldn't participate, and at least one of them (and probably both) are made better off.

58. a. is correct. It's the only choice that shifts the supply curve rightward, increasing quantity purchased and decreasing the price. This will increase the area under the market demand curve and above the market price. Choices b, c, and d either shift the supply curve leftward (increasing price and decreasing quantity) or shift the demand curve leftward, reducing the area described above.

59. d. is correct. Each of the choices a., b., and c. are examples of "market failures" that cause economic inefficiency, as discussed in Chapter 15. While there are no externalities in choice a., monopoly itself is a market failure.

60. a. is correct. Since a regulated monopoly is guaranteed a given rate of return, it has no incentive to minimize cost of any output level, because that will not effect its profit. (See Chapter 14 of your text)

61. b. is correct. When a good provides benefits to third parties, the market will not produce less than the efficient amount. Of the choices listed, only a subsidy will result in increased production, which is needed for efficiency.

62. d. is correct. It takes fewer hours to produce either good in country A, so it has an absolute advantage in both goods. However, the opportunity cost of one guitar in country A is only 4 bicycles (producing one more guitar requires taking 100 hours from bicycle production, which reduces bicycle production by 4), while the opportunity cost of a guitar in country B is 5 bicycles (producing one more guitar in Country B requires taking 200 hours from bicycle production, which reduces bicycle production by 5). Since Country A has the lower opportunity cost for guitars, then by definition it has the comparative advantage.

63. c. is correct. Choices a. and b. are wrong because the tariff will do the *opposite* of what these choices say. However, a tariff raises the cost of buying imports, and raises the price that domestic producers can charge.

64. d. is correct. a. and b. are incorrect, in part because free trade, although it harms some people within a country, provides gains to the country as a whole. b. (like c. and d.) is also incorrect because absolute advantage does not determine either the likelihood of trade or the gains from trade. Comparative advantage is what drives trade.

65. a. is correct. Complete excludability assures that private firms can limit consumption to those who pay, so that the private sector *can* provide the good and collect a price for it. But because of nonrivalry, efficiency requires that anyone who places *any* value on the good at all, no matter how small, be able to consume it. However, if the private sector provides the good, it will not be free, so an inefficiently small quantity will be produced. In choices b. and d., the private sector could *not* produce the good due to complete nonexcludability. In choice c., the private sector *can* produce the good, but choice a. is still better, because the rivalry in choice c. assures us that a price must be charged to get the efficient quantity. (The quantity of the good in c. *might* not be efficient—for example, if there are market failures. But choice a. is still better, because private provision of the good under its conditions *could never* be efficient.) Choice e. is a joke.